AMERICAN INDIAN NATIONS

CONTEMPORARY NATIVE AMERICAN COMMUNITIES
Stepping Stones to the Seventh Generation

Acknowledging the strength and vibrancy of Native American people and nations today, this series examines life in contemporary Native American communities from the point of view of Native concerns and values. Books in the series cover topics that are of cultural and political importance to tribal peoples and that affect their possibilities for survival, in both urban and rural communities.

SERIES EDITORS:
Troy Johnson
American Indian Studies
California State University, Long Beach
Long Beach, CA 90840
trj@csulb.edu

Duane Champagne
American Indian Studies Center
3220 Campbell Hall, Box 951548
University of California, Los Angeles
Los Angeles, CA 90095
champagn@ucla.edu

BOOKS IN THE SERIES
1. *Inuit, Whaling, and Sustainability*, Milton M. R. Freeman, Ingmar Egede, Lyudmila Bogoslovskaya, Igor G. Krupnik, Richard A. Caulfield, and Marc G. Stevenson (1999)
2. *Contemporary Native American Political Issues*, edited by Troy Johnson (1999)
3. *Contemporary Native American Cultural Issues*, edited by Duane Champagne (1999)
4. *Modern Tribal Development: Paths to Self Sufficiency and Cultural Integrity in Indian Country*, Dean Howard Smith (2000)
5. *American Indians and the Urban Experience*, edited by Susan Lobo and Kurt Peters (2001)
6. *Medicine Ways: Disease, Health, and Survival among Native Americans*, edited by Clifford Trafzer and Diane Weiner (2000)
7. *Native American Studies in Higher Education: Models for Collaboration between Universities and Indigenous Nations*, edited by Duane Champagne and Jay Stauss (2002)
8. *Spider Woman Walks This Land: Traditional Cultural Properties and the Navajo Nation*, by Kelli Carmean (2002)
9. *Alaska Native Political Leadership and Higher Education: One University, Two Universes*, by Michael Jennings (2004)
10. *Indigenous Intellectual Property Rights: Legal Obstacles and Innovative Solutions*, edited by Mary Riley (2004)
11. *Healing and Mental Health for Native American: Speaking in Red*, edited by Ethan Nebelkopf and Mary Phillips (2004)
12. *Rachel's Children*, by Lois Beardslee (2004)
13. *A Broken Flute: The Native Experience in Books for Children*, edited by Doris Seale and Beverly Slapin (2005)
14. *Indigenous Peoples & the Modern State*, edited by Duane Champagne, Karen Torjesen and Susan Steiner (2005]
15. *Reading Native American Women: Critical/Creative Representations*, edited by Inés Hernández-Ávila (2005)
16. *Native Americans in the School System: Family, Community, and Academic Achievement*, by Carol Ward (2005)
17. *Indigenous Education and Empowerment: International Perspectives*, edited by Ismael Abu-Saad and Duane Champagne (2005)
18. *Cultural Representation in Native America*, edited by Andrew Jolivétte (2006)
19. *Social Change and Cultural Continuity Among Native Nations*, by Duane Champagne (2006)
20. *Drinking and Sobriety Among the Lakota Sioux*, by Beatrice Medicine (2006)

AMERICAN INDIAN NATIONS

Yesterday, Today, and Tomorrow

EDITED BY
GEORGE HORSE CAPTURE,
DUANE CHAMPAGNE, AND
CHANDLER C. JACKSON

ALTAMIRA PRESS
A Division of Rowman & Littlefield Publishers, Inc.
Lanham • New York • Toronto • Plymouth, UK

AltaMira Press
A division of Rowman & Littlefield Publishers, Inc.
A wholly owned subsidiary of The Rowman & Littlefield Publishing Group, Inc.
4501 Forbes Boulevard, Suite 200, Lanham, MD 20706
www.altamirapress.com

Estover Road, Plymouth PL6 7PY, United Kingdom

British Library Cataloguing in Publication Information Available

Library of Congress Cataloging-in-Publication Data

American Indian nations : yesterday, today, and tomorrow / edited by George Horse
Capture, Duane Champagne, and Chandler C. Jackson.
     p. cm. — (Contemporary Native American communities)
  Proceedings of a symposium held at the University of Great Falls, Montana, July 2005.
Includes bibliographical references and index.
  ISBN-13: 978-0-7591-1094-6 (cloth : alk. paper)
  ISBN-10: 0-7591-1094-8 (cloth : alk. paper)
  ISBN-13: 978-0-7591-1095-3 (pbk. : alk. paper)
  ISBN-10: 0-7591-1095-6 (pbk. : alk. paper)
  1. Indians of North America—Social conditions—Congresses. 2. Indians of North
America—Government relations—Congresses. 3. United States—Ethnic relations—
Congresses. 4. United States—Race relations—Congresses. I. Horse Capture, George P. II.
Champagne, Duane. III. Jackson, Chandler C., 1949–

  E98.S67A43 2007
  305.897'073—dc22
                                          2007008441

Printed in the United States of America

♾™ The paper used in this publication meets the minimum requirements of American
National Standard for Information Sciences—Permanence of Paper for Printed Library
Materials, ANSI/NISO Z39.48-1992.

CONTENTS

Preface

GEORGE HORSE CAPTURE

THE ORIGINAL INHABITANTS OF A COUNTRY should enjoy eventual acceptance, but that isn't always true for people of color. It is even more insulting when those people are American Indians who have been on this continent for many thousands of years longer than anyone else. It is understood by most that a high wall of differences still separates the Indian people from the others. When we were segregated on the reservations, our world was still Indian. So we managed to manage, but that soon changed. Non-Indian schools and other forces, both near and far, nearly devoured our children and we began to lose them as distance and technology overwhelmed tradition.

One demographer estimates the population of the Indian people in the contiguous United States at the time of Columbus at more than 5 million; by the early 1900s we were down to only 250,000. As the Europeans and other foreigners arrived, we became an invisible minority in our own country. But in spite of genocidal efforts, broken treaties, land loss, Christianity, fading blood quantum, and all the other efforts to rub us out, we hung on, and we adjusted.

Then another unanticipated, insidious force confronted the Indian people. Because of extremely high unemployment, poor housing, ineffectual governance, and lost hope, many Indian people began to migrate to the cities to better their world for themselves and their children, but in the process unity in the Indian world would further erode. It is said that over 50 percent of us now live off reservation.

It would seem that, with all of these destructive forces at work, the Indian people would only be a lost memory, but we fooled them. Because of the strength of our brave ancestors, our traditional beliefs, our grandmothers, our stubbornness, our commitment, and our hope, we still survive as a people by adjusting and uniting our forces as one when the cause is just. This natural strategy has proved effective several times over the years, highlighted in the Native American Graves Protection Repatriation Act of 1989, and the National Museum of the American Indian Act in 1990. Our Indian world is changing for the better.

This symposium is a part of that same movement and adjustment. In the late 1980s, there was a flurry of Euro-American centennial activities in the Northern Plains states as they celebrated their 100-year birthday. Few care to remember that they were built on the graves of the Indian people. In order to add an "Indian Voice" and balance to these activities, a large museum in Cody, Wyoming, where I was a curator, working with Sioux people in 1990, organized a museum exhibit and catalog entitled "Wounded Knee: Lest We Forget," featuring the Ghost Dance and the Massacre at Wounded Knee, South Dakota, in 1890. Before we had time to heal after that reminder, we had to endure the country's Euro-American celebration of the 500-year anniversary of the arrival of Columbus. The Indian people again had little to celebrate. Then a few years ago, after we somewhat recovered, it started again, only on a smaller scale, with the 200-year, Euro-American celebration of Lewis and Clark's expedition up the Missouri River to the Pacific Ocean. By now, we had adjusted and realized that the general public often celebrates activities and people who have, among other things, inflicted immense loss on the American Indian nations. Our Indian Voice had to be heard once again to add perspective to these "activities."

The Lewis and Clark Bicentennial Committee, working closely with the Lewis and Clark Interpretive Center on a "Signature Event" for Great Falls, Montana, asked a number of Indian people to work with them organizing an Indian presentation for the event just before the Fourth of July 2005. The Indian people included Duane Champagne (UCLA), Murtin McCluskey (Great Falls), Linda Juneau (Missoula), and myself. After introductions and polite discussions, I outlined a scenario that I have been considering for years. That is, with some adjustments, we could organize a gathering of American Indian thinkers similar to the effort that anthropologist Sol Tax organized in 1961 in Chicago. Although strategic politics guided the earlier effort, this one would be entitled "American Indian Nations: Yesterday, Today, and Tomorrow." All of my enthusiastic fellow planners are my friends and we have known each other for years, so they let me run.

Our structure would divide the Indian world into vitally important categories or subjects that are necessary to our survival as Indian people. Some of those categories would be our land base, water rights, demography, multi-jurisdictions on reservations, the importance of Indians in politics, civil rights, Indian health, the Bureau of Indian Affairs, the importance of Indians in science, Indian education, repatriation, tribal traditions, the state of American Indian studies programs, voting, and many more. Defining and updating the categories was easy; the difficult part was to locate Indian experts for all of them. As a contrast to the fur-clad mountain men and hobbyists at the regular Lewis and Clark activities, our speakers would be, for the most part, American Indian scholars, attorneys, curators, teachers, and other professionals, and traditionalists who are well known, respected, and published in their field of expertise.

With the exception of a few with prior commitments, the invited speakers, with great enthusiasm, all signed on. These Indian scholars came from all parts of the country and shared with us the current facts of these subjects. Of course, with so many diverse topics, we discovered that Indian scholars were not always available to cover a subject, so to achieve my personal goal, my family "adopted" all of the non-Indian speakers for three days, the length of the conference, to make all the speakers "Indian" people. It was an incredible experience to meet all of them and hear what they have learned on these vital subjects. Some are old friends, some are new, and they were all very good and all giants in the Indian world. We must realize that the buffalo days are gone and, in order to survive and even excel, the methods of struggle and dedication must change as well, from the grassy plains to the courthouse and classroom. These new heroes of ours with their briefcases must replace the brave warriors of the past, and the world and our children must know these things.

The great success of our endeavor is found in two quarters: the speakers and volunteers. The first, of course, lies with the character and quality of the speakers. Without exception, they were great. We are so proud of them. Audio records preserved each session, and a good friend from Washington, D.C., made sure they were all recorded on DVDs as well (available at cost from M. Severson, 406-899-8918). Their presentations are also recorded in this publication and are a document of this time, with Indian people telling how they see their world. Talk about the "Indian Voice" presented by our Indian heroes!

None of this could have taken place without our volunteer staff that, in many cases, worked day and night. Much appreciation goes to Mayor Randy Gray of Great Falls and Peggy Beltrone, Cascaded County Commissioner; Dr. Eugene McAllister, president of the University of Great Falls; the National Museum of the American Indian; the Lewis and Clark Bicentennial Commission; Fort Lewis College, and the many others who helped. Special thanks to the key players and workers: Jane Weber, director of the Lewis and Clark Interpretive

Center, who kept us all going; Chandler Jackson, director of the library, Fort Lewis College, the willing workhorse of the group; Dr. Duane Champagne, who assisted everywhere; Carol Franco, who does it all, and all the others I have temporarily forgotten but who were responsible for making this an outstanding success. We all hope that some large associated organization, such as the National Museum of the American Indian, will continue this effort in the future. May you all walk in sunshine. We made history.

George P. Horse Capture
Curator Emeritus
Great Falls, Montana

We would also like to thank the sponsors of the symposium in Great Falls, Montana, for their support.

National Museum of the American Indian
National Park Service
USDA, Forest Service
Qwest Communications
Council of Tribal Advisors (COTA)
Explore! The Big Sky National Signature Event
Indian Land Tenure Foundation
International Traditional Indian Games Society
Montana Tribal Tourism Alliance
Opportunity Link Project
Fort Lewis College
University of California, Los Angeles
University of Great Falls

Opening Keynote Address: Activating Indians into National Politics

BEN NIGHTHORSE CAMPBELL

THANK YOU, IT'S NICE TO BE HERE in Montana for a few days. During the years I was in the U.S. Senate, I was often referred to as Montana's third senator because of my ancestral roots with, and my frequent visits to, the Northern Cheyenne tribe.

For twenty-two years I served in public office—over half that time in the United States Senate, where one of my duties was to chair the Senate Committee on Indian affairs. In that capacity, you might say I inherited a national constituency. In fact, many elderly Indian people believed I was elected by and for Indian country. Perhaps, in a sense, I was. One elder, upon seeing me at the Denver powwow, happily exclaimed: "Finally we have one too." Since I am the first speaker, I would like to set the stage, so to speak.

Since 1977, I have lived among the Southern Ute people in southwest Colorado, not very far from Mesa Verde National Park. According to historians, Utes migrated into that area roughly 500 years ago. I go there often as both a point of inspiration and a place of remembrance. Ancient peoples lived in their cliff houses and in the valleys below them for over a thousand years. Not unlike the people of Tenochtitlán, the predecessor to Mexico City, and Cahokia, near the city of St. Louis, they were there before Christ walked the earth. Their towns, as large and more enlightened than communities in Europe at the time, were inhabited with teachers, religious leaders, farmers, astronomers, craftsmen, and people of many talents that you might find in a community of today. They lived there four times longer than we in the United States have had a system of government and twice as long as all of post-Columbian history. In the case of Mesa Verde's cliff dwellers, their descendants are the present-day Pueblo Indians of New Mexico. The so-called

"Anasazi" are not extinct—they are "ancestors." Think of this. During all that time, they had no sickness or disease such as TB or AIDS or smallpox or polio: not even the common cold. They had no jails because they had no crime. They had no poverty or unemployment, or any of the social vices that afflict modern civilization. They lived by four tenets. One, take care of your family; two, participate in your community; three, be a part of earth mother; and four, honor the Creator. We can learn much from them. They left the area in about 1100 AD because of drought, not discord.

And yet, the history of our people in post-Columbian times and at the hands of the U.S. government has been what some describe as a 400-year holocaust. To many, our post-Columbian history sounds like a bad play. Let me review some "Acts."

Act I: The Removal Act

The Removal Act forced native people from their aboriginal homelands which, to this day, they are still trying to recover. The Cherokee, Seminoles, Delawares, Choctaws, and Creeks didn't start out in Oklahoma. They were relocated at gunpoint. Times had been bad before 1834 but, with the Removal Act, it got worse. The federal government gave up any pretense of honoring treaties and treating tribes as sovereign nations and began to isolate them by herding them onto reservations. During the ensuing years, the federal government "acquired" an additional 174 million acres. Subsequent treaties entered into between tribes and the government were driven by duress and complicated by westward migration by everyone from land speculators, gold seekers, and buffalo hunters to trappers and farmers. If the government had any intention of honoring them at all, it is open to debate. The beginning of the end of freedom for tribes began with the Removal Act. It was conveniently forgotten that the U.S. Constitution recognizes only four governments: (1) the United States; (2) states; (3) foreign; and (4) tribes. All others are chartered and recognized by law. Counties and municipalities are not recognized as constitutional or sovereign governments. In the ensuing years after the Removal Act, somewhere the notion got started that the federal government had "granted" sovereignty to tribes rather than recognizing the sovereignty was an inherent and historic right. It follows that, if the federal government did not "grant" sovereignty to tribes, it could not be eroded or revoked. But they did and in some cases, through accident or intent, still do.

Act II: The Assimilation Act

The Assimilation Act operated under the premise "If you can't change them, absorb them until they simply disappear into the mainstream culture."

The phrase "kill the Indian to save the man" was coined. My father was known as "blackie" in Cheyenne circles when he was in Crow Agency boarding school. It was a time of forced immersion of Indian children into white society. Haircuts and beatings were the order of the day to bleach the red out of those redskins. It didn't work. The Creator put the Red in—no man can take it out. And, by the way, "red skin" is offensive to many Indians if used as a team name. Just as "squaw," "buck," and "savage" are also offensive to them.

Act III: The Reorganization Act of 1934

The Reorganization Act of 1934 stripped tribes of their traditional way of selecting their own leaders and substituted Washington's mandate of how we choose our leaders. How would America react if Russia tried to do this to America? It was a way of dealing with "sympathetic" Indian leaders rather than the likes of Red Cloud and Geronimo.

Act IV: The Termination Acts

In Washington's infinite wisdom, it was decided that tribes should no longer be tribes, never mind that they had been tribes for thousands of years. It is analogous to the federal government mandating that black Americans can no longer be black. Many tribes are still trying after years of work to be reinstated as a federally recognized entity. The reason is that the federal government has a contractual obligation through treaties to perform "trust responsibility" to tribes—not individuals—rather an ingenious manner of avoiding responsibility. If we get rid of "tribes," we can avoid responsibility to individual Indians and save lots of money.

Act V: The Allotment Act or Dawes Act

The most notable of the Allotment Acts opened Oklahoma territory to thousands of people—many who were called "Sooners" because of their creative way of circumventing Washington's effort to administer an organized system of disenfranchising native people. After all, if we're going to steal their land, we should do so in a civilized and coherent manner, rather than a stampede.

The Allotment Act was another of Washington's attempts to destroy the sovereignty of tribal government by substituting in its place private ownership of land to a people who historically and philosophically had no understanding of private ownership. The land was part of the Creator's domain. We may occupy it, but people cannot usurp the Creator by claiming title to it.

Act VI: The Relocation Act

Relocation was, under the guise of improving job opportunities, a process by which the federal government would send an Indian person to trade school in Los Angeles or Chicago or Detroit or elsewhere, give them some skills, and then dump them on the streets to fend for themselves. Some found their way, but too many fell into the depression of unemployment and were mired in a dead-end existence on skid row. In the two years of 1957 to 1959, 35,000 Indians left the reservations. A decrease in federal funding at the same time was a subtle motivation. To eat, go to the city. Besides, that one-way ticket we issued should discourage you from coming back.

All these "Acts" sound like a bad play, but they weren't part of a play. It was a tragedy, but not a play. It began during a time of westward expansions; proceeded through the boarding-school days where Indian children were shorn of their hair, beaten for speaking their language, and stripped of their dignity; and became more subtle in red-lining by banks or subtle discriminating for voting rights or job applications. Through it all, we became an American endangered species. Even though we paid our fair share in millions of lost lives and hundreds of millions of lost acres of pristine land. Even though we paid our fair share with hundreds of new contributions to the world of new foods and medicine that were unknown in Europe. Even though we paid in billions of dollars of lost resources under our lands and even though our Indian veterans paid the ultimate sacrifice in places they had never heard of called Normandy and Anzio, Battan and Inchon, and others where the bones of our warriors still lie, we still were not even considered citizens and allowed to vote until after women were.

Throughout history, the underlining motive for separating Indians from their land and culture was simple—it was pure greed. Efforts along these lines were cloaked in catchphrases like "Manifest Destiny," "Divine Right," and "Westward Expansion," but they were really code words for taking away the possessions of native people. Perhaps the great Sioux Chief Red Cloud described it best when he said: "they made us many promises and they broke all but one. They promised to take our land and they took it."

Let me fast forward, however, to a new era in which Indian leaders have learned well the "rules of engagement" on the new fields of battle. Now we must defend ourselves in the courts and the halls of Congress. The lance and the war pony have given way to education and voting rights and, as of the 1980s, a new act has been added to our repertoire of acts. Under the Nixon policy, a new concept called "Self Determination" was coined and the ensuing pieces of legislation, including the Indian Gaming Regulatory Act (IGRA), to name just one of many, ushered in an era in which the federal government has begun to recognize that, through compacting and contracting services, Indian people can best run their own lives and their own affairs.

The success of IGRA cannot be minimized. Between 1990 and 2005, we have come from nowhere to a $19 billion a year industry hiring 557,000 employees. With gaming profits, tribes have begun to diversify into resorts, manufacturing, tourism, and retail. But even more importantly, they have strengthened their cultures by building schools, initiating traditional language and art programs, improving the health and well-being of tribal elders, and sending more youngsters to college. To be sure, all tribes have not prospered equally and, in fact, most still suffer from high unemployment, high suicide and incarcerations rates, poor health, and few opportunities. But I believe the stormy past our people have experienced is beginning to wane and, given more hard work on our part and a little more tolerance, understanding, and latitude in running our own affairs, a new dawn for Indian people is on the horizon.

The point of my presentation can be summed up this way. After 200 years of the failed policies of the U.S. government toward tribes, perhaps out of frustration and exasperation, someone in Washington in the 1970s came up with a novel and untried approach to the Indian problem. Since nothing else has worked, how about letting them run their own affairs? And, in my view, Indian leaders have risen to the occasion. This, coupled with both a rise of militancy in the 1960s and a determined effort by Native people to effect public policy bills, the Native American Graves Protection and Repatriation Act, the National Museum of the American Indian, the Little Big Horn National Park and Memorial, the Indian Lands Consolidation Act, to name a few, were written in a cooperative fashion by Indians and their representatives in Washington. We have come a long way, to be sure. In looking over the list of presenters here in Great Falls and knowing both their credentials and their determination, I am convinced that the age of reemergence of Red people, that is spoken of in Hopi prophesy, is now taking place. We owe so much to both those who went ahead of us and sacrificed so much and to those who will follow us to fulfill our dreams. Our age group will not personally know either, but we are that link between the past and future that makes the ageless existence of Native peoples.

Are we "out of the woods yet?" Can we relax our vigilance? Absolutely not. Even today, bills are introduced that would reverse the positive trend we have worked for. As an example, one bill dealing with off-reservation gaming, which is for tribes building casinos on lands not contiguous to their reservations, has a section which gives cities and counties veto powers over tribes who have gone through the federal process and jumped through all the bureaucratic hoops, before tribes can build a casino on their own land. It is probably not a defensible position in courts. But since almost half of all Indian decisions which had formerly been heard in the Supreme Court are now routinely being remanded to the appellate courts, we are at risk because we are losing more than we are winning in the appellate courts. But to these people, both Indian or not, there is still much to do before we rest. The difficulties we face are less violent than they were when bounties were put on us. But many are there just the same. Yes, my friends, we still have a long journey to go.

AMERICAN INDIAN IDENTITY   I

Activism: Time to Change Native American References in Sports

2

SUZAN SHOWN HARJO

I AM HERE TODAY TO TALK ABOUT NATIVE AMERICAN REFERENCES in sports. This is not my favorite topic. It is something I have been saddled with, actually, because there is a case called *Harjo et al. v. Pro Football, Inc.*[1] I am that Harjo, and Pro Football, Inc., is Washington's professional football team. I like Jay Leno's joke a few years ago where he said, "Did you hear that the Washington professional football team changed its name? They no longer call themselves professional."

We filed our suit in September 1992, and the team has not gone to the Super Bowl since that year. Now, I am not saying there is a cause and effect; I am just stating a fact. I think it is a little karma and they probably won't go to the Super Bowl again until they change the name. They have fought us tooth and nail since 1992. Now, how much have they fought? They have dragged their feet every step of the way. They have slowed us down any possible way. There are seven of us who brought this lawsuit and they have investigated us up one side and down the other—all our families—and looked at everything we might have said. I guess they looked through our garbage for pictures of us sitting around the house wearing their jerseys and ball caps. I don't know what they were looking for—maybe some signed confession stating that I really do love the name "Redskins." They have been intent on winning this lawsuit.

What is at stake for them? They say that the name is a tradition, that it honors us, and that it is too expensive to change. The previous owner said that. The owner before him said that. We have been in litigation with three owners—Jack Kent Cook, John Kent Cook (the son), and now Daniel Snyder. We did not get a chance to interview or depose Jack Kent Cook, because they dragged their feet too long and then he got sick and passed away. The son said, when asked if he had ever met a Native person, "I think so." The lawyer asked the circumstance. "Along the side of the road, it was selling a pot." "Was this a man or a woman?" "I don't remember. I think it was a Cherokee." Gender just slipped his mind. "It" sold him a pot. I always found that fascinating.

We won our case before the U.S. Patent and Trademark Board in 1999. Our case is a pocketbook incentive lawsuit, and that means we are not taking a straight ahead, civil rights kind of approach. We are saying it's a racist name. It is disparaging. It does all sorts of bad things to people when they least expect it. And, we are saying the team can call itself, the owners can call their team, any racist thing they want, but the federal government cannot sanction that. They cannot provide their imprimatur, their exclusive privilege of making money. That's what happens when the federal government puts its stamp of approval on something like that. They can't do it because of the trademark laws that say you cannot trademark something that is disparaging, that holds a people up to contempt, that holds a people up to ridicule, or that is scandalous. There are four things you can't do and, if you do any one of those, you don't get a license.

So we brought our suit in 1992 saying that, when the team owners brought their bid for a license in 1967, they should have been refused. There should have been no license granted because they offended these four prongs of the Lanham Act, the Trademark Act.[2] Periodically, they received licenses, trademarks, up until 1992 when we filed suit. What our suit is saying is that all of those licenses should be cancelled. There are three trademark judges who looked at the case from 1992 to 1999. Finally, in April 1999, they agreed with us. All three of them, a unanimous decision, a 145-page decision, and they basically said that that word, that team name, in this context disparages Native Americans and holds us up to contempt and holds us up to disrepute. They did not agree with us that it was scandalous. We didn't really think it was scandalous broadly, but we thought it should be and had thrown that in. We didn't get all four. We got three out of four. That ain't bad. So, we won in 1999 and the licenses were cancelled, pending appeal—an important thing.

The federal district court judge reversed those three trademark judges' ruling in October 2003, saying that we were too late and we are not bothered. That is basically it. She said we are not disparaged and we should have brought this suit in 1967, when the team owners initially filed for license protection.[3] Only one of the seven of us was twenty-one years old in 1967 and the youngest one, Mateo Romero, was in diapers. It was interesting how the judge ruled, because she presented a kind of trademark system that this country doesn't have. She was presenting it as if there were a trademark in perpetuity. But there is not. You get trademarks periodically and you go for revisions or extensions of trademarks. She didn't take that into account. Now, we have appealed that. We are in the U.S. Court of Appeals[4] and we could have a decision as early as next week. There will be a decision one way or the other, or splitting the difference, by the end of July, and I think it will be sooner than later. The Circuit Court of Appeals for the District of Columbia Circuit will be making their decision, and you couldn't tell from the hearing that we had on April 8th. They were asking questions from every direction. Basically, they were asking if there were a team called the n-word, would that be offensive? Would that be disparaging? And the lawyers for the Washington football team said no. One of the judges, who had asked the question, nearly fell out of his seat. "What did you say?" The lawyer said, "No, it wouldn't be disparaging, because we have a different meaning. It would have a different meaning because it was the name of a team." So, they are saying it has a secondary meaning.

I remember during my deposition, they kept showing me photos of program covers that had Sitting Bull on the cover and it said "Redskins." And they said, "You don't find this disparaging, do you?" "Well, yes I do. If you put Martin Luther King Jr. on the cover of the team brochure with the n-word, it would not have secondary meaning." This is what is really at issue here. It's fascinating hearing people tell us what we are bothered by, which is the whole crux of the lawsuit. We say we are offended. The Washington team owners say, no you are not; you are honored. We say, no, we are offended. And they say, shut up. That is the lawsuit, and they really don't like to talk to living Indians and have gone out of their way not to. They have kept us out of any deposition and negotiations—it can only be the lawyers present and not any of us— as they call us the activists, the militants. I'll tell you who "we" are:

Vine Deloria, who has written twenty-five books and he's a lawyer; myself;
Norbert Hill, who is an educator who runs the American Indian Graduate Center, which gives out the Gates Millennium Scholarships all around the country, and ran AISES for a while;
Ray Apodaca, who is the governor of Ysleta del Sur Pueblo and is a federal employee now in the TANF program in Washington;
Bill Means, who actually is an activist, and this is the first time he has been a plaintiff in a lawsuit, so he was very happy about that, but he too is an educator and was the first person in his family to get a college degree and ran one of the first survival schools, the Heart of the Earth Survival School in Minneapolis, and has done many things in the area of education;

Mateo Romero—I selected him because he is an artist—whose main point in all of this is that you have to get rid of all of the underbrush of stereotypical images before our actual personae, images, symbols, can shine through. People don't know who we are or what we look like, what our symbols are, what is real and what is not, which is why you can have so many phony baloney, profit-seeking medicine people with sweat lodges who charge people and people think they are getting the real deal, they are getting the genuine thing; and Manley Begay, who is at the University of Arizona and used to be at Harvard and is a Doctor of Education.

These are the people that the other side has no problem in court documents calling the "activists," the "militant cohorts."

Pro Football, Inc., also refers that way to the National Congress of American Indians, the National Indian Education Association, the National Indian Youth Council, Tulsa Coalition Against Racism—the groups that have joined as *amici curia*. And the other side objected to their appearance as friends of the court, and then, when the court said let them appear, they objected to the brief that was filed. The court is still reading the brief and, when they finish reading it, they will rule on it. At that point it really doesn't make a whole lot of difference about what they have said. The Washington football team owners and lawyers have been adamantly opposed to any Native people who do not agree with them that the name of their team is an honor to us. They don't listen, no matter how many Native people, or how many groups, or how many segments of Indian society that you put up before them. All of those people are wrong. The lawyers have even gone out to Pine Ridge and to Rosebud looking for the relatives and descendants of "Lone Star" Dietz. They say the team was named after him. He is someone who went to Carlisle, was said to have been a full-blooded Sioux (and you always have to perk up your ears when anyone says "full-blooded" anything, because that usually means phony baloney). Lone Star went to Carlisle and became an assistant coach of the Washington football team, and they say the name of the team came about because of Lone Star Dietz. It turns out the guy was German, was not Lakota by any stretch of the imagination, had no Indians in his background, and was brought into Carlisle football as a ringer because he was a good football player. He went on to marry an Indian woman from Carlisle, who very suddenly, just before a lawsuit in Washington State involving this man, filed for divorce. She was a famous Winnebago woman and she, I think, although we have found no material to support this point in writing, discovered that he was indeed German and was not Indian and was faking it. It seems it was a little more serious than just faking it. It seems that he was a true identity thief and the person whose name he borrowed disappeared mysteriously. So, it is an entire mystery and the court case was establishing that he indeed was not really one James One Star and asking where was James One Star.

So, you have this myth about how the name came about—that it came about as an honor to a full-blooded Sioux, the beloved coach, who turns out to be not at all Indian. So it is a lie on top of a lie on top of a lie. In the court records in our case, we are derided when we point out these kinds of things and we are accused of being the people who fictionalize things as opposed to these people who are propagandists and mythologizers of the first order. I have begun to see this issue as something much more fundamental than in the day when Kevin Gover was working with people in the early 1970s in Washington, D.C., to get rid of this name, and had a very important meeting with one of the owners at the time, Edward Bennett Williams. Williams also represented the *Washington Post*, which did not take a position against the name and call for the name to be changed until he died. And then the *Post* took the position that at whatever level you take offense here, you certainly wouldn't call a team the Washington "Darkies." So, think of it in those terms. We think of it as a little worse.

The Native people have been working against this name for a long time, especially in Oklahoma. The University of Oklahoma became the very first one to drop its "Native" references in sports. I am very happy about that, being from Oklahoma myself. There was a lot of activity in the 1960s against these sports names at a lot of big schools—Stanford, Dartmouth, Syracuse—who used to be the Saltine Warriors. The myth was that they had dug up in a development an Onondaga chief on the grounds of Syracuse University and they dubbed him the "Saltine Warrior." Why? I don't know. "Indians" at Stanford grew out of "Cardinal." All of these schools grew out of colors. Stanford was "Cardinals"—the color, not the bird. The University of Oklahoma was "Big Red," so they had "Little Red," who became the little Indian mascot who danced around like an idiot. It was always a white guy dancing around. There were huge Indian protests, so the school announced that it would make a big change and now it would be an Indian guy dancing around. There were three of them, and it got so bad that the thing eventually died off, after a few takeovers of the chancellor's office. So, the University of Oklahoma became the first school to drop its "Indian" reference, in 1970, followed shortly thereafter by Stanford and Dartmouth and Syracuse. Dartmouth was "Big Green" and there is a great t-shirt with "Big Green" and the banker guy from the Monopoly set, which I thought was highly appropriate for the Ivy League.

The good news—and it really is good news—is that in 1970, when OU dropped "Little Red," there were over 3,000 "Native" references in American sports, both educational and professional. Today, there are fewer than 1,000. Isn't that amazing? Two-thirds of the maturation of America has been completed in this area. That is really terrific news when you think about it—in thirty-five years for two-thirds of the "Indian" sports references to be dropped, that is a huge societal change. That has happened—as all things happen—school by school by school. Little Arvada High School in Colorado— they were called the Arvada "Redskins"—had to go through a twelve-year process and finally they changed. And they changed their entire history. I talked to the principal two years after that change was made (and he was a new principal). I just wanted to see what the story was after the big change and how they referred to things, and he said, "We had a beloved coach"— these stories always begin with a beloved coach—"at the turn of the 1900s and he was someone who bought the boys brand-new jerseys. Their colors were cherry and white. The jerseys were cherry, and it rained that first football game, and the cherry jerseys bled into the skins of the children who were playing football; hence, the term 'Redskins.'" Anyone who buys that . . . ! They had never come up with that during the entire time of the contest of whether they should drop "Redskins," and it doesn't quite explain how it went from that sweet story to having a mascot with feathers and a huge nose (as they always do) and big lips—this grotesque caricature of a Native person.

All over America, you have these kinds of de-mascoting activities taking place and, one by one by one, the names are changing. Now we are down to 900 and some. That's really terrific. Along the way it raises consciousness about a lot of other things. There is one school in North Dakota that wanted to drop its name "Redskins," so they went through all sorts of gyrations to find a new name, and one of the new names they came up with was "White Knights." The cheerleaders didn't like that. They said, "What are we then? Are we the 'Damsels in Distress'?" It started a whole other thing. And then they went to Bulldogs. Again, "What are we?" When you shine a light on an injustice in one corner, it sort of seeps in and illuminates injustices in other places, and people start asking questions and assert themselves, and I think that is a good and healthy thing.

I still run into people on the airplane, going to Oklahoma, who will say: "I sure miss 'Little Red.' I just liked him, he was so cute." And they go on to talk about how great "Little Red" was. Well, he wasn't cute and he did some damage, and the people who liked him want something that is easy about Indian affairs. They want something that is easy about treaty rights. They want something that is easy about who Native people are. They like the cigar-store Indian. I am looking at a cartoon by Richard Crewson from the *Wichita Eagle* and he has a boy fancy dancer, all fancied up, and there are two white kids—one with a backwards ball cap and a "Go Redskins" shirt, and a smaller person, a girl, whose shirt says "Pocahontas." The boy is saying, "Way cool outfit. Which are you, a sports team mascot or a Disney character?" That is sort of how things are these days. People really don't know—going back to Mateo Romero's point about the underbrush of stereotypes—people don't know who we are and they don't know when they are looking at the authentic or the genuine article. They don't understand our diversity and they don't understand our inconsistencies. They don't understand our humanity. And we play into that so much by dressing in predictable ways or by selling the things that are the easy Indian things, like dream-catchers. Now, name the place that that came from. Whose tradition is that, but people are selling traditional dream-catchers?

The first *Oprah Winfrey Show* that she did on Native people—I was on that show—was on stereotypes. The chairman for the Eastern Band of Cherokee—who make the rubber tomahawk that the Atlanta Braves started doing the tomahawk chop with—said that "We make these tomahawks and we are laughing all the way to the bank." So, he was making a point of how they cash in on stereotypes, and he came up to me afterwards and asked if I wanted a tomahawk. I said, "Yes, I have this mantel of shame, Jonathon Ed. I'll put it right on there with the 'Treaty Beer.' " He said, "This ain't beer." I said, "Sure, give me two."

During my deposition for this lawsuit, Jonathan Ed Taylor's name came up in the lawsuit as one who had written a letter to the Washington Redskins saying "Don't listen to those militants, we don't agree with them. Do you have any scholarship money?" I was happy, not about the circumstance, but for the purpose of the deposition and the point, to be able to say, "Oh yes, this is the tribal chief who, shortly after he wrote that letter, was indicted for embezzlement of tribal funds."

They handed me another letter from another person who was one of the principal chiefs of one of the nations in eastern Oklahoma. "Yes," I said, "he was indicted as a sexual predator." It is interesting that there were four letters and all four were written by offenders of their people when they were in positions to be protectors of their people. That was a fascinating lesson to me about who is with us and who is not. In all of the time of our lawsuit, the other side has not produced a single person to come into court, with the exception of those letters produced at my deposition, who will agree with them. Not a single Native American person. And there are some, we all know them—like the lady I keep meeting on the airplanes who misses cute "Little Red"—a lot of people, especially those who went to BIA boarding schools, do miss their Indian imagery. I remember friends of my mother—they kind of liked it all because they remembered the little cartoon image above Pocahontas Hall, which they called "Pokey Hall," at Haskell University. That was their way of remembering something that was good about the school. All of the BIA schools were named the "Indians," "Braves," "Warriors," even when they were the ringers brought in from other races. These people remember those experiences in the only good way they can, by these little cartoon images. As people say, if you don't have anything good to identify with, you will identify with anything. That's what happens to people in these schools. So, you have a lot of Native people who just want to identify with something that is Indian, so they will bead the Washington football team logo, the disembodied head, or even the name. Or they will have their patch from their boarding school.

This is something that is a reality. I believe you can draw a distinction between the Indian schools that named themselves and their teams and the name-calling from outside. Here's the problem with that though. It is not just your side of the issue that you are dealing with. You go into a sports place, you go into the basketball arena, you go onto the football field, there is another team whose job it is to yell at your team, to beat your team, to demean your symbols, and their fans are going to be very insulting if you are the "Indians" or the "Warriors." You are supposed to be yourselves. You are the Indian people and there are all of these other people demeaning you. How is that separable from them demeaning you as a person and them demeaning you as a people? They don't draw those lines, and when you are on the receiving end when you are a kid, you don't draw those lines, either. It is something that I think the Indian schools are going to have to get real about and eliminate these. I hear a lot of throwback talk these days from some of these schools—"Oh no, it's fine, we are the Indians so we can have these symbols." And you see some of the worse stereotypes—the "Chief Wahoo" kind of things.

As far as the language, they are right. They are not demeaning themselves, so you can liken them to the "Fighting Irish" at Notre Dame. But the "Fighting Irish" really were Irish, before Knute Rockne. They named themselves. They were proud of that. Not too many years ago, when they played Marquette University, the Marquette fans sent out a kid who was supposed to be a drunken leprechaun, onto the football field. There was a huge uproar—the game stopped—and they didn't play Marquette again until they had an official apology. That is the same sort of thing and you could make the case that the Indian schools should keep these names, these symbols, if they want. It is only non-Indians that have to give them up. But I really think the Indians are going to have to bite the bullet on this one and say, we don't want the stereotypes here. There are lots of other things we can call ourselves and people have gotten very creative around the country—like the Michigan team that calls themselves the "Lugnuts."

Little Siena College, in the early 1990s, went to number two in the basketball championships the year that they dropped "Indians." They had two top favorites—they had a measles epidemic so about 49 percent voted for "Measles" and the others voted for "Saints," so they are the Saints. But people showed up for their games at the championship with dots all over their faces, and we almost went to dangerous diseases. That was fun, and I think that, whatever the schools want to call themselves, they should keep in mind that there is no reason to pick a fight. That is the important thing. That is especially important in an educational setting. There is just no reason for any school to sanction this kind of emotional attack on Native people for the recreational use of these images.

In professional sports, no professional team has changed its name and I don't think anyone will until someone actually wins a lawsuit against one of the pro teams, so everyone is looking at our lawsuit to see if that is the one. It doesn't matter if we win or we lose. If we lose, and we may, I have kids, and all of us bringing this lawsuit have, in our families, lawsuits stacked up to infinity, I'm happy to say. This isn't the only suit. This isn't the only possible way to do this and, depending on what kind of response we get, we could continue this very lawsuit but with a different cast of characters, just filing anew. If we win, other groups—the Native people in Cleveland—could file suit using the same kind of theory, the same forum, to get rid of "Chief Wahoo," which is the graphic equivalent of "Redskins," if you think about it.

That is where we are with our lawsuit. We are on the verge of the step below an absolute final decision, although the decision by the Court of Appeals might not be absolute. It could go with us on disparagement and the other side with laches, meaning passage of time. One thing no one has ever considered in this is how long it took the Washington team to file for federal protection. They had this name in the 1930s and didn't file until 1967. I think they filed because of the uproar all around the country on college campuses in the 1960s and they wanted some sort of federal protection. I think that is why they filed, although we have not been able to prove that, or make that assertion in court, but here, just talking, I think that is what happened.

What happened when they came up with the name? We know it wasn't because of the beloved coach, the German "Lone Star" Dietz. It came at a time when Indian dancing was outlawed. From 1880 to 1936, under the "Civilization Regulations," Indian people could not dance on reservations, and the only "Indian dancing" that was able to be done in America was in the sports field, which is so interesting. You had non-Indians dressing up like Indians, in some sort of "way cool acting," and going in as mascots at a time when Indians could be called hostiles, or fomenters of dissent, or ring leaders, or trouble makers, or any other charges that could get them killed, or at least starved and put in prison under the "Civilization Regulations," were not able to dance. Real Indians couldn't dance and the people who were pretend Indians, in "Indian" outfits, could dance, could be mascots. I am not suggesting that people really understood that was what was happening, but it was a marked shift, if you will. If people didn't want to go to the Southwest, where they felt the Indians were, they could go to a football game and see the "Indians" there at halftime. That really is where we are today, except that Indians are allowed to dance today. Some of the dancing that is done is also very stereotypic, and what we are seeing is Native people who are not Native culturally, copying the mascots, copying the kinds of outfits that were developed by the non-Indians to approximate Indians—dyed turkey feathers, primary colors. It is fascinating how much Native people have taken on stereotypes about us and perpetuated those, especially those who are marketing, are selling Indian religion, selling Indian culture, and trying to make a name for themselves.

This really is part of the image problem that we have generally, about who is a Native person, who gets to decide, how can you tell, and does it matter. What does it matter? It matters because what people write about us, what we write about ourselves, what is taught in schools, what ends up in libraries, what ends up on television, all present a problem for us if it is not authentic. It presents a problem for us because it is another overlayer of imaging, and most of these images are not favorable images. You have the savage savage, the noble savage, the good stereotypes, the bad stereotypes—and, as far as I am concerned, there is no such thing as a good stereotype. A stereotype is a negative influence, period.

What we are seeing today is almost a replication of what happened in the late 1800s and early 1900s with all of the show Indians. Some of them were in my own family. I had Cheyenne relatives who were living exhibits at the St. Louis World's Fair in 1904, where they had them on a scale as to how close you were to the monkeys. How low on the evolutionary scale were you, and they said that the Native people of this hemisphere were closer to the animals. My family, coming from the bears, didn't mind the animal part so much—it was the monkeys that they really didn't like. We think that is only in the past. But, it isn't that long ago that the Bureau of Indian Affairs developed a list of three different kinds of Indians. The ones that were closest to the white people were the ones who were put on the first termination lists. What did that mean? The people who were the lightest, the people who spoke English to the exclusion of their Native language or were predominantly over the Native language, and who were primarily Christian. Indians by religion, by language, by appearance—those were the people who could be terminated. I am Cheyenne and Muskogee, and all of our relatives were on that last list. They were kind of hopeless and had to stay under the BIA. Don't terminate them because they still speak their language, they look pretty Indian, and they are not Christians. They were on the last list.

Then you had the middle list. They really didn't get to the middle list. They just started terminating the ones on the first list. The thing about appearance—by whose standard? Who decides about appearance? There are whole nations of people who are much lighter or much darker or started out about the same color before they started intermarrying with this and that other kind of people. Who decides what Indians look like? The more we give over our imagery to non-Native people—and to Native people who are willing to stereotype ourselves and distort our images—the more likely we are to have distortions in policy about us and reactions to us when we try to assert ourselves on something very important. We get laughed at when we are talking about important treaty rights, or any kind of rights really. When we are dealing with something that is very, very serious, we are made light of because of this objectification. It is almost as if we are not people who can hear. We are not the people who can see what people are saying about us. Or see the way people are reacting to us. That is a very interesting dynamic, and any of you who have been in negotiations with non-Indians knows what this is like. You are sitting on the other side of the table and people make cracks about you as if you can't hear what they are saying unless they are addressing you directly. If they are making an aside, it is as if you can't hear, because you are the object that they turn on and off by their attention. It is a very interesting dynamic, and once you are in a position to see these kinds of aberrations that occur because of stereotyping, it makes you want to be a zealot about this issue.

When we filed the lawsuit in 1992, a friend of mine, Michael Dorris, who had been the person at Dartmouth College to get rid of the "Indians" imagery and name—said to me, "What you have given up is your right to be a public person who can laugh." He was explaining what he had found at Dartmouth, that he couldn't crack jokes because it went against the grain of the serious nature of the effort and that the people he was trying to convince only accommodate one attitude at a time from Native people about any given subject. It is a fascinating glimpse into the way that non-Native people deal with Native people who are asserting a right. What is the right here? The right to be treated in a dignified manner. That is the right. I am so interested in this latest move by Florida State University, with their Plains Indian "Osceola" mascot. Osceola was a great, great man, a Muscogee-Seminole man. He would not accept the Seminole removal treaty. When the removal treaty was put in front of him to sign, he stabbed the treaty. Isn't that a strong thing? And he has been reduced to a mascot for a football team. This is a school that went into the Patent and Trademark Board and got licenses for the name "Seminole." They own the name Seminole. With recent examinations of this issue by the NCAA, the Oklahoma Seminoles who represent the majority of the Seminoles don't want Florida State to be called the "Seminoles." FSU doesn't have the right to trademark our names. The Florida Seminoles went to Florida State University and gave them a resolution, saying, roughly, "We are fine with it. We like it. Keep on with it (and by the way, don't touch our gaming)." That is really what is at stake here for them. Florida State University, rather than saying, "We are so glad having a minority opinion," or saying that at least they have the Seminole people living in Florida supporting them and there are more Seminoles in Oklahoma that oppose us, they didn't even acknowledge that. They just said "Great, we have someone who supports us." It reminds me of when the white men would come and ask for this land or that land, and when everyone would say, "Why don't you move over there," they would find the one guy who would say, "Sure, no problem," and they would make him a chief and say, "Sign here." That would be the thumbprint on their deed. Even though there were lots of other Native people (and it may not have even been this guy's land), that was the one entity, the one person who mattered. I see that very starkly by the Florida Seminole situation, where anyone who says yes to the white man must be the exalted chief. Anyone who says no is the troublemaker, the activist, the militant, the cohort. That is how it has been in the past, and that is how it will be in the future.

I hope that we are going to win our lawsuit. If we don't, it's okay, because we made a lot of changes and there have been a lot of changes and they are going to go on. And there will be other lawsuits because there are about ten theories going around and a lot of good people who are standing by us to take on this issue of the professional sports references of Native Americans. I will warn you, if you are thinking about a lawsuit, consider that you might be in a situation that I am in and the other six people who have this lawsuit against the Washington football team. Thirteen years of having to behave in a certain way—there are certain things you can't do—of having to be under a certain kind of scrutiny (imagine having your garbage gone through with regularity). You are putting yourself in a situation where you are inviting stalkers into your house. It is a very difficult thing, to have that kind of lawsuit for a prolonged period of time. I am very proud of the group that we have, who have stuck with it for thirteen years, and maybe in the next five years we may have an absolute end to it.

I want to refer you to something that is coming out this year called *For Indigenous Eyes Only: A Decolonization Workbook*.[5] I have a chapter in that called "Just Good Sports" about this subject. I interviewed a lot of young Native people to look at the impact of "Native" sports references on Native young people who have tried to make a difference in their school; people who have gone into their own schools and changed something. They won something. How empowering was that? Even for those who didn't win 100 percent, it was greatly empowering. I hope you will read that chapter. I really loved the people I interviewed. One of them picked up a doctorate, and she said the difference is now she goes into these schools and tries to get people to change, and when they call her a bitch, she gets to say, "That's Dr. Bitch to you, sir." I commend that chapter to you and the entire decolonization workbook. It is a fun topic, but it is also a very serious topic because it is really the atmospherics, the context, the foundation, for all that we do in Indian rights. It really colors everything, and if you go into any office in Congress, and if there is someone who is still operating on the Boy Scout, Eagle Scout, Indian merit badge level, playing Indian level, the sports team level, they are not the ones who are going to make great Indian policy. They are not the ones who are going to uphold treaties in your home area. They are not the ones who are going to do things that last for Indians, because people don't make good and lasting and thorough policy for cartoons or for mascots or for disembodied heads. That simply is not who gets good policy made for them.

People don't even know this is an affront. If you look at the uproar about the stamps in Mexico of late—which show caricatures of black people in a cartoon context—people in Mexico are making excuses for the stamps, saying this is a beloved character who is teaching people about racism, and we are proud to have this lesson from this set of cartoon characters and it is not racism. It just sounds so much like the Washington football team, like any school around the country with these "Native" references. It is almost word for word the way they are explaining away their position on "Native" references in sports. It is indefensible, but they are defending it. Sometimes it is hilarious, and sometimes you have to be very serious about it and honor the people who are on the other side of the table and not laugh in their face. But it is enough to make a cat laugh.

Notes

1. *Harjo et al. v. Pro-Football, Inc.*, 30 U.S.P.Q.2d 1828, 1831 (TTAB 1994), and *Harjo v. Pro-Football Inc.*, 50 U.S.P.Q.2d 1705 (TTAB 1999).
2. Lanham Trademark Act, 15 U.S.C. §§1051–1127, 1141.
3. *Pro-Football, Inc. v. Harjo*, 284 F. Supp. 2d 96 (D.D.C. 2003).
4. *Pro-Football, Inc. v. Harjo et al.*, 415 F.3d 44 (D.C. Cir. 2005).
5. Angela Cavender Wilson and Michael Yellow Bird, eds., *For Indigenous Eyes Only: A Decolonization Handbook* (Santa Fe: School of American Research, 2005).

3

What's in a Label?
Native American Identity and
the Rise of a Tradition of Racism

GREGORY R. CAMPBELL AND S. NEYOOXET GREYMORNING

N APRIL 1804, Captains Meriwether Lewis and William Clark ventured out from North Dakota into a territory previously uncharted by Euro-
American explorers in search of a water route that would allow passage to
the Pacific Ocean. The peoples the expedition encountered represented numerous distinct cultures and societies. While Lewis and Clark have been lauded for
opening up a nation's knowledge of a previously unknown territory, after the
fabric of that era was rewoven, and although descendants of many of those societies maintained distinct features of their cultures into the twenty-first century,
ironically, many of those peoples have been politically disenfranchised of land,
resources, and identity. Another impact of contact, and perhaps among the most
divisive issues afflicting contemporary Native North Americans, stems from the
questions "Who has a legitimate right to proclaim being American Indian?" and
"By what criteria is such a claim to be made?" Such queries hold deep, important bearing as they impact at least 2 million individuals nationwide. They also
stand as a barometer to which some form of self-determination can be exercised
by more than 500 indigenous nations. It is at this intersection, between individual ethnic identity and a federally recognized tribe's right to determine its own
membership, that emerges a volatile social and political arena. The purpose of
this essay is to explore one emerging area of conflict, that of identity versus the
legitimacy of who can identify themselves as a Native American.

The Traditional Way

Despite the cultural diversity of pre-contact Native North America, there has
never been much genetic distinction between America's Indigenous peoples.[1]

More to the point, Native peoples, despite the relatively high degrees of so-ciocultural inclusiveness, have also maintained a high degree of marriage ex-change among different tribes and cultural groups.

Aboriginally, kinship rather than biology was the core component of both societal composition and individual ethnic affiliation. Every indigenous soci-ety had sociological mechanisms for the incorporation of individuals and, sometimes, whole groups by adoption, naturalization, or other ethnogenetic processes. Over the course of a society's history, most indigenous nations, pe-riodically or continuously, integrated people from other societies.[2] Such so-cial processes negated genetic distinctions.

Once non-Indians appeared on the American landscape, the same kin principles prevailed. Numerous Europeans and Africans were incorporated into indigenous societies by various sociological mechanisms such as mar-riage, adoption, capture, and naturalization. Escaped African slaves for exam-ple typically were accepted among Native peoples. These societal members, whether African or European, became fully integrated into their host societies without any phenotypic or cultural stigma.[3]

Hence by 1830, the criteria of defining "Indianness" in terms of racial phenotype had been rendered absurd.[4] There is little, if any, indication that indigenous societies tended to view this increasing admixture as peculiar, much less threatening, in and of itself.

Racial Dimension of Divide and Rule

The United States' intellectual establishment played a major role in promulgat-ing the pseudoscientific disciplines of craniometry, phrenology, and eugenics from the early nineteenth century onwards.[5] These pseudoscientific disciplines established a racist project that has lasted into the twenty-first century. Some current scholars are still committed to devising "objective" criteria by which the human species can be subdivided into distinct races according to heritable, empirically demonstrable characteristics.[6]

With publication of Morton's *Crania Americana* in 1839, it is no overstate-ment to suggest that the Euro-American intelligentsia stood at the vanguard of "scholarly" efforts to posit an attractive veneer to a white supremacist ide-ology that played to both the Eurocentric imperialism of academic re-spectability, and an aura of sheer inevitability in the popular consciousness.[7] That is, America's "Manifest Destiny" to extend uninterruptedly "from sea to shining sea," could only be attained at the direct expense of North America's indigenous populations.[8] It is instructive that United States policymakers em-braced racism on both scientific and philosophical grounds, standpoints that directly impacted federal Indian policy.

Blood Quantum and Rise of Traditional Racism

Since European colonization, there existed a political strategy to use the incorporation of Anglos and "mixed-bloods" as a wedge to pry indigenous societies apart by favoring them in various social arenas. Predictably, this bias translated into a privileging of phenotypic-looking "white" mixed-bloods, in both political and material terms, while relegating full-bloods to the periphery of their own societies.

While the history of Indian–white relations is fraught with examples of this divide-and-conquer strategy of privileging mixed-bloods, the hallmark of regulating Indian identity was the passage of the 1887 General Allotment Act.[9] The bedrock upon which the allotment process was built was the compilation of formal rolls listing those belonging to each federally recognized tribe on a reservation.[10] While the Act itself posited no specific criteria by which this would be accomplished, Indian Agents used the blood quantum standards already evident in treaty language.[11]

This racialist reconfiguration of Indian identity also presumed that full-bloods were racially incompetent to manage their own affairs and be issued trust patents for their allotments.[12] Mixed-bloods, by virtue of their white heritage, were deemed to be more competent and therefore issued patents in fee simple. This, along with other blatantly preferential treatment bestowed upon those of mixed ancestry, drove the final wedges into indigenous societies. By the turn of the twentieth century, virtually every indigenous society had, by way of a substitution of federal definitions for their own, been stripped of the ability to determine for themselves the internal composition of their constituencies. Blood quantum had become the litmus test for "Indianness."

Blood quantum criteria became further internalized among Indian communities with the passage of the 1934 Indian Reorganization Act (IRA). Most IRA constitutions simply aped the prevailing federal quantum standard, advancing racial standards as the linchpin of ethnic and national identity.[13] Since then, a majority of Indians have been indoctrinated into assessing each other in terms of blood quantum. This in turn led to the creation of what some have labeled a "purity police force," designed to evaluate biological and cultural competence and pass judgment among its societal members. The result has been a steadily rising tide of infighting between and among Native peoples.[14]

Paralleling the rise of multiculturalism during the 1990s, issues of social affiliation and ethnic identity in Indian country became truly pathological. The passage of the 1990 Act for the Protection of American Indian Arts and Crafts, for example, made it a criminal offense for anyone not enrolled in a federally recognized tribe to identify as an Indian while selling artwork.[15] Within months, ad hoc patrols of "identity monitors" were prowling selected museums, galleries, and powwows demanding to see pedigree documentation of Native artists. Thus if one could not produce the proper papers, a nebulous "purity patrol" screamed ethnic fraud at many respected Indian writers, educators, filmmakers, journalists, and scholars.[16] Anyone who did not fall within the acceptable range of phenotypic variation could be suspect. Many felt compelled to carry written documentation in many arenas to prove immediately their identity to other Indians or be publicly challenged for not being an "official Indian."

Meanwhile, back on many reservations, there have been movements afoot to purify the rez! Demographic data, pertaining to those who are federally recognized, reveal that during the twentieth century and beyond, there has been an increasing mixture between tribal members and non-Indian peoples. Such trends have not only continued but have also accelerated, raising concerns among some about preserving biological and cultural purity.[17]

Some reservation tribal leaders are arguing that tribal constitutions should be amended, this time to disenroll members who married non-Indians or raise blood quantum levels on the premise that such measures had become vital "to protect the purity of our Indian blood."[18]

Most tragic is the banner of racial politics that has been taken up by some traditionalists on various reservations. Ignoring long-held principles of kinship affiliation and other cultural practices for the incorporation of other people, some traditionalists have adopted the antiquated notion of blood quantum as a traditionalist belief. At one northwestern reservation, a traditionalist told news reporters that he prayed in his sweat lodge that a tribal amendment would not pass to re-assess blood quantum on his reservation. If this passed, he said, "We'd be adopting everyone into the tribe."[19] Another boldly proclaimed: "If I had one drop of white blood . . . that doesn't make me white. Right?"[20]

Others are pointing fingers at those who may not fit the phenotype of a full-blood, publicly calling them "wannabes," the "new Indians," "casino Indians," or saying they do not deserve to lay any legitimate claim to their tribal ethnicity because they did not suffer the emotional toll that their "darker" brothers and sisters had to endure living in America. The rise of "traditional racism" effectively denies many their ethnic identity by equating cultural competence with phenotype.

The internalization of Euro-America's conception of race by Native peoples, and the virulence with which it is now being manifested in indigenous communities, represents a culmination of federal policy initiatives originating nearly 500 years ago. To all appearances, Native North America has been rendered effectively self-colonizing, and if present attitudes persist, it stands to become self-liquidating as well.

Fortunately, there is a redirection among a minority of tribal nations. The Cherokee Nation of Oklahoma, in its 1975 constitution, took the unprecedented step of completely dispensing with blood quantum requirements in its enrollment procedures and resumed its reliance upon a more traditional genealogical mode of determining citizenship.[21] This had the effect of increasing the number of persons formally identified as Cherokees from fewer than 10,000 during the late 1950s to slightly over 300,000 today.[22] While much has been made about how this course of action was "diluting" whatever was left of "real" Cherokee culture and society, the precise opposite result was obtained in practice.

Plainly, such initiatives have neither ended the internecine bickering over identity, nor established the basis upon which to free even the Cherokees from internal colonial domination by the United States. It does, however, represent a substantial stride toward self-determination and a direction in which the Cherokee are in control. If the model it embodies is ultimately seized and acted upon by a broadening spectrum of indigenous nations in the years ahead, the tools required for liberating Native North America may at long last be forged. Should the current alternative and predominating racialist perspectives prevail, however, a road toward extermination will be traversed rather quickly.

Notes

1. See Joseph H. Greenberg, *Language in the Americas* (Stanford, Calif.: Stanford University Press, 1988); L. S. Cressman, *Prehistory of the Far West: Homes of Vanquished Peoples* (Salt Lake City: University of Utah Press, 1977); Richard Wolkomir, "New Finds Could Rewrite the Start of American History," *Smithsonian* 21, no. 12 (1991): 130–132, 134–144; Theodore Schurr et al., "Amerindian Mitochondrial DNAs Have Rare Asian Mutations at High Frequencies, Suggesting They Derived from Four Primary Maternal Lineages," *American Journal of Human Genetics* 46, no. 3 (1990): 613–623. Also see Satoshi Harai et al., "Peopling of the Americas: Founded by Four Major Lineages of Mitochondrial DNA," *Molecular Biology of Evolution* 10, no. 1 (1993): 23–47.

2. Fred Eggan, ed., *The Social Anthropology of American Indian Tribes* (Chicago: University of Chicago Press, 1955).

3. Jack D. Forbes, *Black Africans and Native Americans: Race, Color, and Caste in the Making of Red-Black Peoples* (London: Routledge, 1988). Also see William Katz, *Black Indians* (New York: Macmillan, 1986); Bell Hooks, "Revolutionary 'renegades': Native Americans, African Americans, and Black Indians," in *Black Looks* (Boston: South End Press, 1992), 179–194.

4. Jack D. Forbes, *Africans and Native Americans: The Language of Race and the Evolution of Red-Black Peoples*, 2nd ed. (Urbana: University of Illinois Press, 1993), 249–264. At least one credible analyst has gone further, asserting the "available evidence indicates that the ethnic mixture between Indians and Negroes is of vastly greater proportions than has hitherto been realized. . . . The American Negro population of today is a composite of African, White and Indian elements." See M. F. Ashley Montagu, "Origins of the American Negro," *Psychiatry* 7 (1944): 163–174.

5. William Stanton, *The Leopard's Spots: Scientific Attitudes Towards Race in America, 1815–1859.* (Chicago: University of Chicago Press, 1960). Concerning phrenology in particular, see John D. Davies, *Phrenology: Fad and Science: A Nineteenth Century American Crusade* (New Haven: Yale

University Press, 1955). On the especially sinister role played by American intellectuals in developing the concept of eugenics ("racial hygiene"), see Stefan Kühl, *The Nazi Connection: Eugenics, American Racism, and German National Socialism* (New York: Oxford University Press, 1994).

6. Richard J. Herrstein and Charles Murray, *The Bell Curve: Intelligence and Class Structure in American Life* (New York: Free Press, 1994). For further analysis, see Russell Jacoby and Naomi Glauberman, eds., *The Bell Curve Debate: History, Documents, Opinions* (New York: Times Books, 1995). Broader perspectives on the implications of contemporary racial/biological scientism will be found in Troy Duster's *Backdoor to Eugenics* (London: Routledge, 1990) and R. C. Lewontin's *Biology as Ideology:The Doctrine of DNA* (New York: Harper Perennial, 1992).

7. Samuel George Morton, *Crania Americana, or, A Comparative View of the Skulls of Various Aboriginal Nations of North and South America to Which Is Prefixed an Essay on the Varieties of the Human Species* (Philadelphia: John Pennington, 1839); also see his *Inquiry into the Distinctive Characteristics of the Aboriginal Race of America* (Philadelphia: John Pennington, 1844) and *Observations on the Ethnography and Archaeology of the American Aborigines* (New Haven: Yale University Press, 1846). Morton's "craniometric method" was to fill specimen skulls with various materials—seeds were used at one point, buckshot at another—in order to measure cranial capacity, the premise being that this would correspond to brain size (true), and that this, in turn, would correspond to innate intelligence (false). By computing average cranial capacity by race, he claimed to have thereby empirically demonstrated the inherent intellectual superiority of whites as compared to American Indians (and eventually all other non-whites as well). Although widely acclaimed at the time—by whites—the idea ultimately reduces to the absurdity that, even within the same race, a larger person "must" be smarter than a smaller one simply because his or her head is bigger. Whether or not Morton himself actually believed such patent nonsense is questionable insofar as he demonstrably rigged his measurements to obtain the desired results. See Stephen Jay Gould, *The Mismeasure of Man* (New York: Norton, 1981), 57–60. Be that as it may, the extent to which his and a raft of comparably pseudoscientific claptrap was popularized at the time is well-examined in Madeleine Stern's *Heads and Headliners:The Phrenological Fowlers* (Norman: University of Oklahoma Press, 1971). On the permeation of basic academic texts with racist pseudoscience, see Ruth Miller Elson, *Guardians of Tradition: Schoolbooks in the Nineteenth Century* (Lincoln: University of Nebraska Press, 1964).

8. Reginald Horsman, *Race and Manifest Destiny:The Origins of Racial Anglo-Saxonism* (Cambridge: Harvard University Press, 1981); George M. Fredrickson, *The Black Image in the White Mind: The Debate on Afro-American Character and Destiny, 1817–1914* (New York: Harper and Row, 1971).

9. Ch. 119, 24 Stat. 388, now codified as amended at 25 U.S.C. 331 et seq., also known as the Dawes Act or Dawes Severalty Act; D. S. Otis, *The Dawes Act and the Allotment of Indian Land* (Norman: University of Oklahoma Press, 1973); Wilcomb E. Washburn, *Assault on Tribalism:The General Allotment Law (Dawes Act) of 1887* (Philadelphia: J. B. Lippincott, 1975). On the "Friends," who were by this point organized as the "Indian Rights Association," see Francis Paul Prucha, ed., *Americanizing the American Indian: Writings by the "Friends of the Indian," 1880–1900* (Cambridge, Mass.: Harvard University Press, 1973); William T. Hagan, *The Indian Rights Association: The Herbert Welsh Years, 1882–1904* (Tucson: University of Arizona Press, 1985); Vine Deloria Jr., "The Indian Rights Association: An Appraisal," in *The Aggressions of Civilization: Federal Indian Policy since the 1880s*, ed. Sandra L. Cadwalder and Vine Deloria Jr. (Philadelphia: Temple University Press, 1984), 3–18. Concerning the explicit intent of Dawes and others of his group to undermine and destroy any autochthonous sense of identity among native people, see Wilbert H. Ahern, "Assimilationist Racism: The Case of the 'Friends of the

Indian,'" *Journal of Ethnic Studies* 4, no. 2 (1976): 23–32; Alexandra Harmon, "When Is an Indian Not an Indian? The 'Friends of the Indian' and the Problems of Indian Identity," *Journal of Ethnic Studies* 18, no. 2 (1990): 95–123.

10. See the relevant material in Charles C. Royce, *The Cherokee Nation of Indians, A Narrative of Their Official Relations with the Colonial and U.S. Governments* (Washington, D.C.: Bureau of American Ethnology, Smithsonian Institution, 1887).

11. See Naomi Zack, *Race and Mixed Race* (Philadelphia: Temple University Press, 1993).

12. Vine Deloria Jr. and Clifford M. Lytle, *American Indians, American Justice* (Austin: University of Texas Press, 1983), 10.

13. Russell Thornton, *American Indian Holocaust and Survival: A Population History Since 1492* (Norman: University of Oklahoma Press, 1987), 190–200.

14. See Patricia Penn Hilden, *When Nickels Were Indians: An Urban Mixed-Blood Story* (Washington, D.C.: Smithsonian Institution Press, 1995).

15. See Public Law 101-644, enacted Nov. 29, 1990; Herman J. Viola, *Ben Nighthorse Campbell: An American Warrior* (New York: Orion Books, 1993).

16. Ward Churchill, "Nobody's Pet Poodle: Jimmie Durham, an Artist for Native America," in *From a Native Son: Selected Essays on Indigenism, 1985-1995* (Boston: South End Press, 1996), 483–499.

17. Thornton, *American Indian Holocaust and Survival*, 174–175; "Tribal Membership Requirements and the Demography of 'Old' and 'New' Native Americans," *Population Research and Policy Review* 16, no. 1–2 (1997): 33–42.

18. Conversation with Twila Martin Catawba, at the time chair of the tribal council at the Turtle Mountain Chippewa Reservation in North Dakota, May 1992 (notes on file).

19. Hector Tobar, "Thinning Bloodlines," *Missoulian*, January 23, 2001, B1.

20. Tobar, "Thinning Bloodlines."

21. Even this instrument fails to go the whole distance, making no provision for naturalization by marriage, adoption, or petition. Moreover, it takes as its point of departure the Dawes Rolls; it explicitly excludes the descendants of Cherokee resisters who refused to move to Oklahoma from Arkansas, Missouri, Kansas, and Texas at the outset of the twentieth century. Still, the present Cherokee Nation of Oklahoma constitution accords much more closely with actual indigenous tradition than any other presently in existence. The constitution of my own Keetoowah Band follows not far behind, providing for enrollment based upon genealogy to anyone who can document it, but restricting voting, the holding of office, and receipt of benefits to those on one-quarter or greater blood quantum. The Band also makes provision for "Honorary Members" who demonstrate no genealogical connection, but who provide service/display loyalty to the group.

22. U.S. Bureau of the Census, *1980 Census of the Population, Vol. 2, Subject Reports: American Indians, Eskimos and Inuits on Identified Reservations and in Historic Use Areas of Oklahoma (excluding Urbanized Areas)* (Washington, D.C.: U.S. Government Printing Office, 1985), 99.

Tribal Nationalism: 4
The Concept of Governmental Recognition of Tribes and the Little Shell Chippewa Tribe

JAMES PARKER SHIELD

T HE LITTLE SHELL CHIPPEWA TRIBE'S EFFORT to gain recognition, indeed restoration, actually predates the creation of the Bureau of Indian Affairs administrative process for acknowledgment.

The History

Originally, the Little Shell Chippewa were members of the Pembina Chippewa who migrated to western Minnesota and on into what is now the state of North Dakota. The Pembina Chippewa had adopted the Northern Plains lifestyle and culture. They were signers of the 1863 Old Crossing Treaty, where half of their territory in North Dakota was given up to the United States government. Among the signers was Chief Little Shell II.

In 1892, the United States government was back, this time with an "agreement." U.S. policy had been revised from "treaty making" with tribes to a process termed "agreements." The Pembina, in 1892, were asked to give up more land in the McCumber Agreement. Chief Little Shell and other leaders and their followers walked out of the agreement negotiations. They refused to give up more land.

Government representatives also attempted to exclude from the agreement mixed-blood, or "Metis," Chippewa. In a now legendary statement, Chippewa leader Red Thunder responded to the McCumber Commission by saying: "When you [white men] first put your foot upon this land of ours, you found no one but the red man, and the Indian women, by whom you have begotten a large family. Those are the descendants of that woman: they must be recognized as members of this tribe."[1]

After Little Shell and the others would not sign the agreement and left to hunt buffalo in Montana, the government representatives appointed a hand-picked committee of Chippewa who signed the agreement. Little Shell and the others returned to North Dakota and were informed that they were no longer recognized by the government as part of the Pembina Chippewa. In following years, Little Shell and fellow Chippewa (and mixed-bloods) migrated to Montana and western Canada as virtually homeless people.

In the late 1800s, the buffalo had disappeared and traditional lifestyles came to an end for the Chippewa who followed Chief Little Shell. The defiant members of the Pembina Chippewa were reduced to seeking shelter and assistance from other tribes. Some tribes did what they could, letting the Chippewa reside on their reservations until ordered by the government to have these "landless" Indians move on.

In 1896, political pressure in Montana resulted in Congress allocating funds for the deportation of landless Chippewa, Cree, and Metis (mixed-bloods) to Canada. In August of that year, troops gathered the Chippewa and Cree from various communities. Some were forced to walk overland. Surrounded by army troops, they were loaded onto railroad boxcars (much like the Nazis did to the Jews in Germany) and transported to Canada. By that same winter, the vast majority of the deported Little Shell Chippewa were back in Montana and living on the outskirts of communities in north-central and central Montana.

The Chippewa under the leadership of Chief Rocky Boy, as well as the "landless" Cree, were finally given a reservation in 1916. Unfortunately, only 452 of 658 applicants were enrolled on the newly established Rocky Boy's Reservation. Most of those left off were Chippewa followers of Chief Little Shell and Metis. These Chippewa continued to live in shantytowns, digging in garbage dumps, and eating refuse from slaughterhouses.

The Struggle with the United States Government

Joe Dussome took over leadership of the Little Shell Chippewa in the 1920s. He and other leaders continued to press the case for federal recognition throughout the next few decades.

I would like to include a summary of our tribe's historical "Now we see you, now we don't" relationship with the U.S. government since the early part of the twentieth century. This summary was part of the written testimony provided by Larry Roberts of the law firm Patton and Boggs in Washington, D.C., to a congressional committee's Oversight Hearing on Federal Recognition of Indian Tribes held on May 11, 2005:

In the years that followed, Little Shell Leader Joseph Dussome pleaded for help from the Commissioner of Indian Affairs explaining that tribal members lived on the "dump piles of our towns . . . going to the back alleys, digging down the swill barrels for their daily bread." Less than two weeks after receiving our plea for assistance, Interior callously responded:

> The Indians referred to are Chippewa's of the Turtle Mountain Band. They were under the leadership of Little Shell who became dissatisfied with the treaties of the United States and the Turtle Mountain Band of Chippewas. He accordingly refused to accede thereto. . . . The disaffected band, by its failure to accede to the terms of the treaty and remove to the reservation is now unable to obtain any rights thereon for the reason that the lands of this band are all disposed of, and the rolls became final. . . . There is now no law which will authorize the enrollment of any of those people with the Turtle Mountain band for the purposes of permitting them to obtain either land or money.

According to Interior, because we were severed from the Turtle Mountain Tribe, we could not receive assistance as Turtle Mountain Chippewas. Thus, like many other tribes in the late 1920s, Interior at worst effectively terminated our federal relationship and at best left us in limbo . . . closed off from the rolls of our Turtle Mountain brothers.[2]

With the passage of the Indian Reorganization Act, the Little Shell people held out great hope that the United States would reaffirm our federal status and secure a land base for our people. During this period, the Chief of Interior's Land Division reassured us that a land base would soon be established.

> This office in general and the commissioner in particular are thoroughly cognizant of the unfortunate situation in which these landless Indians find themselves. To no other groups of Indians is so much constructive thought and persistent effort being directed, for it is fully recognized that theirs is the greatest need.
>
> All government enterprises move slowly in spite of the best intentions, but it is hoped and believed that in the not too distant future a satisfactory plan will be consummated for landless Indians in general, including, of course, the group to which you belong.[3]

Shortly thereafter, the Bureau of Indian Affairs acquired a forty-two-acre tract of land in Great Falls, Montana. The land was acquired for the benefit of landless Indians located in the vicinity of Great Falls. Although we were ready to move to the parcel, Interior explained that "local public opinion forced abandonment of the project. Local residents of the vicinity did not wish the Indians as their neighbors." In 1950, during the Termination Era, Congress enacted legislation providing for the sale of the lands acquired "for the benefit of certain landless Indians in the vicinity of Great Falls."[4]

In the 1950s, the Indian Claims Commission accepted us as an identifiable group of Indians that could bring a claim against the United States. After prevailing in that litigation, Congress enacted the Pembina Judgment Fund Act of 1982 and identified us as a group eligible for receipt of the judgment funds awarded by the Indian Claims Commission. The Pembina Judgment Fund Act required the Secretary of the Interior to report to Congress on the status of our petition for acknowledgement if we were not recognized by September 30, 1985. We again were hopeful that Interior would make a timely decision. Instead, Interior informed Congress that it would require us to do additional work before the petition could be placed under active consideration.

Interior's report to Congress triggered a series of consultations in which Interior continually required more and more documentary information. Five years later, BIA determined that the petition was ready for active consideration. However, after all of this lost time, the Tribe was forced to identify new researchers and asked that the petition be removed from active consideration. The tribe, with the financial assistance of the Native American Rights Fund (NARF), hired new researchers and, beginning in 1993, a series of meetings were held with Branch of Acknowledgement and Research (BAR) staff. Two years later, Interior determined that the petition was ready for active consideration. Over the course of the next five years, BAR staff conducted field research for additional documentary materials and interviews. During this period, BAR requested more materials from the tribe and provided itself with numerous extensions in which to make a determination.

In July 2000, Interior finally issued a proposed favorable finding to acknowledge the tribe. Interior's proposed finding documents a 234-page technical report accompanied by a 67-page bibliography. Yet, even in its proposed *favorable* finding, Interior yet again identified areas of additional research that would strengthen the petition. The tribe took these suggestions to heart. However, the burdens imposed by this proposed favorable finding required our researchers to spend an additional five years, including travel to Canada and England to locate materials, to respond to Interior's requests.

Compared to other petitions that are under the national spotlight, our petition is noncontroversial. Neither the State of Montana nor the local governments have filed any opposition to the tribe's petition or Interior's proposed favorable finding. Indeed, the Turtle Mountain Band of the Chippewa of North Dakota, every tribe in Montana, and many local Montana governments have actively supported our federal recognition through resolutions and official letters of support. Yet we are still waiting for the Interior Department to affirm its proposed favorable finding issued five years ago. We were told by Interior that, because of the present backlog, it will likely be several more years before they make a final determination on our petition. Because of Congress's long history of providing appropriations and subsequent attempts to establish a land base for us, we believe that Congress should affirm our government-to-government relationship through federal legislation.

A Congressional "restoration" bill has been crafted and is currently being reviewed by Congress's Legislative Council. Two of Montana's three representatives have indicated their support and a meeting is planned with the third to elicit his support as well.

The Little Shell Chippewa Tribal Council and our attorneys have serious concerns about proposed changes to the process for recognizing Indian tribes. We feel that growing concern over Indian gaming and recently recognized tribes may have a detrimental effect on those tribes awaiting a decision on their petition for recognition. Even though we are a tribe that is rural and isolated, we are impacted by the political ripple effect of Indian gaming discussions and the linkage to recognition.

This morning, I took part in a sunrise pipe ceremony conduced by Little Shell spiritual leader Henry Anderson. The ceremony took place in a Little Shell tipi, which was one of many tipis from many different tribes at the tipi encampment as part of the tribal events at the "Explore! The Big Sky Commemoration" this week. No one, especially no government agent, came to our tipi and told us that because we were not recognized, we could not hold a pipe ceremony, light sweetgrass, or pray in the tipi. As far as I know, none of this is mentioned in the detailed criteria for federal acknowledgment. When our Tribal Council holds a meeting and issues a call to tribal members and makes decisions on behalf of tribal members, we are not told that our meetings are unlawful assemblies and that the Tribal Council deliberations are meaningless.

So taken, what constitutes true and actual recognition? Is it the recognition the state legislature of Montana granted us that, to this point, is not accompanied by formal agreement or conveyance of programs and services to our tribe as a local unit of government or in adherence to a government-to-government relationship? Or is recognition understood and accepted in only the U.S. government's meaning of the term? Whereby we, the Little Shell Chippewa, would have government-to-government relations with the U.S. government, programs and services would be made available to our tribal members, and we would magically appear on everyone's radar screen as an Indian tribe after all? In a sense then, does federal recognition ultimately amount to programs and services?

In Montana and a couple of other Northern Plains states, and in Canada, we have Hutterite colonies. They live in communities on farmland they own. Hutterites practice their own customs, language, and religion. They dress according to their customs. They interact with the outside world according to their terms. People in Montana know about the Hutterites, can point out a Hutterite colony when they drive by one, and recognize them by their language and dress. Doesn't that sound like "recognition" to you?

As Native Americans, and as Little Shell Chippewa, I feel it is imperative that we not rely solely on the U.S. government's determination, one way or the other, of who is a "recognized" Indian tribe. "Recognition" starts at home, among ourselves as a people. Thus is also true "self-determination."

Notes

1. Senate Document 444, 56th Congress, 1st Session, 33–36.
2. Hearing Before the Committee on Indian Affairs, U.S. Senate, 109th Congress, 1st Session, on Oversight Hearing on Federal Recognition of Indian Tribes, May 11, 2005.
3. Ibid.
4. P.L. 714, 81st Congress, 2nd Session, August 18, 1950.

The Chinook Nation and Its Struggle for Federal Recognition

5

RAY GARDNER

T HE CHINOOK NATION COMPRISES THE CATHLAMET TRIBE, Wahkiakum tribe, Clatsop tribe, Willapa tribe, and Lower Chinooks. I am a descendant of the Willapa tribe. My mother was Lois Robinson, my grandmother was Dora Clark, and my great-grandmother was Annie Hawks. We are all descendants of Huckswelt, the last chief of the Willapa tribe and a signature signer of the Treaty of 1851.

History of the Tribe

A many of you are aware, we were the tribe that met Lewis and Clark at the mouth of the Columbia River at the end of their journey. We are the ones who found them when they were in a dismal niche. We were also the first ones to meet Robert Gray in 1792, when he first sailed into the Columbia River and established trade. We have a long history in our area. I think it would be very hard for people to dispute the fact that we have been there and are still there. As we go forward in time, in 1851, the Chinooks signed a treaty, but for some reason, and we have never been able to find the answer to that, that treaty was never ratified. They came back to the tribe in 1855 and asked us to sign another treaty. That treaty would have relocated us north out of our aboriginal area and would have put us with the one tribe in the whole area we did not get along with. So obviously, we did not want to be put with a tribe that was not our friends and did not want to leave our aboriginal homelands. So we refused to sign that treaty. When we refused the government at that time, then Governor Stephens stormed out of the negotiations and that was the last we heard officially from the government as far as treaty negotiations.

As we go forward beyond that, we were still receiving services from the federal government. We were still receiving health care. All of our members had their blue card. We were doing all that the recognized tribes in our area were doing and should be doing. As time went forward beyond that, in 1962, someone in the Bureau of Indian Affairs was going through a list of tribes that they worked with, and there were a number of tribes across the nation and many in Washington and Oregon that were crossed off the list. Now, I am sure most of you are aware that it takes an act of Congress to legally terminate a tribe. That was never done to our tribe. Someone just took our name off the list. That was very disconcerting to us for many reasons. For one, we were never notified that we were being taken off the list. All of a sudden, an article came out in the paper, which my mother has a copy of, that said the Chinook tribe was extinct. That was hard for all of us to address. The article came out saying we were extinct when we still had a very active government. We were still involved in our community. We had not gone anywhere. We still have one of our tribal elders with us—the last of our elders born on Long Island. We had three village sites on Long Island in Willapa Bay. When he was six years old and living with his grandparents, federal marshals came up and said they were taking that parcel of land. They gave them two weeks to pack up their belongings and leave or they would come back and remove them. So they left. We have another elder who is the last one alive who was born in Goose Point. This was a community we had down by the center of Washington on the Willapa Bay. That person can still to this day go down to Goose Point, although there is not a single structure left, and actually walks that daily, because he is a diabetic and has to exercise, and he can tell you where every home was and who lived there, where the church was; everything that was in that area.

The Recognition Process

We have struggled while trying to regain our recognition from the time we found out that we were classified as extinct. We have been in several different processes. The first one with the Bureau of Indian Affairs lasted for approximately ten years and ended with the fact that they said we could not meet the requirements we have, so therefore, we will not be able to be listed. We started another process that actually ended in January 2001 when Dr. Kevin Gover signed our recognition and put us back on the federal register. That was a huge day in Chinook land. We were finally able to come back to our people and say guess what, we are recognized. The government finally believes we are still here even though we have never left. This was exciting because we had, during that interim, so many of our elders who passed over without the ability to say "I am from a recognized tribe." When we were placed back on the federal register, that decision was appealed. That put us back into a long process and we were sitting there again, saying, "What will happen next?" We found out two years later, when the chairman of our tribe was back in Washington, D.C., by the invitation of George and Laura Bush, attending the kickoff for the Lewis and Clark Bicentennial. Before he could get back on the plane and come back home, he received a call from the Bureau of Indian Affairs saying that they had overturned the decision, taking us back off the federal register. We are no longer recognized. That was very definitely a very disheartening day in Chinook land. After all of our struggles to get there and finally achieving it, to have it snatched away that quickly. Since that time, we have continued to pursue our efforts for recognition. We have worked with members of the Senate, members of the Congress, trying to get them to put a bill on the floor to get us our recognition. They have failed to do that. Unfortunately, the only step we have left at this point is to take the federal government to court and sue them for our recognition. One of the things I will say, during all of the years that we have been struggling to do this, the one plus side to all of that is that we have more documentation for our existence than most tribes that are recognized. So the government did force us to do that which is a plus for us.

I would like to say that it is very disheartening to have a government that does that. Just read the history books. Read what is being taught to our children today. Read the Lewis and Clark journals; we are there. Go into our local community—they know we have never left. Thirty percent of our local schoolchildren are Chinooks—that school is very aware of our existence. We have kept our culture intact. I was very happy, just two weeks ago, when we had our first salmon ceremony. The next day we had our annual meeting with our elections. We are a very solid government. I would hold our council up to any council of any tribe. We have a lot of things we are doing in our community. I know one of the things we are very proud of is that we have a scholarship program set up with $48,000 in scholarships. We are working now to get grants to provide a health clinic in our area. We have a lot of tribal members, as well as other people in the community, who are very low income. We are seeing if there is a way that we can put a clinic to service all of those people. Locally, there is not an argument that we were there, and we are still there, and we have never left.

For any tribe or any group that is in that situation, one thing I can say is: don't give up. You will do a disservice to your ancestors to give up. We have to honor them. We have to move forward. We have to get them back to their place in history as soon as possible.

An Overview of Indian Populations

6

C. MATTHEW SNIPP

THIS ESSAY PROVIDES A BROAD OVERVIEW of the demography of Native America. About half of this essay deals with the historical demography of Native America, and the remainder is devoted to more contemporary issues.

American Indian historical demography—this is a burgeoning area of study. There are many researchers working on this subject, mostly historians and anthropologists. Their work involves trying to estimate the number of American Indians who inhabited different parts of this country and other parts of the continent, including Mexico and Latin America. The historical demography of the Native Americans can be viewed in at least three distinct periods. One is the pre-Columbian population. The second is the population of American Indians during the colonial era in the early periods of contact, particularly with the English, the French, the Spanish, and the Dutch. More recent historical demography focuses on the demography of American Indians as the United States expanded across the continent.

How many Indians were here when Columbus arrived in the Caribbean basin? At first blush, this sounds like a very esoteric question. But the numbers of American Indians present in the western hemisphere around the time that Columbus arrived in 1492 are very important for how we understand American Indian people, how we understand the nature of contact with the Europeans, and how we interpret basic myths of Western society. These are the folklore we encounter on a daily basis—that is, widely held beliefs that are deeply imbedded in the American psyche and deeply imbedded in the American culture in terms of how this nation thinks of itself. There are three aspects of pre-Columbian historical demography that deserve mention.

There is a direct relationship between population size and societal complexity. Small populations spend most of their time seeking sustenance and shelter. With larger numbers, there are more hands to do the work of keeping body and soul together, and surpluses begin to develop. Surpluses lead to other activities. A surplus allows time for the decoration of pots and other housewares. The time can be spent carving wood or stone. Stories can be devised to educate children, and stories can be carefully crafted to explain the nature of the universe.

Surpluses also provide commodities that can be traded with neighbors. A community might have some extra firewood or extra pots that might cause them to travel some distance and meet with their neighbors, to exchange goods and share ideas. Over time, a base of cultural information and knowledge begins to accumulate. Cultural development and the acquisition of more knowledge means increasing sophistication and greater cultural complexity.

As societies grow larger, managing unwanted behavior becomes a larger and more complex problem. Strategies for managing unacceptable behavior and ways of dividing and creating authority within the group—deciding that certain groups are going to make certain decisions under certain circumstances—must be devised. This also leads to more complicated societies in terms of government and a system of allocating authority within the community.

The implications of population size for how we understand the pre-Columbian world of the American Indian should be obvious. If one believes that American Indians, at the time they encountered Columbus, were a handful of people, it is almost certain that they were living in Stone Age conditions, they had very little in the way of culture, and the arrival of Europeans might even have been a blessing for the tools and technology they brought with them. Small numbers mean that Indian people were living in very primitive conditions, with very simple primitive cultures, with very little to recommend it in terms of material comforts and possessions—a people living in primitive Stone Age conditions.

But there is an accumulation of evidence to the contrary. One such place is the site of a once great city known as Cahokia. It is located across from St. Louis, Missouri, on the east side of the Mississippi River. At its peak, it was one of the largest cities in the world. In the 1100s and 1200s, it was probably significantly larger than the cities of Berlin and London, and virtually any of the cities in Europe at the time. It also may have been on par with several significant cities in the Middle East.

Cahokia was a large settlement with a huge mound in its center known today as Monks Mound. This mound is about 100 feet high and is entirely manmade. There was a large palisade that surrounded it, a playing field in the interior of the city; there were many smaller mounds inside and outside the palisade. A village inside the palisade was ringed by a stockade. The people who were wealthy and well-to-do lived within the stockade, and the less wealthy lived outside its protection. Cahokia was a large, complicated city and inconsistent with any notion of very small numbers. But Cahokia was a co-nundrum, a puzzle for many years, because nineteenth-century American and European settlers had no concept of its significance. Furthermore, Cahokia is just one, albeit the largest, of numerous sites located throughout the Mississippi River and Ohio River valleys.

A clear understanding of the significance of the Cahokia site did not be-gin to emerge within the scientific community until the 1920s. Among their discoveries, archeologists found evidence that Cahokia had a "woodhenge"—a large calendar outside the village. This was not a structure typically associ-ated with Stone Age people. Illustrating the lack of knowledge about the nature of the mounds, a piece of pottery recovered from a mound in the Southeast has an engraving that shows a farmer in the early nineteenth cen-tury plowing around the mound. As the European settlers arrived and ob-served that the Indians occupying the land had not built the mounds, there was considerable speculation about their origins.

Small population numbers also provide a convenient fiction for the politi-cal doctrine of *terra nullius*. In the eighteenth century, the doctrine of *terra nul-lius* was articulated as the justification of taking land occupied by indigenous people. It rested on the principle that when the land is unoccupied, it is avail-able for the taking. As Europeans came to understand that the land being taken was inhabited by indigenous people, the doctrine evolved. *Terra nullius* became land that was not just unoccupied, but uncultivated land. This notion of *terra nullius* and the idea of uncultivated land became very important in the early nineteenth century with the Free Soil movement, which becomes the basis for the homesteading movement, for opening the lands in the West for settlement, because if land is not cultivated by the Indians, it must be there for the taking.

Finally, there is the American mythmaking connected to the rise of the United States in the nineteenth century. Rendering an account of America was the inevitable settling of the unsettled frontier, taming the rivers, and conquering the wilderness. This was made inevitable by what most believed was the irresistible engine of modern human progress. By the late nineteenth century, when American Indians were almost extinct, the notion of the van-ishing American Indian became a fixture in nineteenth-century American culture. The march of progress and the irresistibility of Western civilization became the justification for measures designed to humanely facilitate the ex-tinction of American Indians.

These myths dominated the public discourse about American Indians in the nineteenth century. In the late nineteenth and early twentieth century, the question emerged: "How many Indians were present before the arrival of Europeans?" Anthropologists began working on this problem, and one of the first and best-known estimates was published by an anthropologist, James Mooney. He had spent much of his career collecting documents and records that would give him some insights as to the numbers of American Indians. He finally published in 1916 a very short article in the Bureau of Ethnology based on the records he had accumulated. From this information he suggested that there were slightly over 1 million American Indians in 1600, which he reckoned as the first year of significant contact between whites and Indians.

Mooney died in 1922 without completing his work, but he had a colleague at the Smithsonian, John Swanton, who after years of editing published Mooney's notes and papers. In the 1928 version of the *Handbook of North American Indians*, Mooney and Swanton's work reviewed the number and characteristics of tribes known to exist in 1600. In the foreword of this volume, Swanton stated that, based on Mooney's records and notes, there were about 1 million Indians present in North America in 1600.[1]

Alfred Kroeber, another distinguished anthropologist at the time, reviewed Mooney's work and Swanton's work in 1939. He concluded that Mooney probably overestimated the numbers of American Indians in North America; particularly his estimates in California were much too low. He ventured a lower number and guessed that there were probably only about 900,000 American Indians in North America.[2]

Given these small numbers, a population of 900,000 scattered across the territory north of the Rio Grande could support only the most rudimentary culture. Assuming these small numbers are accurate, there is no reason to believe that there was anything remotely resembling a complex culture. Many other scholars examined these numbers, and most of them offered estimates that differed little from the Mooney/Swanton/Kroeber figures. However, these very small numbers published in the 1930s, 1940s, and 1950s were fundamentally inconsistent with what was accumulating in terms of the archeological record. In the 1920s, archeologists began to understand the significance of Cahokia, and by the 1950s most experts could appreciate the magnitude of this site. Archeology in the Southwest grew rapidly in the 1930s and 1940s, and the archeological record that was emerging from the Southwest, the Mississippi and Ohio River valleys, from the Southeast, and parts of the Northern Plains, was completely at odds with these small numbers. How could the small population estimates be reconciled with a contradictory archeological record?

There are a number of different explanations. One explanation offered was that, because there were only small numbers of people here when the Europeans arrived, the people who built the mounds and the towns like Mesa

Verde must have left and moved somewhere else. Perhaps they went to the lost continent of Atlantis and sank beneath the sea. Although humorous in the present, there were individuals who earnestly believed this theory. Others suggested that there was a mass emigration—that the people who left these sites left in boats and settled elsewhere. One strain of thought is that the people who built these structures were space travelers who built pyramids around the world, Mexico as well as Egypt. Others suggest that there must have been a massive population collapse before Europeans arrived, akin to the manner that the dinosaurs disappeared.

An anthropologist and historical demographer, Henry Dobyns, tackled this puzzle in the early 1960s. Dobyns came to realize that the Columbian Exchange entailed a transfer to Europe of corn, potatoes, tobacco, chocolate, and many other things that the Europeans took from the western hemisphere. In exchange, Europeans mostly brought, at least initially to the western hemisphere, contagious diseases: smallpox, influenza, cholera, diphtheria, typhus. These diseases originated in the Middle East and spread to Europe. These diseases had never reached the western hemisphere. When the Europeans arrived with smallpox or cholera or influenza, Natives populations absolutely possessed no immunity whatsoever. They had no knowledge about these diseases.[3]

The first of these epidemics probably took place around 1520 and began in the Caribbean basin around Vera Cruz and spread north and south in the western hemisphere. These diseases produced spectacular mortality: upwards of 50 percent to 90 percent, sometimes destroying entire communities.

The artist George Catlin witnessed an epidemic among the Arikara and recorded the events connected with it. According to Catlin, the Arikara were surrounded by another tribe and under siege when smallpox broke out in the community. When the people realized they had contracted this disease and knew how horrible and painful it would become, they committed suicide rather than let the disease take its course.[4]

Unlike researchers before him, Dobyns realized that diseases spread far ahead and far faster than direct contact. The Europeans arrived with their diseases and Native people began dying from them long before they ever encountered a European. Taking account of the impact of disease, Dobyns published a revised figure for the pre-contact population of North America. He argued that the Mooney/Swanton/Kroeber numbers were fundamentally flawed. The correct number was not 1 million, but probably ten times that—closer to 10 million people in North America.

This caused enormous controversy within the literature and especially among anthropologists. Douglas Ubelaker, an anthropologist working at the Smithsonian Institution, reviewed Mooney's notes and found that his notes actually suggested a number closer to 2 million.[5] It is also important to remember that Mooney was working with information collected about 100 years after contact with European diseases. Thornton and Marsh-Thornton used another source of data and found that even a conservative approach such as linear extrapolation yielded numbers close to 5 million.[6] Another anthropologist, William Denevan, looked at another set of numbers and concluded that, taking the most conservative number possible, there would be at least 4 million in the North American pre-contact population.[7] Gradually, scholars came to understand these pre-Columbian societies in a much different way: the consequences of the arrival of the Europeans, the complexity of the cultures, and the amount of knowledge that was lost.

Dobyns was extensively criticized for about fifteen years. In 1983, he published a book in which he argued that his earlier numbers were underestimates.[8] He presented evidence that led him to conclude the correct numbers were closer to 18 million for North America. People have continued to debate this controversy. The very conservative estimates say there were 2 to 5 million. Plausible arguments that hardly anyone would disagree with are in the neighborhood of 5 to 7 million, and maybe millions more.

Table 6.1 shows a series of these estimates, including the numbers produced by anthropologist Harold Driver. Driver adjusted Dobyns's numbers for errors that he believed were contained in Dobyns's data. Recorrecting and imposing a set of very conservative assumptions about the data still yields population estimates of 5.0 to 5.2 million American Indians.[9] One interesting aspect of Dobyns's numbers is that when populations collapse, particularly when they collapse from exposure to disease, it is not a steady linear progression. It is a precipitous collapse followed by a slow decline. Dobyns

Table 6.1.   Estimates of the North American Native Population circa 1492

	Publication date	Population estimate
Mooney	1910, 1928[a]	1.1 million
Sapper	1924	2.5 to 3.5 million
MacLeod	1928	1.0 million
Villcox	1931	1,002,000
Kroeber	1939	900,000
Rosenblatt	1954	1.0 million
Aschman	1959	2.24 million
Dobyns	1966	9.8 million
Driver	1969	3.5 million
Ubelaker	1976	2.2 million
Denevan	1976	4.4 million
Thornton and Marsh-Thornton	1981	1.8 to 5.13 million
Dobyns	1984	18 million

[a] Published posthumously by Swanton.

approximates this massive decline in the early years of contact, and it becomes a very steady downward trajectory until it reaches a bottom in 1890.

The Native population of the Americas were exposed to a variety of diseases originating in Europe. Smallpox was the deadliest of these diseases, and
historians have compiled lists of known epidemics, including smallpox. The first
smallpox pandemic lasted from 1520 to 1524 and probably ranged all the way
from Chile to the Artic Circle. Some of these epidemics were more localized;
others were massive in terms of the area they covered (see table 6.2).

As a transition to the contemporary demography of American Indians, the
eighteenth and nineteenth centuries were also a period of sustained decline
in the population of American Indians. There were a number of factors that
accelerated this decline, but likely the single most important thing was that
Spain, and later Mexico and France, decided to abandon their claims in the
western hemisphere, particularly in North America.

During the seventeenth and eighteenth centuries, massive colonial expansion by any single nation wasn't possible because the competition between
France, Spain, and England checkmated one another. This competition, and

Table 6.2.   Probable Smallpox Epidemics among North American Indians, 1520–1797

1520–1524	Total geographic area unknown; possibly from Chile across present United States
1592–1593	Central Mexico to Sinaloa; southern New England; eastern Great Lakes
1602	Sinaloa and northward
1639	French and British Northeastern North America
1646–1648	New Spain north to Nuevo Leon, western Sierra Madre to Florida
1649–1650	Northeastern United States, Florida
1655	Florida
1662–1663	Mid-Atlantic, Northeast, Canada
1665–1667	Florida to Virginia
1669–1670	United States and Canada
1674–1675	Texas, northeastern New Spain
1677–1679	Northeast in New France and British territory
1687–1691	Northeast in French and British frontiers; Texas
1696–1699	Southeastern and Gulf Coast
1701–1703	Northeastern to Illinois
1706	Texas and northeastern New Spain
1715–1721	Northeast to Texas
1729–1733	New England; California tribes; Southeast
1738–1739	Southeast to Hudson Bay; Texas peoples
1746	New York, New England; New Spain
1750–1752	Texas to Great Lakes
1755–1760	From Canada and New England and Great Lakes to Virginia, Carolina, and Texas
1762–1766	From Central Mexico through Texas and the Southeast to Great Lakes; Northwest Coast
1779–1783	From Central Mexico across all of North America
1785–1787	Alaskan coast across Northern Canada
1788	New Mexico Pueblos
1793–1797	New Spain

competing claims, prevented massive numbers of people arriving in the western hemisphere from Europe. But, ironically, Europe was, in the seventeenth and eighteenth centuries, experiencing a population boom. One of the reasons Europe experienced a population boom was because they found a cheap food source—the potato. It allowed European families to grow very large and still be able to feed themselves.

As Spain and France withdrew from North America, this enabled England to claim much of North America and use it as a dumping ground for various undesirables such as paupers, religious dissidents, and criminals. Furthermore, after the United States declared its independence, this created a single political hegemony that was determined to possess all of the territory between the Atlantic and Pacific Oceans. This sparked an escalation of conflicts with American Indians which accelerated after the War of 1812, and reached a peak in this part of the continent in the 1850s and 1860s. Disease, warfare, and dispossession from the land continued the steady decline in the American Indian population. Population estimates from 1790 to 1890 show the decline from approximately 760,000 in 1790 down to about 228,000 in 1890.

This fueled romantic nineteenth-century ideas about the vanishing American Indian and that Indian people were destined for extinction. Like the carrier pigeon and the buffalo, it appeared that American Indians were headed for extinction by the late nineteenth century. At the same time, the U.S. population was growing very rapidly. It expanded from 3.9 million in 1790 to 63 million by 1890. By the late nineteenth century, Indian people are on the verge of extinction, and by 1890, most observers predicted that Indian people would soon disappear.

Something very remarkable happened in the late nineteenth century. At the end of hostilities between the United States and the Indian people, which took place in 1890, people began to think differently about the Indian problem. Decades earlier, in the 1860s and 1870s for example, the Indian problem was how do you contain these people, how do you isolate them, how do you move them off the land, how do you put some sort of buffer between them and the United States? This was the original thinking behind the creation of the Indian Territory in what is now Oklahoma. This was the logic behind creating reservations: you give them their land, you put them on a reservation, and, hopefully, they will stay there until they finally vanish into history. But, Native people did not die and disappear. Consequently, by the turn of the twentieth century, people began thinking that the Indian problem was not a problem of containment and isolation, but indeed a humanitarian problem.

American Indians on reservations were starving to death; disease, alcoholism, and "demoralization" were pervasive on reservations. This led to the conclusion that Indian people need not be physically exterminated, simply assimilated instead. This led to a dramatic change in public policies affecting American Indians. The federal government introduced public health measures, and inoculations became regularized. This improved reservation living conditions, particularly improved the survival of children.

In the nineteenth century, what has been described as one of the great demographic disasters in human history was reversed. After a long 400 years of decline, the American Indian population stabilized. Sometime in the 1890s or early 1900s, the Indian population hit its bottom and started to come back. From 1900 to 1930, the growth was slow and flat, then from 1930 to 1950 it picked up a little, a big jump between 1950 and 1960, and a huge jump between 1960 and 2000.

One development between 1950 and 1960 was that the Census Bureau changed its method of counting Indians. Before 1960, a person's race was assigned to them by an enumerator. A Census Bureau employee would come to your house, look at you, and decide whether you were white, black, or whatever. The Census Bureau decided this approach did not work well for American Indians. It seemed that they counted Indians reasonably well on or near reservations, where enumerators were expecting to meet American Indians, but they made substantial errors in cities and places where they did not expect to encounter Indians.

In 1960, the Census Bureau used individual self-identification that allowed people to just check off the box that corresponded to their race. This produced the first large increase in the American Indian population. In 1970, 1980, and 1990, the numbers continued to grow. In 2000, the Census Bureau introduced a new innovation that allowed people to check more than one race if they were so inclined. This has resulted in two numbers for the American Indian population. One is based on multiracial people—roughly 4.1 million—and about 2.5 million who checked only American Indian as their race.

The growth of the American Indian population in the 1970s, 1980s, and 1990s was most striking because these growth rates are biologically impossible. According to standard demographic theory, population growth (and decline) consists of three components: births, deaths, and migration into and out of the population. For American Indians, it is fair to assume that immigration is negligible. To obtain these growth rates, American Indian women would display impossible levels of fertility. In reality, much of the growth in the American Indian population was due to people changing their identity from white or black or something else to American Indian. This dramatic increase is also due to the fact that Indian people have relatively large families, particularly in reservation areas, and significantly larger than whites, blacks, and Hispanic families. Another factor is better coverage in the census. The Census Bureau also does a better job of finding Indians, even Indians who prefer not to be found. Finally, another cause is that in many parts of the country, it is no longer a shame or embarrassment to admit that you are an American Indian.

In the most recent census (2000), how do we count Indians and what do we mean when we talk about American Indians as manifest in the most recent count? The numbers collected by the Census Bureau are the most comprehensive source of information and demographic data about American Indians. Yet it is important to understand how this information was obtained and what it reflects. We know that what it means to be Indian can signify different things to different people. In 1977, the federal government published a document indicating that there were five races of interest in the United States and these would be the only racial groups for whom information would be gathered: black, white, American Indian, Hispanic, and Asian. This classification remained in place for about twenty years. In 1997, the federal government issued a new set of guidelines and indicated that statistical information would be collected for six groups. They added Hawaiian and other Pacific Islanders as a separate category, separately from Asians. They kept American Indians and Alaskan Natives, but added the qualification that included Central and South American Indians. They also added instructions that allowed individuals to check more than one box to indicate a multiracial heritage. These rules significantly impact the way American Indians are counted and who we understand to be Indian people.

Demographic data show the growth in the American Indian population throughout the twentieth century, culminating with the 2000 census. Because a sizable number of persons checked "American Indian" in combination with other races, there are two, very different numbers for the American Indian population. About 2.6 million persons checked American Indian only, and did not identify any other races. These individuals are more likely to be found outside of urban areas, living on or near reservation land, and they tend to be less educated, with less employment, and poorer than Indians elsewhere, and significantly different from persons who identify themselves as American Indian in combination with another race. Multiracial American Indians, those who identify another race in combination with American Indian, are more likely to live outside of Indian Country, most likely in cities, and are better educated, less likely to be unemployed, and less poor than monoracial American Indians.

These numbers might leave one to be skeptical about who identifies as American Indian, and especially to doubt the authenticity of the claims to an American Indian identity by persons who report more than one race. Specifically, this group may contain a substantial number of persons who are not "real Indians." While this suspicion may ring true to many in Indian Country, and while it may also be true that this mixed-race population may contain many persons who are not identifiably Indian using the usual markers of phenotype and cultural behavior, disputing the ethnic authenticity of this group does require a benchmark standard of who is a real Indian and who may not be included. This remains one of the most contentious and most controversial issues facing modern Indian communities today. Yet until this matter is resolved unambiguously, the ambiguity and uncertainty of the data reflected in the census are virtually certain to linger far into the future.

Notes

1. James Mooney, "The Aboriginal Population of America North of Mexico," *Smithsonian Miscellaneous Collections* 80, no. 7 (1928).

2. A. L. Kroeber, *Cultural and Natural Areas of Native North America* (Berkeley: University of California Press, 1939), 131–181.

3. Henry F. Dobyns, "An Appraisal of Techniques with a New Hemisphere Estimate," *Current Anthropology* 7, no. 4 (1966): 395–416.

4. Michael Macdonald Mooney, ed., *George Catlin: Letters and Notes on the North American Indians* (New York: Clarkson N. Potter, 1975), 229.

5. Douglas H. Ubelaker, "Prehistoric New World Population Size: Historical Review and Current Appraisal of North American Estimates," *American Journal of Physical Anthropology* 45, no. 3 (1976): 664.

6. Russell Thornton and Joan Marsh-Thornton, "Estimating Prehistoric American Indian Population Size for United States Area: Implications of the Nineteenth Century Population Decline and Nadir," *American Journal of Physical Anthropology* 55, no. 1 (1981): 50.

7. William M. Denevan, *The Native Population of the Americas in 1492* (Madison: University of Wisconsin Press, 1976), 1–12.

8. Henry F. Dobyns, *Their Number Became Thinned: Native American Population Dynamics in Eastern North America* (Knoxville: University of Tennessee Press, 1983), 34–44.

9. Harold E. Driver, "On the Population Nadir of Indians in the United States," *Current Anthropology* 9, no. 4 (1968): 330.

ART AND EXPRESSION

II

Native Art

7

DAVID PENNEY

I WILL BEGIN BY SAYING THAT "ART" IS JUST A WORD, a word we use to categorize different kinds of things and activities. Its meaning changes all the time. From my point of view, when thinking about American Indian art, it is not a matter of identifying those kinds of things made or performed by Native people that resemble someone else's definition of art, but redefining the word "art" to fit the practices of Native people, practices of the past, today, and the future. This is what artists do, redefine what we mean when we say the word "art." And Native artists have always done so: they do it today, and will do it tomorrow. I will speak to you about how Native artists have changed, have recreated, the definition of art, and how they continue to do so now.

First, let us step back for a moment. I am beginning with a premise that the notion of "art" is not a universal human concept. And here, I don't mean to get into the business of "there is no American Indian word for art," but something, I think, a little deeper and more fundamental.

I do believe that human beings, generally speaking, are social creatures who have evolved the amazing ability to delight, inspire, and influence each other with their expressive capabilities: through performance, oratory (and its written corollary), and by making things. The power of these expressions, and their usefulness, lies in the values they represent. Values are slippery concepts (family values, for example); they are contingent to time and place. And I say this taking a broad historical and anthropological viewpoint. But values are most powerful when they are shared: among family, communities, nations, potentially among all the citizens of the world. Parenthetically speaking, it is tempting, perhaps more hopeful, to think that we recognize universal human values, but again, a broad historical and anthropological viewpoint argues against it. Our ability to express ourselves serves the purpose of putting those values out there for others to share or dispute. In one sense, cultures are composed of systems of shared values: what is good, what is bad, what is beautiful, what is ugly, what is appropriate or inappropriate. We may call such systems ethics or aesthetics (or politics or capitalism, for that matter), but such a system is never static. Human beings wield their many different expressive abilities to explore the dimensions of the values they hold dear, to assert some, to challenge others, and in cumulative effect, to shape them in ways to fit the circumstances of their time and place.

So there is no universal notion of what art should be or could be. But the ability, the need, to express to others fundamental values that inform and guide social life is indeed a basic and universal condition of humanity, in my view. This is what artists do. And we are all artists on some level, as part of the condition of being human. It is just that some of us are better, more expressive, more skilled, as artists than others. And with the word "art," we also privilege certain means of expression and the attendant skills to create them.

Now, let us address the issue of who gets to say what art is, or will be, and how that term might be deployed to promote some values or repress others. Consider for a moment two works of art that William Rubin, former curator of painting and sculpture at the Museum of Modern Art, wished to display in his 1984 exhibition, "Primitivism and Twentieth Century Art." One is a so-called "war god" made by members of the Zuni Bow Priest Society; the other is a painting by the German artist Paul Klee. Rubin saw that one resembled the other. He wished to make the point in his exhibition that Klee had seen the Zuni object in the displays at Museum für Völkerkunde in Berlin prior to his creating the painting in 1932. Klee had interpreted the Zuni object as if it were a work of modern art, seeing in it visual qualities that evoked for him a kind of psychological foreboding and menace which he borrowed for his visual expression about paranoia in early fascist Europe. He titled his painting *Mask of Fear*. In fact, Rubin had organized the exhibition around the premise that it had been customary for the great masters of European modernism—Klee, Picasso, Matisse, and others—to borrow and modify the visual qualities of objects that had been collected from indigenous peoples all over the world—North America, Africa, New Guinea, and elsewhere—in their project of changing the way that Europeans thought about art.

It could be that this is one way that Native artists have changed the definition of art, but inadvertently and only superficially so. It took another fifty years after Klee's painting for the penny to really drop. In 1984, Rubin was discouraged from including the Zuni object in his exhibition, and in the end, he reluctantly chose not to do so. He did this because he had been informed that his desire to display the Zuni object in the exhibition, like Klee's act of borrowing the image in the first place, ignored the Zuni values of which this object was an expression, and ultimately, its display in a museum was disrespectful of those cultural values. The object had been created as an expression of the community's desire for spiritual peace and physical safety. Its material and visual qualities had been selected and crafted expressly to fulfill this purpose. But the expression of these Zuni values lay not only in its physical creation, but also through performative actions. As a kind of prayer or offering, it had been placed in an outdoor shrine where it must remain until its physical materiality weathered back into the earth. The recognition that the artfulness of this object lay in the cultural values that informed its creation and not in any superficial resemblance to the modernist or surrealist agendas of European artists—that is the real and profound change in our collective understanding of what art is, and what art can be.

Not all art belongs in museums. Some kinds of artistic expression are undermined or even lost when translated or transported. I am reminded of a crisp but sunny New Year's Day in 2004, where I watched some 1,200 dancers of San Domingo Pueblo dance in the plaza—men, women, and children of all ages. I was one of many spectators, feeling welcome and yet respectful. Everyone there, I am sure, felt awed and inspired by this collective expression of community solidarity. I ask you, how many towns are there in the United States where twelve hundred residents aged three to ninety-three organize themselves to all do the same thing at the same time? But no photographs, please. This experience cannot be translated, exported, or otherwise rendered in facsimile.

I think about these as community-based art, and they are all over the world. They are endangered. Their safety is dependent upon the safety of the communities in which they are performed. All of the economic issues, the social issues that we have been discussing all weekend, would play into the viability of community arts in the future. But don't underestimate the power of these community arts to support those economic agendas, to support the community sense of well-being and value.

It is no coincidence that the National Museum of the American Indian (NMAI) and the Native American Grave Protection and Repatriation Act were both created at practically the same historical moment, between 1989 and 1991. I see both as evidence of shifts in attitude on a broad, national scale: a recognition that customary ways of thinking about art were in the process of changing; attitudes that had helped fuel trafficking in looted archeological artifacts and sacred objects, for example, were beginning to change. And, closely related, I see a recognition that the artfulness of many kinds of collective community expression are diminished or distorted if alienated from the communities that created them (the lesson William Rubin learned twenty years ago). The community galleries at the NMAI are conceived to help broaden this perception among a large and diverse public who arrive at its doorstep, one hopes, primed for a change in attitude.

Let me change tack, at this juncture, and invite you to think about another way Native artists have changed the definition of art. Native artists have always made things for other people, as gifts to forge relationships and for exchange. With the introduction of a cash economy to North America, the creation of things to sell became an opportunity to earn money. For Navajo women, for example, Anglos are just the latest of a long line of customers for their weavings, stretching back many hundreds of years: people of neighboring Pueblos, Utes, and other Plains tribes from the north, Mexicans whose ancestors came from the south, and eventually, the tourists who arrived on trains and the traders who sold their things through mail-order catalogues. Native artists from all over North America made such things: beaded purses and handbags of the Haudoshawnee and Micmac, argillite smoking pipes of the Haida of Haida'gwaii, or the Queen Charlotte Islands, and weavers of baskets from all over North America, from Maine to San Diego, from Louisiana to Alaska.

They were often called "curios" or "trinkets." The early generations of field anthropologists largely ignored them, feeling, somehow, that this commodification of craft did not fall within their pseudo-scientific scope. When native artists engaged with the marketplace, it had always required a kind of dialogue between creator and customer: educating the consumer, on one hand, to the values of the craft; adapting the craft, on the other hand, to the demands of the marketplace. It had grown customary among early anthropologists to think of such a dialogue as a form of assimilation, a troublesome term that implies the one-way melding of one culture into another. This kind of thinking prompted John Wesley Powell, of the Bureau for American Ethnology, to write of trinkets, as he called them, in 1893, "They chiefly embody the ideas of the white race and in no proper sense represent Indian arts."[1]

More recently, Nelson Graburn initiated a reconsideration of so-called curios and trinkets, from an anthropological perspective, when he assembled a number of fellow anthropologists to contribute to a volume of essays about what he called "tourist art" in 1976.[2] Although many of the consumers of Native baskets, Navajo weavings, Pueblo pottery, and such, can be accurately characterized as tourists, the term "tourist art," to my ear, still trivializes these things with implications of curios and trinkets. I prefer the term coined by my friend, Anishnaabec artist and author Lois Beardslee. She calls the things she and her family make "market art."

Black ash baskets and birch-bark boxes decorated with porcupine quill are the principal market arts among the Anishnaabe in the part of the country where I live, Michigan and the surrounding Great Lakes region. These things have been made here for many centuries, by generations of artists. I read in Thomas McKenney's narrative of his Great Lakes travels in 1827 that Anishnaabe artists at Sault Sainte Marie made small "mococks" of birch bark, ornamented with porcupine quills and packed with a few teaspoons of fine maple sugar for sale to the "curious," as McKenney put it.[3] When I look at the pattern of who makes these things and where they live on a map, it stretches along the old portage and trade route starting with the Micmac of the lower Saint Lawrence, the Abnaki of the lower Ottawa River, the Anishnaabe and Odawa of Georgian Bay, Manotoulin Island, Sault Sainte Marie, and the Straits of Mackinac.

Making quill boxes, as they are called, requires great skill and knowledge. It can be learned only through direct, hands-on training. It requires detailed knowledge of the local environment, where to find the materials, when, and how to properly harvest and prepare them. This special knowledge and skill resides within families and is passed from elder to younger, generation to generation. The history of this art is a genealogical history, who learned from whom, the lineage descent of knowledge that connects practitioners of today to untold generations of ancestors.

At least 125 artists make quill boxes in Michigan today, and there are perhaps twice as many more in southeast Ontario. Yvonne Walker Keshick, of the Little Traverse Bay Band of Odawa, is probably the most skilled and accomplished of those now working. Her grandmother, Mary Anne Kiogima, was similarly regarded in her day. Yvonne learned from her aunts, Irene Walker and Susan Kiogima Shagonoby, and she taught many of the younger artists currently active in Michigan. Yvonne innovated her own unique style of pictorial imagery, avoiding dyes and exploiting the feathery gradations of black, brown, and white in each individual quill to create subtle shadings and textures. Her own style developed after working alongside her aunt Susan for two years and learning her aunt's designs. Quill box artists recognized a largely unspoken protocol, learning and using the designs of their elders only with permission, a kind of intellectual property right that extends throughout an artist's lifetime. Many of the floral designs that had been popular in the past had been learned and executed with the help of paper stencils. Yvonne is now leading a project to find and catalogue these paper stencils (many of them still belong to artist families), match them up with boxes in old collections, and reconstruct the lineage ancestry of artists, their designs, and the boxes they made.

Economically, at best, quill box makers enjoy marginal success. For most, it provides a welcome and necessary supplement to family revenue. Artists bring their creations to powwows and craft shops at the casinos and cultural centers. A few artists, like Yvonne, have been able to command higher prices and she is assisted by the promotional efforts of the Odawa owner of the Indian Hills Trading Company, Victor Kishigo. The economic viability of this market art, I predict, will grow to the degree that it exerts a power to change how their potential consumers think about art. And I choose to be optimistic. Within a nation hungry for experiences of the "authentic" but often confused or ignorant of the real life histories and experiences of Native people in their midst, market art like quill boxes offers a powerful expression of authentic and traditional artistry. A parallel history of multigenerational pottery-making families among the Pueblos of the Southwest now enjoys broad recognition and economic success. The Santa Clara potter Sara Fina, who brought her creations to Santa Fe in a wagon to sell, her daughter Margaret Tofoyo, and their descendants Nathan Youngblood and Nancy Youngblood Lugo, and their success, is one such history. There are countless traditions of market art throughout North America, locally rooted, descending through generations of extended artist families: potters, basket makers, bead workers; carvers of ivory, bone, stone, and wood; painter and sculptors; some traditions growing strong, others fading, still others being revived after periods of dormancy. These histories, these futures, reflect unique and particular Native experiences. They redefine art as a multigenerational endeavor, culturally based, but individually created, traditional and yet capable of startling innovation, often rooted in local environments, but globally relevant in its insistence upon the value of local knowledge. They possess a profound ability to shape the ways we think about art and what art can be.

Let's change tack again, because there is one more thing I would like to talk about. I think of the early twentieth-century project of modern art as social critique symptomatic, in a sense, of Europe's profound anxiety about the notion of progress and all its alternatively utopianist and nihilist implications. Certainly, this played out in Europe with disastrous and tragic result. But the earnest practitioners of modern art, deploying the practices of abstraction, collage, assemblage, and so on, pursued a relentless exploration of one's self, of personal experience, ability, vision, and individuality. That twentieth-century tradition of social critique and personal vision has been strengthened by several generations of Native artists who seized the contemporary art practices rooted in the studio and the gallery for themselves. George Morrison, Alan Houser, Jaune Quick-to-See Smith, George Longfish, Kay WalkingStick, Frank Lapena, Jolene Rickard, Gerald McMaster, too many to mention. All of these artists make art as a process of self-exploration, cultural inquiry, and visual discourse.

The practice of contemporary art making, with its traditions of studio training, the gallery exhibit, the literary critique, had been created principally by men in Paris, New York, and other urbane locations. The reins of control, the mechanisms of critical evaluation, the structures of its economy, the means of patronage and support, still reside there. Some might see the system as restrictive and myopic, and increasingly distant from values familiar to a mainstream public. From the vantage point of a large civic art museum in Detroit, Michigan, it sometimes looks that way to me. On the other hand, I see the rise of a broad global movement, of many artists, from many diverse backgrounds and locations—Asia, Africa, Australia, throughout the Americas—whose engagement with the contemporary art system challenges its Eurocentricism.

My museum, in the tradition of art museums 100 years old and a city-block long, hopes to offer, in a thoughtful afternoon, an overview of world art on the broadest scale: ancient to contemporary; Paris to New Zealand. As is the case with most museums like mine, the experience of global expanse narrows to the two shores of the North Atlantic when a visitor enters the modern and contemporary art galleries. I think this will change. I think that soon, the experiences in our galleries of contemporary art will offer works of art from artists as diverse as the polyglot identities of present-day Detroit. My model for this, the source of my vision, is an event that happens every summer in Detroit, down on the river in Chene Park. It is called "Concert of Colors," organized by ACCESS, North America's largest Arab American cultural organization based in Dearborn, Michigan. Musicians from all over the world are invited here for three days of free performances. And all of Detroit turns out. At no other single event in that city can one sense the vast number of diverse communities that reside there. They come to celebrate and experience the value of difference. That is what art can do. Someday, my museum will offer an experience like that, without historicizing it in the past. And the work of contemporary Native artists will be part of it.

Art, as we have discussed here, possesses great power to affirm cultural values or challenge them. It is no coincidence that many Native artists working today are also powerful spokespeople, advocates, activists, writers, and cultural critics. Their work, alongside that of other indigenous artists the world over, offers alternative ways of seeing, of knowing, of being—their perception, change in understanding for all who look earnestly, and think. And on a world stage, the indigenous artists of North America enjoy tremendous advantages over their colleagues in Africa, South America, and Asia: schools, galleries, museums, foundations, and other kinds of patronage, even if now their work is too often visible only in some contemporary art Indian corner, so to speak. But I feel confident that will change, over time, because even now, as I speak, Native artists are redefining and recreating what art can be and will be.

Notes

1. John Wesley Powell, *Annual Report of the Bureau of Ethnology 1893* (Washington, D.C.: U.S. Government Printing Office, 1896).

2. Nelson H. H. Graburn, *Ethnic and Tourist Arts: Cultural Expressions from the Fourth World* (Berkeley: University of California Press, 1976).

3. Thomas McKenney, *Sketches of a Tour to the Lakes, of the Character and Customs of the Chippeway Indians, and Incidents Connected with the Treaty of Fond du Lac* (Baltimore: F. Lucas, 1827), 194.

Challenges in Managing Culturally Sensitive Collections at the National Museum of the American Indian

8

JAMES PEPPER HENRY

ONE OF THE GREATEST CHALLENGES for the National Museum of the American Indian (NMAI) is the physical translation of its philosophy into the daily work of the museum. This philosophy, as articulated by the museum's mission statement, recognizes a "special responsibility, through innovative public programming, research, and collections, to protect, support, and enhance the development, maintenance, and perpetuation of Native culture and community."[1] Preservation and perpetuation of "living culture" is the NMAI's guiding principle—a concept that diverges from traditional museum principles that focus primarily on the acquisition, preservation, and interpretation of collections. Collections, along with research and programming, are seen as tools to illuminate living culture rather than as living culture being used to augment collections. When the NMAI was established through an act of Congress in 1989, it did not come with a prescribed manual that showed how to integrate this contemporary perspective with standard institutional practices for the maintenance of culturally sensitive collections.

Wealthy New Yorker George Gustav Heye assembled the original collections of the NMAI during the first half of the twentieth century. What began as a hobby for Heye soon became a lifelong obsession. Heye collected for the sake of collecting, unlike his contemporaries who believed that Native culture would be extinct by the twenty-first century. With the enlistment of a small army of collectors deployed throughout the western hemisphere, Heye amassed a private collection of approximately 800,000 material objects representing nearly 1,000 distinct indigenous cultures. These acquisitions included human remains, funerary materials, and religious and ceremonial objects. Many of the practices and transactions to acquire these cultural materials were legitimate, but others were ethically challenged. In fact, in 1914 Heye himself was arrested for grave-robbing an ancient Munsee-Delaware burial ground in Sussex County, New Jersey, but the charges eventually were dropped.[2]

The entirety of Heye's collections would become the Museum of the American Indian–Heye Foundation (MAI), formerly located at 155th Street and Broadway in New York. In the three decades that followed Heye's death in 1957, the foundation struggled to maintain financial stability. To preserve the integrity of the collection and avoid the sale or auctioning of objects to keep the organization afloat, the foundation initiated a series of negotiations and events that culminated in the 1989 transfer of its assets to the Smithsonian Institution and the establishment of the National Museum of the American Indian. Ironically, what once was perceived by many as an epitaph to indigenous cultures of the western hemisphere is now an invaluable resource to Native communities seeking to revive and renew ritual and ceremonial activities. This is possible through the auspices of the NMAI act that established not only the museum but also the first legislated repatriation requirement for a federally funded institution. The resulting Native American Graves Protection and Repatriation Act (NAGPRA) would affect all federally funded institutions and agencies possessing Native American cultural materials, human remains, and funerary objects.

Understanding and acknowledging its inherited history is a critical first step for the NMAI in its endeavor to establish trust with its primary constituency, the Native peoples of the western hemisphere. The museum believes that retaining ancestral human remains and funerary objects of Native peoples is a transgression of human dignity and counterproductive to its mission, and it has proactively mandated their repatriation and respectful disposition. It has established a Repatriation Office to fulfill this mandate and to respond to requests from Native groups for the return of certain sacred and ceremonial objects and objects of cultural patrimony where the museum's title of ownership is unclear.

Building long-term relationships with indigenous communities is a priority for the museum, and much of its work is executed in collaboration with Native community representatives. Inherent since the NMAI's inception is the conviction that first-person perspective, or "Native Voice," is a driving force behind the museum's activities, including policy development, public programming, exhibition development, and collections management. The NMAI has an "open book" policy, providing its Native constituents with unfettered access to collections and information in its possession. Official Native representatives frequently visit the NMAI's Cultural Resources Center (CRC) facility in Suitland, Maryland, to review collections and archival information for research and repatriation purposes. The museum also invites Native representatives to review collections for the development of exhibitions and public programs, and to provide assistance and advice in the conservation of certain objects.

The museum recognizes that its Native constituents have an absolute interest in the management, interpretation, and disposition of collections associated with their respective communities. Pursuit of understanding of the cultural contexts and perspectives of Native community members enforces NMAI's belief that the museum's staff are merely the stewards of these collections, not the owners.[3] Authority over the collections must be shared with the Native constituency to remain true to the museum's mission and enhance the programmatic aspects of the museum's work.[4] With shared authority and stewardship comes the responsibility and burden of managing collections in unconventional ways in accordance with the wishes and concerns of affiliated Native communities.

The stewardship approach to collections management translates into the notion that the physical preservation of an object is not synonymous with the preservation of its cultural integrity. This is not to say that the physical preservation of objects is not a priority for the museum, but rather that certain standard museum practices for managing collections may be inappropriate from a cultural perspective. For example, a Native representative visiting the CRC facility to review collections may tell staff that warrior society items associated with his tribe should not be handled by any woman during her menstrual or "moon" cycle. From his cultural perspective, there is conflict between a woman's procreative powers during this time and the "life-force" or power of the warrior-society item. Any interaction between these two conflicting forces may bring harm to his community or to people associated with the infractor. But honoring the request may violate the museum's gender discrimination rules. An uneasy dilemma exists for the museum as it is caught between two mindsets, with potential consequences for dismissing either protocol.

The mere fact that the museum possesses such culturally sensitive items may be viewed as inappropriate by certain Native constituents. One consistent belief among the museum's culturally diverse Native constituent base is that objects are living entities or retain a living spirit. These spirits are believed to be conscious beings with human-like emotions that, in some instances, require feeding and human interaction to remain healthy. Keeping these items healthy from a cultural context adds to the complexity of managing collections in an institutional setting. Many NMAI staff use the term "cultural risk" to describe potential consequences for the culturally inappropriate care and handling of sensitive collections in the museum's possession.

Some Native representatives also have expressed the concern that the museum is artificially extending the normal life cycle of certain items that, in their original cultural contexts and under normal use, would have worn down over time through use or been claimed by the elements. For example, the NMAI's Integrated Pest Management (IPM) system monitors and prevents pest infestations from damaging collections. However, some Native representatives believe that pest infestations are part of an object's normal life cycle and should not be prevented. For example, one preventative technique to mitigate a pest infestation the museum might normally employ would be to freeze the item at very low temperatures over an extended period; another would be to place the object in a low oxygen tent or CO_2 chamber to suffocate the living organisms. Some Native representatives view either technique as harmful to the living spirit of the object. But to allow a pest infestation to continue unabated would violate the museum's fiduciary responsibility to protect and preserve the collections. Weighing "cultural risk" factors communicated by Native representatives to the museum's staff regarding the management of collections with standard institutional protocols is an ongoing challenge for the NMAI.

Museum staff frequently use the word "respect" when describing the NMAI's management of collections. However, "respect" has distinct meanings and varying connotations for staff and for Native representatives. Physical anthropologists may believe that they are treating human remains with respect by refraining from using any destructive forms of analysis, while Native representatives may regard any handling at all or simply the possession of an ancestor's human remains as disrespectful. From my perspective, the best definition of "respect" is to create a comfortable environment for the objects and to handle collections as little as possible and only when necessary, especially with regard to human remains.

The NMAI regularly receives feedback, suggestions, and requests from Native representatives concerning the management of culturally sensitive collections. Many times this information is relayed to individual staff members in a casual and sometimes confidential manner. In particular, Native staff members are selectively approached with this kind of information because of cultural and ethnic familiarity. In the past, Native and non–Native staff members have often felt an obligation to honor these requests and have taken on this burden themselves. Through experience, the NMAI has come to realize that it is the responsibility of the museum, and not the individual staff member, to consider and act upon these requests. This approach allows museum staff to share the responsibility for the request, maintain consistency in honoring the request over time, and avoid situations that might make individual staff members uncomfortable.

To respond to concerns Native peoples have about the maintenance of culturally sensitive materials and information in the museum's possession, and to mitigate potential incompatibilities between museum practices and Native requests, the NMAI is now in the process of implementing an active Culturally Sensitive Collections Care Program. The program will establish a committee to consider and implement workable solutions to sensitive and/or problematic issues or situations in this area. A long-term goal is to establish a working committee as a permanent and regular part of the NMAI's organizational structure.

This is not the museum's first attempt to establish such a program. In fact, over the past decade there have been at least half a dozen similar attempts— to manage the influx of information NMAI staff receive from various Native representatives, to formulate an internal process to review this information and make informed decisions concerning regular collections management practices, and to determine an effective method of distributing this information across various departments. But previous efforts have been inconsistent.

One major obstacle is the sheer size of the NMAI's collections, which represent such a large cross-section of cultures. Museums and cultural centers housing collections that are associated with only one culture or a group of cultures from a specific region have a great advantage in developing a collections management strategy tailored to address the concerns of those Native constituents. But implementing general guidelines for collections care does not often work for the NMAI, since many of the cultures represented in the museum's collections have conflicting perspectives. In addition, the NMAI employs more than 300 people, many of whom have frequent contact with Native community representatives through diverse and unrelated activities. The lack of broader staff input in the decision-making process was another obstacle hindering a sustained program. These factors highlight the difficulties and complexities involved in formulating a formal structure for managing intangible ideas and beliefs in such a large and dynamic museum setting.

To help address these challenges, the NMAI is implementing a Collections Information System (CIS), a central database where staff can record sensitive collections information received from Native community representatives and post decisions concerning the special care or handling of culturally sensitive collections. A central server and NMAI Intranet offer an effective way for people to access this specific information. There are circumstances when Native representatives provide confidential and/or sensitive information that is not intended for wide distribution to the staff or public, including the location of burial sites of human remains and funerary objects repatriated by the museum, the contents of ceremonial bundles, and the disclosure of ritual or ceremonial activities associated with collections in the museum's possession. The CIS provides a way to control sensitive collections information through a hierarchy of access controls.

A regular and inclusive committee or working group also will address some of the problems of the past. Having a centralized decision-making body comprising Native and non-Native male and female museum staff representing the museum's various departments and units will ensure a balanced and democratic approach to considering and implementing sensitive collections guidelines. The committee's responsibilities are:

1. To develop guidelines and standards for a Culturally Sensitive Collections Policy consistent with the museum's collections policy and institutional rules and regulations.
2. To gather and record sensitive collections information through consultation with Native constituencies.
3. To develop a schedule and identify personnel to execute maintenance of sensitive collections in compliance with the requests of official Native community representatives, given the obvious and reasonable limitations of the museum.
4. To inform and educate museum staff concerning sensitive collections activities, sensitive objects handling guidelines, and collections handling restrictions through the CIS, regular staff meetings, the museum Intranet, and printed materials.

Neither the committee nor any museum staff member is to serve as a surrogate for indoctrinated Native traditional leaders or religious society members who want to carry out ceremonial activities or practices involving objects in the collection. To do so may not only be offensive to other members of the particular Native community, but also may conflict with the personal beliefs or convictions of museum staff members, who have varying cultural and religious backgrounds. Many requests from official tribal representatives for special handling or treatment of objects—including gender restrictions and ethnic preferences—may not be enforceable, even those accepted by the committee. In these circumstances, the committee asks that museum staff voluntarily abide by these requests and/or remove themselves from any uncomfortable situations. Collections are available for ceremonial use by authorized Native representatives at the CRC facility and in special circumstances are loaned out to communities with the assistance of museum personnel.

When there is insufficient information to make an informed decision, the committee will solicit the advice and perspectives of official Native community representatives. In the event that a request is beyond the museum's capacity to honor, the committee will investigate alternative approaches that will be satisfactory to both the museum and the Native communities. The committee also acknowledges the political and cultural dynamics of Native communities and understands that Native community authority will change over time, as will the advice and opinions of the Native community representation. The CIS must be flexible enough to incorporate changes in information affecting the care and handling of specific objects.

An important advantage of having a Culturally Sensitive Collections Care Program, as well as a working committee to facilitate it, is the potential for consistency and continuity over time. As staff members come and go, the program will provide a recorded history of the interactions between the museum and its Native constituents. There will be no need to reinvent a program each time there is staff turnover. The CIS database will continue to evolve and will become an invaluable resource, not only for the museum but also for its Native constituencies.

The management of culturally sensitive collections will involve compromises for the NMAI, which will never be able to approximate the objects' original cultural contexts. The makers of the vast majority of these cultural materials did not intend for them to be placed in a museum or any repository. The NMAI is committed to building and maintaining relationships with the cultures associated with the collections and to maintaining a comfortable and culturally sensitive environment while these items are in its care.

Notes

1. Mission Statement, Board of Trustees, National Museum of the American Indian, 1991.

2. Kevin Wallace, "A Reporter at Large: Slim-Shin's Monument," *New Yorker*, November 19, 1960.

3. Bruce Bernstein, citation from transcript, Museum Partners Project Symposium, Suitland, Md., December 16, 2003.

4. W. Richard West, "American Museums in the Twenty-first Century: By Whose Authority?" lecture, National Museum of Australia, Canberra, February 26, 2002.

Repatriation in the Twenty-first Century: Are We Still Fighting the Skull Wars?

9

DAVID HURST THOMAS

S INCE THE DAYS OF THOMAS JEFFERSON—America's first scientific archeologist—American Indians have been studied as part of the natural world. Like mammoth bones and the fruit trees in Jefferson's own garden, American Indians were "specimens," to be empirically investigated and objectively understood. Following the Jeffersonian model, nineteenth-century anthropologists studied American Indians by digging up their graves and exhibiting Indians in the "ethnographic zoos" that were popular additions to several World Fairs. Sometimes Native people became "living fossils" tucked away in the museums of America; sometimes, when these "museum Indians" died, their bodies were not buried at all, but rendered into bones, numbered and stored away as part of America's greater heritage.[1]

By 1900, American Indians seemed to be vanishing as surely as the American bison, and so too were the archeological vestiges of Indian history. As museum anthropologists hurried to document and collect the last of Indian culture, the United States Congress passed the Antiquities Act of 1906, legislation crafted to preserve America's remote past and to ensure its continued study by a rapidly growing scientific community. The archeological record was seen as a critical part of America's national identity because it documented its progression from savagery to the most civilized place on earth and, in 1906, this heritage was formally entrusted to science. Whatever Indians had to say about their past was irrelevant to the American narrative.

But American Indians, of course, refused to vanish. Their numbers bottomed out in the 1890s and have dramatically increased ever since. Particularly since the 1960s, Indian people have stepped up their fight to reclaim and reinforce their treaty-guaranteed sovereignty, borrowing strategies and guidelines from the world of international law. Such Indigenous ideologies assert an essential Native subjectivity, promoting themes of self-worth and cultural preservation, and suggesting that Indian culture could help correct some problems of the modern mainstream.

Achieving power over their own history has tangible payoffs in the everyday life of Indian people, where life is still subject to long-conflicted federal policies. Economic development in Indian Country remains integrally connected to politics—intertwined with issues of sovereignty, tribal identity, access to resources, cultural issues, and ideology. By emphasizing histories absent from white-dominated curricula, Native people are attempting to build institutional mechanisms to help their communities and reassert their rights. By taking hold of the imagery that still frames negotiations with state and federal governments, they seek to translate historical and cultural identities into tangible political power.

The bottom line is defining which history gets taught and who gets to teach it. In seeking identities independent of non-Indian historians and anthropologists, many Native Americans have come to resent the appropriation of their ancient artifacts and ancestral bones by "experts" claiming an authority denied to the Indians themselves. As Native people across the land try to recapture their own language, culture, and history, they are increasingly concerned with recovering and taking control of tribal heirlooms and human remains.

Congress responded to these sensitivities in 1990 by passing the Native American Graves Protection and Repatriation Act (NAGPRA). This legislation marked a significant shift in the federal stance toward the rights of Indian people and a sea change in the perception and practice of American archeology. As in 1906, the federal government asserted its right to legislate access to the American past. But the 1990 law explicitly acknowledged that Indian pasts are relevant to the American present. This public and visible benchmark reflected a deep-seated shift in thinking, emphasizing America's self-perception as a multifaceted, pluralistic society. The American Creed shifted away from the time-honored melting pot to newer perspectives recognizing the merits of a multicultural society.

Such an interpretation of the American character was unimaginable in 1906. The Antiquities Act of 1906, which legally transferred the Indian past on the American public domain, was crafted without Indian involvement and with no suggestion that Indian people might have spiritual affiliations with that past. In 1990, for the first time, Native people were empowered to question mainstream American ownership of the Indian past, both literally and metaphorically. No longer were Indian bones found on public lands automatically defined as natural resources, as federal property to be safeguarded in scientific custody. No longer did science have a monopoly on defining the meaning of archeology; instead, Native groups were invited to assign their own spiritual and historical meanings to archeological sites and their contents. It is hard to overlook the sense of loss among mainstream scientists and historians who see their power and authority eroding as late twentieth-century America experiments with multicultural alternatives to the traditional melting pot imagery.

The multicultural tug-of-war over Kennewick Man raises deep questions about how the past can serve the diverse purposes of the present, Indian as well as non-Indian. The Kennewick conflict has often been portrayed as a face-off between science and religion, a reprise of the famous Scopes trial of the 1920s—except that Red creationists have now assumed the role of Christian fundamentalists. But the facts of the case indicate otherwise.

At the heart of the matter, the Kennewick dispute boils down to issues of power and control. Who gets to control ancient American history—governmental agencies, the academic community, or modern Indian people? To understand the deeply political nature of the Kennewick conflict, one must remember the long-term interactions between Euro-American and Indian populations. Over more than five centuries, several distinct American Indian histories have developed, of which three are especially critical: a larger national narrative that glorifies assimilation into the great American melting pot; an academic discourse written by anthropologists and historians who view Indians as subjects of scholarly inquiry; and an Indigenous insider's perspective long maintained in the oral traditions of Indian people themselves. Although sometimes overlapping, these distinct histories often paint quite different visions of America, past and present. Proponents of each strongly believe that "their" history is the correct one, the version that should be published in textbooks, protected by law, and defended in the courtroom.

The Kennewick controversy clearly highlights the difficulties in asking the court system to resolve disputes involving cultural heritage and intellectual property rights. To be sure, the eight scientists filing the Kennewick Man lawsuit felt a sense of urgency, even desperation. But as the argument over Kennewick Man came to be viewed in terms of "winners" and "losers," it overshadowed the search for a relationship based on mutual respect and consensus.

Robert McLaughlin speaks of "a more introspective" brand of museum anthropology that is being practiced during the NAGPRA era.[2] Although Kennewick Man has generated headlines for nearly a decade, archeologists and Native Americans increasingly agree on the importance of the past and the necessity to cooperate to understand it and to preserve whatever remains of it. Some tribes have used their own archeology to promote tribal sovereignty, a critical social and political issue throughout Indian Country. Many tribes and First Nations today maintain large and effective archeology programs employing both Indian and non-Indian archeologists. Some Native groups are conducting archeology to encourage tourism, to inform educational programs, and to preserve sacred sites on their own land. Several tribes sponsor their own museums that display archeological materials. The Society for American Archaeology (SAA) sponsors a Native American Scholarship Fund—named after Arthur S. Parker, an American Indian who served as the SAA's first president— encouraging Indian people to train as professional archeologists and funded, in part, from royalties earned on books written by archeologists about the Native American past. Throughout Native North America, Indian people are increasingly involved in archeological meetings and publications—not merely as "informants," but participants and collaborators.

Perhaps the lasting legacy of the Kennewick Man dispute is that of negative role model. Litigation and legislation appear to be increasingly unattractive ways to settle conflicts over cultural patrimony and intellectual property rights. Over the past decade, we can document literally dozens (and dozens) of cases in which American Indian and scientific interests have elected to work together to resolve their differences amicably, doing what ethnologist Michael Brown characterizes as "thoughtful people coming together to negotiate workable solutions, however provisional and inelegant."[3] Perhaps the Kennewick case will be viewed as a worst-case scenario—quite literally, a court of last resort—for resolving disputes between American Indians and the non-Indians who wish to study them.

Notes

1. For more on Jefferson and the early history of American archeology, see David Hurst Thomas, *Skull Wars: Kennewick Man, Archaeology, and the Battle for Native American Identity* (New York: Basic Books, 2000).

2. Robert H. McLaughlin, "NAGPRA, Dialogue, and the Politics of Historical Authority," in *Legal Perspectives on Cultural Resources*, ed. Jennifer R. Richman and Marion P. Forsyth (Walnut Creek, Calif.: AltaMira, 2004), 185–201.

3. Michael F. Brown, *Who Owns Native Culture?* (Cambridge, Mass.: Harvard University Press, 2003), 9. See also Thomas, *Skull Wars*, 254–267.

Today's American Indian Tribes and Their Museums

10

LISA J. WATT

THE TRIBAL MUSEUM MOVEMENT is not a new phenomenon. In fact, it started at least seventy years ago and has picked up speed, particularly since 1991. One colleague surmises that the creation of tribal museums is the fastest-growing segment of this country's museum world. I don't know whether that's true or not, but I wouldn't be at all surprised if it is.

This paper explores three aspects of tribal museums: a brief history of tribal museums, the tribal museum movement today, and models for tribal communities to consider as they plan their own facilities. Unfortunately, there isn't enough space to discuss each and every tribal museum, but I hope readers will seek out these institutions as they travel throughout this country and get to know them better.

A Brief History of Tribal Museums

As early as the 1930s and 1940s, tribal museums started to appear. The Osage Tribal Museum is reportedly the oldest tribal museum in the country, founded in 1938 in Pawhuska, Oklahoma. Then ten years later, in 1948, the Cherokee Historical Association opened the Museum of the Cherokee Indian in Cherokee, North Carolina.

I suspect many tribes had similar goals and desires of having a tribal museum in those early days. My own nation, the Seneca Nation of Indians in western New York State, started its conversation about a museum in the 1930s, but the Seneca-Iroquois National Museum did not open until 1977.

The tribal museum movement took off in the 1960s and 1970s, during a time of American Indian activism which called national attention to tribal issues and, in particular, the need to honor Indian treaties. A collective pride in Native heritage arose. It was during this activism that tribes began to question the authority of museums as purveyors of tribal culture. Museums had to re-examine their relationships with tribes and understand that they—the museums—were not the experts on tribal culture.

During Richard Nixon's presidency in the 1970s, the Economic Development Administration viewed tribal museums as a vehicle to create jobs and stimulate and diversify tribal economies. Four pilot projects were approved and constructed with federal funds: the Yakama Nation Cultural Center in Toppenish, Washington; the Makah Cultural and Research Center in Neah Bay, Washington; the Seneca-Iroquois National Museum in Salamanca, New York; the Native American Center for the Living Arts in Niagara Falls, New York. Soon, more and more tribal museums started to pop up all over the country, nearly twenty of them in the 1960s and 1970s alone.

The next wave of new tribal museums occurred in the 1990s. Between 1991 and 2002, a total of nineteen facilities opened, with the highest concentration of openings occurring between 1993 and 1995 with at least eight. They opened in all areas of the country, from coast to coast. The fact that more and more tribes are now planning and/or opening new museums speaks to their increased sophistication, resources, and ability to implement their long-term, community, comprehensive plans that address cultural needs and concerns. In other words, where tribes have the money, resources, knowledge, and desire, they are creating museums.

Today, there are approximately 120 tribal museums in the United States. Some estimates are as high as 170 to 250, but those numbers, in my opinion, are inflated. Why? Because I called each and every tribe that stated they had a tribal museum. While the original lists were long, the final list boiled down to approximately 120 in total. During this exploratory phase, when tribes were asked about their museums, many stated their "museum" consisted of one or more display cases with objects and more often than not were found in the main lobby of tribal administration buildings. Staff was not assigned to maintain the cases, and many of the objects were on loan from local tribal individuals and families. The tribes would ultimately decide they did not have a "real" museum but expressed a desire to have one.

What Is a Tribal Museum?

One definition of a tribal museum is a museum, cultural center, heritage center, history center, or interpretive center that is owned and operated by any one or more of the federally recognized or unrecognized American Indian tribes, either on or off reservations. This is an expansive and inclusive definition that not only recognizes the several different types of interpretive and cultural facilities but the variety of tribal groups no matter their location.

"Owned and operated" are the key words here, because there are mainstream museums that are dedicated to American Indian history, art, and culture but are operated by non-Indian groups, such as the Heard Museum in Phoenix, the Eiteljorg Museum in Indianapolis, and even the new National Museum of the American Indian in Washington, D.C., although each of them has close ties to contemporary tribal people. There are other institutions that display tribal objects but may have little or no connection to the tribal groups whose objects they own. For the purposes of this paper, ownership and control by Native people are the keys.

Like all museums, tribal museums come in all shapes and sizes, and they are in varying stages of development and in many different locales. There are tribal museums that occupy their own buildings, some of which are secure and climate-controlled. Some have state-of-the-art exhibition spaces and other visitor amenities. Other buildings are refurbished, fashioned out of old churches or other community buildings. Still others consist of a dedicated space in tribal administration office buildings. There are tribal museums on and off reservations, and even in urban Indian centers, such as those found in Seattle, New York City, and Minneapolis. All three of these facilities are controlled by Native people and serve large urban Native populations.

Then there are the new cultural centers located on each campus of the thirty-three tribal colleges nationwide. In recent years, a generous donor of the American Indian College Fund donated a beautiful log cabin building to each tribal college for the purpose of creating a cultural center. Some have done just that. Others have created multipurpose facilities, combining a cultural center with classrooms or bookstores or administrative offices or galleries or some other combination. No two log cabins are alike. The range of these facilities is still emerging.

There are also three museums that have Native collections and are owned and controlled by religious groups located in or near tribal communities: the Heritage Center at Red Cloud Indian School, located on the Pine Ridge Reservation in South Dakota; the Atka Lakota Museum and Cultural Center, located on the campus of the Saint Joseph Indian School in Chamberlain, South Dakota; and the Buechel Memorial Lakota Museum on the Rosebud Reservation in Saint Francis, South Dakota.

Then there are the three museums owned and operated by the Indian Arts and Crafts Board, which is a program of the Department of the Interior. These museums are the Museum of the Plains Indian in Browning, Montana; the Southern Plains Indian Museum in Anadarko, Oklahoma; and the Sioux Indian

Museum, which is located inside the Journey Museum in Rapid City, South Dakota. Each of these museums has displays, permanent collections, and gift shops where local tribal people sell their arts and crafts.

While not tribal museums by the above definition, these last six museums are recognized as part of the tribal communities they are located in or near. The best part of all is that, in each instance, the collections remain in or near the communities from which they came.

Reasons to Exist

So why do tribal museums exist? They exist for the same reasons that mainstream museums exist: to preserve, protect, educate, interpret, communicate, stimulate, and so forth. Lots of adjectives can apply here.

But there are other reasons for tribal museums to exist, and when I asked tribal museum professionals around the country "Why?" this is what they said:

- A tribal museum may be the only place where you can learn about a particular tribe.
- To perpetuate tribal culture and traditions.
- To hold what little some tribes have left of their material culture.
- To instill a healthy tribal identity, so that Indian children gain a deeper understanding of who they are and where they come from.
- To communicate what is important to their community.
- To serve as a public relations vehicle for the tribe.
- To tell their story in their own words.
- To remind the mainstream world of a tribe's presence.
- To define tribal territory.
- To exert tribal sovereignty.
- To reinforce treaty rights.

In an interview with Bobbie Connor, director of the Tamástslikt Cultural Institute, she expressed the idea that a tribal museum may be a benchmark or milestone of a tribe's collective self-worth. It is a public declaration of "we are important"; "we are culturally worth maintaining."

Now, lots of museums can make these same or similar claims, but yet it is different for American Indian tribes and their museums. No other ethnic and racial group in the United States has a trust relationship with the U.S. government, a relationship that is recognized in the Constitution and reflected in our treaties. When we talk about "Indian Country," Indian Country is a real place. It is a legal term that recognizes claims to original ownership and autonomy.

Thus, one of the key differences between tribal and mainstream museums comes back to our status as sovereign nations. Tribal museums do help define our territories, they are expressions of treaty rights, they are expressions of sovereign nations. In the same way that the British Museum is the national museum of Britain, the Canadian Museum of Civilization is the national museum of Canada, and the Smithsonian Institution is the national museum of this country, so too are tribal museums a cultural, historical, and artistic expression of each sovereign tribal nation.

Challenges Facing Tribal Museums

Museums are desirable. They are very desirable to tribes. In fact, I always say that despite the great cultural diversity of tribes in the United States, there are really two and *only* two types of tribes—those that *have* a tribal museum and those that *want* a tribal museum. I tested this observation on a group of tribal leaders a few years ago, and while the statement was met with laughter, there was also universal agreement. I suspect if you review the development or master plans of nearly every tribe in this country, there would be mention or discussion about the desire or goal to have a tribal museum.

Here are some of the issues that face tribal museums today:

- The unfounded belief that "if we build it, they will come" (which rarely, if ever, happens).
- The desire/need to serve both the tribal community and the general public (which is a delicate balance difficult to achieve).
- The notion that a museum will be self-sustaining (they rarely are).
- Confusion about the best governing structure (tribes have more options when it comes to nonprofit status).
- Lack of internal understanding of what a museum does (the notion that filling display cases is all that's needed to be a museum).
- Unrealistic expectations placed on staff (to be self-sustaining and at the same time serve multiple audiences and needs).
- Limited funding and resources (which means the difference between surviving and thriving).

These problems are very common, not just for tribal museums, but for many museums across the country today. Practically every museum in this country is in the same boat to one degree or another.

Tribal museums, though, are faced with a unique opportunity and a challenge. Tribal museums have two distinct audiences: the tribal community and the general public. The first priority is the tribal community. Nearly all tribal museums see their mission as preserving and perpetuating tribal history, culture, and traditions for members of their community through the collections they hold and the programs and activities they conduct. Whether they get the resources from the tribal government to do this important work is another matter. On the other hand, when it comes to the general public, a tribal museum's goal is much simpler and apparent: to educate visitors about the history, art, and culture of that tribe. Again, the question of having the resources to meet this goal is another question.

Balancing these two distinct audiences is delicate and difficult, and what happens is that one audience is often sacrificed for the other, not by design but by default. To successfully address the needs and expectations of both audiences, tribal museums require lots of money, time, and resources.

The most successful tribal museums I've seen are those where the tribal government and community have a clear understanding of what they want their museum to do and for whom. They answer the questions: Why does this museum exist? Who does it exist for? What do we want this institution to do? Are we willing to give it the resources it needs to be successful and to do all that we want it to do? The tribes and tribal communities are clear about roles, responsibilities, and expectations.

Models to Consider

The following is a very small sample of the 120-plus tribal museums in the United States. I wish I could recite the unique qualities of each and every tribal museum I visited, but it's just not possible. My apologies to those museums not represented here. I hate to say I have a favorite tribal museum, because each museum is distinct and has something wonderfully unique and special to offer, no matter how professionally orchestrated or offbeat. There are a few tribal museums, however, that stand just a little taller. These are just a few.

Tamástslikt Cultural Institute, Pendleton, Oregon

This wonderful facility was created by the Confederated Tribes of the Umatilla Reservation, which is a confederation consisting of the Cayuse, Umatilla, and Walla Walla tribal peoples of eastern Oregon.[1] It opened to the public in July 1998 and contains 45,000 square feet. *Tamástslikt* means "to interpret" or "to follow" in the Waluulapam language.

The impetus for this beautiful institution was the national 150th anniversary of the Oregon Trail. The national observance traced the Oregon Trail from its starting point in Missouri to the settlement of the Oregon Territory and the places we now know as Washington, Oregon, California, Idaho, Nevada, and Utah. The Oregon Trail is the story of the more than 300,000 pioneers and settlers and their arduous journey west between 1810 and 1860, with most of the migration occurring in the 1840s. In certain sections of the Oregon Trail, you can still see the wagon ruts.

Four museums and interpretive centers were constructed along the route, each telling a different aspect of the Oregon Trail story. Tamástslikt Cultural Institute is the only institution that tells the story of the Oregon Trail from a tribal perspective. It's a vital part of this national story and, to me, the most interesting.

Today, Tamástslikt is much, much more than just the Oregon Trail and its impact on these three tribal groups. Tamástslikt shares the history, art, and culture of the Umatilla tribes, but more importantly, its greater vision is "to become the foremost trusted source of knowledge on the culture and history of the Confederated Tribes of the Umatilla Reservation."[2] What a bold vision! For this reason alone, I consider Tamástslikt to be a leader in the tribal museum field. Whereas nearly all tribal museums say their vision or mission is to preserve, protect, and perpetuate tribal culture, Tamástslikt is one of the few tribal museums that has publicly proclaimed authority and ownership of its own history and culture. That role may be implied for tribal museums, but Tamástslikt publicly states it. The staff has a healthy respect for formal scholarship and gives equal voice and credence to community knowledge and oral history. This tribal museum and tribal community have set the bar high and are striving to reach it.

Tamástslikt has an active, changing exhibition program, one of the best tribal museum gift shops in the country, a community storage area, a new outdoor tribal village, and one of the best permanent installations with themes of "We Were," "We Are," and "We Will Be."

Challenges in Alaska

Alaska has several tribal museums, and those institutions face a unique set of challenges. The majority of facilities are seasonal because winter comes early and lasts for several months, making the tourism season just a few months long. Sustainability is difficult because of the lack of steady revenue streams year round. Construction costs are double those in the Lower Forty-eight and are further complicated by the short building season and the isolation of Native villages. It is difficult to get quality museum training, which usually means Native and non-Native museum professionals must travel to the Lower Forty-eight to get it, thereby having to invest both time and considerable money. Distance learning is not an option now, due to the lack of an infrastructure, especially in the bush where the villages are located. (This is a problem for all of Alaska in general.) Moreover, the needs of Alaska Natives are often overlooked when it comes to resources and finding out needs. In many instances, Alaska Natives are often, for lack of a better word, an afterthought.

But there are a couple of Alaska Native institutions that are addressing or overcoming these obstacles, in part by creating unique partnerships with outside agencies. In fact, in Alaska more than anywhere else, you will find interesting collaborations.

Southeast Alaska Indian Cultural Center, Sitka

The Southeast Alaska Indian Cultural Center (SEAICC) is located on the island of Sitka in southeast Alaska.[3] It sits in the heart of the Sitka National Historical Park, where the Tlingits battled the Russians in 1804. The area tribal groups are the Tlingit, Haida, Tsimshian, and Eyak. The SEAICC opened to the public in 1969 and today has over 300,000 annual visitors.

This amazing facility has had a wonderfully unique partnership with the National Park Service for more than thirty years. In 1969, when the original visitor center was being planned by the National Park Service, it was designed with the tribal cultural center component in mind, as that being a place to pass on Tlingit, Haida, and Tsimshian traditions to the Native community and to educate the general public about these beautiful cultures.

Today, the visitor center is operated by the National Park Service, while the cultural center component is managed by an independent board of trustees as a 501c3 nonprofit organization with funding provided by the National Park Service. The cultural center houses four artist studios where local Native artists demonstrate and teach carving, weaving, silversmithing, beading, and other artistic traditions. At least two artists are on-site every day during the tourist season. Through these demonstrations, the SEAICC has amassed one of the largest collections of contemporary Tlingit, Haida, and Tsimshian art in the world.

The most interesting thing about this facility is that the National Park Service provides all of the funding for a full-time cultural center director and four full-time artists, as well as programming during the summer months. Plus, the National Park Service provides office and storage space at no cost to the SEAICC. The National Park Service is responsible for the upkeep of the grounds and building, which was recently expanded and updated. The SEAICC is only required to present artists and programs. The SEAICC is not a National Park Service entity, nor is it directed by the National Park Service. It is a Native-directed program that facilitates interaction with and celebrates Tlingit, Haida, and Tsimshian art and culture and serves as a place to pass on important tribal traditions.

In addition to the visitor center, the park site contains two miles of walking trails where fifteen replicated totem poles are interspersed among tall stands of spruce and hemlock. The original poles are now the centerpieces of the newly renovated center. This renovation also included updated and larger artist studios, an improved display and exhibit area, and more visitor services. The site is exquisite, with the center situated on a beautiful rocky shore. It has got to be one of the most beautiful sites for a cultural/visitor center anywhere.

Alaska Native Heritage Center, Anchorage

Founded in 1989 and opened to the public in 1999, the Alaska Native Heritage Center (ANHC) in Anchorage is an exceptional facility.[4] The building consists of 26,000 square feet, with 15,000 dedicated to museum functions. Over 110,000 visitors walk through its doors each year.

Surrounded by the majestic Chugach Mountains, the ANHC is located on a twenty-six-acre wooded site about a ten-minute drive from downtown Anchorage. The center consists of a 26,000-square-foot Welcoming House and five outdoor traditional home sites situated around a beautiful manmade lake. A tour of this facility allows people the world over to see and hear living Alaska Native cultures.

Alaska is divided into five cultural regions: (1) the Athabascans, (2) Aleuts and Alutiiqs, (3) Inupiats, (4) the Yupik and Cupik, and (5) the Tlingit, Haida, Tsimshian, and Eyak. Each cultural group is represented in the ANHC by five cultural advisory committees. These committees provide guidance and assistance in programming. Every year a program theme is chosen and explored in depth when the center is open. When I was there in 2001, the theme was traditional clothing in "Fur, Feathers, Fiber: Covering Native Alaska." In 2002, the theme was "Healing Ways," an exploration of how traditional knowledge helped Alaska's Native people achieve a healthy harmony of mind, body, and spirit.

The center's hallmark is its emphasis on experiential, interactive learning. On any given day, visitors can view one or more dance performances, hear stories, witness a wide array of demonstrations such as kayak construction using traditional methods, or hear discussions on hunting or fishing, all conducted by Alaska's Native people. Many of these activities take place in a large performance space known as the Gathering Place or in any one of the five traditional home sites during the summer months.

Visitors may also interact with traditional and contemporary artists in any of the three artist workshops and studios found in the Hall of Cultures, which also contains an exhibit area that explains the different cultural groups. This is an intimate exhibit space, where the topics are chosen by each of the five cultural advisory committees. There is also a film that is shown several times daily.

The center has a beautiful gift shop that features authentic arts and crafts created by Alaska Natives from across the state. Alaska Natives are serious about ensuring Native arts and crafts are appropriately identified and promoted as such.

The ANHC is not a collections-based institution. It is not a traditional museum. It is a heritage center that celebrates the cultures and traditions of Alaska's Native people. Its emphasis is on the experiential and educational, and it succeeds very well.

Ak-Chin Him-Dak EcoMuseum, Maricopa, Arizona

The Ak-Chin Indian community is located in Maricopa, Arizona, just south of Phoenix.[5] As the discussion of a museum evolved, the community decided this institution would be an ecomuseum, a concept that originated in France in the 1960s by George Henri Riviere. Its principal idea is a museum without walls, where the land and community replace the building. Tribal members are the curators as well as the audience.

The Ak-Chin Him-Dak EcoMuseum is one of my favorite tribal museums for several reasons, but mostly for a single, critically important one. When the tribal council committed to creating this museum, they decided the primary audience and focus would be the Ak-Chin community. But they also knew in making that determination, they would more than likely have to fund it in its entirety, and they have. While staff are encouraged to pursue grants and outside funding, the tribal council understood their responsibility to their museum from the beginning and provides the funding and support it needs.

The museum is located in the center of the Ak-Chin community. On the day I visited, I couldn't find any signs pointing the way to the museum. That alone told me a lot about this facility and for whom it exists. Just by quietly walking through the gallery, you can see just how closely this facility interfaces with the tribal community. They had lovely exhibits on diabetes and archeology, plus community quilt and tribal-member art shows. A new tribal veterans' exhibit had just been installed. The community emphasis here is palatable and inspiring.

The building is beautifully designed. In fact, it's deceiving, giving the impression it is much larger than it is. It just seems to go on forever.

The entire staff is professionally trained and is clear about their mission. In other words, they know why they exist and for whom. To me, the Ak-Chin Him-Dak EcoMuseum is an important model for existing and potential tribal museums nationwide.

Akwesasne Library and Cultural Center, Hogansburg, New York

The Akwesasne Library and Cultural Center is located in the Mohawk community of Hogansburg, not far from the Saint Lawrence Seaway in far upstate New York.[6] The Mohawks are one of the Six Nations of the Iroquois Confederacy and are known as Keepers of the Eastern Door. Akwesasne is a small community where tribal culture and tradition are strong.

The facility is a library and a cultural center combined. Founded in 1971, the library/cultural center is an independent 501c3 nonprofit organization with its own board of directors, which means it is separate from tribal government and immune to the sometimes unpredictable nature of tribal politics. The library/cultural center thrives and is embraced by the community.

On the day I visited, the place had just tons of foot traffic. Tribal members were stopping in to check their e-mail on a bank of computers donated by Microsoft. They were also doing Internet research, reading the paper, browsing the stacks, visiting the cultural center, and visiting with one another. This place is a precious refuge in the community. The staff works hard at that, making sure that everyone in the community feels welcome. In fact, staff members are expected to serve as ambassadors for the library/cultural center and would personally invite tribal members whom they hadn't seen in a while to visit, and those who do visit to visit more often.

The library is on the top floor, but on the bottom floor is the cultural center/museum. It is a neat, small, lovely space, filled with well-loved objects and cases. This is one institution where I would love to see what the staff and community would do if they had lots of money and resources. How the community has embraced the library/cultural center is a lesson for all tribal museums.

Birthing New Tribal Museums

There is another category of tribal museums which we haven't discussed yet: the ones that are currently in the planning stages. The Agua Caliente Cultural Museum[7] is one example. It is being planned by the Agua Caliente Band of Cahuilla Indians in Palm Springs, California.

The tribe currently operates a temporary museum facility located on the main strip in downtown Palm Springs. The museum is highly visible and is one of the only places in the region where you can learn about the Cahuilla people in and around Palm Springs. While the museum sits in a prime location, it's a very small building with a small exhibit area and gift shop. They also have a growing collection that has been donated or purchased. This is one of the best benefits of having financial resources for many tribes nationwide: the ability to purchase objects of their cultural patrimony.

Recently, the Agua Caliente broke ground for a new 88,000-square-foot solar-powered, energy-efficient facility which will be located in downtown Palm Springs. The total cost is $41 million, of which the tribe is contributing $20 million. The rest is being raised in a capital campaign. The new museum will contain 20,000 square feet of permanent exhibition space, 3,700 square feet of temporary or changing exhibition space, four education classrooms, a 4,250-volume research library and archives, a 150-seat multipurpose theater, an outdoor learning garden, . . . the list goes on. Granted, not all tribal museums in the planning stages are as ambitious as this one, but when you have the resources, knowledge, and desire, why not think big. This tribe has.

Conclusion

Tribal museums can be found all over the country and, like the tribes themselves, are amazingly diverse. As more and more tribes start to implement their long-term goals and have more resources, we will see more and more tribal museums constructed in the future. It's a movement that's not about to stop anytime soon.

The formal lessons that existing tribal museums have to offer are beneficial to those in the planning stages. But at the most fundamental level, tribes need to be aware that for a tribal museum to be strong, be successful, and fulfill its mission for multiple audiences, it needs both sustained tribal government and tribal community support. That is critical. Government and community must also have a clear and unwavering understanding of what their museum does and for whom. A tribal museum can be a dynamic and vital place in a community—just as it is in Ak-Chin and the Mohawk community of Awkwesasne. It can also serve the interests and needs of the wider general public. It is a delicate, yet critical balance, but with the commitment of a tribal government and community, a tribal museum can be an incredibly valuable resource.

Notes

1. Tamastslikt Cultural Institute, www.tamastslikt.com. Websites for each of the museums and cultural centers are cited so readers may learn more about each of these facilities from the source. All were accessed 12 September 2005.
2. Tamastslikt Cultural Institute.
3. Southeast Alaska Indian Cultural Center, www.nps.gov/sitk/home.htm.
4. Alaska Native Heritage Center, www.alaskanative.net.
5. Ak-Chin Indian Community, www.itcaonline.com/tribes_akchin.html.
6. Akwesasne Culture Center, www.nc3r.org/akwlibr/index.html.
7. Agua Caliente Cultural Museum, www.accmuseum.org.

EDUCATION III

Indian Education: State and Federal 11

EARL J. BARLOW

THE SINGLE MOST IMPORTANT INGREDIENT for quality education for Indian students is a qualified classroom teacher. The goal of Indian education should be to produce an educated person equipped to make decisions in his or her best interest. If the educated Indian person chooses to live among his or her people and live according to tribal values, customs, beliefs, and traditions, he or she could do so with peace of mind, dignity, pride, and self-respect. Or, if the educated Indian person chooses to leave and seek his or her fortune in higher education, vocational technical training, or the world of work, he or she can do so with the tools and confidence to succeed. For too long, Indians have been denied the basic right to make such decisions because the system has failed them.

During my career, I expended much time and effort to make the two primary educational delivery systems, state and federal, more user friendly. I was not involved to a great extent with private schools. I concluded that the highest quality of education for Indian students does not depend upon the delivery system so much as it does upon the interest, involvement, and commitment of Indian people. Approximately 80 percent of all Indian students attend public elementary and secondary schools, 15 percent attend federally operated schools, and 5 percent attend private or tribally operated schools. Today, I will relate some of my trials and tribulations, successes, and failures.

I began my teaching career in a public school on the Salish-Kootenai Indian Reservation. Ideas about Indian education were not in my thinking. Why was this so? I was born on an Indian reservation. My parents were Indian. I attended a federal boarding school and graduated from a public high school on the reservation. I didn't realize I was a highly acculturated product of the system. When

I was in the second grade, the teacher had us learn about the Belgian Congo. The unit was based on a young African boy and his life. My peers groused and were not much interested. I told them to hush and we must do what the teacher wanted. It was ironic that during my formal education I learned more about African natives than my people.

In those years, I perceived my job was to educate students and motivate them to achieve their potential. I was not oblivious to the plight of Indian students and had a natural rapport with them. I was determined to help them without knowing how. By dint of hard work, many of the Indian graduates went on to become doctors, lawyers, and Indian chiefs. At the end of my first year, the school board informed me that a non-Indian parent requested I be fired because he didn't want an Indian teaching his daughter. The trustees laughed and gave me a contract with a $100 raise!

My elation was short-lived when I discovered secondary teachers had been given raises of $200. The school superintendent explained that high school teachers had to know more than elementary teachers. I succeeded in persuading the administration and school trustees to adopt a single salary schedule based on education and years of teaching experience.

In 1968 Dolores Colburg, a dynamic young educator, was elected Montana State Superintendent of Public Instruction and hired me as State Indian Education Supervisor. My career took a dramatic change and I was apprehensive as the first Indian to fill the position. I felt an obligation to make a positive impact. Before I accepted, Ms. Colburg agreed that Indian people would be consulted in the management of Johnson-O'Malley Act funds; Indian education committees would be organized in school districts to plan, implement, monitor, and evaluate JOM programs. As I began to concentrate on the problems of Indian education and solutions, the arcane and bizarre factors and forces in play frustrated me. It was obvious we had to learn the existing political, economic, and social systems and use them to our advantage.

The Johnson-O'Malley Act was enacted in 1934 to provide education services for Indian children. The JOM Act authorized the Secretary of the Interior to contract with any state for the education, medical attention, agriculture assistance, and social welfare, including relief of distress, of Indians through qualified agencies of the state. Education funds were available to public school districts on or adjacent to Indian reservations and were used primarily for basic support of the general fund budget. In 1936 the Act was amended to authorize the Secretary of the Interior to contract with a political subdivision of a state, university, college, or school, or with any appropriate state or private corporation, agency, or institution. In 1934 Montana school districts contracted with local Indian agencies for JOM funds. In 1946 the Superintendent of Public Instruction contracted with the Bureau of Indian Affairs for JOM funds and managed the programs in the local school districts. At that time the funds were used for basic support in the general fund budget and benefited all students, Indians and non-Indians. This use was justified as necessary because of the low tax base resulting from nontaxable Indian lands. Neither individual Indian people nor tribal governments participated in the process.

This funding scheme began to change in 1952 when P.L. 81-874, Impact Aid, was extended to Indian reservations. Federal funds through P.L. 81-874 began to replace JOM funds for basic support. JOM funds were used mainly to pay for school lunches for indigent Indian students living on Indian land. The 1958–1959 school year was the last year JOM funds were used for basic support.

I telephoned Dwight A. Billedeaux, a Blackfeet Indian who was teaching in Las Vegas, where he had achieved national prominence in the field of curriculum development. He began his teaching career in Sunburst, and his mentor, Duane Taft, Superintendent of Schools, influenced his work and philosophy. Dwight came to Helena, was interviewed and hired. Montana's JOM programs attracted national attention. In response to feedback from teachers, we published *The Indian in the Classroom: Readings for the Teacher with Indian Students*.[1] We were off to a good beginning, but needed information and direction for Indian education.

In November 1969 a U.S. Senate Special Subcommittee on Indian Education published a report, *Indian Education: A National Tragedy—A National Challenge*.[2] The report was dedicated to the memory of the first chairman, Senator Robert F. Kennedy, a man who cared deeply and spoke out. Indeed, he did. And I vividly recall a news story about his visit to a public school on the Fort Hall Indian Reservation. He asked to see their library books about Indians. After a frantic search, one book was found. Senator Kennedy opened the cover, and the front piece was a picture of a Delaware Indian scalping a young white girl. Senator Kennedy was outraged and delivered a blistering lecture to the school authorities. He was succeeded as chairman by his brother, Senator Edward M. Kennedy. The report was invaluable to me, and I frequently used it to justify my initiatives to improve Indian education.

The Robert F. Kennedy Journalism Award was founded in 1968 by his widow, Ethel, and is given to outstanding reporting on the problems of the disadvantaged. This spring the University of Montana School of Journalism won the award for a series on tribal sovereignty. The series was written by fourteen student reporters in UM's Native News Honors Report.

The Kennedy Report, as I call it, is an examination of a major failure of the American vision—the education of Indian children. The senators listened to the Indian people speak for themselves. Time does not permit a comprehensive discussion of the findings; however, the senators concluded that the responsibility for the Indian children is primarily in the hands of the federal government and the federal government has not lived up to its responsibility. They cited the failure of national policy, failure of public schools, and the failure of non-education Indian programs. The report is well documented, and recommended remedies are well stated. I recognized the enormity of the challenge to develop educational programs for culturally different children and educationally disadvantaged children.

The Kennedy Report has a section entitled "The Failure of National Policy: An Historical Analysis." The report called it 400 years of failure. I deem it important to give you a brief overview of the history.[3]

The Mission Period, 1500–1897. The goal from the beginning has been not so much to educate Indians as to change them.

The Treaty Period, 1778–1871. Nearly 400 treaties were executed. Treaties are the supreme law of the land. One billion acres of Indian land were ceded by treaties to the U.S. government. Treaties are the primary legal basis for federal policies. In 1845 the term "Manifest Destiny" was coined to justify the hunger the white man had for Indian land. They convinced themselves they were ordained by destiny to rule all of America from the East Coast to the West Coast. Some spoke of America from the North Pole to the South Pole. The belief developed that what white Americans upheld was right and good and that their God had designated them the chosen people. In a speech delivered before the U.S. Senate in 1846, Senator Thomas Hart Benton, Missouri, said the white race was far superior to the yellow, black, brown, and red races. He said the white race alone received the divine command to subdue and replenish the earth!

Allotment Period, 1887–1934. Designed to dissolve the tribal land base; 125 million acres were reduced to 50 million acres during this time.

Meriam Report and the New Deal Period, 1930–1950. 1920s corruption, exploitation, mismanagement, and failures became a national scandal. The Meriam Report of 1928 was devastating in its criticism of two areas: (a) the exclusion of Indians from the management of their own affairs; and (b) the poor quality of services, especially in health and education. The report was critical of federal boarding schools; it stressed the need for a relevant curriculum adapted to the individual needs and background of the students; it stressed the need for schools to adapt to the language of the child; and it stressed community participation in the direction of schools. The report stated distrust for state supervision and the ability of states to meet special needs of Indian pupils.[4]

During the 1930s, President Franklin D. Roosevelt's Secretary of the Interior, Harold Ickes, and Commissioner of Indian Affairs, John Collier, were active in Indian Affairs. Legislation included the Indian Reorganization Act of 1934 and the Johnson-O'Malley Act of 1934. The IRA provided for tribal self-government, Indian preference, and tribal economic development, and it ended the General Allotment Act of 1887.

Termination Period, 1950–1970. The U.S. Congress in 1944 announced "the final solution to the Indian Problem" and named education as the primary means. It advocated acculturation and assimilation. The goal of Indian education should be to make the Indian child a better American rather than equip him simply to be a better Indian. In 1948 the Senate put in motion a program to "terminate" tribes, that is, remove them from government supervision. One criterion for termination was the degree of acculturation.

In 1950 Dillon S. Meyer was appointed Commissioner of Indian Affairs. During World War II he masterminded the relocation of Japanese Americans from West Coast cities to internment camps in the interior. In 1952 the voluntary relocation program for Indians was launched. Indian people were enticed to relocate into urban centers in the western and mid-western United States.

The Self-Determination Period, 1970–1975. President Richard Nixon announced a policy of self-determination without termination.

I deemed it important to describe Indian education prior to 1492 and wrote "The Indian Period, BC to 1492."[5]

Prior to the arrival of white men, the Native Americans who inhabited the North American continent evolved a civilization which was well suited to meet their needs. They lived in close harmony with nature, were on the verge of eliminating warfare as a means of diplomacy, had democratic governments, and developed freedom of the individual to a degree unknown anywhere in the world.

Education has always been a need of human society, and every society evolved a process of educating its youth for active adult participation in that society. Every society devises means for socializing the youth and transmitting its culture.

Prior to the arrival of white men, Native Americans existed in tribal entities and established functional societies. An integral part of the Indian society was an education program designed to meet the needs of the young and to prepare them for adult participation in the tribal society. The educational process was active and not passive. The boys and girls learned by doing. The process was not highly structured and was dependent upon parents, relatives, and tribal elders for implementation. The curriculum could be described as informal but relevant. The lifestyle of Indians was tuned to the natural forces surrounding them, and the overall goal of education was to preserve and maintain their way of life. Indian children were expected to grow up as their parents did and to perpetuate tribal customs, values, traditions, and ethics. Indians of that era were profoundly spiritual.

Because American Indians did not have a written language, much of what was learned was by word-of-mouth transmission. The basic thrust of Indian education was traditional in the sense that the past was revered.

Among certain tribal groups, corporal punishment as a form of child discipline was virtually unknown. Instead, praise or ridicule or peer-shaming techniques were utilized extensively. Other tribal groups utilized whip men or motivated the children through fear.

Further, the tribes had little formal structured government. Men became leaders through exemplary action rather than through formal election. The headmen were moral and spiritual leaders as well as political leaders. The important difference between Indian and white government, however, lay in the authority exercised by the leaders. Decisions were arrived at in consultation with the heads of various families or clans. Indian leaders remained leaders only so long as the wisdom of their actions held the respect and support of the people.

Beginning in 1969, JOM programs began to have an impact on Indian education in Montana. In 1969 the JOM allocation for Montana was $180,000 serving 3,111 students. The state plan was revised to reflect the services recommended by Indian parents. Twenty-eight JOM Education Committees were established. In the beginning, the committees were 100 percent Indian women and, later, men joined in. In 1973 the JOM allocation was $1,080,000 serving 7,163 students. Montana became a national model. Annual state conferences were initiated and attracted several hundred participants. State and federal decision-makers began to take notice.

We were continually looking for ways to enhance Indian education and build on our base. An opportunity to crack the political system that was generally closed to us came about in an unexpected way.

In 1970 the citizens of Montana voted to convene a constitutional convention to revise the 1889 state constitution. One hundred delegates were elected to do the revision and not one was an Indian. I decided to try to persuade the delegates to incorporate language requiring the state to recognize the cultural heritage of American Indians and to preserve our cultural integrity. I was courteously received and given the opportunity to testify. However, the committee chairman informed me a constitution would be drafted that would preclude the need for specific reference to any ethnic group or minority. We were persistent and, in a surprise move, I was invited to address the convention. My message centered on the cruel and demeaning remarks about Indians made by the delegate from Ronan and reported by the *Great Falls Tribune*. When I finished, the chamber erupted with thunderous applause and I was stunned. I was asked to meet with delegates the next day and make plans for an amendment for their consideration. During my previous testimonies, I had recommended a clause in which the state acknowledged the cultural heritage of Indians and pledged to preserve our cultural integrity. During one of my meetings with the Montana Inter-Tribal Policy Board, their attorney, Donald Marble, crafted the version I would offer. I was accorded another signal honor when the delegates invited me to join them on the floor of the convention on March 10, 1972, the last day amendments could be introduced. Delegate Dorothy Eck, Bozeman, asked to introduce the amendment. Delegate Gene Harbough, Poplar, moved to add the words "in its educational goals." I accepted the change and the amendment was adopted by a vote of 83–1. The delegates warmly applauded, and I was emotionally drained and wept tears of gratitude on behalf of all Indian people: past, present, and future. Article X, Section 1 (2), of the Montana State Constitution states, "The State recognizes the distinct and unique cultural heritage of the American Indians and is committed in its educational goals to the preservation of their cultural integrity."[6]

The opportunity to capitalize on this monumental accomplishment was to come with the first legislative session in 1973 under the new constitution. My research, the Kennedy Report, the Meriam Report, and the doctoral dissertation "A Study of the Attitudes of Selected Elementary School Teachers toward American Indian Students in the State of Montana," by Don E. Hjelmseth, University of Montana,[7] and others convinced me that teacher attitudes, knowledge, and understanding were key ingredients for improving Indian education. Teachers are the solution, not the problem. I testified and proposed an Indian Studies Law be enacted. Several former constitutional convention delegates were now legislators, and they good-naturedly chided me and said the constitution took care of the need. That gave me the opening to explain the constitution must now be implemented. H.B. 343 passed and was signed by Governor Tom Judge, who gave it a ringing endorsement.[8] Remember this. In 1979 the law was amended and made the provisions permissive. Governor Judge signed the bill and wrote, "I do not believe that this should only apply to American Indians in Montana, but to all minorities in our state." We were relegated to our previous status as invisible Americans outside the melting pot. The AP called me for comment and I said, "The new law is a loss of a small battle in a big struggle."[9] I placed my trust in future Indian leaders to remedy this wrong.

In 1986 Indian educators in Wisconsin asked me for advice on how to improve Indian education in their state. I gave them a copy of the original Montana Indian Studies Law. They presented a bill patterned after it to the Wisconsin legislature and it was enacted into law.[10]

Today, my heart is uplifted with good news from my native state. I commend Representative Carol Juneau and others for their recent success. The Indian Education for All Act is a positive step.[11] The Montana Supreme Court

Decision to fund the clause in the constitution is just.[12] To each of you fighting for what is right, never despair. This spring the State of Washington adopted legislation "advising" public schools to teach tribal history, culture, and government.[13]

In my testimony in 1973, I said: "A teacher is disadvantaged in the same way that a student is disadvantaged. First, if the disadvantaged child is one who has a negative self-concept, the disadvantaged teacher is one who has a negative concept of the child he is supposed to help. Second, like the disadvantaged child, a disadvantaged teacher has a value scale very much limited by his own cultural or class orientation. Third, the disadvantaged teacher lacks adequate background to help him understand the nature of language and the functions of literature and their unique place in the education of the disadvantaged child.[14] Effective education for Indian children demands a special kind of teacher sensitized to Indian culture.

It is necessary to examine appropriation bills when reviewing Indian education. Congress established the quarter-blood requirement for higher education assistance in an appropriation bill early in the twentieth century. During the 1960s two landmark federal laws were enacted. P.L. 92-318, Education Amendments of 1972, was enacted and had a major impact on Indian education in public schools. Title IV, the Indian Education Act, established the Office of Indian Education headed by a Deputy Commissioner in the U.S. Office of Education. A National Advisory Council on Indians consisting of fifteen members to advise the Commissioner of Education was established. In my estimation, Section 453, Definition, was a pleasant surprise. Eligibility was extended to members of tribes terminated since 1940 and to members of tribes recognized now or in the future by the state in which they reside.[15] The 35,000 Lumbees recognized by North Carolina, but not the federal government, won a great victory.

Who is an Indian? There has never been a statutory or legal definition of "Indian" and I prefer not to have one. Our enthusiastic response to this landmark legislation was dampened when the director of BIA education announced that JOM was no longer needed and would be ended. I was incensed and organized a protest that convinced the BIA to rescind their action.

My office was asked to assist in education programs for migrant farm workers involving Indian children, and we were happy to do so. The overall program was one of the best federal programs I ever witnessed. Information on each child was collected and stored in a central office. School authorities could access the information instantly by computer. This was a boon to schools as the children moved from school to school every few weeks. I proposed the BIA set up a similar program to track Indian students who frequently transfer between BIA and public schools.

The Kennedy Report concluded that the responsibility for the education of Indian children is primarily in the hands of the federal government. I agree with this and sought to find out why it was not so in Montana. I reviewed the treaties between tribes and the United States. Treaties are the supreme law of the land and superior to the laws of any state and protected by Article VI of the U.S. Constitution.[16] The treaties support the conclusion of the Kennedy Report.

The transition of the responsibility for Indian education from the federal government to the individual states was the direct result of two basic events: the organization into states of all lands within the continental United States formally in territorial status and the Indian Citizenship Act of 1924.

A provision of the first Montana Territorial school law of 1865 created school districts. Later, the Montana Legislative Assembly contemplated that Indian lands be in a school district and that Indian children be counted in apportioning school moneys. Further, the county superintendent of schools was given authority to attach territory on an Indian reservation to an adjacent school district. All of this was done without formal consultation with the tribes.

When Indian communities told me of their concerns about education in high schools located off reservation, I explained the option of creating a high school district on reservation and starting a high school. Three high schools— Hays-Lodge Pole, Plenty Coups, and Rocky Boy—were created.

The Meriam Report of 1928 and the Kennedy Report of 1969 reported serious deficiencies in BIA education programs. They said the present organization and administration of the BIA system could hardly be worse.

The BIA was created in 1824 by John C. Calhoun, Secretary of War, without authority of the Congress. When the Department of the Interior was established in 1849, the BIA was transferred and is still there. The BIA was officially authorized by Congress in 1934. Title IV, Indian Education, P.L. 92-318, Education Amendments of 1972, addressed problems in Indian Education in Public Schools. Title XI, The Indian Basic Education, P.L. 95-561, Education Amendments of 1978, provided for substantive structural and procedural changes in the administration of Indian education programs in the BIA.[17] The House Committee on Education and Labor appointed a subcommittee that sponsored the legislation. Counsel Alan R. Lovesee was the point man. He had a passion for upgrading BIA education and skillfully worked with lay people and educators to frame the reforms. I was asked to head the Bureau's Office of Indian Education. I took several weeks to decide. I was well aware of the problems. There had been nine directors in the past five years, and the BIA testified in opposition to P.L. 95-561. The Assistant Secretary for Indian Affairs assured me the BIA would be directed to implement the law and I would have his support. I accepted the assignment and resigned as superintendent of schools in Browning. Tribal leaders, relatives, and friends held two ceremonies in my honor. The first was an inspirational religious ceremony and the second was a ceremony preparing me for battle. An ancient Indian name was given to me and Peter Red Horn II wrote an honor song, "The Lone Warrior." I did not get the connection between such honors and going to Washington, D.C. How prophetic my people proved to be.

My immediate task was to develop rules and regulations for implementing eight mandates in the new law—and I added a ninth mandate, School Boards. Task forces were empanelled to assist with this. Federal operations are defined in manuals. Department manuals and BIA manuals had to be revised. I will list a few of the changes that were made.

1. Direct line authority from the Director of Indian Education to the schools. Education was removed from the BIA line of authority. We named the new division Ed (Education) and the other division Bob (Balance of Bureau). The battle for turf was bruising.
2. Decentralized central office functions to local schools, i.e., delegate my authority to local offices.
3. Mid-level Area Offices were bypassed.
4. Utilized Bureau administrative support.
5. A school equalization system with formula funding for distributing funds directly to schools. A child's programmatic needs determine the amount of money a school receives. First system of its kind in the nation. Greatly simplifies and facilitates budget requests to Congress. Maximum local control. Allocating funds appropriated by Congress directly to schools eliminated "slush" funds that historically had been siphoned off as the moneys went through the bureaucratic system.
6. The law exempted education personnel from civil service requirements. Civil service was replaced with a personnel system designed to enhance recruitment and retention of qualified education personnel.
7. School Boards established and trained for every school.
8. I retained authority to allocate funds to schools and I retained the student audit function in the central office.
9. Management Information System installed.

I moved quickly to place qualified educators in administrative positions in the new line authority. The BIA resisted and argued that an administrator need not be trained and experienced in the field of education. I rejected that argument for obvious reasons.

In early 1980, a representative from the General Accounting Office informed me that Senator Abraham A. Ribicoff, Chairman, Committee of Government Affairs, had ordered a review of BIA education operations. He matter-of-factly said that past GAO reviews during the 1970s found that the BIA failed to provide Indians a quality education and that severe management problems had persisted for years. Further, he had already decided to recommend transferring BIA education to the recently created Department of Education. I was disappointed but pledged full cooperation.

The GAO report dated April 23, 1980, was delivered to me and stated the BIA has responded to the Indian Basic Education Act by taking positive steps to correct deficiencies; therefore, a transfer to the Department of Education would not be appropriate at this time.[18] Privately, GAO told me this was the only positive report the BIA ever received. My hardworking staff and I were euphoric. During this time, the *Washington Post* published encouraging accounts of improvements in BIA education.[19]

In an audit report dated May 2, 1982, the Office of the Inspector General praised the Student Membership System of BIA schools. The report stated, "We are pleased to report the BIA has done an excellent job in implementing its Student Membership System which is one of the requirements of P.L. 95-561."[20] This is significant because student membership determines school funding and must be uniformly accurate.

I perceived the BIA did not enjoy respect in the Department of the Interior and I was determined to change that. Secretary Cecil Andrus generally lent me a sympathetic ear since he was familiar with Indian issues in his home state of Idaho. Early on I briefed him and his staff and he responded by memo dated June 27, 1979, and said:

> The briefing this morning on Indian Education was timely, informational and presented in the proper manner. Frankly, it was the best briefing I have had on a subject matter in a long time.
> Thank you,
> Cece

A handwritten note from the Office of Public Affairs was attached and said, "the briefing was absolutely excellent."[21]

The Office of Equal Employment gave the BIA a commendation for employing Indian women in administrative positions. Ninety percent of them were in education and reflected my program to recruit and hire qualified Indian women administrators.

Shortly before the 1980 presidential election, Vice President Walter Mondale invited me to meet with him and discuss Indian education issues. His concern was about the large number of Navajo students in BIA boarding schools. He was very knowledgeable and knew that 60 percent of the total boarding school students were Navajo. Then I remembered that when he was a senator he was a member of the subcommittee that issued the Kennedy Report. The report had recommended that, as rapidly as possible, the elementary boarding schools on the Navajo Reservation should be replaced by day schools. I told the Vice President that I favored closing all boarding schools and educating the children in their communities. However, red tape and resistance by communities where the boarding schools were located created obstacles. Also, persons who attended boarding schools were very loyal to them. I proposed that my office commission a study of the Navajo and make recommendations for his review. The Navajo Day School Study was not completed until after the administration change. The study showed an absence of suitable roads and bridges were the main obstacles to building day schools because students could not be transported to them. The study estimated $1 billion would be required to build sufficient roads and bridges.[22] The incoming administration would not release the report, and the Assistant Secretary said he feared they would be blamed for the problem. On my watch, Chiloco and Seneca boarding schools were closed on June 15, 1980. Fort Sill and Stewart were closed on September 30, 1980.

James Watt was named Secretary of the Interior, and he selected Ken Smith to be his Assistant Secretary for Indian Affairs. I organized briefing sessions that did not go well. Mr. Smith said he had been told Indian education was a can of worms. His deputy said he attended Bureau schools for his first five years and never learned to read. Another deputy fell sound asleep. Shortly thereafter Ken Smith removed me from the position of Director of Indian Education without giving his reason. This key position was not filled for several years until Dr. Henrietta Whiteman was appointed upon my recommendation.

I am satisfied with my accomplishments, and the system required by P.L. 95-561 is still intact today. My tenure of three years was a record for longevity. Ross Swimmer replaced Ken Smith and twice asked me to return as Director and I declined.

Now that I am retired, and if I were a king or chief and were omnipotent, here are some changes I would decree:

1. There will be a cabinet level Department of Indian Affairs and Indian Education.
2. All federally operated off-reservation boarding schools will be phased out as soon as suitable alternatives can be utilized near the homes of the students.

3. There will be an Indian and Alaska Native National Education Assembly consisting of delegates selected by their peers and empowered to negotiate with federal and state governments in all matters of education.

4. There will be two seats reserved for Indians and Alaska Natives in each house of the U.S. Congress.

5. There will be a federally funded foundation program in order to provide operation expenditures that are sufficient to provide for the educational programs in public schools on or adjacent to Indian reservations.

6. Indian education will be a federal trust responsibility as legally established by a U.S. Supreme Court decision in 1831.

I will continue to advocate that the federal sector continue its role in Indian education and ultimately decide that Indian education is a trust responsibility. I will continue to advocate that the federal government provide the resources and leadership to ensure a basic quality education for identified Indians regardless of where they live, regardless of their tribal affiliation and regardless of their socioeconomic status, so that each may be inspired to develop to his or her fullest intellectual, emotional, social, moral, and ethical stature. This can be best accomplished by giving Indian education back to the Indians.

Notes

1. Robert Bigart and Earl Barlow, *The Indian in the Classroom: Readings for the Teacher with Indian Students* (Helena: Montana Office of the Superintendent of Public Instruction, 1972).

2. U.S. Senate, Special Subcommittee on Indian Education, *Indian Education: A National Tragedy—A National Challenge* (Washington, D.C.: U.S. Government Printing Office, 1969).

3. U.S. Senate, *Indian Education*, 10–17.

4. Lewis Meriam, *The Problem of Indian Administration: Report of a Survey Made at the Request of Hubert Work, Secretary of the Interior, and Submitted to Him, February 21, 1928* (Baltimore: Johns Hopkins University Press, 1928).

5. Earl J. Barlow, "If a Man Loses Something" (paper presented at Fifth Annual State Indian Education Conference, College of Great Falls, Great Falls, Montana, April 3, 1975).

6. *Montana Constitutional Convention Proceeding, 1971–1972* (Helena: Montana Legislature, 1981), 6:1952–1957.

7. Donald Erwin Hjelmseth, "A Study of Attitudes of Selected Elementary School Teachers toward American Indian Students in the State of Montana" (Ed.D. diss., University of Montana, 1972).

8. Montana Legislature, *Indian Studies Law*, H.B. 343, Chap. 464, Laws of 1973.

9. AP News Release, published by Montana Press when the Indian Studies Law was amended in 1979.

10. State of Wisconsin, Revisor of Statutes Bureau, Wisconsin Statutes 1985–1986, Chap. 115, Subchap. IV.

11. Montana Code Annotated 2005, 20-1-501.

12. *Columbia Falls Elementary School District No. 6 v. State*, 326 Mont. 304, 109 P.3rd 257 (2005).

13. Revised Code of Washington, Title 28A, Chap. 320, Sec. 170.

14. Personal testimony before the Montana State Legislature, 1973. See also San-su C. Lin, "Disadvantaged Student? Or Disadvantaged Teacher?" in *Teaching English in Today's High Schools*, ed. D. L. Burton and J. S. Simmons (New York: Holt, Rinehart and Winston, 1965), 419–427.

15. *Education Amendments of 1972*, P.L. 92-318, *U.S. Statutes at Large* 86 (1972), 339–345.

16. Article VI, Clause 2, states: "This Constitution, and the Laws of the United States which shall be made in Pursuance thereof; and all Treaties made, or which shall be made, under the Authority of the United States, shall be the supreme Law of the Land; and the Judges in every State shall be bound thereby, any Thing in the Constitution or Laws of any State to the Contrary notwithstanding."

17. *Education Amendments of 1978*, P.L. 95-561, *U.S. Statutes at Large* 92 (1978), 2313–2333.

18. U.S. General Accounting Office and U.S. Senate, Committee on Governmental Affairs, *Should the Bureau of Indian Affairs Continue to Provide Educational Services to Indian Children: Report to the Chairman, Committee on Governmental Affairs, United States Senate* (Washington, D.C.: General Accounting Office, 1980).

19. For example, see Charles Babcock, "Signs of Hope Rise in Indian Schools: Signs of Hope Arise in the Education of Indians on Reservations," *Washington Post*, December 27, 1981, A1.

20. "Review of Selected Aspects of Elementary and Secondary Education within the Albuquerque Area, Bureau of Indian Affairs," Audit Report of the Inspector General, Department of the Interior, May 1982.

21. "Secretarial Policy Briefing—Indian Education," memorandum from Cecil Andrus, Secretary of the Interior, to Forrest Gerard, Assistant Secretary, Indian Affairs, June 27, 1979; "Secretarial Policy Briefing—Indian Education," memorandum to Earl J. Barlow, Director, Office of Indian Education Programs, from Forrest J. Gerard, Assistant Secretary, Indian Affairs, July 2, 1979; handwritten memorandum to Forrest J. Gerard, Assistant Secretary, Indian Affairs, from Office of Public Affairs, Department of the Interior, June 27, 1979.

22. "Navajo Day School Study Report," Earl J. Barlow, Director, Office of Indian Education Programs, Bureau of Indian Affairs, Department of the Interior, January 1981.

What Can Universities Contribute to Indigenous Language Immersion Programs? A Case Study from Southern California

12

MARGARET FIELD

I WOULD LIKE TO PRESENT AN OVERVIEW of language immersion as a teaching methodology, with examples drawn from my own personal experience as a linguist in an American Indian Studies department in Southern California. First, I'd like to review what language immersion is, then why it is a useful methodology for teaching indigenous languages, what some drawbacks may be, and finally, how universities, and in particular linguists, may be of assistance to community-based immersion language programs.

What Is an Immersion Language Program?

In Hinton and Hale's excellent book *The Green Book of Language Revitalization in Practice*,[1] Ken Hale discusses five types of immersion programs:

Level one: A child learning their first language within their family. This is the best possible immersion context.

Level two: Preschool/kindergarten children being cared for by people who speak to them always in the indigenous language at school. This is a more limited context, but still excellent, as children this age learn languages very quickly and easily.

Level three: A situation where an adult native speaker of the indigenous language spends a great deal of time together with an adult learner of the language. This situation varies greatly, but in general is not as ideal as the first two levels of immersion. As Hale points out, this context also describes how most linguists learn about a language they are studying, with the learner using his/her language (usually English) to elicit the indigenous language, until finally, ideally, all communication takes place only in the indigenous language.

Level four: A course where the target language is used as the language of instruction, but the content deals with something other than the language itself. This is similar to level two, but the time is shorter and the learner is older, so it is not ideal.

Level five: A monolingual language class in which only the indigenous language is used, but the content also deals with the structure of the language. This context for immersion, more than any of the others, requires the teacher to have some training in the structure of the indigenous language, or at least to have as well-developed lesson plans as possible. This level is also the one which I have been asked to assist with most recently, and which most of the rest of my presentation will refer to and draw examples from.

Why Is Immersion a Good Methodology for Indigenous Languages?

Although immersion has become a very popular teaching method for use in bilingual education programs nationwide ("dual immersion programs"), which are typically not aimed at indigenous languages, it has obvious immediate relevance for American Indian languages, in that most of them do not have a tradition of literacy. Using immersion as a teaching method allows the teacher and learner to get directly down to the business of language learning without having to worry about a writing system at all. This is especially crucial when the language is extremely endangered and there is no time to waste, as is the case in the American Indian community I currently work with in San Diego, where the language is called Kumeyaay, or, depending on the dialect, Ipaay or Tiipaay. Currently, there are approximately ten native speakers of Kumeyaay still living on this side of the border, and many of them are either too elderly or too busy running tribal governments to become language teachers. There are more Kumeyaay speakers in Mexico, but we are not sure how many, but it is probably less than one hundred. Although many middle-aged, and older, Kumeyaay people grew up hearing Kumeyaay spoken by their elders, no children today are native or fluent speakers of Kumeyaay, and it is definitely a dire situation which everyone is aware of. There are several small language classes happening in different places across the ten different Kumeyaay reservations in San Diego County, as well as at the Kumeyaay Community College, which offers a night course taught by various speakers, mostly from Mexico. To my knowledge, there are currently no immersion language courses specifically targeting small children.

Kumeyaay has a writing system, or orthography, which was created by a linguist, Margaret Langdon (now retired), in the 1960s, but almost no one in the Kumeyaay community uses it. It uses symbols which are all found on English keyboards, but Kumeyaay does have some sounds which English does not, and for these sounds, English letters are doubled or combined. My own personal experience has been that most people trying to learn Kumeyaay, and especially the elders trying to teach Kumeyaay, would rather avoid the writing system entirely because it confuses them. But still, when I visit Kumeyaay language classes, I see several people taking notes on the oral lessons, and I can't help wondering how they are spelling things, and if it is helping them. Although immersion as a language teaching methodology does not preclude the use of literacy, it is not required. This makes immersion the ideal method for use, both with very small children as well as for communities who do not have a written tradition, or are not sure they want one.

Some other principles of immersion language teaching include:

- Use complete sentences.
- Repetition is key: in order for a learner to master vocabulary, they must hear it twenty times in twenty different situations (400 times).
- Do not use English or other nontarget languages.
- Use nonverbal communication.
- Embed learning into real activities.[2]

What Are Some Possible Difficulties in Using Immersion as a Language Teaching Methodology?

One major problem for the Kumeyaay language classes I have observed, and which elders have also told me about, is the degree of dialect diversity, and how this should be handled in Kumeyaay classes. Although Kumeyaay dialects may not be so different across reservations located next to each other, they are pretty different in Mexico, especially compared with the northernmost Kumeyaay dialects spoken in San Diego County. Although some linguistic research has been done on Kumeyaay dialect variation, this work has not yet been made available in a form that nonlinguists can understand, and especially not in any kind of teaching material format. It seems to me that this is one area where linguists can be of assistance to indigenous communities—that is, in helping to explain, in nontechnical terms, exactly what dialect differences there may be in any language, and helping address these differences through the creation of language teaching materials and/or working with language teachers to help them become more conscious of how their dialects may differ from each other. In my own previous experience studying the Navajo language, where literacy in Navajo is emphasized and students are often fluent native speakers, I found that instructors often told students "just to write it like it sounds." But unless instructors are familiar with all the forms of dialect variation that are out there, they may not recognize what their students write, although it may in fact look like the students' local dialect pronunciation. In Kumeyaay country, where there is a great deal of dialect diversity, misunderstandings and concerns about it probably even prevented some Kumeyaay people from either taking Kumeyaay classes taught off their particular reservation or from hiring speakers with other dialects to teach in their communities. And, at this late stage, that is not a good thing, as any Kumeyaay language learning going on anywhere can only help the situation.

Another common difficulty I have observed, and which elder speakers and teachers have complained to me about, is the need to develop a varied and interesting series of immersion lesson plans. Just being a native speaker of a language is not necessarily enough to make someone a good language teacher, and elders especially need all the help they can get in putting together the content for language classes, even if they are all oral and immersion based. As one of the principles of immersion language teaching is to embed lessons within real activities, ideally each lesson would center on some kind of activity which people do every day, such as cooking, eating, getting dressed, taking care of babies, playing a game, or doing everyday tasks. Although these activities don't necessarily need to deal with traditional cultural activities, it is probably a good idea to steer away from talk about modern contexts, such as offices or schoolrooms, where much of the vocabulary is relatively new and words may still need to be created for things in indigenous languages, like computers or blackboards. On the other hand, if the language in question is spoken well enough by students for them to be ready to make up words in it, then lessons probably should deal with modern contexts, and this would be an excellent way to involve students in a creative use of their language. Another simple solution for language lesson plans might be to collect props for discussion during each lesson, such as articles of clothing, or types of food, or things which can be found in the garden, or the woods, or the ocean, etcetera. Collected items, or pictures of them, could be kept in the classroom and used in future lessons as memory aids or as points of further departure. Students could also be asked to bring to class examples of things which are yet to be discussed—for example, if everyone brought in a type of plant, the lesson could cover cultural categories for different types of plants (flowers, weeds, cactus) or colors, or textures, or other relevant words, such as "delicious" or "poisonous." If the class is taught by an elder, as is often the case in Kumeyaay country, one person in the class could be in charge of keeping track of all of the vocabulary covered in each course, in any language, as an instructional form of assistance to the elder speaker/teacher. Lessons can also be tape-recorded or video-recorded, if everyone present is comfortable with this use of technology, and the recorded lessons could then be used as the basis of further language teaching materials, which brings me, finally, to the topic of my presentation, "How can universities be of assistance?"

The form of language teaching assistance which I have provided to a couple of indigenous communities has been in multimedia format, and I would like to show you a couple of examples.

Example One: A Navajo Coyote Story

My first example is a spoken version of a Navajo coyote story told entirely in Navajo, with illustrations, and written Navajo, but with no English (except in the comprehension questions at the end, which teachers may assign and/or translate as they see fit for their communities). I recorded this story in a Navajo preschool classroom in which very few of the children understood spoken Navajo fluently. The classroom had a computer where this little story software was placed for the children to explore on their own. The general idea is that they play with it together and scaffold each other (in this case, mostly in English) in mastering the content of the story. It could also be used in upper elementary and high school classrooms with more specific literacy goals assigned. I consider this an example of immersion methodology because it is entirely in Navajo language, as is my next example, from Kumeyaay country.

Example Two: Kumeyaay Colors

This very simple little multimedia lesson presents all of the verbs which refer to colors in nature as well as the Kumeyaay word for "multicolored" (which can mean striped, polka-dotted, or what have you—any combination of colors). The colors in Kumeyaay do not map exactly to English words for colors as, for example, there is one word which must do double duty for both blue and green. The same thing is true for brown and yellow or red and orange. Nowhere in the lesson is this specifically stated and, so, learners must figure this out for themselves as they work through the lesson, which also has some simple instructions, such as "point to the red flower" in Kumeyaay. Where necessary, video segments are also embedded on a page, illustrating verbs, such as "point to X," which we decided was the best way to translate the English verb "click on X." The dialect used in this lesson is from Mexico and will probably vary from those spoken in San Diego County to some degree. This lesson is a pilot in a series which will be created for the use of all education centers across all ten Kumeyaay reservations in San Diego County, with the assistance of the local "Tribal Digital Village" (created through a grant from Hewlett-Packard).

The next step in this process, for me as a linguist working in an American Indian Studies department, will be to help local communities identify specific differences between their local dialects and that used by the speaker in the lessons, resulting in more community-specific language lessons, as well as a much better understanding on everyone's part of the nature of dialect diversity across these communities, and a proliferation of language lessons.

Another reason why multimedia, or computer technology, is a good form for language lessons to take is that it is inexpensive, at least to produce multiple copies of lessons or to make them web-based, as compared with the cost of printing actual books. The main expense lies in purchasing a computer on which to put the software. For this expense, I refer tribal offices interested in this technology to explore library grants for small communities, which provide the funding for technology. Digitizing language, through importing it into a computer and burning it onto a CD or DVD, is also a much more reliable format for archiving language for posterity than audio tapes or Hi-8 tapes are, as these may degrade over time. Finally, integrating technology, such as computer software or web-based lessons, into language teaching, in my opinion, may make it more exciting for children, as they are often fascinated by computers. It is a simple way of integrating indigenous language into modern contexts, which may appeal to children as well, and if a multimedia can result from video recordings of the content of every live language immersion lesson, then it need not replace live language instruction, which of course is always more basic and preferred, but rather can be used to supplement it. Remember, it takes 400 repetitions to truly master a new word!

Notes

1. Leanne Hinton and Kenneth L. Hale, *The Green Book of Language Revitalization in Practice* (San Diego: Academic Press, 2001), 227–228.
2. Hinton and Hale, *The Green Book*, 183–184.

Observations on a Tribal Language Revitalization Program

13

DARRELL ROBES KIPP

I WANT TO SHARE WITH YOU SEVERAL OBSERVATIONS and questions concerning tribal language revitalization on my reservation. The first question is why would a predominately English-speaking Indian community want to mess around revitalizing a language thousands of years old when we all struggle to speak and write English correctly? Why would we want to hinder ourselves further by adding the learning of our tribal language to our list of linguistic challenges simply to "save" our original language? The salespeople don't speak the Blackfoot language, and you can't order anything at Red Lobster in Salish, so what's the point? This is how monolingual America sees it. Yet there is a common history in America when English was not the first language of countless families in this country. The demand for a common language in an emerging America became so powerful, the home language of the immigrant usually disappeared within three generations. So America, which could have been a polyglot country with countless languages spoken, instead ended up as a monolanguage-speaking society, with English the only acceptable language for all citizens. As a once upon a time English teacher, I can verify the school subject almost all students disdain is English. Yet, as Americans, we fully support an English-only society almost without question. A major lobby group in America raises millions of dollars to advance English as the official language of the United States. In fact, the State of Montana passed legislation, several legislation sessions ago, making English the official language of commerce and government. You might want to keep that in mind the next time you hear someone chatting in Cree, Salish, or some language other than English somewhere in the state.

Knowledgeable sources estimate that when first contact was made during the Christopher Columbus adventure, there were a thousand-plus languages and dialects thriving in North America. Today, according to Michael Krauss at the University of Alaska, about 185 Native American languages remain in tribal communities in North America.[1] Krauss, and others, estimate the majority do not have children speakers. A significant number also are down to less than a dozen speakers, and in some cases, a mere one or two.

The *New Yorker* magazine ran an article in 2005 chronicling the story of a woman in Alaska who, on the death of her sister, became the lone speaker of her tribal language. Years ago, at a large indigenous language conference in New Mexico, the audience listened spellbound to a similar account. The fact that stories of the last, lone speaker of a tribal language are becoming commonplace is alarming. If a descendant of any of the immigrant languages became so moved to learn their original language, they can easily book a flight to their homeland and learn the language. If you are a Native American tribal member though, and there are no longer any speakers of your tribal language, there is no place to go to retrieve it. It becomes an irrevocable loss, and irretrievable. Some tribes without speakers are utilizing linguists in an attempt to regenerate their languages, but this might be indeed quite a stretch without fluent speakers to assist. Still, it illustrates the importance members in such a tribe attribute to their language, despite waiting too long to revitalize it. Considering the lack of resources, especially the total absence of a funding base to support revitalization efforts, it is likely the number of viable Native American languages will become drastically small in the next twenty years. Several tribes will continue to have a significant number of speakers because of current large populations, and geographic isolation in parts of their homelands. Even these tribes, unless they are initiating revitalization programs today, will ultimately experience the demise of their language. Most tribes in North America will soon be without speakers of their languages, often sooner than anyone in the tribe realizes, or cares.

So the question is always there: faced with the abundant difficulties associated with tribal language revitalization, why bother? It is a profound question, not easily answered. Everett T. Hall, the noted anthropologist and author of *The Silent Language*, one of his many books on culture, states, "there is no way to *teach* culture in the same way that language is taught."[2] It is my interpretation that tribal culture derives from tribal language, and the quintessence of a tribe is found in their language, not their culture. Their tribal language is the unique factor distinguishing them, whereas many tribal cultural elements, such as dance and music, are now pan-Indian and not exclusive to one tribe. Indian people are always talking about preserving their culture, which I consider a highly unreliable term, but seldom specify what they mean.

A tribal language is the most dynamic aspect of tribal culture, but if it is neglected, essential tribal elements are lost forever. Museums preserve culture artifacts and icons in a static replication of bygone tribal days, but hardly represent present-day tribal life. On the other hand, tribal languages have been adapting forever to changes in tribal lifestyles; material acquisitions from horses to computers, and countless innovations which constantly refresh the original and essential knowledge base of the tribe.

It is common at tribal conferences to hear the speakers extol preserving or strengthening tribal heritage and ways. How exactly is one supposed to accomplish their advice? Most solutions offered are centered on theories for economic development, housing, drug and alcohol prevention tied to educational refinement for our students, and health or social issues. Seldom is it ever mentioned how important tribal language revitalization is, and how it should be included in planning for long-term tribal benefits. So, it is clear many advocates of tribal progress have not taken time to think through how important a tribal language is to a tribe. This void in thinking is derived from long-standing assimilation dogma imposed on tribal people, deeming their languages worthless and unnecessary in the modern day. Consequently, tribal language revitalization is not part of the eloquence of most tribal spokespeople, which is part of the dilemma of language revitalization.

I share an analogy with you. Say you are walking down a beautiful path, somewhere in your homeland, and you come upon an older couple, tired and alone, sitting on the ground. Let's say they represent your tribal language and all the unique qualities of your tribe. Will you stop and assist them to a safe haven? Will you be willing, if you had to, to pack them on your back, or will you inform them, although you care, you are too busy, and need to hurry along your trek? That is what it is really about. Most people probably will say they would like to assist the revitalization of their tribal language but are too busy with too many other things. They don't have the time but do have a bumper sticker on their car saying, "Proud to be an Indian." How is that for a trade-off?

The choice is up to tribal members in the community to advocate, and educate their fellow membership of the importance of tribal language revitalization. If you are one of those who refuse to walk past the older couple, and do stop to do whatever it takes to help them to a safe haven, then you have the awareness to help your tribe keep their language healthy. Those who are too busy, too weak, or simply do not care to help, and walk on by the couple, unfortunately represent those people who have put their tribal language behind them. Then one day, when there are no older couples available to christen their child with a tribal name, pray in the language for their ceremonies, or grant any of the many other favors expected, it will be too late to go back to get the old couple sitting along the path. I think that is the basic question when it comes to language revitalization. Some tribal people see the importance; they embrace it in life, and give it importance. They will do what they can. I always say the language will choose you; you will not choose it. The language will come upon you, and choose you.

The Piegan Institute is approaching its twentieth birthday. The term Piegan is a derivative of Pikuni, or Far Off Spotted Robes, our ancestral name. Today, we are referred to as the Blackfeet Tribe of Montana, which is our corporate name as a tribe. The institute is a private nonprofit located in Browning, Montana. It was founded by tribal members, two who were nonspeakers of the language, in response to an awareness of the language slowly disappearing from use within the community. In 1985, a seminar on the tribal language was so poorly attended, and misunderstood, it became clear the community had accepted the imposed order against the maintenance of the language. A survey in the same year revealed the youngest fluent speakers of the language were all in their late fifties. Few under the age of fifty were speakers of the language, and most assuredly no children spoke the language. The founders chose a private nonprofit format, since none of the community institutions were interested in the language. The institute chartered itself, *to research, promote, and preserve the Native American Languages*, and has done so since 1987.[3] During the first years, extensive retrieval and collection of tribal language materials took place. Countless dictionaries, grammars, and related studies on our language were collected and studied. It is common among tribes to believe little information exists about their languages in written form, but this is usually a mistake. Our tribal language turned out to be well documented and recorded beginning as early as 1878, but guess where all the documents were? Almost without exception they were stacked on some dusty shelf in archives and libraries across North America. This is likely the case with most tribes.

In 1994, a private school was built by the institute in the town to test out our theories, if you may, or to answer our questions. We wanted to know if a tribal language could be revitalized; taught to children, and experience a restored status in the community. The quick answer to our questions is a resounding yes, but countless obstacles remain. At this point in time, only 150 or so fluent speakers remain out of an enrolled membership of 18,000 Blackfeet Indians. All of the speakers are part of the oldest generations of the tribe, with a handful of exceptions. You don't have to be a mathematician to figure out how long our tribal language has left on this earth.

This is quite similar to the status quo of several other tribes in Montana, and elsewhere. The important finding through our work is that a tribe can teach their language to children and produce proficient speakers. These young speakers slowly begin to supplement the diminishing number of older speakers. The school program has now assured the community of approximately thirty young speakers of the language, and these students will remain the keepers of the language in the years to come.

The key to success is in the school program format. A private school where the language can be taught all day long is crucial. Second, if the school can teach primarily in the tribal language for the most of the school day, the student's ability to master the tribal language is greatly enhanced. The simplest outline is a classroom, a fluent speaker, and several small children, staying in the tribal language as much as possible throughout the day. The Nizipuhwahsin (Real Speak) School, designed by the institute, recently completed a ten-year operational run in May 2005, with successful results. Designed as a private elementary school program for forty K–8 students, operational funds were obtained exclusively through private foundations and donors. One of the true obstacles to tribal language revitalization, especially with instructional programming, is the lack of funding sources. Most tribes do not have the resources to fund a private school, or are simply overwhelmed with other expenses to adequately contribute to a private school. Almost all successful tribal language schools are privately funded and operated by community members. Those tribes, or tribal members, waiting for a federal or state grant to get started are wasting valuable time. It is important to begin as soon as possible with whatever means are available. Also, it is unlikely public schools on reservations will take up a serious attempt to teach the tribal language, since most of them barely teach foreign language requirements dictated by the state. They are not likely going to be bothered to teach the tribal language except in a perfunctory manner, which will not produce speakers.

In ten years of Real Speak school operation, eleven students graduated from the K–8 program. The majority became honor-roll students in English-speaking public high school programs. This is a crucial selling point to educators, and others, in terms of advocating tribal language instruction as an extremely efficient learning model for Indian children. Students from the school also are sought out to participate in tribal ceremonies, openings, and related community activities because of their tribal language abilities. It is now common to have young students of the school conducting opening prayers in the tribal language for many of the community gatherings.

Many individuals, especially educators, early on surmised the school was just for saving the language for its own sake, and in fact, many questioned the merits of the program. Yet it is an established fact of science that, when Indian children are taught exclusively in their tribal language, they also become highly competent students in English-only school programs. It is about language acquisition skill-building and the merits of students experiencing success in language utilization in varied forms, including the teaching of sign language into the format further increases student language acquisition skills, and is a tactile form of instruction capable of internalizing language for long-term recall.

I end with this. Native languages can be revitalized. For the most part, those being revitalized at present are being done by small groups of tribal members taking it upon themselves to do so. They will do so without a great deal of encouragement from the education or greater community sector. Nor will they get much support from the financial dispensers of operational funds and will, too often, find themselves in a fantastic struggle to survive. They will also find abundant reward for their work and, often in the most unusual ways, be bestowed signs acknowledging their work. The beauty of a young child praying eloquently and sincerely in their tribal language, hearing children speaking the language with each other, or with an older couple, are just a few of the countless daily, but powerful, indicators of success.

There are rules conducive to success in tribal language revitalization efforts. First of all, never ask permission to save your language. Do not go to the school board. Do not go to the tribal council. Seek no one's permission. If there are three or four of you in the community who want to start a small tribal language school, then go ahead and do it, but if you ask permission, what do you think you will be told? "You better not do this. It will hurt the children. They will never learn English and they will flunk out of regular school." Some will tell you it is against their religion, philosophy, or vision for Indian people. Official records from the Montana Office of Public Instruction indicate close to 60 percent of Indian children never finish the tenth grade in the public school system. Now there is a program I would worry about sending my children to. Tribal language immersion schools have much better records of achievement, yet they remain questionable in the eyes of many so-called education experts.

Second, don't wait around for some big federal grant. Do it on your own and start as soon as possible. Start with what you have available. Also, stop debating the fact our tribal languages have been deemed worthless and of a past age. When someone demands an explanation, or wants to debate the merits of your choice, send them away and conserve your energy for the tasks at hand. Last of all, show, don't tell. Teach a child even the rudiments of the tribal language and the child becomes the most powerful representation of the good work you are doing. A young child speaking the tribal language is a rare, precious child, and even the cold-hearted critics will change their advocacy in their presence.

If one studies how other languages of the world have endured through cycles of oppression, neglect, and condemnation, it becomes clear that efforts to revitalize a tribal language are not without promise for a future time. The

Hebrew language was once spoken by only a few thousand individuals, yet it was chosen to be the national language of Israel and today is spoken by millions of people. It was preserved by a small number of individuals primarily for ceremonial reasons. When the time came, it was intact and today is spoken by generations of Jewish people. Today, many assume the long-standing ceremonies of the Blackfeet Tribe are gone, or diluted, but this is not true. Within the four tribes of the Blackfoot Confederacy, important ceremonies are still in a purest state because people in charge of keeping them are strict and refuse to change, or alter, any of the ritual or language. So today, you find that children and adults closely aligned with the language revitalization movement are also aligned with the ceremonies of the tribe. The spectrum of language revitalization ranges from educational value on through to ceremonial promise, with every human quality in between.

An older friend of the language came to the Real Speak school one day from a relative tribe in Canada. He saw and heard the wonderful things the children were doing with the language, and he asked if anyone ever complimented the staff, parents, or students? Who gives compliments anymore on an Indian reservation? He laughed and said years from now, when people come to Browning and hear the tribal language still being spoken, they are going to be shocked. They will say, after all these tribes in America have lost their languages, how can it be this tribe still has speakers? The answer will be: many years ago some people put up a tribal language school, and grandma and grandpa went there, ended up marrying each other, and taught all their children and grandchildren, who taught their children. There are valid and spiritual reasons to revitalize a tribal language, and it will be in the hands, minds, and hearts of a small number inclined to do so. The final resolution of what shall result from their noble efforts to revitalize their tribal language will not be revealed until many years from now. Those tribes who do nothing to revitalize their languages will know the results of their oversight much sooner.

Notes

1. Michael Krauss, "The World's Languages in Crisis," *Language* 68 (March 1992): 4.
2. Edward T. Hall, *The Silent Language* (New York: Anchor Books, 1973), 25.
3. Piegan Institute Mission Statement, www.pieganinstitute.org/pieganindex.html.

Since Lewis and Clark: Are Tribal Colleges Meeting the Challenges of the Twenty-first Century?

14

GERALD E. GIPP

Y NAME IS GERALD GIPP; I am a member of the Standing Rock Sioux Tribe, traditionally known as the Hunkpapa Lakota. My Indian name is Tatanka Hunska, or Long Bull, the name of my great-grandfather. Thank you for inviting me to participate in this discussion. I will take this opportunity to share my perspectives about the American Indian Higher Education movement in America, its development, and continuing challenges since the days of the Lewis and Clark expedition.

First, in discussing the American Indian tribal college movement, one is quickly reminded of the impetus for the development of these institutions. I believe it is important to understand the context of this phenomenon and the contemporary issues facing our communities. Therefore, I will provide a brief historical context from which they originated. Second, I will discuss the status of the tribal colleges movement, and finally share some of the challenges that our communities and tribal colleges confront in today's political environment.

Before the coming of the white man, the traditional lands of the Lakota, Nakota, and Dakota people and several other tribes extended from the western woodland area of Minnesota, across the great plains of North and South Dakota, into parts of Nebraska, Wyoming, and the mountains of Montana. Much of the terrain that was crossed by the Lewis and Clark expedition was land of the Lakota and other neighboring tribes. Today the landholdings of the Lakota have diminished into much smaller parcels of tribal reservation lands in several states. The land of the Hunkpapa Lakota straddles the central part of the states of North and South Dakota on the western banks of the Missouri River.

Since the beginnings of this nation as we know it today, the Native people of this land have not had the opportunity to reap the benefits of the prosperity of this great nation, which has emerged as a world leader on all levels. Native people have in fact paid an extreme price in the development of this nation in terms of loss of land and natural resources; not to speak of the human devastation through the destruction of cultures, languages, and breakdown of families and community infrastructures. Native people with few exceptions continue to be among the most impoverished in the nation.

American Indians and Alaska Natives have experienced and survived a number of eras of the past centuries, among them war and genocide; a period of removal from ancestral lands, as in the Trail of Tears and Indian Territory; a time of reconciliation; and a treaty era, where some 300 treaties were signed but never honored; an Allotment era, which sought to break up our tribal lands that were set aside for tribal people; a brief period of understanding in the 1920s and 1930s, when American Indians became citizens and educational leaders sought to recognize the value of Native culture in schools. Unfortunately, that lasted only a millisecond in the history of time. This was followed by an era of termination of the 1950s, when the federal government sought to extinguish the federal tribal responsibility: in effect, to sever the federal relationship and its responsibility, to buy out tribal sovereignty and force assimilation of tribal people into mainstream society through relocation programs into urban centers—cities such as Los Angles, Chicago, Denver, and Cleveland—in addition to a variety of other programs.

The federal policies that have governed tribal lives over the past centuries are like a slowly meandering river, switching back and forth, covering much time and distance, yet hardly going anywhere.

Tribal Languages and Culture

Throughout the westward expansion of this nation, the stories are replete with conflict and change for Native people. The devastating effects on the lifestyles and cultures of indigenous people are well documented. The stories may differ, but they share the common theme: the destruction of a way of life. In the end, the Native people of this land have experienced a significant loss of language and culture at the expense of developing the United States of America. For the people of the Plains, much devastation followed the expedition of Lewis and Clark.

There are wide variances in the level of these losses within the tribal communities nationwide. In many cases, whole languages and cultures have disappeared. In others, languages and traditional practices have thrived despite the edict of federal officials to abandon a way of life. Ironically, a cultural bastion of hope can be attributed to the isolation factor of Indian reservations established by the federal government. Most reservations are located in remote rural areas of the country, where there has been little access and influence by mainstream society. As a result, many tribal cultures and languages were maintained despite the efforts to eradicate them by the federal government. However, on a cultural continuum, many native communities are somewhere in the middle, with losses of language continuing because of pressures of white society and other intervening variables, such as the symptoms of poverty and their devastating effects on family structures, decades of irrelevant education programs, the impact of television, the Internet, and other contemporary influences.

With the destruction of a traditional, extended-family learning process, over the past century there has been an erosion and absence of informal or formal structures to facilitate and allow tribal languages to grow and flourish. Today Native families and tribal communities require a rebuilding of these support mechanisms if tribal communities are to undo the destructive processes of the past.

Until recent decades, white policymakers and educational institutions have purposely overlooked and ignored the importance of tribal language and culture in the learning environment. The consequence of this tactic has been destructive among American Indian and Alaska Native students, leading to poor self-esteem, high dropout rates, and low achievement.

Tribal educators have long recognized the importance of Native language and culture in the learning process that was commonly practiced throughout the historical past, when Native people were able to live and enjoy a lifestyle that melded the world of knowledge with the traditions of spirit, language, and cultural practices.

Since formal education was systematically introduced in the 1800s, it has been a destructive process for Indian people. It has left in its wake a trail of failure and tragedy that continues today. It has only been since the 1960s that Native people began to see an environment conducive to change that would allow for tribal control over educational institutions through school boards and the creation of tribal colleges. Native people are now exercising the right to provide an educational process that centers on creating a culturally hospitable environment to provide quality relevant education to native students.

Since Lewis and Clark

Where has all this left tribal people in the twenty-first century, two hundred years after the expedition of Lewis and Clark? It has left Native people as the most undereducated and underserved population in the United States. Confronted with poverty, the problems are compounded by health issues, alcoholism, suicide, high dropout rates, lack of opportunity, and internalized oppression, which breeds a sense of hopelessness.

While Native people are still left impoverished, with the overwhelming majority of people living in some of the most isolated and poorest economic conditions in the richest nation in the world, we have great hopes for a new beginning as we continue to gain control over our educational institutions.

A New Beginning: The 1960s

In the 1960s, tribal communities entered an era of self-determination with the federal government. During this time, Congress recognized the documented failures of the past federal policies and the value of Native cultures and traditions in the learning process. It also marked the time for Indian people to assume greater control over programs affecting their people. This era has been a more positive time across all levels of American Indian and Alaska Native education.

We have realized the passage of the Indian Education Act of 1972, recognizing the needs of Indian students attending public schools. Nearly half of the 400,000 students are attending these schools in small cities or major urban centers. The remainder are in public schools on or adjacent to Indian reservations where there tends to be a lack of Indian representation on local school boards.

We have witnessed the passage of the Indian Self-Determination and Education Assistance Act of 1978. We have seen the formulation of school boards and greater control of K–12 schools funded and operated by the Bureau of Indian Affairs (BIA). For the first time in the history of formal education, Indian parents were being welcomed into the school and given a clear role and voice in the operations of the BIA schools. Since that time, we have seen tribal communities take over the complete operation of Bureau of Indian Affairs schools as tribal and contract schools.

The Creation of a Concept: Tribal Colleges

The idea of providing higher education programs for Native students through an American Indian university was proposed as early as the turn of the twentieth century. However, it was not until the 1960s, during President Johnson's "Great Society" and war on poverty, which promoted community action programs on Indian reservations, that a social and political environment was more conducive to the radical notion of tribal governments chartering and operating schools of higher education for their own people.

One of the solutions to address the failures of the past has been the establishment of tribal colleges and universities. In the late 1960s and early 1970s, we witnessed the growth and development of the tribal college movement from the original six colleges in 1972 that established the American Indian Higher Education Consortium that now has thirty-six member institutions. The catalyst for the tribal college movement was in large part the lack of attention to and failure of mainstream institutions of higher education to address the unique needs of American Indian and Alaska Native students.

This new enterprise within Indian Country is allowing Native communities and new leadership to emerge and begin to design programs that consider a cultural perspective that seeks to "Indigenize" American Indian higher education by providing culturally relevant education. The goal of providing cultural programs is tied to the revitalization of tribal languages, which will be challenging because it will require the commitment of the entire tribal community.

The tribal college movement was initially championed by a handful of dedicated educators, Native and non-Native, who committed their professional careers to the success of educating Native American youth. Despite numerous continuing challenges and barriers, tribal colleges and universities have proliferated since that time through their tenacity and unwillingness to fail. In 1973, the leadership of the six original colleges created a parent organization, the American Indian Higher Education Consortium (AIHEC) to serve and represent them in that nationwide movement. AIHEC in turn created the American Indian College Fund (AICF) in 1989, and later was instrumental in the development of the Student Congress in 1990, and the Alliance for Equity in Higher Education, all of which have contributed to the development and success of the colleges and the students they serve.

Through the organizing mechanism of AIHEC, a small nucleus of individuals worked tirelessly in the halls of Congress, advocating for the support of the tribal college movement. Finally, a level of stability was reached when federal legislation was enacted in 1978 through the Tribally Controlled Community College Assistance Act, renamed in 1998 the Tribally Controlled College or University Assistance Act, to provide funding for the core operations of the colleges.

Since the 1970s, the success of the original schools has led to the growth of thirty-five tribal colleges and universities in the United States, with the promise of more to follow. New colleges and educational satellites have been organized in several states—across Alaska, New York, Oklahoma, Wyoming, Idaho, and Washington. The Native people of Hawaii have also expressed interest in joining the tribal higher education movement.

Many accomplishments have been realized since the Navajo Nation created the first tribal college, the Navajo Community College, in 1968, now known as the Diné College. Since that time, the number of colleges has multiplied; programs and the quality of offerings have increased; colleges have expanded into four-year and graduate programs. The number of students entering tribal colleges and universities directly from high school is on the upswing, and colleges are playing a more significant role within their respective communities and tribal governments, as well as in regional and national arenas, serving over 30,000 full- and part-time students.

Despite the success of the movement within the tribal communities, tribal colleges and universities continue to be the most underfunded institutions of higher education in the United States, which has hindered their ability to gain parity with their mainstream sister institutions. Continual financial stress threatens the caliber of the programs they offer, and their ability to attract qualified faculty and staff. In partial response to this financial stress, AIHEC and the tribal colleges and universities presidents promoted major policy initiatives in the early 1990s to increase funding from the federal government agencies.

Two of the most important successes of these initiatives include the 1994 legislation that bestowed land-grant status to twenty-nine tribal colleges and universities. In addition, on October 19, 1996, President Bill Clinton created an important partnership between the tribal colleges and universities and federal agencies by signing an Executive Order to establish a White House Initiative on Tribal Colleges and Universities (WHITCU). The Executive Order mandates all federal agencies to develop strategic plans to increase services and resources to the tribal colleges. More recently, President Bush reaffirmed the initiative by extending the Executive Order for the White House Initiative on Tribal Colleges and Universities.

Over the past six years, as a result of the Executive Order, the tribal colleges and universities have realized a dramatic increase in federal funding from a variety of government programs. However, while this infusion of resources has been extremely important for the developing institutions, these funds are more often competitive, supplemental, and short-term, and therefore tend to come with restrictions and limitations that can stifle innovation and creativity. Consequently, all colleges may not benefit equally from this initiative, nor do they always have the necessary flexibility to address colleges' basic needs. An additional concern with this type of funding is that it may detract from the colleges' primary mission, that is, to provide culturally relevant quality education.

The success of the tribal colleges and universities is also dependent upon their individual ability to create partnerships outside the federal sector. Among the most significant of these private-sector partnerships has been that with the W. K. Kellogg Foundation. This foundation has been instrumental in supporting several important tribal colleges and universities initiatives over the past decade, most notably, their support has helped the individual tribal colleges and universities and their national organization, AIHEC, strengthen their governing structures and fiscal capabilities. The funding demonstrated how private philanthropic organizations can make an important contribution to build and enhance quality and sustainable programs within the tribal colleges and universities. A recent book, *The Renaissance of American Indian Higher Education: Capturing the Dream*, edited by Maenette K.P. Benham and Wayne J. Stein, tells the story of the Kellogg initiative.[1]

New and Continuing Challenges

As the tribal colleges and universities enter a new era of greater accountability and increased expectations, there are new challenges to be met. Tribal colleges and universities must maintain a delicate balance as they move forward in developing quality education that reflects the needs and culture and traditions of their tribal communities. The following are a few of the challenges that will continue to be addressed in the struggle to maintain quality higher education programs.

Resource Parity

Throughout the history of the tribal college movement, the colleges have never reached a level of funding equal to similar public and private institutions. As a result, the tribal colleges are forced to carry the extra burdens of being resource poor. This dilemma forces tribal college and university faculty and staff to carry additional responsibilities by focusing on the developmental activities to bring in additional resources for the colleges. The future ongoing challenge will be to convince the decision-makers at the federal and congressional levels to provide increased resources to provide quality educational programs.

Language and Cultural Maintenance and Revitalization

Tribal colleges and universities have two major challenges in trying to undo the cultural genocide of the past federal policies. One is to help tribal communities capture and document to the greatest extent possible their languages, culture, and traditions. Two, and perhaps the greatest challenge and barrier that our communities face, is how we use it. Tribal educators need to develop our own experts to build upon the traditional epistemology of their elders in translating native knowledge and its relationship to Western thinking.

For example, the unique aspects of Indian Country present challenges that are not adequately addressed by the federal mandates of "No Child Left Behind" (NCLB). Areas of particular concern include: (1) culturally relevant programming and (2) adequate yearly progress.

Culturally Relevant Academic Programming: The incorporation of Native American culture and traditions into academic curriculum and education programming is essential to success in Indian education. The study and development of sound, culturally relevant curricula should be supported to ensure effective implementation of education programs and requirements in Indian country. NCLB formally recognizes the federal government's support for culturally based education approaches as a strategy for positively impacting the achievement of Native American students.

Yearly Progress: However, the time frame for results under NCLB do not adequately account for the investment in time and resources required to develop effective culturally based education approaches or to develop curricula that reflect the cultural and linguistic heritage of the community.

Lessons Learned

Tribal colleges and universities and AIHEC must capture and institutionalize the lessons learned from their experience of developing institutions of higher learning to ensure the sustainability of their work and to share this new knowledge and wisdom to widen the circle of partnerships with other tribes, federal agencies, and philanthropic groups.

Accountability

Today, with the federal government demanding greater accountability through K–12 initiatives like "No Child Left Behind," there is increasing pressure to provide empirical data for programs receiving federal funds. Internal federal program assessments like the Office of Management and Budget's Program Assessment Review Tracking (PART) instrument is demanding new information from federal agency programs for determining future budgets. In the final analysis, tribal colleges and universities will be required to demonstrate progress by providing quantified data streams beyond numbers of graduates. The AIHEC is addressing this matter by developing a databank to better measure the progress of tribal colleges through a data initiative called American Indian Measures of Success (AIMS). These data, based on "indicators of success," will be gathered, compiled, and reported on an annual basis to the federal government and other funding entities. The AIMS initiative seeks to capture these efforts and measure the success of the tribal colleges and their communities by demonstrating that they are more than degree-granting institutions, providing training programs, health and wellness programs, economic development opportunities and training, leadership development, and a wide array of community based programs.

Closing the Gap

Throughout the history of formal education, there has been a major disconnect in what was taught and its relationship to the Indian community. Only until recent decades was there any mention of Indian values, history, or culture in the classroom. There was no place for it in Indian schools. Students were often punished for using their language and discouraged from participating in cultural activities. Fortunately, while language and culture were not permitted in the schools, they were quietly carried on and shared by elders and family members; as a result, much of language, culture, and traditional ways were being maintained during those decades of prohibition.

Today, we have many more experts on hand to help address this issue. However, it is one thing to have documentation; it is another to use it effectively so that it is passed on to the next generation. The challenge for our tribal institutions is to create processes, approaches, and learning environments that integrate our native ways of knowing into the learning environment. We must address the issue of *relevant education* if we are to be successful. We must engage parents, elders, teachers, tribal leaders, and administrators to lead and participate in this educational effort. There must be a total commitment to merging our native knowledge base with Western math and science and education if our students are to compete successfully in this fast-paced, ever changing society. If we are successful, our tribal governments will continue to be strengthened with new, better-prepared leaders to ensure the progress and survival as tribal people in a nation that seeks to exploit our tribal resources.

Diversity: A New Challenge

The concept of diversity is interesting, challenging, and for most of the time difficult. We face it in our everyday lives as we decide how to act or react as the dominant society moves and dictates. It is intertwined within our informal interactions both on a friendly and sometimes challenging circumstance. We know that diversity among the indigenous people of the Americas was always here. Diversity among tribal people and diversity among the people of this nation bring new and special challenges for Native people and the tribal colleges.

The 2000 U.S. Census indicated a Native American population of 2.5 million; the population of those who are multiracial with Native American heritage had grown to 4.1 million; and more than 7 million claim some "Indian ancestry."[2] Our tribal reservation populations are composed of predominantly Native people with limited interaction on a daily basis with the larger white society. Our encounters with diversity on the reservation were often limited. Until recent times, our communities were isolated with a sense of insulation and safety from the outside world. Times have changed in the recent decades, with greater modes of transportation, better highways, and the proliferation of technology, with television and computers bringing greater interaction, exposure, and influence from the dominant society.

A Different Worldview

As Native people of this land, we are here despite a history of tragedy and conflict with this new nation. Because our people have been so overwhelmed by the dominant society and the federal government, many Americans believe that Native people think and act like them. This is one of the first and continuing challenges for tribal communities as they seek to control their own destiny. In actuality, tribal people think and often act in a different fashion, stemming from their own traditional intellectual base. Historically, many intellectuals have disavowed or given short shrift to Indigenous traditional knowledge, beliefs based on the wisdom and epistemology of our traditional elders.

An important and key factor in the diversity discussion is that Native people hold *differing worldviews* and values than the dominant society. There is a common belief that the land is sacred and cannot be owned and must be respected and cared for, to ensure a healthy environment for future generations. There is a belief that all things are related—animals, plants, and the earth must be respected and be in harmony to be honored for the good of all.

Such values were part of the traditional, everyday life built upon the foundation of Native peoples' respect and value of living in harmony with their environment—Mother Earth. Understanding that we had a special relationship to the land where we lived meant not exploiting it, and giving thanks for what it had to offer. We have always felt a special relationship with this country because it is our homeland, even though the federal government has taken most of it away.

Native people comprise a small and diverse, but resilient segment of our nation's population, a "minority among minorities," to the point of being nearly invisible over the past several decades. These factors have caused demographers to classify our people as "others" within American minority populations. Thus, the needs and concerns of Native people have often been misunderstood, misrepresented, and ignored through benign neglect, and in many cases through blatant illegal actions and gross mismanagement of "trust responsibilities," such as the taking of land and loss of billions of dollars of "trust funds" by the federal government.

Diversity: A New Definition

Today, there is much concern over the issue of diversity and its relationship to affirmative action and equality. Peter Wood, in his book *Diversity: The Invention of a Concept*, states that diversity is a set of beliefs wholly distinct from its original meaning of variety and multiplicity. In his discussion, he offers a contemporary view that has evolved over the past quarter-century: that diversity is not a single meaning, but divided into separate groups based on race, ethnicity, or sex, and other categories—some of which, he argues, have enjoyed privileges that have been denied others. According to Wood, diversity is more than emphasizing differences and separateness; it is a political doctrine asserting that some social categories deserve compensation for prejudice and social inequities of the past and to address continued disadvantages. Wood also believes this new doctrine works against the old ideas of liberty and equity. Obviously, these arguments have implications for the Native American community in a variety of ways.[3]

While Native people are interested in the ideal of equality, which grows out of the goals of diversity, one major difference to be noted is the fact that the struggle for equality and equity for Native people is also based on treaties as *sovereign Tribal Nations* with the federal government and not based on race. The future challenge for the tribal colleges and universities will be to bring greater understanding of these important differences to the dominant society that can enhance the nation's economic competitiveness, social stability, and cultural richness while contributing to the concepts of freedom and equality.

Conclusion

In conclusion, the tribal college movement, which is still young in the history of time, will have much to offer in our future struggles for self-determination. While the tribal college and university movement represents only a speck of time in the history of our world, they are in fact an established tool for the future, to be used by students, parents, educators, and tribal leaders. Tribal colleges and universities represent bright lights of hope in the skies over Indian Country as they bring a new dawn to a vision that benefits the seventh generation.

Notes

1. Maenette K. P. Benham and Wayne J. Stein, eds., *The Renaissance of American Indian Higher Education: Capturing the Dream* (Mahwah, N.J.: Lawrence Erlbaum, 2003).
2. Linda P. Morton, "Targeting Native Americans," *Public Relations Quarterly* 47, no. 1 (2002): 37.
3. Peter Wood, *Diversity: The Invention of a Concept* (San Francisco: Encounter Books, 2003), 11.

American Indian Issues for the Next Fifty Years

15

JAMES SHANLEY

MOST OF MY REMARKS ARE GOING TO BE ABOUT MONTANA, because I don't get many other places probably. When I was first asked to speak here, they said it was going to be about Lewis and Clark, so my whole orientation, at least for a couple of months, was on Lewis and Clark. I didn't know anything about Lewis and Clark. I read the Lewis and Clark journals. So I thought I could have some fun and talk about things that I usually don't get a chance to talk about. Usually I get to give the speech that Jerry [Dr. Gerald Gipp] just gave, with the statistics and talking about government programs and how terrible the world is, and so I thought that I could talk about the things that are going to be happening in the future. He has covered the present. I am going to go back and cover the past and then jump forward and cover the future. To start this, there is a little video I want to show you.

[The Video][1]

This was a video representation of a non-event, something that didn't happen. They were never in contact with Lewis and Clark, but this film—does it represent reality? Maybe, maybe not. It's based on some tenuous tracks of oral tradition. Does it have some truth in it? Perhaps it does, perhaps it doesn't. There is one section in there where they say that perhaps they should kill these white fellows. Perhaps that is a twenty-first-century afterthought. I don't know if they really thought about killing them—no one really does. The people who made this film at Fort Peck probably were thinking, "Damn, I wish they had killed them then." But that didn't happen. Anyway, I thought that would be a good prelude into the short conversation I am going to have with you today. Don't take it too seriously.

I have been logging onto this website called edge.org. What they do is they pose a question; every year they have a question on their website, and people respond to it—scientists, philosophers, average people, some very illustrious people respond to their question. Their question for this year is "What do you think is true but you can't prove it?" Well, my whole talk falls into this classification. I may think some of it is true but I can't prove any of it. I hope I don't offend anybody or that anyone gets upset about some of the things I say.

I want to talk about Montana and this [the film] is one part of Montana. The stuff you saw at the end—that is very nice, but I am not sure it is part of the coming reality. A lot of people have called Montana the "Last Best Place." And they put out a book five or six years ago called *The Last Best Place* that was full of Montana writers.[2] But what is going to happen to Montana in the next fifty years? And what is going to happen to American Indians in Montana in the next fifty years, in particular? There are a few things. I enjoyed Janine's [Dr. Janine Pease] talk on Indian voting rights, and she mentioned population. Let me start with the reservation I live in—Fort Peck. We have two different tribal groups. There has been a lot of intermarriage between those two tribal groups because we have all lived on the same reservation for a hundred years and we are linguistically related to each other—the Assiniboine and the Lakota and Dakota. There has always been some understandability between the two languages. We have between 6,500 and 7,000 enrolled members who live on our reservation, yet our Indian Health Service Clinic treats a little over 9,000 Indians, as there are some 9,000 Indians who live at Fort Peck out of a population of about 12,000. What does that say about our population and how does that transfer to other tribes and reservations in the state? For one thing, those 2,000 Indians are either marginal Indians—in other words, they don't have enough Indian blood in them to be enrolled—or they are Indians from other tribes. Primarily, they are Indians from other tribes, because our people have been going away to marry, to boarding schools, to Haskell, to Billings, to Great Falls, and marrying other people and bringing them back. So we have a large portion of our population who are nontribal members at this point in time. I think that is true for the remainder of the reservations in the state. That is something I think is true that I can't prove. Actually, you could prove it if you wanted to dig into the statistics enough. Another thing is that, of the people who are enrolled tribal members who reside on the reservation, I would hazard a guess that at least 50 percent of them have some other type of Indian blood, other than Fort Peck Assiniboine or Sioux, in them. That is true for every tribe in the country. We are lovers, we've got everything, and I don't think that is untrue for other tribes as well. How long has that phenomenon been occurring? I would guess at least fifty years.

So what is going to happen in the next fifty years? Janine mentioned it today. Indian population is growing in the state. What is going to happen on reservations? At one time, and in the film they were talking about the early 1900s, the population of Fort Peck was about 60 percent non-Indian and 40 percent Indian. Now it is about 85 percent Indian and 15 percent non-Indian. In twenty years, almost everyone who lives on the Fort Peck Reservation will have Indian blood of some quantum. And that is true on almost every reservation in the state, except possibly Salish. Why is that not true for Salish? It is because of the huge influx into this last and best place, Montana, by people from California, Washington, other places in the West. These are people who have money, want to live in a nice place, and don't want to have to put up with the problems you see in urban areas, nor the cost in urban areas. They are buying up our last best land in this state at a rate that is tremendous. Indian people are going to find themselves squeezed in, and the Salish, who are in one of the most beautiful places, are going to be in more trouble than Fort Peck. The Indian people as a whole will grow in Montana over the next several generations.

What is going to happen to the rest of the population? When I started doing this thing and I was thinking what would happen in the next fifty years, I had a couple of different methods of research. First of all, I got on the Internet, went to the Census Bureau, and ordered a bunch of population manuals. I looked at global warming. I looked at a whole series of things. And then I said I needed to have my own unique methodologies, so I started asking people in bars what they thought it would be like in fifty years, and I got a lot of really good answers. Janine mentioned the changing population in the United States. What used to be the minority is going to become the majority. In other words, people of color are going to become the majority population in the United States in the next fifty years. That is primarily driven by the Hispanic people. I have some relatives who live in Arizona, and I used to live in Arizona, and I drive back and forth through this intermountain corridor to Arizona all the time. And again, this is something I can't prove but I know in my heart is true: we are getting a vast movement of people from Mexico and South America that are moving, migration-wise, into the United States, and they are moving in the West through a western corridor that is kind of limited to the Montana border and going straight down through Colorado. Many of you who are older may have been in Denver many years ago. Remember, Denver was kind of a lily-white town at one point. Denver is majority Hispanic now. Reno, Nevada, is about 70 percent Hispanic. I have been on a lot of reaccreditation visits over in Washington State. The whole tri-city area, Yakima, all the way up from Oregon, there is a vast influx of Hispanic people. That is going to happen in Montana as well. That is good news and bad news. Number one, they are not coming with a lot of money, so they can't buy the best places. And number two, these people are primarily the same people we are. They are Spanish and they speak Spanish, but they come from Indian heritage. And at least in some ways, they have a Native viewpoint of the world. So they are people like us and they are coming into Montana in the next fifty years.

What else is going to happen in Montana? I mentioned global warming. There are a lot of predictions that there aren't going to be any glaciers in Glacier Park and that is happening fairly rapidly. Yet scientifically, global warming is still one of those debatable types of things and it's kind of like the true-believers syndrome. There are the true believers that global warming is happening on one side, and people who say the evidence isn't there are on the other side, and the sides won't coincide at all. People on the scientific side are not sure what it will do to regional climates even if it occurs. They know that much of it has to do with affecting the ocean currents, and then ocean currents affect precipitation patterns and so on. We had a really wet year this year in Montana, we have had droughts in years past, but we have had wet years and droughts before. We have cold and we have heat. We have mosquitoes. We have a lot of things. Will regional global warming make us hotter or wetter, colder or drier? We really don't have any idea. It will affect how Montana is set up economically and the different geographic regions. I don't expect that the American Indians will leave the reservation much. We will live in the cities as well, but we will still be the primary population on our homeland.

Going back to the issue I brought up before, about all of the different tribal blood that is going to be populating our reservations. Indians have a good sense of humor. They laugh and they talk all the time, and they joke about themselves, but when we get into professional settings, we tend to get politically correct, and if you start talking about Indian traditions, Indian culture, Indian languages, if you say anything that seems to be contrary to current beliefs, people begin to beat you up. We have moved into an area of political correctness in terms of our own politics that I think sometimes is scary and self-defeating. But how do you teach a culture or a language to a people that are going to have five, six, seven different tribes in them in fifty years? Your grandchildren could essentially have many different types of tribes. Which language do you teach them? Does everything become the generic powwow culture? We made a representation when we made this film. It was done in the best of intentions, with great heart. But you noticed probably as people were speaking, the way they were using their Indian language in a very elementary manner, like children were speaking, that was because most of these people were not fluent speakers. What is the reality for Indian languages? Some say that if you have a group with a language with less than 10,000 native speakers, it is going to be lost shortly. We have one language that is on the endangered language list here in Montana now. We probably have three or four or five others that are borderline or close to it. Is there any hope for Indian languages? I was watching TV last night, and I saw a thing on George Carlin; they were showing clips out of the biography of his life, and he was talking to this woman, and she was saying something about "Since this stuff has happened, I have just given up hope." He said, "Good for you." He said, "Hope is highly overrated in my book anyway." Sometimes, I think Indians end with that attitude that hope is highly overrated. I'm just going to blurt it out and we will see what happens. But in terms of languages, I saw Darrell Kipp up here yesterday. We have had some tremendous people doing tremendous things in preserving and sustaining languages. Is it real? I really couldn't say. I hope that it is, regardless of what I think about hope. The reality is that the McDonald world, globalization, may not allow us to keep our languages. A good friend of mine, who also happens to be a medicine man, said it is very likely that our great-grandchildren are going to be speaking Spanish, that I will have grandchildren who will have Spanish surnames. He said that, when those other brown people come up to Montana, we are going to marry them. Things are going to change.

Are there other things that are going to enter Montana that are going to make a difference? I think we are so parochial, we look at our own communities, at our own tribes, and our own little world, that we don't see what is going on in the world as a whole. We are going to pack up our boys and send them off to fight whatever war comes along, and our girls. But other than that, we don't seem to give a damn about what other people in the world are doing. Here are some of the things that are happening. The Europeans have banded together as a trading unit with a common currency. If you have been to Europe, you will find that, if you speak English, you can go just about anyplace in Europe. If you speak French, you can go just about anyplace in Europe. If you speak German, you can go just about anyplace in Europe. The languages are becoming so interchangeable that they are becoming more and more a unit where they are comprised of different nationalities and ethnic groups. We have the whole of the southeast part of the globe, particularly China but also India, that are going to become huge economic powers. China is already a huge economic power. What I see that doing, in order to compete globally and politically, militarily, and a lot of other ways, I see it forcing a North America. And I have always been an advocate of that anyway. I have always wanted to see Mexico, the United States, and Canada become more of one unit, the whole of North America. For Native people, again, there is good news in that. Fifteen percent of Canada is Native. Many of our tribes' brothers and sisters and cousins, I mean actual brothers and sisters and cousins, that live across that line have been able to preserve their language and their culture in a much more intact way than we have been able to. And if we can merge with them in some way, if we can open up grandmother's medicine line, it is going to help us. I think that naturally that is going to occur, because the economic pressures from other areas of the world, coming from the East, coming from Europe, will make us come closer. The Canadians are ready. In fact, there were three or four provinces that wanted to join the United States if Quebec had gone French. The Canadians are willing to be much more close to us. It is the people of the United States that are jingoistic. And the people of Mexico are already closer to us. They are becoming part of us. So why don't we face up to it and bite the bullet and take all of these people into the family and make the best place we can make?

There are a lot of other things that are going to happen, and a lot of other things that those people are hoping to get by us that I probably can't tell you here, but I would be happy to tell you at some other time. Thank you.

Note

1. Dr. Shanley showed the video *Assiniboine Chief Rosebud Remembers Lewis & Clark*, produced by Mary Helland (Glasgow, MT: Valley County Historical Society, 2004). This video is a dramatization of the story, originally told by Chief Rosebud and passed through Assiniboine oral tradition, of the Assiniboine watching the members of the Lewis and Clark Expedition travel along the Missouri River. It depicts Assisniboine life and culture at the beginning of the nineteenth century before there had been much contact with white culture. The narration is in English, but most of the dialogue is in Nakoda. The Assiniboine never met or saw Lewis and Clark during the expedition of the Corps of Discovery, but Chief Rosebud told this story anyway.

2. William Kittredge and Annick Smith, *The Last Best Place: A Montana Anthology* (Helena: Montana Historical Society Press, 1988).

The Rise and Fall of Native American Studies in the United States

16

DUANE CHAMPAGNE

THE TOPIC AND TITLE FOR THIS PAPER were given to me by my colleague George Horse Capture. Most likely I have not written what he thought I should. I believe an argument can be made for decline in American Indian Studies during the 1990s, at least in organizational and resource terms. However, I will argue that there is great promise for American Indian Studies in the twenty-first century as a new and substantial paradigm that will help understand the collective and individual motivations, social and cultural change, and policies for the indigenous peoples of North America and around the world. Native studies, focusing on the continuity of land, community, self-government, and culture, presents a new and alternative way to understand social groups, mainly indigenous peoples, and their struggles in the contemporary context with nation-states. The indigenous paradigm is only now gaining some attention and theoretical articulation, but it is grounded in the experiences, history, and contemporary struggles of indigenous peoples in the United States and elsewhere. Just as the social movement of indigenous peoples around the world gained international and national status in many countries, indigenous studies, or American Indian Studies in the United States, has arisen to reflect, analyze, and support the policies, interests, and aspirations of indigenous peoples. The indigenous movement is without great political power, and does not have the favor of nation-states in the international arena, yet it is grounded in the values, cultures, histories, and governments of indigenous peoples, and is not well explained by the usual studies based on class, race, ethnicity, or cultural studies. In my view, the indigenous peoples movement, especially since the 1970s, but in principle since the time of first European colonial contact, requires more precise conceptualization on its own grounds as an international social movement of like cases that deserves greater analysis and policy discussion. The indigenous movement will not go away, and therefore the indigenous paradigm, or the need for American Indian Studies, or indigenous studies, will not recede. The development of an international indigenous perspective is as strong as any time in history, but the national and international context for the indigenous viewpoint is not favorable, both in the United States and on the international scene. American Indian Studies, its rise and fall, in many ways mirrors the political struggles of the indigenous movement, in times when there is less nation-state support from mainstream institutions. Nevertheless, some unique history and circumstances have affected the rise and development of American Indian Studies and continue to inhibit the development of an American Indian Studies discipline.

American Indian Studies, or Native American Studies, I use the terms interchangeably, is a field in formation. American Indian Studies programs and departments first emerged during the later 1960s and early 1970s. Native American Studies is the smallest of the historically American ethnic studies programs, and increasingly the intellectual and policy stepchild of the ethnic studies movement. Nevertheless, practitioners of American Indian Studies are articulating a viewpoint on indigenous communities that emphasizes central roles of sovereignty, land, cultural preservation, and continuity. Native American Studies is premised on the view that no other discipline studies its areas of interest. Indeed, Native American Studies proposes a perspective that includes institutional, cultural, holistic, and ethnographic understanding of community, but within the context of indigenous worldviews, and relations to nation-states, the world-system, and cultural globalization. Native American Studies, or perhaps better, American Indian communities, propose that their status and interests require an understanding of their community organization and culture, goals of maintaining self-determination, cultural autonomy and continuity, land, and their own modes of accommodating to nation-states, global markets, and trans-societal information transfers. American Indian communities can be studied from their own points of view, values, and understandings in ways that will give greater analytic power and empowerment to the communities. Native American Studies is working toward an indigenous paradigm with a focus on the patterns of cultural and community continuity, while at the same time making culturally and institutionally informed decisions and strategies for accommodating to a changing and globalized environment. American Indians are about preserving culture, community, land, and ensuring rights to self-government for future generations. Native American Studies is developing points of view and conceptualizations drawing on the everyday strategies and conceptions of American Indian communities that require mainstream academics and policymakers to rethink and extend the views of indigenous groups, as a means to include their views and social-cultural actions outside of the use of class, ethnicity, race, and even nationality. Native American Studies, and more generally indigenous studies, calls for conceptualizations and strategies that encompass indigenous issues, rights, and strategies of political, cultural, and territorial survival.

I will develop the argument that a paradigm for indigenous studies has intellectual and policy promise, although the resource and organizational efforts of U.S. universities have not kept pace with the intellectual developments, and have inhibited the development of American Indian Studies as a fully developed discipline and paradigm.

The Beginnings of Native American Studies

American Indian Studies programs arose within the context of the civil rights movement, and the protest about the Vietnam War, and were accompanied with a demographic shift among Native Americans toward urban life. During the 1950s many American Indians moved to cities, looking for employment and opportunities. Many began to attend colleges in larger numbers, and found that university curricula did not cover American Indian history, culture, and policy in familiar or useful ways. Consequently, American Indian students and communities sought to convince university administrations that American Indian studies needed to include more content about American Indians. The rise of American Indian Studies programs and departments coincided with the rise of ethnic studies programs, usually composed of the major, recognized, historical American minority groups, Afro-American, Asian American, Chicano/Latino, as well as American Indian. Many universities and colleges moved to create ethnic studies departments and programs, and generally American Indian Studies was included in the movement. The programs reflected the social movement and social change trends of the 1960s and 1970s by efforts to bring more inclusion to members of historically excluded and disadvantaged groups. Minority groups struggled for more inclusion, and ethnic studies programs and departments were a means for introduction of new curricula, research, publications, faculty hiring, and student recruitment. American Indian students entered colleges and universities that heretofore had given them little attention or attention from an outsider's point of view.

Most likely, without the alliance to the larger and more visible ethnic and racial groups, many American Indian Studies programs or departments may not have been established, or at least established in the ways they started, largely as a small ethnic group, with interests of intellectual and social inclusion. The prescribed ethnic studies model, with emphasis on assimilation, inclusion, or perhaps renationalization,[1] proved only a partial model for American Indian points of view. While national trends led toward establishment of ethnic studies, their organization and relations within university administrations varied considerably. The relative success of a program or department often depended on the attention provided by university administrators. Often a successful program needed strong support from well-placed administrators who encouraged new faculty, research, and student recruitment. Administrators, however, come and go, and programs at times had attention and could grow, and at other times, administrations turned attention to other issues, and ethnic studies programs often languished in those contexts.

The trends that led toward contemporary American Indian Studies, however, arose from multiple currents. While the flow of national events toward ethnic studies was critical, there were several undercurrents that help define American Indian Studies and often threw it in intellectual and policy contention with ethnic studies and mainstream intellectual perspectives. Other trends that contributed to the present state of American Indian Studies include the Self-determination Policy (1960s to present), the history and attention of anthropologists, historians, and the rise of ethnohistory, and the American Indian movement toward self-determination and assertion of political and cultural autonomy since the 1960s. While each of the historical American ethnic groups have a unique story and relation with the United States, American Indians fit least into the ethnic group and studies conceptualization. American Indians are composed of hundreds of cultures that have had self-government, territory, and an associated form of community from time immemorial. American Indians do not have an immigrant experience during the past 500 years, as do all other ethnic groups, and American Indian governments, communities, and claims to territory predate establishment of the U.S. Constitution. American Indians are not parties to the Constitution, and most became citizens only in 1924 by an act of Congress, but did not thereby give up rights to membership in an American Indian community. American Indians are more like hundreds of small nationalities rather than an ethnic group. They do not share a common religion, culture, language, territory, or form of government. From the early colonial period in the 1600s to 1871, the European colonial powers and then the United States made government-to-government treaties with American Indian nations.

While American Indians generally have pressed their indigenous rights to territory and self-government, the most recent policy period of self-determination is related to changing mainstream American views toward minorities, ethnic groups, and poor people's movements, most prevalent during the 1960s and 1970s. Policy and some legal victories encouraged greater assertions of self-government. Tribal governments were encouraged to manage their own affairs, organize tribal government staffs, develop economic market opportunities, and secure wider ranges of federal funding. Increasingly, tribal communities sought restoration of lands, federal recognition of government-to-government relations, legal and political participation and inclusion enough to negotiate their interests and rights. Many American Indian communities that were terminated from federal relations since the 1950s sought congressional acts to restore their rights and status as American Indian communities, and most succeeded. Over 300 federally nonrecognized Indian nations sought federal recognition, while about 560 American Indian communities are currently recognized by the federal government. Native communities sought to control their own schools, established tribally controlled community colleges, and some began to engage in high-stakes casino establishment. After some legal and political maneuvering, American Indian government rights to manage gaming on tribal lands were upheld, but with negotiated agreements or compacts with their surrounding host states. In the middle 1940s, American Indian leaders and tribal governments formed national organizations like the National Congress of American Indians (NCAI), primarily a Washington lobbying group, all of which is a measure of increased American Indian participation in U.S. civil society. American Indian communities generally are committed to retaining culture, communities, and political processes that are informed by their cultural traditions, but at the same time live in the twenty-first century and want to meet the challenges of globalization and social change on their own cultural terms. Many tribal communities are currently looking for economic opportunities that will give them greater control over resources and support their communities, while many are rethinking their current governing organizations to make them more effective in managing contemporary political challenges, but at the same time responsive to their cultural values and community norms and political processes.[2] This movement toward greater community control and decision-making is one of the primary issues that American Indian Studies has taken up as central to establishing a discipline. Much of American Indian Studies is about contemporary American Indian life, community, and processes of change and cultural continuity. There are hundreds of American Indian communities, and there are many issues confronting the communities, such as education, nation building, contemporary art, the restoration of ceremony, use of traditional art, protection of legal rights, land protection and acquisition, protection of sacred sites and the remains of ancestors, ecological issues, economic development policy, and many more.

American Indian Studies seeks to create a discipline of study about social and cultural change that encompasses the point of view of American Indian people and communities. While the practice of ethnic studies for Afro-Americans, Asian Americans, and Chicano/Latinos generally has risen with the establishment of ethnic studies programs, there is a long historical record and scholarship about American Indians before the 1960s. Jesuit missionaries, traders, colonial officials, trade companies, and colonial governments kept records, wrote reports, and sometimes published their work.[3] In the 1720s, the Jesuit missionary Joseph-François Lafitau wrote about egalitarian and consensual American Indian political processes and cultures, directly contrasting them with the hierarchical, class-based, absolutist monarchies of Europe.[4] His work had some influence on the political theories and Enlightenment viewpoints in France and Europe. Some of the founding fathers, such as Thomas Jefferson, studied American Indian cultures and languages. Benjamin Franklin, among others, had knowledge of American Indian political processes and diplomatic patterns.[5] As early as the 1830s and 1840s, there was considerable speculation about who built the many earthen mounds and remnants of towns found in the eastern United States and Mississippi Valley. Lewis Henry Morgan, who in the 1850s published a book on the Iroquois,[6] did extensive kinship studies among American Indians.[7] Morgan is often considered the father of modern American anthropology and ethnography. Friedrich Engels and Karl Marx used Morgan's work to describe the Iroquois as a classless, precapitalist social organization, where women had political power in a consensual, egalitarian political organization.[8] The egalitarian gender, classless, and consensual political relations became a model for human social organization at the end of history within Marx's evolutionary vision. Franz Boaz and his students formed the School of American Anthropology and practiced salvage anthropology, trying desperately to record language, social organization, and culture before they vanished.[9] The Bureau of American Ethnology within the Smithsonian Institution dedicated a book series and other publications to researchers who were focused on histories and ethnographies of Indian communities.[10] Since the 1960s and 1970s, interest by anthropologists has receded, although there are still many practitioners of American Indian communities. In part because of the Boasian view that American Indian cultures were only significant for research in their pre-European-contact state, most anthropologists started looking for their material in other parts of the world, envisioning that few communities of interest remained in North America. Furthermore, Vine Deloria wrote critiques about anthropological methods and humanist interests[11] that led anthropologists to shy away from study of American Indian communities, although Deloria wanted the anthropologists to stay and assist contemporary American Indian communities with their present-day issues, such as poverty, retaining culture and language, political sovereignty, and the legal and legislative issues confronting Indian communities.[12] In more recent years, armed with new theoretical perspectives and viewpoints, many anthropologists have reengaged the study of American Indian societies and are researching contemporary language revival, cultural and political change,[13] tribal federal recognition, intellectual property rights,[14] repatriation,[15] economic development, urbanization,[16] tribal cultural resource management,[17] and other issues.

There is a long record of colonial history and diplomacy that American historians have taken as their area of study. American Indian history has developed as a subarea within American history. Relations with American Indians are a central part of early U.S. history and colonial relations, and much history is devoted to localities, fur trade, diplomacy, treaties, wars, legislation, U.S. policy, legal case history, and more recently, histories of tribal communities. During the 1970s there was an outpouring of historical works about American Indians, often within the context of military and policy mistreatment.[18] The critiques of U.S. policy toward Indians helped frame the debates about self-determination, and comprised a literature that was indirectly a critique of U.S. policy in Vietnam.[19] While the outburst of historical scholarly attention declined by the 1980s, the subarea of American Indian history within U.S. history changed dramatically. By the 1990s, there was less output but more attention to Native cultures, tribal histories, Indian voices, and a more clearly organized subdiscipline.[20]

Both history and anthropology have their own disciplines, and many anthropologists and historians were not entirely satisfied with the mainstream orientations of the fields. During the 1930s and 1940s, anthropologists and historians began to develop ethnohistory—a synthesis of historical documentary and anthropological ethnographic approaches—and established a society for the study of ethnohistory in 1954. The group established a journal, *Ethnohistory*, and concentrated on the study of the history of American Indians in North America, and in more recent years has expanded its range to include cultures and communities throughout the world. The ethnohistorians focused on detailed histories and cultural studies of social and cultural change. Nevertheless, the ethnohistorians have provided a rich literature that often put Native people and communities at the center of the analysis and described them in continuous and changing social and political contexts that were often missing in the mainstream disciplines.[21] Ethnohistory explores tribal histories,[22] and religious and revitalization movements,[23] and attracts scholars from cultural anthropology, linguistics, archeology, ecology, history, and related fields. In more recent years, American Indian Studies scholars have joined the ranks of ethnohistorians. Ethnohistory seeks to develop a multidisciplinary and inclusive approach to the study of American Indian communities, and in more recent years to indigenous peoples around the world.

The Rise of American Indian Studies

When American Indian Studies programs emerged in the early 1970s, there was already a large amount of literature about American Indians in many fields. History, anthropology, and ethnohistory had dedicated subfields, or primary interests, in the study of American Indians. In addition, many other disciplines also had literatures about American Indian issues. The history of art, ethnomusicology, law, linguistics, increasingly political science, public health, English, and education contained literature or practices that included material about American Indians. Before the 1970s, few American Indians were employed as scholars. While in more recent decades the pipeline has increased, a great many postgraduate degrees for American Indians are in education, law, and professional fields, perhaps reflecting concerns for improving everyday life in Indian communities. In the early 1970s, many Afro-American, Asian American, and Latino/Chicano Studies programs moved to create a literature where there had been relatively little interest from mainstream disciplines. Since then, the ethnic studies programs have made strong arguments, and increasingly their material is entered into the mainstream disciplines. For American Indian Studies, there was already a large and in some ways centuries-old literature, although generally written and conceptualized by several fields, and generally with little intellectual input or vetting by American Indian communities or approaches. Anthropology, U.S. history, and law all had substantial American Indian subfields but nevertheless maintained theories and conceptualizations that were fostered by intellectual and other interests from the mainstream of U.S. society or within the discipline. In many ways, scholars of American Indian culture and history were taught to believe they had the best-informed understanding of American Indians.[24] American Indians were studied because they fit into a theoretical or methodological frame, and the theories and outcomes of studies generally addressed issues in U.S. society or policy. Such orientations are to be expected, and theories and studies often have goals or outcomes that have ramifications beyond the interests of the subjects. Nevertheless, many of the disciplinary academic positions could not be said to constitute American Indian Studies or an American Indian perspective. The long history of colonial and U.S. relations created images that are part of U.S. culture and identity. While few mainstream American citizens are knowledgeable about the histories, cultures, and legal status of American Indian individuals and communities, they often have formed conceptions from mass media and mythology about American Indians. For better or worse, American Indians are a central part of U.S. past relations and nation building, and a significant part of U.S. history.

American Indian Studies began as interdisciplinary programs. Unlike other historical ethnic groups, there were few American Indian scholars available to immediately take the mantle of a new discipline. Furthermore, there were many academics from several disciplines who were engaged in work about American Indians. American Indian Studies, with a few exceptions, has taken an interdisciplinary approach and, unlike other ethnic studies programs, has been managed by scholars from a variety of disciplines. This approach had the advantage that programs could be constructed from long-standing disciplines, and often seasoned scholars could be called upon to provide guidance and support. This approach, however, did not allow a coherent presentation of a Native Studies voice or perspective, and inhibited discussion and development of American Indians Studies as a coherent disciplinary endeavor.[25] Native Studies needs faculty who are trained in the emerging discipline of American Indian Studies, or scholars who are willing to commit to a Native American Studies point of view. Like all other academic disciplines, American Indian Studies should not be a field of scholars of American Indian descent, that will doom it to a cacophony of multidisciplinary approaches, or the study of American Indians from a variety of points of view, none representing the Native point of view of themselves or their interests either future or past. A scholar of Native descent who works within contemporary mainstream disciplinary worldviews, such as, say, economics or political science, can make contributions to that discipline, and perhaps to Native peoples and issues, but is not taking a Native American Studies approach, and therefore should be supported within a mainstream academic department rather than within Native American Studies. A discipline is an agreed upon way of looking at the world, a generally agreed upon epistemology and methodology, and agreed upon goals and purposes for the knowledge. Native American Studies is not an ethnic diversity program; that view has some advantages of training and integration of scholars, but does not focus on the issues, methodologies, theories, or policies that confront Native communities and peoples in a coherent way. Native American Studies or indigenous studies has all possibilities for developing a coherent paradigm for powerful scientific, humanistic, and policy analysis that will significantly inform current and future scholarship and serve and promote the issues and values of indigenous communities and nations.

The effort to define and form American Indian Studies into a discipline with a well-defined method and epistemological view of American Indian histories, cultures, and processes continues into the present. Mainstream disciplines have strong investments in Native historical and cultural material, but not necessarily from the Native point of view. The entry into academia against well-established paradigms and many practitioners of those paradigms constrains the possibility of developing and introducing alternative Native-focused approaches to Indian studies. The control and ownership of American Indian topics of scholarship require that American Indian Studies needs to more clearly define and develop its own paradigm. The indigenous paradigm must be worked out more clearly by and for scholars, and then Native American scholars need to be produced at the doctoral level to carry on the teaching, research, and policy, and to generate students for the future. There are not enough doctoral programs in American Indian Studies, and we need more, and we need to generate and sustain the scholarly viewpoints and develop an indigenous paradigm. Gaining control of the intellectual process, training of students, recognition of a viable alternative indigenous paradigm are necessary for future development of the field. American Indian Studies and indigenous studies should not be a race-based or even culture-based program, but like all other disciplines is a matter of intellectual and social commitment. Those scholars, Native and non-Native, who can commit to the principles of the discipline, and who are willing to work within paradigms that are meaningful to the cultural, political, policy, and intellectual interests and values of Native communities and nations, should compose the professionals within the discipline.

Since the early 1970s, there have arisen over 100 American Indian Studies programs. The great majority of the programs have not formed departments but are organized as interdisciplinary programs.[26] American Indian Studies departments are rare; most notable are the University of California, Davis, and the University of Minnesota, Minneapolis, which both have departments, and some of the Canadian universities have departments. Very few U.S. American Indian Studies programs have reached departmental status, and most are formed by interdisciplinary arrangements. In general there are few scholars trained in American Indian Studies at the doctoral level, and so colleges and universities draw upon related fields. Furthermore, while most colleges and universities feel compelled to have ethnic studies or American Indian Studies programs, they are prone not to invest heavily in program development. The typical American Indian Studies program is composed of several faculty who are appointed in outside departments, and whose research or interests lay related to American Indian issues. Departments control the promotions and evaluation of research, and most faculty must conform to the rules, procedures, and expectations of their departments and disciplines to maintain successful careers.

The interdepartmental model, where the faculty have different home departments and have only token associations with the American Indian Studies program or departments, is the most common form of organization.[27] Most programs are composed of faculty in non–Indian Studies doctoral degrees who have an expertise in American Indian culture, history, or other fields, and who are willing to teach or cross list their courses in American Indian Studies. This type of organization has the advantage of home departments for the faculty and connections with faculty and organizations outside of American Indian Studies. Faculty gain access to resources and contacts outside American Indian Studies, reducing the possibility of financial and administrative ghettoization. Most Indian Studies programs are organized along the interdepartmental model primarily for economic reasons; it is a way to use existing faculty and not have to invest in more faculty. The major drawback of the interdepartmental model is that there is a weak and underresourced faculty core, and it is difficult to develop a coherent Native perspective in the courses, since the faculty have diverse training and objectives. Faculty can gain tenure in a home department, and that is often considered a strength, but faculty are distracted by departmental demands, and their interests in advancement are usually tied to fulfilling departmental requirements, often leaving less attention for American Indian Studies. Interdepartmental programs are the main way that American Indian Studies programs are organized around the country, especially among smaller colleges that lack resources for a department. Coherent Indian Studies perspectives are hard to maintain and develop in the interdepartmental programs because of multiple disciplines, departmental demands, and generally short resources.

A few universities have adopted departments, and often many Indian faculty see the department as an ideal arrangement for Indian Studies. Departments can hire a core of committed faculty. Although, since few doctorates are awarded in American Indian Studies, it is in practice very hard to identify and hire the scholars who take an indigenous studies approach. Most prospective Indian Studies faculty are trained in mainstream disciplines and often have little training about American Indian topics, unless they choose to include research about Indians in their dissertation and research. Departments have the advantage of possibly creating a core group of faculty who share common understanding of the methods and goals of research and community relations that constitute the field of American Indian Studies. A disadvantage of the departmental model is that American Indian Studies may become ghettoized financially and administratively.

A third model might be called a mixed model, which is a combination of department and associated core faculty. The mixed model works best when it can exploit the strengths of the departmental and interdisciplinary models. Many interdepartmental models may evolve toward departments by creating a mixed model with a small number of core faculty located within a department, while affiliated teaching and research faculty may serve in other departments, cross listing a course within the American Indian Studies program. Mixed models may serve as transitions to departmental status, or as models in their own right. A few faculty can compose the core American Indian Studies faculty which give the program a coherent vision, research, and curriculum about American Indians and congruent with an indigenous paradigm. Other faculty may choose to remain within the discipline and departments of their graduate training, and associate with the American Indian Studies core faculty. The model has a core faculty, but also has faculty who have ties, interests, and contacts throughout the university that may be of value to the American Indian Studies core faculty and department. One of the most successful Indian Studies programs, at the University of Arizona, uses a mixed model of about a dozen core faculty, and another ten faculty who have other disciplinary departments but are committed to teaching and participation in the Indian Studies Department.

Another organizational feature of Indian Studies programs is their relation to ethnic studies departments or programs. Many American Indian Studies programs are embedded in ethnic studies programs. While one can make an argument for an association with ethnic studies, often on financial and university political grounds, the theoretical and policy interests and orientations of American Indian Studies are not compatible with the main ethnic studies approaches. Indigenous rights issues concerning sovereignty, land, self-government, and retention of culture are generally not central issues in the ethnic studies paradigms that emphasize diaspora, immigration, and renationalization. Often an indigenous studies approach has little in common with ethnic studies theory, methods, and policy, and therefore makes substantive research and teaching in common with ethnic studies very difficult, and disorienting for students who want to study indigenous studies approaches. An indigenous studies model is a very different theoretical, policy, and methodological path than the diaspora, immigration, and renationalization models of ethnic studies or race relations. Some notable programs, such as those in the three major Arizona universities, have avoided placing American Indian Studies within pan-ethnic organizations for their campuses. Perhaps because Arizona has a relatively large American Indian population and presence, and less of a racial and ethnic minority presence, the pan-ethnic model does not appeal in Arizona. In a large, ethnically diverse state like California, American Indian Studies centers at UCLA and UC Berkeley are associated with ethnic studies, and that arrangement seems natural for university administrators. The disadvantage of ethnic studies organizations is that the perspectives of an indigenous studies approach can be overwhelmed by the larger presence, resources, and theoretical views of the main ethnic groups.

The Fall of American Indian Studies

Unlike other ethnic studies programs, American Indian Studies has been dominated and controlled by a large body of pre-existing scholarship and scholarly disciplines. Elizabeth Cook-Lynn wrote an essay, "Who Stole American Indian Studies," that argues that Native American Studies has not been fully developed and has not lived up to its potential for supporting the sovereignty and nation-building interests of U.S. tribal communities.[28] The vision of Native American Studies is yet to be realized fully, and in many ways has a long way to go in organizational and intellectual development. In some senses, the intellectual control and dominance of several disciplines have inhibited the rival intellectual and social vision of American Indian Studies to emerge and present a full intellectual point of view. American Indian Studies has not been stolen: it has not been allowed to see the light of day. The Native American Studies paradigm has not been fully realized within the present-day intellectual and ethnic competition that characterized the intellectual and resource politics of contemporary American universities. The continued emphasis on race and ethnic identity in mainstream institutions tends to overshadow the less understood perspectives of an indigenous paradigm grounded in the cultures, sovereignty, identities, land, and nation building of indigenous peoples.

Native American Studies departments and programs are funded largely through private and state funding. The funding of American Indian Studies puts the administration of American Indian Studies programs directly in the hands of university administrators who for the most part are not well-schooled in the history, culture, or law affecting Native Americans. Natives are generally treated as a racial or ethnic group, since that view fits well in mainstream worldviews and everyday understandings. University administrators are mandated by the state government to provide services, research, and teaching under the direction of state guidance. Since American Indian Studies programs and departments are organized within the traditions, administrations, and funding of American universities, they are generally informed by American forms of organization and criteria for knowledge, teaching, and research. U.S. universities serve the culture and interests of U.S. society, and not those of American Indian communities and nations. There is great pressure to serve university guidelines and values, and unlike most university disciplines, American Indian Studies engages in research, teaching, and community relations that necessarily involve interests, cultural orientations, policies, and legal issues that are not in conformity with the values and interests that inform university purposes, goals, and orientations.

Since universities fund American Indian Studies, they tend to believe that they own them and can administer them in ways that serve the interests of the university and its mainstream non-Indian constituency. As long as Native American communities and nations are not in a position to fund their own universities, they will find it difficult to have their interests and viewpoints expressed in university research, policies, and teaching. Tribally controlled community colleges have gone a significant direction in the way of supporting Native community values and culture within the education pathways for Native students. Nevertheless, much of the tribal community college budget comes from federal government allocations from Congress. Tribally controlled community colleges need to conform to accreditation standards, but many have strong programs in their tribal culture, history, and language. It is unlikely that Native communities will anytime soon support universities, but some tribal communities are in a position to support Native Studies programs, departments, and centers. Contributing tribal communities could specify the purposes and outcomes of gifts to universities so that their contributions serve their values and interests. This is what gift givers generally do when supporting universities; they want to see that certain information is collected, or research, teaching, or policy development is undertaken as a result of the gift. Such gifts will support Native Studies perspectives by giving legitimacy and financial support for the perspectives and research that support tribal goals, values, and policy. Without significant financial support and explicit specification by tribal communities about their needs and interests in higher education, indigenous perspectives will have a harder time establishing themselves within the university and academic arenas.

In some ways, American Indian Studies has not risen far enough in the direction of stable paradigm to fall very far. The extensive non-Indian intellectual history and scholarship, the administrative dynamics of state universities, and funding constrain the development of American Indian Studies as a discipline and as strong university departments. In recent years these constraints have ameliorated. Many indigenous scholars are working toward defining an indigenous paradigm tribally, nationally, and internationally. While I have great faith that an internationally recognized indigenous studies paradigm will be worked out and gain broad acceptance, the university bureaucratic environment, weak resource support, the emphasis on race and ethnic paradigms over an indigenous paradigm, and the relegation of Indian Studies to serve general diversity interests for the university will continue to constrain, and often will prevent, full development of indigenous studies departments and programs at many universities. The struggle to establish indigenous studies departments, research programs, and full disciplinary status lies before us, and the movement will continue to be long and hard. As George Horse Capture[29] and Elizabeth Cook-Lynn[30] say that American Indian Studies has not seen the light of day, I think there must be agreement that they are right, and we must look for ways to establish American Indian Studies as a discipline that provides information and supportive policies that will help ensure the continuity of Native cultures and nations many centuries into the future.

Native American Studies Going Forward

Native American Studies is working toward forming its own discipline. There are several journals now established: *American Indian Quarterly*, *Wicazo Sa Review*, *American Indian Culture and Research Journal*, *Journal of American Indian Education*, and *Red Ink*. Relatively new professional organizations of American Indian scholars and the America Indian Studies Consortium have formed and meet annually. There is an ongoing discussion in the literature about how to define Native American Studies. American Indian communities have significantly different worldviews, social and political orders, and are cast in the position of protecting land, self-government, and generally nondifferentiated cultural forms and institutions. Contemporary scholarly disciplines in American universities reflect the highly organized, social-cultural processes and interests of U.S. society. And that is as it should be. In the same way, Native American Studies needs to reflect the social order, values, and interests of Native American communities. In holistic, institutionally nondifferentiated, indigenous communities, knowledge is inherently integrated with community, culture, and political and economic relations. Native epistemologies and cultural and institutional interests need to inform the practice and intellectual production of Native American Studies.

The search for a Native American discipline must necessarily look to international indigenous issues.[31] There are several hundred million people in the world who are living in indigenous communities. They do not share a common culture, race, or ethnicity, but they share common features, such as culturally holistic, institutionally nondifferentiated, self-governing societies engaged in negotiations for preserving land, self-government, and cultural integrity with a surrounding nation-state. The issues confronting indigenous peoples are not reducible to race, class, ethnicity, or other common analytical dimensions in use within mainstream disciplines. Races, classes, ethnicities, especially in the United States, do not aspire to the territorial, political, and cultural claims that are at the forefront for American Indian communities. Therefore direct racial, ethnic, and class analyses of American Indian communities do not measure important issues that are front and center for indigenous communities. The search for Native American Studies is a search for an indigenous paradigm, which may be defined primarily as a negotiation between indigenous claims to autonomy and nation-state efforts at incorporation and renationalization. An indigenous paradigm offers new ways to understand and analyze groups that heretofore have not been central to mainstream scholarship, in part owing to the absence of conceptual and analytical tools. A theory of society or social groups that includes indigenous perspectives and social processes will be more complete and promises deeper and wider understanding of the human experience.

Notes

1. Peter A. Kraus, " 'Transnationalism' or 'Renationalism'? The Politics of Cultural Identity in the European Union," in *The Conditions of Diversity in Multicultural Democracies*, ed. Alain-G. Gagnon, Montserrat Guibernau, and François Rocher (Montreal: McGill-Queen's University Press, 2004), 241–264.

2. Charles Wilkinson, *Blood Struggle: The Rise of Modern Indian Nations* (New York: Norton, 2005).

3. See Cadwallader Colden, *The History of the Five Indian Nations of Canada* (New York: Allentown Book, 1904); James Adair, *Adair's History of the American Indians*, ed. Samuel Williams (Johnson City, Tenn.: Wautauga Press, 1930); Edmond Atkins, *The Revolt of the Choctaw Indians*, Landowne Manuscript 809 (London Museum, 1750s); Edmond Atkins, *Indians of the Southern Colonial Frontier*, ed. Wilbur Jacobs (Columbia: University of South Carolina Press, 1954); and Henry Schoolcraft, *Indian Tribes of the United States* (Philadelphia: Lippincott, 1857).

4. Joseph François Lafitau, *Customs of the American Indians Compared with the Customs of Primitive Times*, vol. 1 (Toronto: Champlain Society, 1974), 293.

5. Donald Grinde and Bruce Johansen, *Exemplar of Liberty: Native America and the Evolution of Democracy* (Los Angeles: American Indian Studies Center, UCLA, 1991), 141–168.

6. Lewis Henry Morgan, *League of the Iroquois* (North Dighton, Mass.: J.G. Press, 1995).

7. Lewis Henry Morgan, *Ancient Society* (New York: Gorder Press, 1977).

8. See Friedrich Engels, *The Origin of the Family, Private Property, and the State* (Zurich: Hottingen, 1884).

9. As an example, see Thomas Buckley, *Standing Ground: Yurok Indian Spirituality 1850–1990* (Berkeley: University of California Press, 2002).

10. As an example, see James Mooney, *The Ghost Dance Religion and Wounded Knee* (New York: Dover, 1973).

11. Vine Deloria Jr., *Custer Died for Your Sins: An Indian Manifesto* (New York: Macmillan, 1973), 78–100.

12. Steve Pavlik, ed., *A Good Cherokee, a Good Anthropologist: Papers in Honor of Robert K. Thomas* (Los Angeles: American Indian Studies Center, UCLA, 1998).

13. See Thomas Biolsi, *Organizing the Lakota: The Political Economy of the New Deal on the Pine Ridge and Rosebud Reservations* (Tucson: University of Arizona Press, 1992) and Buckley, *Standing Ground*.

14. See Mary Riley, *Indigenous Intellectual Property Rights: Legal Obstacles and Innovative Solutions* (Walnut Creek, Calif.: AltaMira Press, 2004).

15. See David Hurst Thomas, *Skull Wars: Kennewick Man, Archaeology, and the Battle for Native American Identity* (New York: Basic Books, 2000), 209–221.

16. See Susan Lobo and Kurt Peters, eds., *American Indians and the Urban Experience* (Walnut Creek, Calif.: AltaMira Press, 2001).

17. See Darby C. Strapp and Michael S. Burney, *Tribal Cultural Resource Management: The Full Circle to Stewardship* (Walnut Creek, Calif.: AltaMira Press, 2002).

18. See Dee Brown, *Bury My Heart at Wounded Knee: An Indian History of the American West* (New York: Holt, Rinehart and Winston, 1970).

19. As an example, see Ronald N. Satz, *American Indian Policy in the Jacksonian Era* (Lincoln: University of Nebraska Press, 1975).

20. As examples, see William T. Hagan, *Taking Indian Lands: The Cherokee (Jerome) Commission 1889–1893* (Norman: University of Oklahoma Press, 2003); Frederick E. Hoxie, *Parading through History: The Making of the Crow Nation in America, 1805–1935* (New York: Cambridge

University Press, 1995); and Richard White, *The Middle Ground: Indians, Empires, and Republics in the Great Lakes Region, 1650–1815* (Cambridge: Cambridge University Press, 1991).

21. Russell Thornton, "Institutions and Intellectual Histories of Native American Studies," in *Studying Native America: Problems and Prospects*, ed. Russell Thornton (Madison: University of Wisconsin Press, 1998), 93–95.

22. As examples, see Georges Sioui, *Huron Wendat: The Heritage of the Circle*, trans. Jane Brierley (East Lansing: Michigan State University Press, 1999); and Bruce G. Trigger, *The Children of Aataentsic: A History of the Huron People to 1660* (Montreal: McGill-Queen's University Press, 1976).

23. As examples, see Anthony F. C. Wallace, *The Death and Rebirth of the Seneca* (New York: Vintage Books, 1972); J. B. Herring, *Kenekuk: The Kickapoo Prophet* (Lawrence: University Press of Kansas, 1988); and Robert H. Ruby and John A. Brown, *John Slocum and the Indian Shaker Church* (Norman: University of Oklahoma Press, 1996).

24. David Hurst Thomas, "The Skull Wars Revisited," presented at American Indian Nations: Yesterday, Today, and Tomorrow: A Symposium, Great Falls, Montana, 2005.

25. Elizabeth Cook-Lynn, "Who Stole Native American Studies," *Wicazo Sa Review* 12, no. 1 (1997): 9–28.

26. Duane Champagne and Jay Stauss, eds., "Defining Indian Studies through Stories and Nation Building" in *Native American Studies in Higher Education* (Walnut Creek, Calif.: AltaMira Press, 2002); and Susan Guyette and Charlotte Heth, *Issues for the Future of American Indians Studies* (Los Angeles: American Indian Studies Center, UCLA, 1985), 1–15.

27. Guyette and Heth, *Issues for the Future*, 74–76.

28. Cook-Lynn, "Who Stole Native American Studies," 9–28.

29. George Horse Capture, personal communication, Great Falls, Montana, 2005.

30. Cook-Lynn, "Who Stole Native American Studies," 24–27.

31. Duane Champagne and Ismael Abu-Saad, eds., *The Future of Indigenous Peoples: Strategies for Survival and Development* (Los Angeles: American Indian Studies Center, UCLA, 2003).

Bibliography

Adair, James. *Adair's History of the American Indians*. Ed. Samuel Williams. Johnson City, Tenn.: Wautauga Press, 1930.

Atkins, Edmond. *The Revolt of the Choctaw Indians*. Landowne Manuscript 809. London Museum, 1750s.

———. *Indians of the Southern Colonial Frontier*. Ed. Wilbur Jacobs. Columbia: University of South Carolina Press, 1954.

Biolsi, Thomas. *Organizing the Lakota: The Political Economy of the New Deal on the Pine Ridge and Rosebud Reservations*. Tucson: University of Arizona Press, 1992.

Brown, Dee. *Bury My Heart at Wounded Knee: An Indian History of the American West*. New York: Holt, Rinehart and Winston, 1970.

Buckley, Thomas. *Standing Ground: Yurok Indian Spirituality, 1850–1990*. Berkeley: University of California Press, 2002.

Champagne, Duane, and Ismael Abu-Saad, eds. *The Future of Indigenous Peoples: Strategies for Survival and Development*. Los Angeles: UCLA American Indian Studies Center, 2003.

Champagne, Duane, and Joseph Stauss, eds. *Native American Studies in Higher Education: Models for Collaboration between Universities and Indigenous Nations*. Walnut Creek, Calif.: AltaMira Press, 2002.

Colden, Cadwallader. *The History of the Five Indian Nations of Canada*. New York: Allentown Book, 1904.

Cook-Lynn, Elizabeth. "Who Stole Native American Studies." *Wicazo Sa Review* 12, no. 1 (1997): 9–28.

Deloria, Vine, Jr. *Custer Died for Your Sins: An Indian Manifesto*. New York: Macmillan, 1973.

Engels, Friedrich. *The Origin of the Family, Private Property, and the State*. Zurich: Hottingen, 1884.

Grinde, Donald A., Jr., and Bruce E. Johansen. *Exemplar of Liberty: Native America and the Evolution of Democracy*. Los Angeles: UCLA American Indians Studies Center, 1991.

Guyette, Susan, and Charlotte Heth. *Issues for the Future of American Indians Studies*. Los Angeles: UCLA American Indian Studies Center, 1985.

Hagan, William T. *Taking Indian Lands: The Cherokee (Jerome) Commission, 1889–1893*. Norman: University of Oklahoma Press, 2003.

Herring, J. B. *Kenekuk: The Kickapoo Prophet*. Lawrence: University Press of Kansas, 1988.

Horse Capture, George. Personal communication, Great Falls, Montana, 2005.

Hoxie, Frederick E. *Parading through History: The Making of the Crow Nation in America 1805–1935*. New York: Cambridge University Press, 1995.

Kraus, Peter A. " 'Transnationalism' or 'Renationalization'? The Politics of Cultural Identity in the European Union." In *Conditions of Diversity in Multinational Democracies*, ed. Alain-G. Gagnon, Montserrat Guibernau, and François Rocher, 243–264. Montreal: McGill-Queen's University Press, 2004.

Lafitau, Joseph-François. *Customs of the American Indians Compared with Customs of Primitive Times*. Toronto: Champlain Society, 1974.

Lobo, Susan, and Kurt Peters, eds. *American Indians and the Urban Experience*. Walnut Creek, Calif.: AltaMira Press, 2001.

Mooney, James. *The Ghost Dance Religion and Wounded Knee*. New York: Dover Publications, 1973.

Morgan, Henry Lewis. *Ancient Society*. New York: Gorder Press, 1977.

———. *The League of the Iroquois*. North Dighton, Mass.: J.G. Press, 1995.

Pavlik, Steve. *A Good Cherokee, a Good Anthropologist: Papers in Honor of Robert K. Thomas*. Los Angeles: UCLA American Indians Studies Center, 1998.

Riley, Mary. *Indigenous Intellectual Property Rights: Legal Obstacles and Innovative Solutions*. Walnut Creek, Calif.: AltaMira Press, 2004.

Ruby, Robert H., and John A. Brown. *John Slocum and the Indian Shaker Church*. Norman: University of Oklahoma Press, 1996.

Satz, Ronald. *American Indian Policy in the Jacksonian Era*. Lincoln: University of Nebraska Press, 1975.

Schoolcraft, Henry. *Indian Tribes of the United States*. Philadelphia: Lippincott, 1857.

Sioui, Georges. *Huron-Wendat: The Heritage of the Circle*. Trans. Jane Brierley. East Lansing: Michigan State University Press, 1999.

Strapp, Darby C., and Michael S. Burney. *Tribal Cultural Resource Management: The Full Circle to Stewardship*. Walnut Creek, Calif.: AltaMira Press, 2002.

Thomas, David Hurst. *Skull Wars: Kennewick Man, Archaeology, and the Battle for Native American Identity*. New York: Basic Books, 2000.

———. "Skull Wars: Revisited." Presented at American Indian Nations: Yesterday, Today, and Tomorrow: A Symposium, Great Falls, Montana, July 2, 2005.

Thornton, Russell. "Institutional and Intellectual Histories of Native American Studies." In *Studying Native America: Problems and Prospects*, ed. Russell Thornton, 79–110. Madison: University of Wisconsin Press. 1998.

Trigger, Bruce G. *The Children of Aataentsic: A History of the Huron People to 1660*. Montreal: McGill-Queen's University Press, 1976.

Wallace, Anthony F. C. *The Death and Rebirth of the Seneca*. New York: Vintage Books, 1972.

Weibel-Orlando, Joan. *Indian Country, L.A. Maintaining Ethnic Community in Complex Society*. Urbana: University of Illinois Press, 1999.

White, Richard. *The Middle Ground: Indians, Empires, and Republics in the Great Lakes Region, 1650–1815*. Cambridge: Cambridge University Press, 1991.

Wilkinson, Charles. *Blood Struggle: The Rise of Modern Indian Nations*. New York: Norton, 2005.

MEDIA

IV

Native News: "Somehow"

17

MARK TRAHANT

I WANT TO START WITH A LITTLE STORY. After you hear what I have to say, you might wonder how Tim Johnson and I could view the world so differently. My wife is Navajo, and we were married in a traditional Navajo wedding. The way that works, there is a time when people from the community come together to give you advice for the future. There are two corns— a yellow corn and a white corn—which are made into mush, and when you eat the mush, you are married. Well, people came to give us advice, and we were crowded into this small hogan in Blue Canyon, Arizona, and it was very crowded inside. In the front was a friend of mine by the name of Jefferson Begay. Jeff cleared his throat to say something. Just at that instant, just when he was about to say something, his wife who was sitting behind him gently pressed her knee into his back, so he didn't say anything. There was a feast outside, and people were starting to get hungry, and again things were starting to wind down, and again people were telling us things, and again Jeff thought it was time to say something. So this time he cleared his throat a little louder, and at that instant, this time with more force, the knee goes into his back, so he doesn't say anything. Well, people are hungry at this point and the feast is outside and it is winding down and Jefferson clears his throat, this time really loudly, and this time with a great deal of force, that knee goes into his back so he doesn't say anything. They were leaving the hogan, and Ella Begay turned to Jefferson and said: "Jefferson, why didn't you say something? I kept kneeing you in the back to say something." He then admitted that he was about to stress the importance of communication in marriage. I like to tell this story to journalists because so often with the stories we are following, if we can't pull back and look at the bigger picture, so often we miss what it's about.

I remember when I was a kid, we went to Idaho Falls, which is the big town not far from Fort Hall, and there was a group of Cub Scouts, or something, and we toured the paper and we were sitting around after the tour. The editor came out to talk to us, and someone asked: "What does it take for one of us to get on page one?" Being of that age, we had great morbid thoughts about "What if we shot somebody? Would that be on the front page? If we had a car crash on the way home and wiped out eight cars, would that be page one?" We kept escalating it until we thought what would it take to get on page one, and he didn't give us an answer that we felt was satisfactory. Whatever we came up with, it wasn't going to be page one. I think about that in my professional generation, people my age, and how much the world has changed, because in my era as a kid, and this was in the 1960s, it was not common to see stories from Fort Hall on page one. Fast forward to these days and it is not uncommon at all to see stories of Fort Hall on page one. From Fort Hall, a kid might think: "What happens if I'm elected governor? Would that be on page one?" Larry EchoHawk ran for governor. He didn't win, but he changed what stories would be covered by the media on the reservation. Other stories that are now routine that make page one are something that people think about. For a long time, at least in Arizona and New Mexico, Notah Begay was on page one. A sports story, an athlete, a successful story, something that was so important that it determines what is on page one. In Idaho, as in many places, gambling has become a page one story. Where I live in Washington, it has been a huge story, particularly with efforts to roll it back in combination of efforts including one successfully stopped.

Again, thinking how the world has changed, some of these changes came about because of the growth and sophistication of the tribal press. You think of papers like *Navajo Times* and the *Cherokee Phoenix*, which have not only put together their own voice, but they went through the process of creating a new tribal law that allowed them to do the legal structure that protects their freedoms. That's pretty extraordinary when you think about it—not only do the papers have a voice, but they went through to take the next step and created a whole mechanism about how those papers were going to be regarded under tribal law. The same could be said for *Indian Country Today* and its ownership as an economic enterprise.

There is also a huge growth in electronic media. I think if you look back at the history of media at least in the 1970s, the big missed opportunity is television. There were a few documentaries and a few this and that, but really Indians never broke into television in a way that changed the story-telling. But the Internet is not like that at all. With the Internet, from the beginning, people have been finding ways to tell the stories in pretty remarkable ways, ranging from Indiansz.com to individual tribal zines that are produced by one person down to the block level. Sometimes, tribal media has become sort of a tip sheet to mainstream media, which is something that didn't occur thirty years ago. A lot of tribal newspapers, as soon as they are published, people in the big city next door read them and figure out what stories they ought to be covering and then send someone to cover them.

I think perhaps the most significant thing that has changed in the decades since I went on that field trip was the number of bylines you see from Indian Country. When I was with the *Navajo Times Today*, it was a daily newspaper and we had an election. This gentleman got elected whose first mission was to fire us all. When I got fired, that is when I went into mainstream, and at that time, I had just been elected president of the Native American Journalist Association (NAJA). At that point, there was nobody else in NAJA, on the board or a member, who was working in mainstream media. I was doing something that hadn't been thought of as being part of the tribal journalism experience. Now, you go to a convention of NAJA and it is about half-and-half or three-quarters mainstream and the growth has just been phenomenal. I will tell you just about a couple of people.

I met Jodi Rave when she was a student at the University of Colorado, and it was the first year they had the convention called Unity, which was bringing together journalists of different minority groups into one. She was a college student and she was doing really well, working on the student newspaper, and you could just see this career getting started. A few years later, I ran into Jodi again. I was with the Salt Lake Tribune Company and I was up in Moscow as the publisher, and she was applying for a job at Salt Lake, so I was telling her who she needed to talk to, and doing other door-opening. Well, she got the job as assistant business editor and could have just done mainstream stuff, but that is not what she wanted to do. Her goal, going into the newspaper business, was to write about tribal affairs, and she wanted to bring the larger story to Native communities. Knowing that, she kept it in the back of her mind, and Lee Enterprises, which most of the people in Montana know about, called her up and said they wanted to hire her and started to talk to her about what jobs they had in mind. She shook her head and said: "I don't want to do that. If you want to hire me, I want to cover Indian Country as a beat and I want you to give me the resources to do it." They did—first in Lincoln and now in Missoula. They created an Indian beat, and she can travel anywhere in the region. She has the resources to cover the stories the way she wants to because she had this idea of what she wanted to do and knew where she was going with her career and she was able to put those things together.

Kara Briggs is another example. She is a Yakima. She started at several suburban newspapers and she worked her way—she was in Wisconsin when I first met her, and a couple of other papers, finally going to the *Portland Oregonian*. And lately she has been writing for *Indian Country Today* an extraordinary series about her experience with breast cancer. There is a long list of people who have changed Indian Country from that perspective.

Someone else I would like to tell you about is someone who has done it through sports. This is Eugene Tapahe. Eugene is Navajo, and I knew his uncle pretty well, so I saw him growing up as a kid. He was working at the *Navajo Times* in a staff job when ESPN called and asked if he would like an internship. It's a bit odd to go from a staff job to an internship, but ESPN was where he really wanted to be, so he said yes. He went to New York City and he was working with *ESPN*, the magazine, and he was surprised to learn that ESPN had never done a story on the controversy on sports mascots. So he pitched the story as "This is something I really want to tell." He researched the topic, and a day went by with no reaction from his bosses, then a week. Then he got up the courage to go ask the producer what was up. The producer told him: "I haven't read that, but it's there, but I will." He implied to give up on the idea—that it wasn't going to happen. But he went over his head and went to the senior producer's office. He said: "I'm only an intern and I'm only going to be here a couple of months, but I have this story that I really think is important. It ought to be told and it ought to be told by ESPN. Will you read what I propose?" Well, his courage paid off, the story was assigned, and the project was a go. A producer was assigned, and they went out and told the story about the Washington football franchise and others in a way that was the first time ever. ESPN got people to explain things in a way of context.

Indian Country is full of such stories, stories that ought to be told with respect. There are complicated histories that defy traditional graphical journalism, so it takes people with a sense of the history to be around to be able to say, "Have you thought of this?" that is not part of the straight story. I think this is where most journalism misses the mark, because we don't get the context right. I will give you an example with the Indian gambling initiative that has been on the ballot the past few years. It is a good example of the gambling story that the context is often missing in. The cartoonist I worked with at *Navajo Times* was Vincent Craig, who has the great comic strip "Mutton Man." But he also has a phrase he uses that I like, and it is "Somehow." "Somehow" is a phrase used in Navajo Country when things are just right—maybe a little bit screwy. The story he uses in a song is about a woman named Rita who asks a police officer to arrest someone for looking at her "somehow." So many of these stories that are "somehow" are told with just a little missing element—they are "somehow." For example, on the gaming story, a usual line is that tribal gaming has become so much more important because so many jobs depend on it. In northern Idaho, for example, tribal gaming is the second largest employer, replacing natural resources and other industries that were long part of the economy. That is a good story, but the "somehow" part of it is the context is left out by us in the press weaving the story together in the larger picture, and that is something we need to work on. One of these days, someone is going to write the story about the strain of gaming initiatives on the state ballot—not just one, but how they all fit together. This is an effort that attracted one fairly positive, making the case for fairness in jobs. I have not seen that story told yet with a national context.

Truth be told, most journalists are not well equipped to uncover major trends that lie below the surface. It's just not part of what we do. Consider this: when the huge immigration wave occurred during the 1990s, most of the story was told after the U.S. Census told us about it as a big deal. Every paper you can think of missed the story. What was reported was the death of cities when, in fact, something very different was happening. We just didn't have a way of getting to that story. That type of disconnect happens all of the time to journalists. We are very good at focusing on an event—something that happens instantly—but we are really lousy at context, pulling back and looking at what the trends mean.

Gambling, I think, is an exact example of that problem. What the press has missed over and over is that America is having a love affair with gambling. It is not Indian gambling, but it is gambling. We haven't been able to pull back and look at the bigger picture of how it is changing our society. Gambling is more popular than sports, movies, or attending church, but it is rarely put in that context. Writing about gambling is one of the things I do in my column. I like to do it as a fight between bookies. It is often which bookies are fighting over which resources, rather than the bigger picture.

This is a great time to challenge journalism. I guess that is the message I want to leave you today, because many journalism institutions are going through a lot of self-introspection about the future and where we are going in the future. This is a good time to call people up and find out where to assign people and where the resources are. So often, how stories are determined is a question of resources. Where do you have your people? When I first became an editor, one of the things that amazed me is that most editors said they didn't want a lot of crime coverage, but yet they had a lot of reporters hanging out at the police shop, so we ended up with a lot of crime coverage. By moving people away from that, you could shift it to other areas. Indian Country has got to make the pitch that there are other areas and get the people moved to that.

I just want to tell one more story. Probably the story that I thought represented both the good and the bad of media in a lot of ways was when the hantavirus episode broke out in the southwest. Here was a disease that in the very beginning nobody knew what it was. It was also when, for the first time, most of the Indians working for mainstream media were called and told: "You go on this story." In fact, I remember having coffee with Hattie Kauffman of CBS News saying there was this disease and all we know about it is that it is killing Indians. So, what does the media do? It sends all the Indians. Yet, because of that, the wording was very different than it might have been before that. *USA Today*, for example, was a newspaper without any Indians working for it, yet it was the only paper that came up with a name for the disease. They called it the "Navajo flu." I remember a meeting, and I was the senior editor there, and at that meeting I decided that I was going to make the case that, as a policy, our newspaper would not cover any of the funerals involved in this episode. I had friends who were Navajo, and I went through the reasons why the newspaper shouldn't even send reporters to the funerals. As part of my preparation, I went through and did database searches of the coverage of legionnaire's disease, which was another mystery disease that had similar patterns. So I went into the news meeting with a stack of documents and said, "I don't think we should cover funerals and here's why," and started going through the case. Even before I could finish the case, everybody agreed with me. As I said, I was a senior editor, so maybe it was unfair, but that sort of thinking wouldn't have happened a generation ago. It was because, on that story, there were seventeen Native Americans as line reporters, producers, or somehow involved in the process. I think that changed the story-telling for all of it, of how that story was covered.

Press Coverage of American Indian Issues

18

TIM JOHNSON

IN THIS DAY AND AGE, I can't think of a more crucial discussion to have. Why is this topic so important? Because the future of a continued and vibrant American Indian existence is linked to how well the American public and its policymakers are informed about American Indian realities. History serves as a looking glass not only into the past, but also into the present and future.

With history as our guide, it must be understood that the challenges and threats to American Indian freedom remain and, in fact, grow in direct correlation to Indian success. Let me repeat that—threats to American Indian freedom grow in direct correlation to Indian success.

During the past few decades, Indian Country has achieved significant advances in tribal self-governance and self-determination. The most publicly visible outcome of these advances has been the growth of tribal economic development—in other words, increased Indian wealth.

Often overlooked in the historical process of dispossession, whereby Indians have been removed from their lands, resources, markets, self-governance rights, and freedoms, is the role the media has played—the role of enabler. In virtually every instance in which dispossession has occurred, preceding it was a public discourse of some sort that contained within it misinformation and rationalizations that served the interests of those who wanted to take what Indians had.

There is a historic formula for this process. It goes like this:

Misinformation × Media discourse = Public policy (theft of Indian land)

Misinformation × Media discourse = Public policy (destruction of Indian rights)

Misinformation × Media discourse = Public policy (theft of Indian monies/markets)

Misinformation × Media discourse = Public policy (theft of Indian identity)

Historic Background

Why is it important and essential that Indian peoples get their stories told accurately in the media? Well, let's pull out our history guide. There exist mountains of information in newspaper archives across this country that provide insight into how the press shaped public perceptions of American Indians and paved the way for human rights abuses, atrocities, and the theft of Indian assets. Writes columnist Suzan Shown Harjo in the pages of *Indian Country Today*: "Historically, the American mainstream press has been our critic, missing and ignoring our story, or deliberately getting it wrong."[1] And they have been doing it for hundreds of years.

In her column, Suzan cites some compelling examples and I'd like to share just a few with you today. She writes that:

> Greed for Indian land, rather than Indian success, was the trigger for negative reporting in the 1800s and 1900s. Most newspaper families—such as the Hearst publishing empire that was built on Black Hills gold—owned the mines and railroads and were an integral part of westward expansion. True believers in the manifest destiny of whites to own the "new world," they advocated and instigated violence against Indian people who stood in their way.
>
> Newspapers were essential to the federal government's 1880–1934 "civilization" campaign to eradicate Indian religions, languages and traditions, including ceremonial dancing. Most of the stories were written in what one federal circular promoted as a "careful propaganda" to "educate public opinion against the dance."
>
> . . . *The Rocky Mountain News* . . . started a drumbeat against Cheyenne Dog Soldiers and other "hostiles" that culminated in the Sand Creek Massacre of a peace camp of Cheyenne elders, pregnant women and children on Nov. 29, 1864. *The News* celebrated the "Battle" of Sand Creek, lauding the Colorado Volunteers' "Bloody Thirdsters" as having "covered themselves with glory."
>
> [Even though] a Senate Special Committee on Indian Affairs investigated federal–Indian relations and reported in 1867 that white aggression was the cause of most armed confrontations with Indians, most editorials dismissed the important report. Newspapers continued to demonize Indians and aggressive whites took more Indian land and murdered more Indian people.[2]
>
> Lt. Col. George Armstrong Custer, on Nov. 27, 1868, invaded Cheyenne land that had been secured by treaty only one year before in what is now Oklahoma. . . . "The End of the Indian War and Ring" was the way *The New York Times* announced the Washita Massacre. . . . *The Times* editorialized: "The

truth is, that Gen. Custer, in defeating and killing Black Kettle, put an end to one of the most troublesome and dangerous characters on the Plains." . . .

L. Frank Baum, the author of the *Wizard of Oz*, was also an editor of *The Aberdeen Saturday Pioneer*. His anti-Indian writings in 1890–1891 were especially virulent. Baum and other newspaper editors in the area contributed to the climate of fear and hatred that led to the massacre at Wounded Knee on December 29, 1890. In one editorial, Baum referred to Indian people as "a pack of whining curs who lick the hand that smites them."

There is one particular quote that I think deserves great attention. Wrote Baum in an editorial: "The Whites, by law of conquest, by justice of civilization, are masters of the American continent, and the best safety of the frontier settlements will be secured by the total annihilation of the few remaining Indians. Why not annihilation? Their glory has fled, their spirit broken, their manhood effaced; better that they die than live the miserable wretches that they are."[3]

Sound a little extreme and, perhaps, unconscionable in today's world? Well, you might want to read the recent Supreme Court decision in the *Sherrill* case.[4] Pay particular attention to Footnote 1.

These are very compelling examples and Suzan continues in her piece to list others. But they are just the tip of the iceberg—an iceberg that has never melted.

Contemporary Media Examples

This historic relationship between media and policy, this dynamic of the media establishing the perceptions and metaphors that define American Indians, has played itself out quite visibly during the past five years. There has been a dearth of slanted coverage and commentary of the Indian world, much of which can be characterized as a backlash, but a backlash against what? Against American Indian success—of course.

Much of the contemporary wave of biased press perceptions about American Indians emerged from the *Boston Globe* in 2001, whose inaccurate reporting was further advanced, in classic derivative fashion, by the *Wall Street Journal*. In a *Journal* editorial of March 1, 2002, that dealt with New York Indian casino issues, the editorial used stereotypical images to strike out at tribal developments. In an editorial, Governor George Pataki was described as New York's "new Indian chief and gambling boss."[5] The appellation of the title "chief" is familiar to every American Indian who has ever been stereotyped, in the workplace or other public situations. Being called "chief" for Indians, when delivered with the same derisive tone as the *Journal*'s editorial, is pejorative and insulting.

Later in the editorial, the *Journal* also calls Pataki the "Great White Father," another term we had thought hackneyed to death long ago. This name-calling in a mainstream newspaper is belittling and prejudicial, and it marks the editorial down to the lowest of journalistic levels. But the *Journal* didn't stop there. Its gratuitous insults were matched by its dishonest arguments. Apparently driven by a nearly religious hostility toward Indian gaming, the editorial made the point that gaming enterprises are bad, bringing "lowlifes and organized crime, drugs, prostitution, loan sharking and money laundering. The mob infiltrates and corruption in local government often follows." This is misinformation of the highest order.

The public perception the Journal *sought to manufacture, mixed in with a heavy application of condescending stereotypes, is that Indian gaming is bad and must be addressed.* Indian leaders across the country condemned the *Wall Street Journal*.

One highly contentious example of the mainstream media fashioning the public's perception was a two-part series published by *Time Magazine* later in 2002. This venerable weekly launched perhaps the most controversial work in its December 16 cover story, "Look Who's Cashing In at Indian Casinos."[6] In what was billed as a "special investigation," the thirteen-page spread served up negative articles about Indian gaming as an economic development rotor for Indian country. A thick layer of antitribal attitude permeated the story, which was intended to prove, once and for all, that Indian peoples and their self-governance rights are unfair, corrupt, and inept. The piece was so far out of balance and gave such a negative take on tribal reality that it seemed strategically intended to directly challenge the positive concept of hard-won tribal gains. Most tribal leaders had a problem with the series' lack of context.

As a result of the *Time* series, members of Congress called for hearings on tribal gaming and federal recognition. Reported Suzan Harjo in *Indian Country Today*, Senator Daniel Inouye, who was vice chairman of the Senate Committee on Indian Affairs at the time, warned tribal leaders at a convention of the National Congress of American Indians. Inouye told the group that their Indian ancestors would say, "You've done well, you've stood tall—you've succeeded." But with success has come a "whole legion of critics," he said, counting *Time Magazine* among them. "Don't let the critics tell your story," said Inouye.[7]

The public perception fostered by the Time *series was one of Indian tribal recognition, economic growth, and advancement as creating more problems than solutions. The few bad examples the reporters highlighted—amid hundreds of successes that went untold—were to become the prevailing public perception.*

Then, of course, there is national political commentator Robert Novak, who still has not apologized to American Indians for his incorrect reporting in late 2003 and early 2004. In another classic case of derivative reporting, Novak resurrected a well-demolished rumor: that South Dakota Senator Tim Johnson's election to the U.S. Senate in 2002 over Republican candidate John Thune was fraudulently "stolen by stuffing ballot boxes on Indian reservations." Novak made these remarks January 6 while appearing on CNN's *Cross-*

fire. Novak had already made a similar remark on *Crossfire,* December 13, declaring: "The Indians, they got the phony Indian votes out there."[8]

Novak holds to his discredited story, even though South Dakota Secretary of State Chris Nelson, a Republican, confirmed that no illegal votes were cast as a result of the very limited voter-registration problems. Nevertheless, the conservative media continued to roll out this false version of events for obvious partisan purposes.

The false perception Novak and others planted in the mainstream discourse was that Indians stole an election—one of the few elections where the Indian vote was, in fact, decisive.

Of course, who can forget California Governor Arnold Schwarzenegger's relatively recent comment that California's Indians are, quote: "ripping *us* off" (emphasis added). "*Us*" meaning non-Indians apparently. You know, Us and Them—Them being the Indians.[9]

Whether spoken out of ignorance or strategically delivered, the result was the same: to reverse public perception about the tribes in California and apply a lever to extract ever more concessions from California Indians with respect to their gaming compacts.

His comment was and is remarkable in at least two respects. First, it lays waste to the language and spirit of the Indian Gaming Regulatory Act—that was crafted to help develop tribal governments, not to bail out state governments in fiscal crisis. Second, it slanders history. Anyone who has studied the brutality experienced by California Indians would find such a statement reprehensible and unacceptable. I don't believe the governor has ever apologized for the comment.

With the assistance of the media the public perception created by Schwarzenegger is that Indians are the bad guys (and certainly the fall guys) who are at least partly responsible for the state's own massive financial problems. But allow me to editorialize on this point: *Every dollar given to a state is one less dollar that could and should be put to better use in Indian country.*

Now, here is a much more sophisticated example of a brewing public perception discourse. Many of you may know of George F. Will. In some respects, Will is regarded as a master thinker on the conservative flank of national pundits. He has a way of lining up his arguments that makes a reader feel intelligent just for following the logic and the obscure references. Indeed, it takes an effort to fully understand the high erudition and sheer intelligence of Will's prose. As *Indian Country Today's* editorialists have scribed, "As one digests it [Will's viewpoint], however, the message often brings up its own difficulty."[10]

Reading further from the *Indian Country Today* editorial on the famed pundit:

In one of his 2002 columns, Will makes the arguments for the view that a uni-cultural America, one with a "unified" point of view, as one of the great results of the 9/11 tragedy. He makes this sound as if this were the return of the natural order of things, that somehow this foreshadowed an America made up of "unified individuals again," rather than, as he expresses it, "coagulated groups." By "coagulated groups," columnist Will means the varieties of cultures and subcultures in American life, some organized as political entities, from nonprofit organizations to interest groups, and, of course, potentially including the reality of American Indian nations, perhaps the ultimate "special interest groups" in some minds. This creative and growing public media discourse, the concept of "One Nation" or "Equal Citizenship," is a major theme of the anti-Indian movement. It is designed to diminish and abolish the inherent self-governing freedoms of American Indians.[11]

The underlying message here is that mainstream American culture is the most legitimate of cultures within the nation. Never mind that American Indians were self-governing peoples long before Europeans arrived.
These are but a few contemporary examples of perception-building and metaphor-crafting going on within the media discourse that are affecting American Indians.

What to Do

So what do we do about this lingering problem? How do we get stories into the mainstream press that are accurate and fair? How do we tell our own stories?

Two weeks ago, at a round table gathering of the new American Indian Policy and Media Initiative at Buffalo State College, several prominent Indian journalists of long standing met together with policy makers—leaders with experience in tribal government and the federal government—to examine this issue of how media perceptions influence and shape public policies that affect American Indians.

The American Indian Policy and Media Institute (AIPMI) is an independent public policy research initiative dedicated to the education and projection of American Indian historical, legal, and contemporary realities within the mainstream public's awareness, knowledge, and generally held perceptions. It has been formed to help reconcile the knowledge divide that exists between those who have disparate understandings of the historical, cultural, and legal realities that define and empower American Indian peoples and their governments.

Distinguished Viejas Chairman Anthony Pico delivered a strong warning to those assembled at the round table. He said the ability of American Indians to tell their stories in the media was no less than a matter of survival.

"The future preservation and prosperity of American Indians," stated Chairman Pico, "will be decided in the court of public opinion. How we are viewed in the eyes of the nation—and our ability to deliver our message to the public, the press, elected officials and federal and state policy makers—is of crucial importance to generations of American Indians to come."

Pico stressed that if tribal governments fail to tell their story and promote an accurate image of today's Indian peoples, "the pillars of economic, social, governmental and political success tribes have begun building over the past thirty years will come crashing down."

Senator Ben Nighthorse Campbell, who was also in attendance, made the observation that intense media competition in recent years has resulted in a general erosion of objectivity. Many "news" stories, he said, offer very little in the way of actual news, substituting instead an array of opinions from various sources. The result is too much editorializing and not enough objective reporting.

"The media must portray positions based upon both sides of the issue. Who gets to define who you are? As Indian people, we must define ourselves," said Senator Campbell.

So how do we do that? Here are some of the recommendations advocated at the Buffalo think-tank:

- Tribes need to write more for themselves. Productivity is the key. Beyond the issuance of press releases, tribal leaders and tribal communicators must write regularly, op-ed columns and cultural columns, for direct submission to local, regional, and national newspapers.
- Tribes can advertise directly in newspapers to get their messages across on a consistent basis.
- Tribes need to "get beyond" the taboo of speaking to the press and build aggressive public and media relations teams.
- Tribes need to hire journalists with solid newsroom experience to tell their stories.
- Tribes must reach out to newspapers' business pages to stress the job creation and economic benefits of tribal business operations, rather than allowing such coverage to remain with political reporters.
- Tribes must make more efficient use of public contacts, to educate patrons who visit their businesses. Millions of opportunities are being wasted every year by American Indian businesses that fail to inform their customers about American Indian governance.
- Indian Country must continue to encourage young American Indians to enter the field of journalism.
- Tribes must build proactive relations with individual local reporters— this was seen as more useful than simply speaking with editorial boards—and help educate those reporters about tribal culture, tribal history, and treaty rights.[12]

Educate America or Perish—*this is the clarion call to this generation.*
Make no mistake, Indian Country. In a cyclical repeat of American history, another attack on tribal rights is coming on full steam. The long, hard fight for the hearts and minds of the American public on the economic reconstruction of Indian Country is not yet guaranteed—not by a long shot. Brace for it, strategize collectively, dedicate and apply significant resources, develop national campaigns to get tribal perspectives heard, get ready to fight the forthcoming media stampede to misrepresent this new era of Indian political empowerment and economic recovery. Every experienced tribal leader cognizant of America's legacy of distorting Indian history and of stealing Indian assets knew this day would come again.

"Public policy is hugely influenced by the media," Senator Campbell stated at the Buffalo round table. *"Tribes must tell their stories. We're making progress, but we have a long way to go."*

The currents gathering in this effort are as wide and voluminous as is the work and legacy of those before us who understood these fundamental truths: *Indian nations are the primary nations of these lands. From our own original societies and cultures did American Indian peoples grow and prosper. Indian nations have every right to our inherent liberty and freedom as confirmed by our own tribal histories, by our own inherent truths, founded upon our primacy on these lands we call Indian Country.*

Notes

1. Suzan Shown Harjo, "A History of Critics Getting Our Story Wrong," *Indian Country Today*, March 3, 2003.
2. Existence of this Senate report—more than 130 years ago—is a very interesting historical footnote and is to be remembered when we come around to a discussion of contemporary issues.
3. Harjo, "A History of Critics."
4. *City of Sherrill, New York v. Oneida Indian Nation*, C. Ct., March 29, 2005.
5. "Big Chief Pataki," *Wall Street Journal*, March 1, 2002, Eastern Ed., A14.
6. *Time*, December 16, 2002, 44–58.
7. Harjo, "A History of Critics."
8. Quoted in "Editor's Report," *Indian Country Today*, January 30, 2004.
9. Quoted in "Editor's Report," *Indian Country Today*, October 29, 2004.
10. "George F. Will's Homogeneous America," *Indian Country Today*, March 31, 2002.
11. Ibid.
12. A roundtable discussion was held on the campus of Buffalo State College on June 15, 2005. The above comments and recommendations came out of that discussion.

POLITICS AND LAW

V

Voting Rights in Indian Country　　19

JANINE B. PEASE

V OTING RIGHTS IN INDIAN COUNTRY pertains to the participation
of American Indians, or Native Americans, in the federal, state, and
local election process. American Indian voting rights are complicated
by legal, historical, and cultural structures that pose formidable barriers to
their full participation in the civic life of the country. The Voting Rights Acts
has added complexity to the situation. American Indians have struggled to
maintain a separate existence as tribal nations, while other American minorities worked to achieve integration into American society. Over the past
twenty years, however, Indian Country has been the scene of extensive litigation over voting rights, at the school board, city, county, and legislative district levels. American Indians make up 1.4 percent of the nation's population,
but are 1 percent to 6 percent of the voters in twelve western states. Height-
ened American Indian voter participation and highly contested elections have
made Indian Country a battleground for American voting rights.

This study poses six questions, to sort through the maze of voting rights
in Indian Country:

1. What historical events form American Indian voting rights?
2. Are there barriers to American Indian voter participation?
3. How does the Voting Rights Act work to protect American Indian
   voters?
4. Which voting rights cases frame Indian Country voting rights?
5. What is the status of voting rights in Indian Country today?
6. What are the future prospects for the Indian Country voting rights?

Sources for this research are standard works in American Indian history, U.S. Department of Justice publications, Indian Country news sources (*Indian Country Today, NCAI News, Native American News, Missoulian, Great Falls Tribune*, and *Billings Gazette*). Further, the American Civil Liberties Union (ACLU) of Montana and ACLU of the Dakotas provide a rich archive of American Indian voting rights. An emphasis was placed on the story of American Indian voting rights, with the voices of plaintiffs, actions with consequences, both good and bad.

An Introduction to Indian Country

American Indian people reside in urban and rural reservation communities, and make up 1.4 percent of the U.S. population.[1] American Indians are those who reported being "all or part" American Indian or Alaska Native. The ten U.S. states with the largest American Indian population (in order) are California, Oklahoma, Arizona, Texas, New Mexico, New York, Washington, North Carolina, Michigan, and Alaska. The largest percentage, 43 percent, live in the West, while 31 percent reside in the South, 17 percent in the Midwest, and 9 percent in the Northeast. There are twenty-eight counties in the country with a majority Indian population.[2] The federal government currently recognizes over 500 tribal nations, and fifty are state recognized (in California and New York, for example).

American Indians are among the nation's poor. In Montana, families living below the poverty line range from 40 percent to 75 percent on the seven reservations, and urban Indian families reflect a similar socioeconomic status. The median American Indian family income (family of four) is $21,000/year, compared to $31,000/year for white Montanans. The Manhattan Institute for Policy Research, which assesses educational achievement in the United States, found a high school completion rate of 54 percent among American Indian youth (compared to 76 percent among white youth, 49 percent among African American youth, and 48 percent among Hispanic American youth), and that only 14 percent of the American Indian high school graduates were ready to enter college (by standardized test scores.)[3] The American Indian age profile is youthful. According to the 2000 U.S. Census, 33 percent of all American Indians are younger than eighteen years of age, compared to the American population with 25.6 percent younger than eighteen.[4] American Indians are young and seriously undereducated.

What Historical Events Impact American Indian Voting Rights?

In 1879, in Nebraska, Standing Bear was found to be human by Judge Dundy, who declared that "Indians were people within the meaning of the laws, and that they had the rights associated with a writ of habeas corpus."[5] No mention was made of citizenship, however. The Congress of the United States granted citizenship to American Indians in 1924, with the passage of the Indian Citizenship Act.[6] Citizenship was not extended to all American Indians with this congressional action, for seven states persisted in restrictions against Indian suffrage until 1938. The change of federal law regarding Indian citizenship did little to rectify the racial attitudes these requirements had perpetrated during the years of their enforcement.[7]

The right to vote has been declared by the U.S. Supreme Court as fundamental, since "it is preservative of other basic civil and political rights." But, for American Indians, there is no one defining moment when the right to vote was secured. Rather, the struggle for that right has been "an extraordinarily prolonged, complex and piecemeal process that has yet to be fully resolved."[8] The states set the requirements for voter eligibility, in local, state, and national elections. Western states imposed severe restrictions on American Indian voting that pertain to residence, competence, civilization, tax status (meaning property owners), or in various combinations of these restrictions (see table 19.1).[9] While the Indian Citizenship Act of 1924 ended most of the state restrictions, seven states persisted in these restrictions until 1938. South Dakota maintained restrictions until 1940, and Utah persisted until 1956.[10]

The Montana Territory denied voting rights to American Indians under the "guardianship" of the government category of restriction, and in the Enabling Act of 1889 (statehood), Montana restricted voting to citizens without regard to race or color, with the exception of Indians not taxed. By 1900,

Table 19.1.   Historic Restrictive Approaches to American Indian Voting

States	Restrictive Approaches
Colorado, Montana, Nebraska, Oregon, South Dakota, and Wyoming	Required that voters be citizens, and Indians were not citizens until 1924. South Dakota officially excluded Indians from voting and holding office until 1940.[a]
California, Minnesota, North Dakota, Oklahoma, and Wisconsin	Required that voters be "civilized," meaning that a person of Indian descent shall have severed tribal relations (North Dakota constitution).
Idaho, Montana, New Mexico, and Washington	Disqualified Indians from the polls; "Indians not taxed."
Arizona, Montana, Nevada, and Utah	Required citizenship, residency, and tax roll listees. Indians were considered under government "guardianship," therefore persons of "disability."
Utah	Disenfranchised Indians by declaring Indian residents of reservations were not state residents.

[a] Laughlin McDonald, "Voting Rights Act in Indian Country," American Indian Law Review 29, no. 1 (2004): 49.

Montana enacted two additional voting qualifications: taxpayers and persons listed on the city/county tax rolls. Again, American Indians were disenfranchised. In 1911, the Montana legislature declared that "anyone living on an Indian or military reservation who had not previously acquired residency in a Montana county before moving to a reservation would not be regarded as a Montana resident.[11]

Are There Barriers to American Indian Voter Participation?

The states' voting restrictions had implications and meaning to American Indians that negatively impacted American Indians from participation in the voting process, long after the Indian Citizenship Act of 1924. The restrictions and their implications for American Indian voters are delineated in table 19.2. For American Indians, the voter restrictions created long-lasting negative associations with voting and voting procedures, with implications that dissuade American Indian voter participation.[12]

The U.S. system of Indian reservations has added to a separation of Indian people from non-Indian people. The voting restrictions are indicators of the distance and separation between American Indians and their (mostly) white neighbors. Legal and political patterns of separation promoted a mind-set and acceptance of these approaches. At its extreme, Indians were set apart and thought of as inferior.[13]

Registering to vote is also an action and a requirement that harkens back to signing up. Under the early reservation system, household censuses were taken. Indian families were "registered" or "enrolled" and subsequently assigned

Table 19.2.   Implications of State Voting Restrictions

State Restriction	Implications of the Restriction
Citizenship	American Indians were not qualified to be citizens if they resided on the reservation.
Civilized	Indian people and their lifeways were "uncivilized, inferior"; to be civilized was to disavow relationships with their families and tribes, and to move off the reservation.
Taxed/Property Owner	Tax roll status required American Indians to move their lands out of trust status into the fee patent or state taxable status.
Under Federal Guardianship	Federal "wards" are incompetent, incapable of conducting business on their own behalf, disabled, and requiring the care of a white "guardian."
Nonresidents	Reservations and their American Indian residents are "out of the state."

Source: Senate Democratic Policy Committee, "The American Indian Vote: Celebrating 80 Years of U.S. Citizenship" (Washington, D.C.: Senate Democratic Policy Committee), 1.

to specific reservation districts, or residences. The reservation system did not allow American Indians mobility among communities, except with permission from the government agent. Requiring an Indian to "sign-here" is reminiscent of land leases or sales, or even the forced removal of Indian children from their families to faraway Indian boarding schools.[14] Registering and signing in have serious and negative associations for American Indian people.

Since the 1950s, many counties limited access to voter registration. In the recent past, Montana counties required "in person voter registration" at the county clerk or auditor's office in the county courthouse, located in a non-Indian border town. South Dakota has three "unorganized counties" that prohibited Indians from voting in elections as late as 1975 and from holding office as late at 1980.[15] Hyper-technical registration was also common, that required the applicant to know the section, township, and range of their residence. Many rural counties and Indian reservations lack an addressing system, making an exact location difficult to complete. Registering to vote was not a matter of addresses by post office box, but by section, township, and range. Registration-form errors were cause for rejection by county officials. Registration deadlines prior to primary and general elections, as well as purging systems, also contribute to this list of barriers to voting and voter registration.

Voter dissuasion has happened at the polls. Rural polling places may be at a considerable distance from an American Indian voter's home, in rural reservation locations. Impoverished American Indian voters may lack transportation to and from the polling places. Rural reservation road conditions in June and November can be muddy or snow packed, keeping voters home on election day. Once at the polls, the election judges may not speak the tribal language, which for older American Indian voters may be a necessity.

How Does the Voting Rights Act Work to Protect American Indian Voters?

The U.S. Congress enacted the Indian Civil Rights Act in 1968, to extend to tribes the constitutional standards of the Bill of Rights and the Fourteenth Amendment. However, Indian civil rights emanate from a nearly opposite direction, from other American minorities. Indian tribes have struggled to maintain separate political entities with their own institutions and beliefs. Through treaties and federal legislation, the tribes have sought to prevent the dismantling of their own systems.[16] In the formative era of American civil rights, American Indian tribes were completely enveloped in civil rights struggles even more basic—their very existence as Indian Nations. The House Concurrent Resolution 108, passed during the Eisenhower administration, unilaterally terminated the special relationship between the federal government and a specific set of Indian tribes. Massive relocation efforts moved American Indian young people from reservations to urban centers.[17] These American Indian civil rights issues have no application to other minority groups in this country, since American Indians have a unique political and legal status, under treaty law. From *The Native Americans*, by Spencer and Jennings, the governmental policy is described:

> During the 1950's there was an unfortunate reversal in governmental proposals and policies for the Indians. It now became the official aim to accelerate the liquidation of the government's responsibility to the Indians as speedily as possible. The idea was to get rid of the Indians by dispersing them and relieving the government of all responsibility for their specific problems. The new aim was to "get the government out of the Indian business". . . by a policy of termination of governmental services to the Indians, by transferring federal jurisdiction of law and order on Indian lands to the states, and by the relocation of as many Indians as possible off the reservations, in order to hasten, once again, their assimilation and to alleviate the pressure of increasing population upon the inadequate resources of the reservation.[18]

Tribes banned together in opposition to these federal policies and, through intensive effort, managed to obtain their reversal. The tribes terminated in 1953 took twenty years to restore their federal recognition. Relocation continued to remove American Indian youth from reservations until 1978. The American Indian tribes and their leadership were entirely consumed with this federal policy reversal, essentially eclipsing their contributions or participation in the civil rights movement in the 1950s and 1960s.

The Voting Rights Act and amendments do provide protections for American Indians and Alaska Natives. American Indians and Alaska Natives are protected from discrimination and intimidation in exercising the right to vote and in becoming candidates for serving in federal, state, and local elected offices. Ten years after the passage of the Voting Rights Act, in 1975, amendments included American Indians, with an expansion of the geographic reach of the special preclearance provision of Section 2, and the requirement of certain jurisdictions to provide bilingual election materials to language minorities.[19] Federal observers may be placed in polling places to make sure minority voters are permitted to vote without discrimination.[20] The amendment of Section 2 of the Voting Rights Act, in 1982, incorporated a discriminatory "results" standard that was a prohibition on the use of voting practices or procedures that "deny or abridge" the right to vote on the basis of race or color.[21] Since 1982, voting rights actions have been brought by American Indians in Arizona, Wisconsin, Nevada, South Dakota, Montana, Nebraska, and New Mexico.[22]

Which Voting Rights Cases Frame Indian Country Voting Rights?

Several voting rights cases build a framework for Indian Country voting rights. Members of the Sisseton-Wahpeton Sioux tribe brought the first case, under the amended Section 2, in South Dakota in 1984. *Buckanaga v. Sisseton School District* of 1985 challenged its school district's voting system, claiming that the at-large election system dilutes Indian voting strength.[23] The federal district court dismissed the complaint, but the Court of Appeals for the Eighth Circuit reversed, and on remand, a cumulative voting system was adopted on settlement, giving voters the option of casting their allotted votes in any combination. In *Sanchez v. King* in 1982,[24] the New Mexico federal court found the state's reapportionment plan violated the one-person, one-vote rule and ordered the state to redraw the districts.[25] In *Windy Boy v. Big Horn County* of 1986,[26] Northern Cheyenne and Crow Indians of Montana charged that the Big Horn County and Hardin Schools 17H and 1 at-large election schemes violated Section 2 of the Voting Rights Act. The lead plaintiff was Janine Pease-Windy Boy (this author), a Crow Indian. The federal district court of Montana ruled a violation and ordered the reorganization of the county and school district into single-member districts or zones, with Indian majorities in one commissioner district (of three) and two school board districts or zones (of five). These cases establish critical precedents in voting systems and state legislative reapportionment plans that violate the Voting Rights Act in Indian Country.[27]

What Is the Status of Voting Rights in Indian Country Today?

Voting rights activities are outlined here for three states: South Dakota, Minnesota, and Montana. This summary will give an overview of the protections sought by American Indian people, and the federal courts' rulings. These illustrate the importance of the Voting Rights Act, Sections 2 and 501, in particular.

In South Dakota, seven voting rights lawsuits have impacted American Indian voters and their rights. The Dakota and Lakota Indian voters have complained to the federal courts about Voting Rights Act violations in American Indian voter dilution in at-large election schemes at the city, school district, and county levels, reapportionment and redistricting actions, and abject neglect of election procedures that impact protected minorities. The ACLU and the ACLU of the Dakotas have been instrumental in the development of these cases:

- The South Dakota legislative redistricting committee proposed the demise of a special Indian majority legislative district with Indian voters from Cheyenne River and Standing Rock reservations in 2001.[28] Tribal members Steven Emery, Rocky Le Compte, and James Picotte filed suit in 2000, challenging the state's 1996 interim legislative redistricting plan.[29] In December 2001, in *Emery v. Hunt*,[30] the district court invalidated the state's 2001 legislative plan as diluting Indian voting strength, and "on the totality of circumstances analysis required by Section 2, the court found there was substantial evidence that South Dakota officially excluded Indians from voting and holding office."[31]

- The South Dakota legislative redistricting committee formed Legislative District 27 by packing Lakota Indian people from the Rosebud Sioux tribe and the Oglala Sioux tribe in Shannon and Todd counties, making a supermajority district. The district had 90 percent American Indian population.[32] South Dakota is one of sixteen states whose political districts are subject to federal review due to a history of discrimination against minority people. In *Bone Shirt v. Nelson*,[33] Judge Schreier ruled in favor of the plaintiffs and found that the South Dakota legislature violated Section 5 of the Voting Rights Act, and ordered the state to propose a plan. It was found that South Dakota sought preclearance only ten times in thirty years. Jennifer Ring, of the ACLU of the Dakotas, observed that South Dakota adopted a renegade position and openly flouted compliance with this important law, the Voting Rights Act.[34] The plaintiffs in the *Bone Shirt* case are Alfred Bone Shirt, Belva Black Lance, Bonnie High Bull, and Germaine Moves Camp.[35] The district lines had not been redrawn by the Legislative Executive Committee even as late as October 2004, due to what the state called "lack of data and authority to redraw lines."

- Indian plaintiffs challenged the Wagner Community School District in Charles Mix County in March 2002 for a voting rights Section 2 violation. Under a consent decree in March 2003, a method of elections using cumulative voting replaced the previous at-large system. The *Weddell v. Wagner Community School District* case resulted in the election of John Sully, an Indian, to the school board.[36]

- In Martin, South Dakota, a town of 1,000 people total, there are three city wards. For ninety years, the boundaries have stayed the same. The city has 44 percent American Indian population, and following the decennial census, the city redrew the ward boundaries with 33 percent American Indian population in each of the three wards. Bryan Sells of the ACLU told the federal court that Martin boundary lines deny minority voters the opportunity to elect a candidate of their choice.[37]

- In Buffalo County, 1,500 of the county population of 2,000 were packed into one county commissioner district, all being members of the Crow Creek Sioux tribe. Whites, 17 percent of the county, controlled the other two commissioners' districts. With representation by the ACLU, the tribal members brought suit in 2003, alleging the districting plan was misapportioned, with a total deviation of 218 percent. Settled by consent decree, the county admitted the plan was discriminatory and submitted to federal supervision of future plans.[38]

- The city boundaries in Lake Andes, South Dakota, were moved in 2004. Mostly American Indian voters received a letter informing them they were no longer within the Lake Andes city limits.
- Yankton Sioux tribal members filed a lawsuit in Pierre charging that Charles Mix County is violating Native American voting rights by using election districts that are unequal in population and divide the Native American community. The total deviation of existing districts in the county is 19 percent, almost twice the legal limit. Located in south central South Dakota, Charles Mix County is rural and is governed by a three-member county commission in single-member districts. American Indians are one-third of the county population. Lead plaintiff Evelyn Blackmoon said, "We have been without a voice in the commission for too long. This is an effort to change that." *Blackmoon v. Charles Mix County* was filed in January 2005.[39]

In Minnesota, the voting rights activity pertains to the legislature's new voter ID requirements, following the federal "Help America Vote Act."

- The ACLU of Minnesota, the National Congress of American Indians, and three Minnesota American Indian voters complained that the State of Minnesota established voting requirements more restrictive than the federal Help America Vote Act, and that unfairly target American Indian voters. The Minnesota law prohibited the use of a valid, federally recognized tribal ID for election-day registration. District Court Judge Rosenbaum issued the order to allow the use of tribal ID cards, with or without addresses, as valid identification for the 2004 general election, and ordered the Minnesota Secretary of State to notify the county auditors of the decision. The plaintiffs were Bonnie Door-Charwood of the Mille Lacs Band of Ojibwe, and Richard Smith, a member of the Fond du Lac Band of Lake Superior Chippewa.[40]

In Montana, the voting rights litigation in the years 2000 to 2005 spans issues of at-large elections in school districts and counties, and the redistricting of legislative districts.

- Tribal members from the Northern Cheyenne tribe and the Salish and Kootenai Confederated tribes filed two lawsuits in the U.S. District Court in Missoula, Montana, in 1999, charging that county and school district election practices diluted their voting strength, in violation of the Voting Rights Act. At issue was the election method of the Rosebud County Commission and the Ronan-Pablo School Board.[41] *Alden v. Board of County Commissioners of Rosebud County, Montana,* and *Matt v. Ronan School District 30* were taken to trial in 2000, and in May of 2000, Federal District Court Judge Molloy ordered local officials to create new boundaries for the 2000 Rosebud County commissioner elections, an order that cancelled a primary election and provided for a special general election for the commission race. The Ronan School District drew new boundaries in a separate settlement agreement, and in early May 2000, two Native Americans were elected to the Ronan school board.[42]
- In 2002, Blackfeet and Salish-Kootenai tribal members, represented by the ACLU of Montana, filed a complaint in federal district court, charging that the 1993 Montana redistricting plan diluted Indian voting strength when it failed to organize Indian majority districts on the Blackfeet and Salish/Kootenai reservations. U.S. District Court Judge Hatfield found the district did not dilute the voting strength of Indian voters, because the percentage of majority Indian districts in Montana is roughly proportional to the number of Indian voters in the state, and that white bloc voting was not significant. The Ninth Circuit Court of Appeals rejected both of these contentions and remanded the case back to district court. On remand, U.S. District Court Judge Pro of Nevada ruled that the 1992 redistricting plan did not dilute Indian voters' ability to elect candidates in Glacier and Lake counties, upholding the original district court decision. Shortly thereafter, the 2003 Montana legislative redistricting plan was adopted, which created additional majority Indian districts on the two reservations. This was the original relief sought by the plaintiffs in *Old Person v. Brown.*[43] The plaintiffs in this case were Earl Old Person, Carol Juneau, Joe McDonald, and Jeannine Padilla.[44]
- The Assiniboine and Gros Ventre tribal members Delores Plumage and Bill Stiff Arm, represented by the U.S. Department of Justice, filed a lawsuit in federal district court asking for the Blaine County commissioner districts to be redrawn. In September of 2000, the Montana Association of Counties and the Mountain States Legal Foundation came to the support of the Blaine County commissioners.[45] Blaine County is 40 percent American Indian in population—the

Assiniboine and Gros Ventre tribes.[46] Fort Belknap tribal leaders issued a strongly worded news release condemning the Blaine County commissioners for being unwilling to settle the redistricting issue.[47] The trial was in October of 2001, and expert witness Theodore Arrington of the University of North Carolina, Charlotte, testified about the racially polarized voting in Blaine County. In June of 2001, the district court ruled that the at-large voting system violated the Voting Rights Act. American Indian Blaine County residents drew the redistricting plan accepted by the court, but the Blaine County commissioners appealed the district court ruling to the Ninth Circuit Court of Appeals. The Ninth Circuit affirmed the district court decision in April 2002. Delores Plumage was elected to the Blaine County commission in the first election under the new plan.[48]

- The Montana legislature, leaders of the majority and minority, appoint the members of the Montana Districting and Apportionment Commission. In 1999, each leader appointed two members, and the four members convened to elect a presiding officer. No candidate acquired a majority vote, and in this stalemate, the Montana Supreme Court, delegated to appoint the presiding officer by the Montana Constitution, appointed Janine Pease-Pretty On Top (this author) by unanimous vote. The Montana Districting and Apportionment Commission, a citizen's commission, convenes for three years, in organizational meetings and public hearings. Here are key points of Montana's redistricting:

- Montana has an American Indian and Alaska Native population of 7.32 percent, an increase of 39.1 percent over 1990.
- The commission began redistricting in north central Montana, the area under litigation in the *Old Person v. Brown* case, and held hearings in Browning and in Great Falls.
- Criteria 3 (of four) was the protection of minority voting rights and compliance with the Voting Rights Act. Criteria 4 was that race cannot be the predominant factor to which the traditional discretionary criteria are subordinated (based on *Shaw v. Reno*, 1993).[49]
- The commission declined to become a part to the *Old Person v. Brown* litigation but adopted Resolution 1, which commended the parties in the case for attempting to settle, and resolved to create an additional Indian majority House District and Indian majority Senate District in the region of Montana, the Blackfeet and Flathead Reservation areas.[50]

- Based on the 2000 U.S. Census data, the commission maintained the existing number of districts, although the districts reflected the required equitable population in each district. The 2003 plan contains six Indian majority House Districts and three Indian majority Senate Districts. House Districts 1 (new majority district) and 2 (existing majority district) combine into Senate District 1 (new majority district) and include parts of the Flathead Indian reservation and the Blackfeet Indian Reservation. House District 18 (existing majority district) includes the Rocky Boy Indian reservation of the Chippewa Cree tribe and the Fort Belknap Indian Reservation. HD 18 combined with House District 22 (existing majority district) into Senate District 9 (new majority district). House District 22 has a portion of the Fort Peck Indian Reservation, which includes the Assiniboine and Sioux tribes. House District 29 includes the Northern Cheyenne and Crow tribes and reservation and is combined with House District 30, which includes the Crow tribe and reservation, for Senate District 12. (All three districts are existing Indian majority districts.)[51]

American Indians in South Dakota, Minnesota, and Montana are actively involved in the protection of their right to vote, and have sought protection under the Voting Rights Act, Sections 2 and 501. American Indian disenfranchisement is a reality throughout Indian Country, and these few tribal groups and individual plaintiffs have challenged their cities, counties, and states election systems and voting procedures.

What Are the Future Prospects for Indian Country Voting Rights?

The 2000 U.S. Census indicated a 38 percent growth in the American Indian population, expanded by 38 percent from 1990. The converse is true of the non-Indian population adjacent or contiguous to many Indian reservations, due to low birth rates, an aging population, and rural population losses. In some instances, this contrasting demographic dynamic exacerbates local issues and the "us and them" characterization referred to in the Martin, South Dakota, litigation over city wards. The American Indian population growth has meant an expansion of the potential and real American Indian voter bloc.

The elections of 2000, 2002, and 2004 demonstrated election results that can be inordinately influenced by 1 percent to 5 percent of the votes cast. The 1996 Pat Williams congressional race in Montana, the 2002 Slade Gorton senatorial defeat in Washington State, and the 2002 Tim Johnson senatorial victory in South Dakota are all cases where the Indian vote was essentially the percentage difference in votes cast. Indian voters that were 1 percent to 6 percent of these states' electorate voted as a bloc and determined the outcome of these elections: Williams won in Montana, Gorton was defeated in Washington, and Johnson was elected in South Dakota. Political competition for the Indian vote, and attempts to control, manage, or suppress the Indian vote, have been and will be heavier where elections are close.[52] Redistricting will be a cyclical concern, and for American Indians, a matter of constant attention.

The American Indian vote has been recognized as a swing vote in close races at many levels. The swing vote has been especially influential when the particular state is not clearly "red" or "blue." The American Indian percentages in western states can make a definitive difference for wins or losses, and in the current state and national political environment, this potential places American Indian voters under increased scrutiny.[53] Candidates will be "courting the Indian vote," and when there is competition, election monitors will probably be required.[54]

The Montana voting rights litigation in the Blaine County commissioner redistricting indicated the support of the Mountain States Legal Foundation and the Montana Association of Counties. The activity and presence of Montanans Opposed to Discrimination and the Civil Rights Organization in Bighorn and Lake counties show that white rights organizations and associations do support election schemes that dilute the American Indian vote, despite federal court decisions to follow the Voting Rights Act and its protections. The western media often express empathy for the cities, counties, and states in the region.[55] Further, the National Congress of American Indians with the Minnesota American Indians and the American Civil Liberties Union clearly demonstrates the allies in Indian Country voting issues. These alliances place American Indian voting squarely in the public arena and into the courts, but particularly with regional and national importance.

The press writers illustrate a huge variation in discussion of voting rights cases, both in Montana and South Dakota. When Blaine County commissioners met the Department of Justice attorneys in court, the *Great Falls Tribune* writer Eric Greene said, "In a lopsided showdown reminiscent of David and Goliath, Blaine County is battling the U.S. Department of Justice over the voting rights of Native Americans."[56] The implication is that Blaine County is the "woe-begone little county" and the Justice Department is the big government beating up on the little county, when Blaine County is associated with the Mountain States Foundation, something of a financial monolith for support and expertise. The real inquiry here must be: where are the American Indians in this scenario, so much furniture? The American Indian voter projects and voting rights initiatives are overlooked in the greater scenario of "big government beating up on the little guy county."

The courts have made voting rights protection something of a "legal paradox." The protection of minority voters, language minorities, is required by the Voting Rights Act, but recent court decisions have required that redistricting cannot be done on the basis of race alone. As Karen Humphrey of *Indian Country Today* points out, "the redistricting issue created a paradox for lawmakers because while the federal law demands the voting rights of racial and ethnic minorities must be protected, the courts ruled in the last decade that race cannot be a primary factor when drawing a given district."[57]

Orlan Svingen, historian and author, poses what he calls "ponderables" from his study of the *Windy Boy* case: the anti-Indian sentiment is strong and defiant; the anti-Indian organizations were intent on countering Indian voter participation in local and state elections, and on criminal prosecution of leading activists and the official obstruction of American Indian voting.[58] The historical roots of anti-Indian sentiment are deep in the towns on/near the reservations in Indian Country. The anti-Indian attitudes were shown to be widespread among county officials, among white ranchers, to the extent of formal and secret organizations. In Montana, the statewide organizations of like-minded non-Indians have affected American Indian voting rights in Big Horn, Blaine, Rosebud, and Lake counties. The prospect for the future is that this anti-Indian sentiment will build as a correlate with the growth of Indian population and levels of voting participation in Indian Country.

Conclusion

A complex series of historical events contribute to American Indian voting rights, including the restrictions by states that barred American Indians from voting and holding office for reasons of noncitizenship, residence, civilization, nontaxpayer status, and wardship. The American Indian Citizenship Act of 1924 ended most states' restrictions, although many persisted into the 1950s. The restrictions, while historic, have served to dissuade American Indian voters from the voting process.

Barriers to American Indian voter participation do exist. The conditions of rurality, poverty, and social and political separation of American Indians from whites, especially in the western states, pose formidable barriers to American Indian voter participation. Recent voting rights cases brought by American Indian plaintiffs have shown voter registration systems and election schemes are further barriers met by American Indian voters.

The Voting Rights Act does protect American Indian voters, particularly Section 501 and Section 2. American Indians were brought under the Voting Rights Act protections with amendments in 1975 and 1982. The isolation of Indian Country, conditions of poverty, and the lasting impact of historic states' restrictions kept American Indian voters from the benefits of the Act until the 1980s. Several voting rights cases frame Indian Country voting rights. *Buckanaga v. Sisseton Independent School District* in South Dakota, *Windy Boy v. Big Horn County* in Montana, and *Sanchez v. King* in New Mexico set precedents regarding school board and county commissioner election systems and legislative districts that dilute American Indian voting strength.

Since 2000, in just the last five years, voting rights in Indian Country has become an especially contested field. Election schemes that dilute American Indian voting strength at the city, school board, county, and legislative districts levels are under scrutiny and before the federal courts in Montana and South Dakota, on behalf of American Indian people. Voting procedures and voter identification have been contested in Minnesota. Tribal nations and their members involved in these suits come from the Dakota, Lakota, Assiniboine, Gros Ventre, Salish and Kootenai, Ute Mountain Ute, Omaha and Winnebago, Ojibway, and Hochunk. Court ordered election scheme reorganization of school boards, county commissions, and legislative districts have resulted in the election of American Indian people to public office. American Indian people are exerting their voting rights, and participating in stronger percentages in the election process.

The prospects for Indian Country voting rights are rife with contests for the states, counties, and cities in the western states where American Indian voters pose a formidable voter bloc. The contentious elections in which Congressman Pat Williams in Montana, Senator Tim Johnson in South Dakota, and Senator Slade Gorton in Washington State were candidates illustrated the power of the American Indian voters and their influence. Election officials and political parties will vie for American Indian voters, making voting processes and election schemes subject to scrutiny and challenge. A growing American Indian population and increasing American Indian voter participation will bring both positive and negative attention to American Indian voting rights with every election year, at all levels. The prospect for American Indian voter participation and the election of American Indian public officers is increasingly strong, and long overdue.

Notes

1. U.S. Census, 2000.
2. Tom Wanamaker, "Census Names Top 10 Tribes," *Indian Country Today*, February 15, 2002, 1.

3. Manhattan Institute for Policy Research, "College Readiness Rates in the United States," 2002.

4. U.S. Census, 2000, "Characteristics of American Indians and Alaska Natives by Tribe and Language."

5. University of Nebraska, Native American Studies, "Native American Citizenship," 1–2.

6. Suzanne E. Evans, "Voting," in *Encyclopedia of North American Indians* (New York: Houghton Mifflin, 1996), 658.

7. U.S. Commission on Civil Rights, *Indian Tribes: A Continuing Quest for Survival*, Report of the United States Commission on Civil Rights (Washington, D.C.: U.S. Government Printing Office, 1985), 32–33.

8. Evans, "Voting."

9. Evans, "Voting."

10. Evans, "Voting," 658–659.

11. Orlan Svingen, "Jim Crow, Indian Style," *American Indian Quarterly* 11 (Fall 1987): 270.

12. Nicole Adams, "Getting Out the Vote in Indian Country," *Winds of Change* (Summer 2004): 3–4.

13. Svingen, "Jim Crow, Indian Style," 270.

14. Senate Democratic Policy Committee, 3.

15. Laughlin McDonald, "Voting Rights Act in Indian Country," *American Indian Law Review* 29, no. 1 (2004): 49.

16. U.S. Commission on Civil Rights, 32.

17. U.S. Commission on Civil Rights, 35–36.

18. Robert F. Spencer and Jesse D. Jennings, *The Native Americans* (New York: Harper and Row, 1965), 501–502.

19. McDonald, "Voting Rights Act in Indian Country," 43.

20. U.S. Department of Justice, Civil Rights Division, "Protecting the Civil Rights of American Indians and Alaska Natives," June 2002, 1–5.

21. McDonald, "Voting Rights Act in Indian Country," 52.

22. U.S. Commission on Civil Rights, 36–37.

23. *Buckanaga v. Sisseton Independent School District*, 804 F.2d. 469 (8th Cir. 1986).

24. *Sanchez v. King*, 550 F. Supp. 13 (N.M. 1982).

25. Evans, "Voting," 659.

26. *Windy Boy v. Big Horn County*, 647 F. Supp. 1002 (D. Mont. 1986).

27. Svingen, "Jim Crow, Indian Style," 268.

28. Kay Humphrey, "Sole Native American District Remains," *Indian Country Today*, October 12, 2001, 1–2.

29. McDonald, "Voting Rights Act in Indian Country," 54.

30. *Emery v. Hunt*, 272 F.3d 1042 (8th Cir. 2001).

31. McDonald, "Voting Rights Act in Indian Country," 61.

32. Kay Humphrey, "ACLU Closely Watching South Dakota Redistricting," *Indian Country Today*, October 9, 2001, 1.

33. *Bone Shirt v. Nelson*, Civ. 01-3032-KES 2004 DSD 18.

34. David Melmer, "Largest Voter Lawsuit Filed against South Dakota," *Indian Country Today*, August 9, 2002, 1.

35. David Melmer, "South Dakota Redistricting Draws Lawsuit," *Indian Country Today*, January 15, 2002, 1.

36. McDonald, "Voting Rights Act in Indian Country," 59.

37. David Melmer, "Voting Rights Violation Argued (Part One)," *Indian Country Today*, July 12, 2004, 3.

38. McDonald, "Voting Rights Act in Indian Country," 59.

39. American Civil Liberties Union, "ACLU Charges South Dakota County Blocking Native Americans from Holding Office," January 27, 2005, 1.

40. American Civil Liberties Union, "Minnesota's Restricting Voter Identification Rules Violate Federal Election Law, ACLU and Native American Groups Charge," October 27, 2004, 1.

41. American Civil Liberties Union, "ACLU and Indian Rights Group Seek to Secure Voting Rights for Montana's Native Americans," July 7, 1999, 1–2.

42. American Civil Liberties Union, "ACLU Victorious in Securing Voting Rights for Native Americans in Montana," May 18, 2000, 1.

43. *Old Person v. Brown*, 312 F.3d 1036 (D. Mont. 2002).

44. ACLU of Montana, "Old Person, et al. v. Brown: The Rights of Suffrage and Equal Protection of the Laws," December 2002, 2.

45. Eric J. Greene, "Counties Band Together to Fight Indian Districts," *Great Falls Tribune*, September 27, 2000, 1.

46. Karen Ivanova, "ACLU Asks to Join Indian Voting Rights Suit," *Great Falls Tribune*, April 9, 2001.

47. Karen Ivanova, "Tribal Leaders Condemn Blaine's Persistence," *Great Falls Tribune*, July 11, 2002.

48. ACLU of Montana, "U.S. v. Blaine County, et. al.: The Right of Suffrage and Equal Protection of the Laws," June 2001, 1.

49. Legislative Services Division, *Legislative Redistricting Plan: Based on the 2000 Census, January 2003* (Helena: Montana Legislative Services Division, January 2003), 12.

50. Legislative Services Division, *Legislative Redistricting Plan*, 16.

51. Legislative Services Division, *Legislative Redistricting Plan*, 18.

52. David Melmer, "ACLU Files Another Suit in South Dakota," *Indian Country Today*, October 29, 2004, 1.

53. McDonald, "Voting Rights Act in Indian Country," 62.

54. Adams, "Getting Out the Vote in Indian Country," 2. See also Geneva Horsechief, "Primaries, Caucuses and Earning the Native Vote," *Native American Times*, February 6, 2004, 3.

55. Eric J. Greene, "Blaine County Resists Federal Effort to Build Indian Representation," *Great Falls Tribune*, February 20, 2000, 1.

56. Greene, "Blaine County Resists."

57. Karen Humphrey, "ACLU Closely Watching South Dakota Redistricting," *Indian Country Today*, October 9, 2001, 1.

58. Svingen, "Jim Crow, Indian Style," 276.

Bibliography

Adams, Jim. "An Indian Country Election Scorecard." *Indian Country Today*, November 1, 2002.
———. "NCAI Conference Has Case of Jitters." *Indian Country Today*, June 28, 2004.
Adams, Nicole. "Getting the Vote Out in Indian Country." *Winds of Change* (Summer 2004): 1–6.
American Civil Liberties Union. "ACLU and Indian Rights Group Seek to Secure Voting Rights for Montana's Native Americans," July 7, 1999.
———. "ACLU Appeals Court Ruling on Indian Vote Dilution in Montana," February 4, 2002.
———. "ACLU Charges South Dakota County Blocking Native Americans from Holding Office," January 27, 2005.
———. "ACLU Secures Major Victory in Landmark Redistricting Case: Federal Court Rules South Dakota Violated Voting Rights of Native Americans," September 15, 2004.
———. "ACLU Victorious in Securing Voting Rights for Native Americans in Montana," May 18, 2000.
———. "Court Rules Voters May Use Tribal ID Cards on Election Day," October 29, 2004.
———. "Minnesota's Restrictive Voter Identification Rules Violate Federal Election Law, ACLU and Native American Groups Charge," October 27, 2004.
ACLU of Montana. "U.S. v. Blaine County, et al.: The Right of Suffrage and Equal Protection of the Laws," February 2001 and June 2001.
———. "Old Person, et al. v. Brown: The Right of Suffrage and Equal Protection of the Laws," December 2002.
Center for Community Change. "Community Voter Project of the Center for Community Change: A Status Report." Center for Community Change, April 11, 2005: 1–5.
Evans, Suzanne E. "Voting." *Encyclopedia of North American Indians*. New York: Houghton Mifflin, 1996.
Greene, Eric J. "Blaine County Resists Federal Effort to Build Indian Representation." *Great Falls Tribune*, February 20, 2000.
———. "Counties Band Together to Fight Indian Districts." *Great Falls Tribune*, September 27, 2000.
———. "Federal Efforts Have Heated Up Debate over Fairness of State's At-large Elections." *Great Falls Tribune*, February 20, 2000.
———. "Feds Threaten Suits over Voting Districts." *Great Falls Tribune*, July 28, 1999.
———. "Majority-Indian District Ordered—Now." *Great Falls Tribune*, May 20, 2000.
Henderson, Wade. "The Voting Rights Act of 1965: 40 Years after 'Bloody Sunday,' A Promise Still Unfulfilled," March 2, 2005, 1–3, civilrights.org.
Humphrey, Kay. "Sole Native American District Remains." *Indian Country Today*, October 12, 2001.

———. "ACLU Closely Watching South Dakota Redistricting." *Indian Country Today*, October 9, 2001.

Ivanova, Karen. "ACLU Asks to Join Indian Voting Rights Suit." *Great Falls Tribune*, April 9, 2001.

———. "Redistricting Debate Coming to Hi-Line Towns." *Great Falls Tribune*, January 14, 2002.

———. "Tribal Leaders Condemn Blaine's Persistence." *Great Falls Tribune*, July 11, 2002.

Johnson, Peter. "Trial Focuses on Strength of County's Indian Vote." *Great Falls Tribune*, October 10, 2001.

Komp, Catherine. "Native Americans Win Minnesota Voting Rights Challenge." *The News Standard*. A Project of PeoplesNetWorks, November 2, 2004.

McCarty, Jason. "Hearing Scheduled in Voting Rights Lawsuit Filed by National Congress of American Indians and Minnesota ACLU." *NCAI News*, October 29, 2004.

McDonald, Laughlin. "Voting Rights Act in Indian Country." *American Indian Law Review* 29, no. 1 (2004): 43–74.

McFarlane, Jane. "ACLU Fights to Join Federal Lawsuit." *Great Falls Tribune*, June 19, 2001.

Melmer, David. "ACLU Files Another Suit in South Dakota." *Indian Country Today*, October 29, 2004.

———. "Illegal Voter Districts to Stand." *Indian Country Today*, October 29, 2004.

———. "Indian Voters Ousted from City in South Dakota." *Indian Country Today*, September 10, 2004.

———. "Largest Voter Lawsuit Filed against South Dakota." *Indian Country Today*, August 9, 2002.

———. "South Dakota Redistricting Draws Lawsuit." *Indian Country Today*, January 15, 2002.

———. "South Dakota Reprieve in Voting Rights Violation." *Indian Country Today*, January 31, 2005.

———. "Voting Rights Violation Argued (Part One)." *Indian Country Today*, July 12, 2004.

———. "Voting Rights Violation Argued." *Indian Country Today*, July 16, 2004.

Pierpoint, Mary. "Haskell Students Exercised Voting Rights." *Indian Country Today*, November 22, 2000.

Selden, Ron. "Montana Leaders Explore Lawsuits, Federal Funding, Legislative Concerns." *Indian Country Today*, January 3, 2001.

Senate Democratic Policy Committee. "The American Indian Vote: Celebrating 80 Years of U.S. Citizenship." Washington, D.C.: Senate Democratic Policy Committee.

Svingen, Orlan J. "Jim Crow, Indian Style." *American Indian Quarterly* 11 (Fall 1987): 275–286.

United States Commission on Civil Rights. *Indian Tribes: A Continuing Quest for Survival*. Report of the United States Commission on Civil Rights. Washington, D.C.: United States Commission on Civil Rights, 1985.

United States Department of Justice, Civil Rights Division. "The Voting Rights Act of 1965." nd. www.usdoj.gov/crt/voting/overview.htm.

———. "Protecting the Civil Rights of American Indians and Alaska Natives: Nondiscrimination Laws Enforced by the Civil Rights Division United States Department of Justice." 2002. www.usdoj.gov/crt/Indian/broch.html.

United States Department of Justice, Civil Rights Division, Voting Section. "Introduction to Federal Voting Rights Laws." 2005. www.usdoj.gov/crt/voting/intro/intro.htm.

———. "Section 4 of the Voting Rights Act."

University of Nebraska, Native American Studies. "Native American Citizenship." Lincoln: University of Nebraska, Native American Studies, nd.

Wanamaker, Tom. "Census Names Top 10 Tribes." *ndian Country Today*, February 15, 2002.

Federal Indian Policy in the Twenty-first Century

20

KEVIN GOVER

T HE CONTEMPORARY PARTICIPANT IN THE MAKING of Indian policy, whether at the periphery of the process or at the center, may be forgiven for viewing policy development as a series of long and difficult efforts made for only the occasional partial success. A more detached perspective, however, especially when had in the context of 218 years of American constitutional policy-making, yields a far different conclusion. The past forty years of policy constitute in many respects the "Golden Era" of federal Indian policy.

We tend to forget, in the daily give-and-take of administering federal and tribal programs for Indian communities, how far we have traveled in reforming federal Indian policy. To gain a fuller appreciation of the profound changes that have occurred, a brief review of the situation at the beginning of the twentieth century is worthwhile.

The Coercive Assimilation Policy: Allotment

In 1900, a policy of coercive assimilation of Indian people was in full swing. The centerpiece of the assimilation policy was the Dawes Allotment Act of 1887. Most of the large reservations had been broken up and parceled out to tribal members and non-Indian homesteaders. Tribal landholdings would fall from 155.6 million acres in 1881 to 104.3 million acres in 1890, to 52.2 million acres in 1934, when the allotment policy was formally abandoned.

By 1934, fully 66 million acres of tribal land had been acquired by non-Indian homesteaders pursuant to the allotment policy. Individual Indian land owners who had been deemed "competent" by the Bureau of Indian Affairs

(BIA) alienated another 23 million acres of allotted land. The government on behalf of noncompetent Indians had sold another 3.7 million acres. The remaining lands owned by the tribes came to only 34.3 million acres, while individual Indian allottees or their heirs owned 17.6 million acres.

A masterpiece of understatement, the famous Meriam Report concluded in 1928 that "Admirable as were the objects of individual allotment, the results have often been disappointing." Far from creating the self-sufficient Indians that the proponents of allotment had predicted, the allotment and assimilation policies left the Indians desperately poor. The Meriam Report noted that, for Indians on several reservations, "the figures for income are reported so low as to be almost unbelievable." Seventy-one percent of reservation Indians lived in communities where per capita income was less than $200 per year; almost one-quarter lived in areas where per capita income was less than $100 annually. The Meriam Report gamely suggested that Indian subsistence practices and Indian disinterest in material goods made the picture slightly less bleak, but it was obvious that forty years of coercive assimilation efforts by the United States had left reservation Indians utterly destitute.[1]

The harm created by coercive assimilation was not limited to the economic sphere. A key feature of the assimilation policy was to educate Indian children in the ways of white Americans so that they might be productive, if not particularly intellectual, members of the dominant society. From the beginning, Indian schools were designed to teach Indians to be white people, and language was the point of the spear in this attack. In 1886, Commissioner of Indian Affairs J. D. C. Atkins said: "The first step to be taken toward civilization, toward teaching Indians the mischief and folly of continuing in their barbarous practices, is to teach them the English language."[2] Atkins prohibited the use of Indian languages in classrooms.

Many Indian schools were located far from the reservations. In 1900, twenty-five off-reservation boarding schools enrolled over 7,400 Indian students. Another eighty-one boarding schools were on the reservations, with enrollments totaling 9,600. Five thousand Indian students attended 147 reservation day schools. Needless to say, cultural pluralism was not a concern in creating the curriculum. Indian Schools Superintendent Estelle Reel wrote, in the 1900 Report of the Commissioner of Indian Affairs, that "With education will come morality, cleanliness, self-respect, industry, and, above all, a Christianized humanity, the foundation stone of the world's progress and well being." Reels defended the limited objectives of the curriculum: "it is not wise to spend years over subjects for which he will have no use in later life and for which he has but little taste now, when the time could be more wisely employed in acquiring skill in the industrial arts, which will also train the judgment, will power, and all that combines to make up strength and character."[3]

By 1928, the situation was grim. The Meriam Report called the care offered the children in the boarding schools "grossly inadequate," a strong condemnation in a report notable for its measured language. The diet fed the children was "deficient"; the dorms were overcrowded and conducive to the spread of disease, especially tuberculosis; the medical care provided the children was "not up to a reasonable standard"; schools were not accredited because the teachers were not qualified; the curriculum did not reflect the needs of the children; the discipline was "restrictive rather than developmental"; the "industrial training" the children received more closely resembled illegal child labor in support of the schools than it did an educational program.[4]

The practice of removing Indian children from their families had impacts we have only begun to measure. The Indian family system—the central cohesive force in any tribal culture—was deliberately attacked. Children were forbidden their languages, their religions, their cultures, even their parents. The family dysfunction and accompanying ills of addiction and violence that are rampant in Indian Country perhaps find their genesis in this organized assault on the Indian family structure.

The era of coercive assimilation was plainly the nadir of the Indian experience in America. Today the tribes survive and in many cases prosper. It is easy to lose sight of the fact that the objective of policy 100 years ago was to dismantle Indian tribes forever. This reality makes what followed so very remarkable. The era of Indian self-determination in which we now live would have been quite simply unthinkable for the policymakers of the coercive assimilation era. The underlying assumptions of current policy—the permanence of tribal existence; an ongoing federal responsibility to Indian tribes and people; that Indian cultures should be actively preserved, taught, and celebrated; tribal control of services in tribal communities—were literally beyond the conception of the makers of Indian policy in 1900.

The Reorganization Policy

The road to Indian self-determination was hardly a straight one. It is fair to say, though, that it began in the 1920s, with the rise of reformers who thought that Indian tribal existence should not be destroyed. Their primary argument in favor of a change of policy was the evident failure of coercive assimilation. The Meriam Report confirmed most of the criticisms of the reformers, who were led by the agitated and often vituperative John Collier. The Indians were poor, many of them very poor. They were ignorant and unhealthy. The Bureau of Indian Affairs deepened the problems with poor organization, bad management, and inadequate funding for its assigned tasks. As a result, Indians made virtually no progress toward integration into the larger society.

These failures of policy were accompanied by events the reformers used to bring their criticisms to a wider American audience. The performance of Indian soldiers in World War I was valiant and demonstrated a perfectly fine capability to deal intelligently with circumstances well beyond the Indians', or anyone else's, prior experience. The valor of these soldiers combined with the policy objective of ending federal supervision of Indians produced the Indian Citizenship Act of 1924. The abject failures of the BIA to protect Indians from sharp dealing in managing their land were an ongoing source of embarrassment to Indian policy officials. Absurd and insensitive efforts by Commissioner of Indian Affairs Charles Burke to suppress certain Indian dances—driven by the considerable lobby of Christian missionaries who made a profession of working in tribal communities—gave the reformers more grist for the mill.

Yet federal Indian policy only changed with the grand and tragic failure of national economic policy that resulted in the Great Depression. The desperate need resulting from the Great Depression overcame the nation's traditional hostility to centralized government. The notion of getting the government out of the Indians' business lost currency when the government started getting into everybody's business with its New Deal programs. The pervasive and intrusive administration of Indian programs by the BIA did not seem so extraordinary when agency government grew spectacularly across the board.

These forces, combined with the appointment of John Collier as Commissioner of Indian Affairs, produced a policy that thirty years before would have been laughable: Indian reorganization. The Indian Reorganization Act (IRA) of 1934 embodied the then-revolutionary idea that Indians themselves should make the important decisions regarding their affairs. The Act authorized tribes to enact constitutions to establish governments that would exercise the inherent sovereignty of the tribes. The legal constructs of tribal sovereignty were examined and embedded into these constitutions. Federal corporate charters were granted to tribes that wished to manage their economic affairs through a corporate entity. Programs were established to purchase land for tribes and individual Indians. Revolving credit programs were established to encourage economic development. An Indian Arts and Crafts Board was established to assist Indian artists in marketing their work and to educate the general public on Indian culture. Finally, a seemingly modest provision for Indian preference in employment in the Bureau of Indian Affairs eventually resulted in a dramatic change in the culture of the bureau that blossomed in the 1970s and 1980s and continues to the present.

The IRA enacted by the Congress fell well short of the more wideranging proposal put forward by Collier. Assimilated Indian land owners and Christian missionaries and their converts railed against the Collier reform program, and Congress enacted only a modest version of the program. Still, the IRA was revolutionary in its time, and without it, the self-determination program that emerged forty years later simply would not have been possible.

The reorganization policy did not realize its full potential for a variety of reasons. Collier himself earned adversaries with his heavy-handed implementation of the tribal constitution provision of the IRA. He alienated the cohort of professional missionaries in Indian country by dramatically reducing their role in BIA social service and education programs, in some cases prohibiting any involvement whatsoever. These missionaries and the assimilated Indian land owners continued to agitate against the Collier program, and their efforts had effect. Within two years, one of the primary sponsors of the IRA was seeking its repeal.

That the policy failed to achieve its potential, though, was well beyond the control of any of the parties to the dispute. World War II absorbed all of the nation's money and attention. The programs Collier administered took reductions in funding, and the additional authorities he sought were not forthcoming. Collier diligently organized Indian support for the war effort, using the BIA to ensure that Indians complied with the Selective Service laws, and managing Indian mineral, timber, and agricultural resources so as to help the war effort. His annual reports read like propaganda tracts, extolling the heroism of Indian soldiers, the diligence of Indian war industry workers, and the patriotism of Indian tribes and individuals for their purchase of war bonds.

In hindsight, Collier's programs peaked in the mid-1930s. He spent much of the remainder of his tenure as commissioner—the longest in the history of the agency—fighting to hold on to the authorities he had gained in the IRA. He was placed at a considerable geographical disadvantage when the BIA headquarters were moved to Chicago so that its Washington offices could be used for the war effort. Isolated and waning in influence, Collier could not accomplish his vision. By 1944, with the reform program severely underfunded, Collier resigned.

Coercive Assimilation Revisited: Termination and Relocation

The return of Indian veterans and war industry workers from their World War II experiences would have a profound effect on federal Indian policy. Their return made all the more evident the economic deprivation that was characteristic of reservation life. The skills acquired in the war effort had little place on reservations where industry and jobs were largely non-existent. Yet the war demonstrated the ability of these veterans and war workers to deal with the non-Indian world. They were hardly incompetents requiring government oversight of their every transaction. They wanted more than the deprived lifestyles the reservations had to offer.

Simultaneously, the Truman administration made important steps toward abolishing de jure discrimination from American life. Truman believed in equality under the law for all races, and the members of his administration were troubled by the presumption of Indian incompetence and inferiority that was the basis of much of the federal–Indian relationship. Not unlike the humanitarians and western land speculators who joined forces to promote the allotment/assimilation policy, believers in racial equality combined with Cold Warriors and conservative advocates for smaller government to create the termination policy of the 1950s.

The idea of reducing the federal role in and responsibility for ensuring Indian welfare had been brewing for some time. The failure of Collier's reforms to work a quick reversal of Indian poverty, along with the growing amount of funds appropriated to meet federal responsibilities in Indian Country, had both the Truman administration and the Congress seeking a permanent solution for the problems of Indian Country. The first step in this direction was the enactment of the Indian Claims Commission Act in 1946. Addressing the historic claims of the tribes had been one of Collier's proposed reforms. Concerns about the potentially enormous liabilities of the United States prevented passage of the legislation during Collier's time. However, with an eye toward settling America's debts to the tribes once and for all, Congress authorized lawsuits against the United States to address the tribes' claims of unfair dealing in the past.

The Bureau of Indian Affairs was also actively pursuing new policies and programs to address the higher expectations that Indian veterans brought back from the war. In early 1947, the BIA began developing lists of tribes that were ready to have federal oversight withdrawn and those that were not. The lists, drawn at the request of Congress, became the blueprint for the implementation of the termination policy of the 1950s.

The BIA was also developing a new approach to addressing joblessness on the reservations, especially among veterans and former war workers. If the jobs could not be brought to the reservations, the Indians would be brought to the jobs. Thus was born the "relocation" program of the late 1940s and the 1950s. The BIA developed "relocation centers" to assist reservation Indians in their transition to working-class urban life in certain western and midwestern cities. Congress and the BIA were enthusiastic about this program, spending millions of dollars throughout the 1950s to relocate Indian families.

With the election of President Eisenhower and a Republican Congress in 1952 came an aggressive new push to get the United States out of "the Indian business." The 83rd Congress quickly enacted Public Law 83-280, which mandated certain states, and gave discretion to the others, to assume criminal and civil adjudicatory jurisdiction over matters arising on the reservations, including matters involving Indians. President Eisenhower, though expressing concern about certain provisions of the legislation, approved the law "because its basic purpose represents still another step in granting equality to all Indians in our nation."[5]

The coup de grace fell on August 1, 1953, with the passage of House Concurrent Resolution 108. There Congress announced its policy that, "as rapidly as possible," Indians should be made "subject to the same laws and entitled to the same privileges and responsibilities as are applicable to other citizens of the United States," and that "at the earliest time possible, [Indians] should be freed from Federal supervision and control and from all disabilities and limitations specially applicable to Indians."[6] These goals of equality and freedom, benign to the uninformed observer, resulted in the withdrawal of federal programs and protections from over 100 tribes over the following thirteen years. Some 11,500 Indians lost their legal status as Indians, and nearly 1.4 million acres of land lost its status as trust land. Most of this land was soon lost to the tribes, and although the tribal members received distributions of the proceeds from the land sales, they failed to prosper. Tribal members became subject to the laws of the states and dependent on the services the states provided. The dislocation of Indian life was profound.

Federal Indian policy had hit bottom again. Termination was yet another effort at the coercive assimilation of Indian people, leading Felix Cohen in 1953 to remark famously: "The Indian plays much the same in our American society that the Jews played in Germany. Like the miner's canary, the Indian marks the shift from fresh air to poison gas in our political atmosphere, and our treatment of Indians, even more than our treatment of other minorities, marks the rise and fall of our democratic faith."[7]

Cohen was right, of course. Indian policy had long been accommodated, if not driven, by considerations other than what Indians themselves believed was in their best interests. Even the relatively progressive reorganization policy was the brainchild of outsiders who thought they knew what was best for Indians. Indians had long been victims of, rather than participants in, the federal political system. Cohen's remark at once laments the political impotence of Indians even as it supports the belief in the ongoing necessity of benevolent outsiders determining what is best for the Indians.

Though termination caused profound dislocation in too many Indian communities, the majority survived intact, if all the more wary of federal policy initiatives. Broad tribal resistance to termination could not prevent many tribes from being terminated, but it did ultimately kill the policy, and within only a few years. This successful resistance marked something of a turning point. Tribes were fighting successfully in the federal political system to protect their interests. While the effort was not a complete success, the many successes that followed indicate that in resisting termination, the tribes learned how to fight effectively in the federal political system. With fifty years' worth of hindsight, we can see now that Cohen's lament, while true in the moment, was not true for very much longer.

The Self-Determination Policy

So unattractive was the policy of termination that all three men who served as U.S. president in the 1960s repudiated it. President Kennedy declared his opposition during the 1960 campaign, and Presidents Johnson and Nixon adopted policy approaches that were entirely incompatible with termination.

Two key events took place in 1961. The American Indian Chicago Conference was a gathering of 450 delegates from tribes throughout the country. The delegates adopted a Declaration of Indian Purpose that called for an end to termination, major educational reforms, and tribal control of resource management and social service programs. The declaration was presented directly to President Kennedy the following year. A Task Force on Indian Affairs appointed by Interior Secretary Stewart Udall submitted its report in 1961. The task force joined the Chicago Conference delegates in repudiating the termination policy. Clearly, tribal opposition was having the desired effect of ending termination.

Even as termination was grinding to a halt, the makings of a new policy were being created in the context of President Johnson's War on Poverty. As Johnson's "Great Society" legislation moved through the Congress, Indian concerns received unusual levels of attention. Tribal needs were specifically addressed in the Economic Opportunity Act of 1964, which made tribes eligible for funding for youth programs, community action programs, and the Volunteers in Service to America (VISTA) program, among others. The Neighborhood Youth Corps, Job Corps, and Operation Head Start brought new programs and funding to the reservations. Unlike BIA and Indian Health Service (IHS) programs, however, Office of Economic Opportunity (OEO) funds were administered directly by the tribes. While OEO funds were hardly sufficient to make a dent in the problem of Indian poverty, they had the collateral effect of increasing tribal government capacity to administer federal programs, and in turn increased the desire of tribal governments to take over other federal programs for the reservations.

The impact of the broader civil rights movement cannot be overlooked either. While Indian activism was driven by a more complex philosophical construct than were African American demands for equal rights, it simply cannot be credibly argued that Indians would have gained the same attention to their issues in the absence of the civil rights movement. Indeed, to the extent one considers the civil rights legislation of the 1960s "fresh air . . . in our political atmosphere," Cohen's observation of the place of Indians in American society held true in the 1960s. The tribes benefited from the happy coincidence of their own political efforts and the environment of change created by the civil rights movement.

The efforts of the Johnson administration in Indian affairs peaked in March 1968. In a Special Message to the Congress, President Johnson marked the change of direction in Indian policy by proposing a "new goal" for Indian policy: "a goal that ends the old debate about 'termination' of Indian programs and stresses Self-Determination; a goal that erases old attitudes of paternalism and promotes partnership self-help."[8] The policy watchword in Indian affairs had become "Self-Determination" and has not changed since.

The new policy flourished in the administration of President Nixon. Nixon had specifically foresworn forced termination during his 1968 campaign. In 1970, President Nixon made the most important statement in the modern history of federal Indian policy. In his July 8 Special Message on Indian Affairs, President Nixon critiqued the termination policy and its consequences as well as the paternalism that had long characterized the federal government's relationship with the tribes. He concluded that neither approach was acceptable as the basis for modern policy. He then offered another approach: "Self-Determination among the Indian people can and must be encouraged without the threat of eventual termination. In my view, in fact, that is the only way that Self-Determination can effectively be fostered."[9]

This, then, must be the goal of any new national policy toward the Indian people to strengthen the Indian's sense of autonomy without threatening this sense of community. We must assure the Indian that he can assume control of his own life without being separated involuntarily from the tribal group. And we must make it clear that Indians can become independent of federal control without being cut off from federal concern and federal support.

President Nixon asked Congress, among other things, to expressly renounce the termination policy, authorize tribes to take control of federally funded and administered programs, authorize Indian control of Indian schools, restore ownership of Blue Lake to Taos Pueblo, enact economic development legislation, and provide assistance to urban Indians. Despite the premature end of the Nixon administration, this policy statement set off an extraordinary period of legislative activity that has changed the face of Indian policy, perhaps permanently.

Self-Determination: Clearing the Wreckage

One of the first orders of business in creating a new policy was to address the ill effects of the termination policy. Congress set to work almost immediately by restoring the Menominee tribe of Wisconsin in 1973. Since the Menominee restoration, a small but steady stream of restoration bills has passed the Congress, including bills restoring the Siletz tribe, the Paiute tribe of Utah, the Klamath tribe, the Ponca tribe of Nebraska, and a dozen others. In addition, approximately twenty small California tribes have been restored to federal recognition by the federal courts. All of the largest terminated tribes have been restored, and Congress has not finally rejected any terminated tribe that has sought restoration.

Congress also has addressed far more ancient grievances of eastern tribes that most Americans would have thought no longer existed. Beginning with the claims of the Narragansett tribe in Rhode Island, Congress passed major land claim settlement bills for tribes in Maine, Connecticut, Massachusetts, and South Carolina between 1978 and 1993.

Self-Determination: Reform of Indian Service Programs

The key changes to federal service programs reflect a belief that has endured for some thirty years now that tribal governments, and not federal agencies, should decide how governmental services would be provided in reservation communities. This is an unremarkable proposition to current tribal, state, and federal policymakers, but it was a revolutionary concept in the 1960s and 1970s. Congress has not retreated from this idea, and it is a sine qua non of current policy.

It began, as discussed above, with the Office of Economic Opportunity providing funds directly to tribal governments in the 1960s. In 1975, Congress aggressively expanded the concept to include virtually all programs administered by the Bureau of Indian Affairs. The Indian Self-Determination and Education Assistance Act of 1975 has thoroughly changed the relationship between tribal governments and the Bureau of Indian Affairs and Indian Health Service. Tribes may, upon request, contract with the agencies to administer programs on their reservations, and the agencies have almost no discretion to decline to enter into such contracts. Though the agencies resisted in the early years of the new law, Congress and the tribes persevered, and the BIA and IHS now boast of the number of programs and the amount of funds contracted to the tribes.

The self-determination program has only expanded, and Congress in 1994 enacted the Tribal Self-Governance Act to further expand tribal discretion in the design and execution of service programs on reservations. Congress even applied the self-determination model to programs administered by the Department of Housing and Urban Development in the Native American Housing and Self-Determination Act of 1996.

In addition to restructuring the administration of service programs on reservations, Congress has made substantive reforms to specific programs—and created new programs for Indian communities as well—in legislation such as the Indian Health Care Improvement Act of 1976, the Tribally Controlled Community College Assistance Act of 1978, and the Indian Law Enforcement Reform Act of 1990. Taken together, this legislation demonstrates unprecedented progress in the provision of governmental services to Indian communities. Note as well that these statutes do not speak of preparing Indians for their liberation from federal supervision and assimilating them into the general population. To the contrary, these statutes assume an ongoing, perhaps even a perpetual, relationship between the federal government and the tribes. The assumption that tribes will ultimately disappear into the great American melting pot is nowhere to be found in the legislation of the self-determination era.

Self-Determination: Cultural Resources and Religious Freedom

Congress responded to President Nixon's Self-Determination Message almost immediately when it restored ownership of Blue Lake to the Pueblo of Taos. Taos had sought the restoration of this sacred site for many years. In 1970, it finally happened.

The restoration of Blue Lake was only the first of ever more expansive legislation addressing Indian culture and language. Recall that in 1900, the United States was pressing an all-out assault on Indian language and culture. By the end of the century, Congress was acting not only to respect and preserve Indian language and culture, but also in some respects to actively promote them.

In 1978, Congress enacted the American Indian Religious Freedom Act, expressing its conclusion that Native American religions were entitled to the same constitutional protections as those imported to North America. In 1989, Congress passed the National Museum of the American Indian Act, using the last open space on the Capitol Mall in Washington, D.C., for a museum for the presentation of Indian cultures. In 1990, Congress passed the Native American Graves Protection and Repatriation Act, requiring that human remains and items of cultural significance in the possession of federally funded museums be returned to the tribes. The Native American Languages Act was passed in 1990 with the objective of preserving threatened indigenous languages. The Religious Freedom Restoration Act of 1993 contained important provisions for accommodating Native American religious practices. The organized, persistent, comprehensive assault on Native culture by the federal government is over, and the tribes have a fighting chance to preserve, as they choose, what is left.

Self-Determination: Economic Development and Natural Resource Management

The problem of Indian poverty has persisted since the traditional tribal economies were destroyed and the reservations established in the nineteenth century. No solution has yet been found for most of the largest tribes, and Indian poverty and unemployment still dwarf those of the public at large. The tribes have made progress, though, with the assistance of the Congress.

In 1974, Congress enacted the Indian Financing Act. The Act created a direct loan program, a revolving loan guarantee fund, and an interest subsidy program to help tribes and Indian business owners borrow money for their enterprises. In 1982, Congress enacted the Indian Tribal Governmental Status Act, extending to tribes several of the federal tax immunities and advantages offered to states. In 1988, the most important economic development legislation of all was passed in the Indian Gaming Regulatory Act. Gaming has provided most tribal communities in the lower forty-eight states with badly needed discretionary income to support tribal government operations. A number of small, fortunately situated tribes have become economically self-sufficient due to their gaming enterprises.

Congress has also attempted to improve management of, and make more valuable, both tribal and individually owned lands held in trust for Indians by the United States. The Indian Land Consolidation Act of 1983, its serial amendments, and the American Indian Trust Fund Management Reform Act of 1994 represent earnest efforts by the Congress to help the tribes make the most of their single largest asset: 55 million acres of land.

The Congress has also made efforts to help the tribes increase their returns on the mineral resources of the reservations. Most significantly, the Indian Mineral Development Act of 1982 authorized creative transactions by tribes, abandoned the outdated and exploitative model of leasing to outsiders in return for insufficient royalties, and reduced federal intrusion into tribal decision-making regarding tribal mineral resources.

Congress also has amended several of the nation's key environmental statutes to enhance the tribes' abilities to improve and protect reservation environments. The Comprehensive Environmental Response, Compensation, and Liability

Act (CERCLA or "Superfund") and the Safe Drinking Water Act were amended in 1986 to permit tribes many of the same authorities as states under the statutes. Thereafter, the Clean Water Act was similarly amended in 1987, and the Clean Air Act in 1990. Finally, Congress enacted the Indian Environmental General Assistance Program Act in 1992, authorizing block grants to tribes to identify and pursue their primary environmental regulatory objectives.

Self-Determination: Law Reform

Extremely important changes to the laws governing tribal court authority have been part of this barrage of legislation in the self-determination era. Even before the Nixon policy, Congress turned its attention to the rights of Indian people vis-à-vis their tribal governments. In the Indian Civil Rights Act (ICRA) of 1968, Congress extended most of the requirements of the Bill of Rights to Indian tribal governments. Most tribes considered this legislation an invasion of their sovereignty, and it was. Yet it is hard to argue that persons under tribal authority on Indian reservations should not have at least the basic rights that Americans enjoy elsewhere. Moreover, the ICRA contained authorization for funds for improving tribal justice systems and, more importantly, prohibited states from further assumptions of jurisdiction in Indian Country under Public Law 83-280 without the consent of the affected tribe. Thus, a centerpiece of the termination policy—subjecting reservation Indians to state court authority with or without tribal consent—was abandoned.

Perhaps the new law most important to the future of the tribes is the Indian Child Welfare Act (ICWA) of 1978. For many years, state, federal, and religious social service agencies and workers had been removing Indian children from their families and their reservations and placing them into non-Indian foster care and adoption systems. Reliable figures on the number of such placements are hard to come by, but easily number in the thousands. The displaced children tended to fare poorly, and the Indian families and communities were devastated by the losses. The ICWA placed primary authority for such placements squarely in forums created by the tribes. It contained extraordinary provisions permitting tribal intervention in state court proceedings and created strict requirements for the adoption of Indian children. The ICWA produced some harsh results for non-Indians who adopted Indian children in good faith, yet Congress has rejected every effort to weaken tribal authority under the ICWA. The tribes once more have control of the one indispensable element to their future.

Self-Determination: Other Government Reforms

A few, seemingly modest, structural changes in the past thirty years to the Indian policy-making machinery of the United States account for the extraordinary pace of these statutory and administrative changes. In 1974, Congress created the American Indian Policy Review Commission, made up of six members of Congress and five Indian people, to review the state of Indian affairs and make recommendations for change. The commission produced a report that was not an artistic success, but did contain most of the current ideas generated by the tribes for meaningful reform.

A key and simple recommendation of the commission was the reestablishment of committees on Indian affairs in the Senate and House of Representatives. A Senate Select Committee on Indian Affairs was established and is now simply the Senate Committee on Indian Affairs. While no similar committee was established in the House, Indian policy has received considerable attention from the chair of the House Interior Committee and its successors, including the current House Resources Committee. This restructuring of congressional processes for considering Indian affairs legislation has changed the political dynamic with which the tribes must contend. Even when the committees are under leadership hostile to tribal rights, most members of the committees will not support legislation that is broadly opposed by tribal governments. This hardly amounts to a blank check for the tribes. Progress remains deliberate, and tribes have to be very organized and very persistent to work changes in the law. However, the bad old days of congressional rule of Indian affairs by fiat appear to have ended. The organs of Indian policy-making respond more to what the tribes desire, and it is hard to imagine a major policy being enacted over the opposition of tribal governments.

The executive branch, too, has changed its Indian policy machinery. Most significantly, perhaps, President Carter in 1977 elevated the head of the Bureau of Indian Affairs from "Commissioner of Indian Affairs" to "Assistant Secretary for Indian Affairs." To the outside observer, this change appears insignificant. The reality in the bureaucracy is that assistant secretaries have more influence over budget decisions, greater standing in interagency contests, and greater access to members of Congress and state and local officials. The Assistant Secretary for Indian Affairs these days is more a politician than bureaucrat and has many opportunities to press for change both inside the agency and out.

Statements of Indian policy by presidents of the United States have become de rigueur. From presidents who made Indian affairs a priority (Nixon, Carter, Clinton) to presidents that did not (Reagan, Bush, Bush), every president in the self-determination era has had *something* to say about Indian affairs. The greatest use of executive statements of policy among recent presidents was by President Clinton, who issued executive memoranda and executive orders regarding subjects such as Indian religious freedom, consultation with tribes by federal agencies, and Indian education.

Indian Policy in the Year 2000: No Longer "the Miner's Canary"

By any measure, and certainly when measured against past eras of federal Indian policy, the preceding list is an impressive accomplishment by Indian tribes and their advocates. In 1900, Indian culture was under attack. Tribal government, to the extent it existed at all, was underground. Indians were uniformly poor, without formal education, and tragically unhealthy. They were to be absorbed into the population at large. The peoples known as American Indians were brought to the brink of destruction. Certainly things have changed dramatically for the better.

This is not to say that there are not daunting problems and challenges for Indian tribes. The legislation described above was far from perfect from the tribal perspective, and the effort continues to improve each of these statutes to more closely reflect tribal aspirations. Moreover, as scholar P. S. Deloria regularly points out, Congress and the courts could do away with tribal government in an afternoon, should they so choose. What Congress hath given, Congress can taketh away.

Yet, it is remarkable that the tribes have succeeded in fundamentally changing the terms of the debate in Indian policy. Indian policy is no longer made with an eye toward the eventual disappearance of the tribes. That tribal governments possess, and should possess, a certain measure of authority is no longer a subject of debate, even though a lively battle continues over the extent of that authority in particular cases. No serious policymaker proposes that the federal–tribal trust relationship be terminated. Indeed, recent federal efforts reflect a sense among policymakers that the federal responsibility is ongoing, perhaps perpetual. When we argue, for example, that the Native American Graves Protection and Repatriation Act should be strengthened to protect ancient human remains from scientific exploitation, it is well to reflect on the fact that this debate could not have even taken place in 1900. The existence of a National Museum of the American Indian on the Capitol Mall celebrating the endurance of living Indian cultures would have been well beyond the contemplation of the makers of federal Indian policy in 1900.

In short, Indians can no longer be deemed "the miner's canary." The tribes have found their voice in the federal policy-making process and are no longer the passive victims of tragic policy errors made by others. They are part and parcel of the policy process, and have the legal, political, and economic wherewithal to defend their interests in the federal and state political systems. If bad policy is made, it is not because Indians had no opportunity to influence the process.

Indeed, it would seem Indian political power is at its peak. This is a function of two related efforts. First, the tribes have become active financial supporters of candidates for public office, especially the gaming tribes. A good many members of Congress have acquired a serious taste for campaign contributions from Indian tribes and their supporters and are extremely unlikely to support legislative initiatives to deprive tribes of their right of self-government. Although this sort of congressional support for tribal causes is shallow, perhaps even cynical, it is as real as the congressional support for unions, pharmaceutical companies, environmental groups, and the extractive industries.

Second, the power of the Indian vote is beginning to be realized. Candidates in statewide elections in states such as Arizona, Montana, New Mexico, Alaska, and South Dakota are loath to antagonize Indian voters due to the sheer number of Indian voters—more than enough to carry the day in a close race. Even in states where the number of Indian votes is only a small percentage of the total—such as Washington, California, and Minnesota—tribes have formed powerful alliances with other groups to defeat disfavored candidates and elect candidates responsive to Indian issues. The relatively low turnout of American voters could permit highly organized Indian voters to have a disproportionate impact on the outcome of an election. In New Mexico, for example, the voting age population of the state is 10–11 percent of the total population. Between 2000 and 2004, the number of voters in reservation precincts increased by 31.5 percent.[10] Should this growth continue while the downward trend in American voter turnout continues, Indians could one day cast votes in amounts disproportionate to their population. A growing tradition of single-issue bloc voting has the potential to give tribes political influence beyond their numbers.

Additionally, Indian progress reflects real change in race relations in the United States in the last forty years. Race continues to be a source of tension; perhaps it always will, even in a country with the noblest of pluralistic intentions. Yet there is a discernable change in how Indians are perceived by non-Indian America. Consider Indian gaming. In some states, tribes had to win statewide referenda in order to legalize their casinos. In every state, had the non-Indian public been deeply antagonistic to Indian gaming, the tribal gaming operations simply could not have survived, let alone flourished as they have. The cynic might interpret this phenomenon as a measure of non-Indian support for gambling, and certainly it is to some extent. More likely, though, is that support for Indian gaming is more truly support for *Indians* rather than support for gaming. Peering into the polling data on the public's attitude about Indian gaming leaves the strong impression that the public simply wants to do something, at long last, that is good for the tribes.

If it is true, as I suppose, that Indians are no longer "the miner's canary," then we live in a momentous time, the time when the place of the Indian Nations as permanent components of the American federalist system was at last secured. Indian tribes have more control of their destinies than they have had in many years. What they will choose to do with this control cannot be anticipated, yet a few themes suggest themselves from the current policy debates.

Federal Indian Policy in the Twenty-first Century: Restoring Tribal Authority

Clearly, the issue most on the minds of tribal leaders is the restoration of tribal governmental authority that has been lost over the past three decades to a Supreme Court that has quite thoroughly redefined the scope of tribal sovereignty. Ironically, even as Congress became increasingly at ease with tribal sovereignty, the Court became uneasy. On the basis of historic doctrine, the tribes clearly have the better of the legal argument. Yet they have suffered a series of defeats in the Supreme Court as impressive as the list of victories they have won in the Congress.

The Court clearly is put off by tribal sovereignty in two key respects. First, conservative members of the Court struggle with the concept of sovereign entities in America other than the states and the United States. In their notion of federalism, there simply is no place for another 560-some sovereigns. Second, the entirety of the Court is clearly offended by the idea of tribal authority over persons having no right to participate in tribal governance. In the absence of at least the constructive consent of non-Indians to tribal jurisdiction, the Court is quite unwilling to subject non-members of a tribe to its jurisdiction.

These are real concerns. It seems rather un-American to subject a citizen to the authority of a government in which she cannot, and can never, fully participate. The concern is made all the more pressing by the none-too-infrequent stories of tribal governments denying basic rights to their members and others. The problem is that the Court's approach is not to search out the abuses and rectify them. Rather, the Court prescriptively addresses the possibility by stripping tribes of whole realms of authority, particularly over non-Indians. Scholars question the authority of the Court to do so, but because Congress has defaulted on its responsibility to manage Indian affairs in this respect, the Court has taken over.

The solution for the tribes is obvious. They must ask Congress to take charge of defining the reach of tribal sovereignty. Congress, and not the Court, is the appropriate body to weigh the advantages of tribal authority in a given situation, consider the possibilities for abuse of power, and provide remedies to address such abuses. The tribes, of course, object to congressional limitations on their authorities, as do critical scholars who have described well a theoretical tribal sovereignty that is limited only by specific tribal cessions of authority. As attractive as such a theory may be, it is wholly unrealistic in practice. Even an Indian-friendly Supreme Court justice, Thurgood Marshall, described such notions of Indian sovereignty as "platonic." And to imagine that Congress will in wholesale fashion restore all of the tribal authorities that have been restrained over the past 218 years is fantasy. A pro-Indian member of Congress may be perfectly willing to defend Indian tax and regulatory immunities and to appropriate federal funds for tribal programs, but that same member of Congress is quite unlikely to subject the non-Indian majority of his constituents to unfettered tribal jurisdiction.

Therefore, if the tribes wish to have Congress restore tribal authorities, they will have to settle for a piecemeal approach. Authority can be restored a bit at a time, as it was when Congress legislatively reversed the Supreme Court's *Duro* decision that tribes lacked criminal jurisdiction over Indians not members of the tribe that brought the charges. The Court in the *Lara* case upheld this congressional restoration of tribal authority last year, opining that "limited" restorations of inherent tribal authority are permissible.[11]

The key is for the tribes to think—and talk—much less about their "power" as governments, and much more about their *responsibilities* as governments. A tribal request for a restoration of authority from the Congress will be strongest in a situation where a tribe has assumed a particular responsibility, has strived to meet that responsibility, and makes a credible case that the responsibility cannot be met without additional authority. In these circumstances, a pro-Indian member of Congress can explain to her non-Indian constituents why the tribe should have authority over them, even though they cannot vote in tribal elections and receive no share of the tribal income.

Moreover, tribes should expect that restored authority would come only with strings attached. Even when Congress reversed the Court's decision in *Duro*, it did so knowing that nonmember Indians were subject to a maximum term of one year in jail under the Indian Civil Rights Act. To expect Congress to restore authority without similar restrictions on the extent of tribal authority is not realistic in the existing, or the foreseeable, political climate. Thus, tribes should be prepared for requirements like federal approval of expanded tribal regulatory programs, more specific performance criteria for the use of federal funds, and federal court review of criminal convictions in tribal forums.

The areas in which tribes should press for additional authority, including authority over non-Indians, is obviously up to the tribes. The case is most compelling when additional authority is needed to meet the most pressing needs of the tribal communities. For example, violence against Indian women is epidemic; recent estimates are that one in three Indian women will be assaulted in their lifetimes. The data also suggest that non-Indians will commit most of these assaults. Here a strong case can be made that a comprehensive program for ending violence against Indian women requires authority over the non-Indians who commit these acts.

Take also the epidemic alcoholism and substance abuse in Indian Country. Reservations have become havens for methamphetamine production and use. Bootlegging alcohol on reservations has an unhappy history reaching back to the nineteenth century. If non-Indians are a major part of these burgeoning problems, and if the tribes demonstrate that they want the responsibility for solving these problems and have a credible plan to do so, what member of Congress is going to favor non-Indian bootleggers and drug dealers over a tribal government earnestly trying to save its community from these scourges?

Federal Indian Policy in the Twenty-first Century: "Customizing" Indian Policy

Federal Indian policy suffers in some respects from an absurd inflexibility. Congress, for obvious reasons, prefers to legislate in omnibus fashion by enacting statutes equally applicable to all tribes, rather than taking into consideration the vast differences in Indian Country. Tribal populations range from less than ten to over 250,000, and reservations vary in size from one-half acre to the size of West Virginia. Tribal physical environments include everything from high desert to rain forest. Their histories are as varied as that of the fifty states. Some have treaties with the United States; others do not. Socioeconomic conditions range from genuine prosperity to grinding poverty. And yet, federal statutes and court decisions treat the tribes largely the same. This is absurd.

Of the 560 or so federally recognized tribes, over 220 are in Alaska, where only one tribe has a reservation. Over 100 are in California, virtually all with small reservations and small populations. Thirty-seven are in Oklahoma, where there are no reservations, though there is trust land over which the tribes have jurisdiction. Fully 60 percent of the tribes are very small, have no treaties with the United States, and have very small reservations. What possible sense does it make to have statutes and court decisions treat such tribes as though they were the same as tribes in Montana, Wyoming, North Dakota, South Dakota, Arizona, and New Mexico? For that matter, what sense does it make to treat *any* two tribes as though they were the same?

The Interior Department made a ham-handed effort at distinguishing among tribes in the early 1990s, when it announced that "historic" tribes (those intact since their contact with Europeans, particularly treaty tribes) had inherent sovereignty, while "created" tribes (those Indian communities cast together from several groups or that were only a part of larger groups from which they had separated) did not have inherent sovereignty. While the facial appeal of the distinction is somewhat understandable, Interior painted with too broad a brush. Congress almost immediately enacted legislation prohibiting such distinctions.[12]

It should also be noted that federal programs for tribes do have some flexibility. Tribes may, for example, choose from the menu of BIA and IHS programs which programs they will contract to operate under the Self-Determination and Self-Governance acts. Similarly, when dealing with the Environmental Protection Agency, tribes may choose from among the various regulatory programs what aspects of the programs they will assume responsibility for. Still, the terms of the arrangements are uniform and treat the small tribe in California as they would the large tribe in Montana.

The considerable obstacle that must be overcome is the preference of the Congress and the executive agencies for the convenience of a single set of rules applicable to all tribes. Certainly, Congress cannot be expected to legislate tribe by tribe as to each federal program for Indians. However, there is no reason the authority to deal with the tribes individually cannot be delegated to the agencies. It will require considerable effort by the tribes to force the agencies to deal on such a basis, but with adequate congressional oversight of agency implementation, it can be done.

The trickier matter of jurisdiction *will* require special congressional attention. Allocating jurisdiction among federal, tribal, local, and state governments requires a balancing of interests that is only appropriately done by the elected representatives of the people of the tribes and states. The agencies can be helpful in facilitating discussions among the affected governments, but actually approving a restatement of jurisdiction probably should be done only on a case-by-case basis with the entire weight of the United States behind it.

Tribes have traditionally found strength in numbers when approaching the Congress, and there will be considerable reluctance among tribal leaders to pursue their objectives in isolation. Moreover, tribes have tended to have an altruistic, "no tribe left behind" mentality about these matters. The reality, though, is that the large tribe in Montana or South Dakota has virtually nothing in common with a small Alaska tribe, save their identity as American Indians. At some point, the Montana tribes or the Alaska tribes may choose to pursue their own interests without regard to whether the tribes of other states receive the same consideration. Indian policy-making necessarily becomes more complex at that point, but it also becomes more sensible when it is customized to meet the particular circumstances of each tribe.

An important caveat is required here. Tribes that choose to pursue their interests separately should never do so at the expense of others. The disgraceful conduct of certain gaming tribes in preventing entry into the gaming industry by other tribes deserves the condemnation of all. Recent revelations in Washington show the consequences of tribes climbing into the political sewer to attain their objectives at the expense of other tribes: they get bitten by rats.

Indian Policy in the Twenty-first Century: Redefining the Trust Relationship

The *Cobell* trust funds litigation,[13] regardless of its ultimate outcome, has had the effect of making clear for both the United States and the tribes that the trust responsibility as currently defined is inadequate in concept and in its implementation. Indeed, the government's performance after eight years of reform efforts suggests that the Individual Indian Money account system cannot be fixed, or can only be fixed at an expense that exceeds the value of the resource.

Moreover, reform of the trust system inevitably will lead to more intrusion by the Interior Department into tribal decisions regarding tribal trust lands. If the department is to be held to the standard of a private trustee, the process will inevitably become more formal and unfriendly to the tribes and individual owners of trust lands. The informal and flexible management of trust funds and trust lands that evolved now haunts Interior. If the response is to impose processes to ensure that the trust is very rigorously enforced in every circumstance, the tribes and the individual land owners face a much different, much less responsive Interior regime for management of trust resources. Delay and inflexibility promise to be the hallmarks of trust administration in the future.

Worse still, there is little to indicate that Interior possesses resources or expertise that the tribes do not in the area of managing trust resources. The Self-Determination Act has had the broad effect of severely diminishing the capabilities of the BIA and simultaneously and dramatically increasing the capabilities of the tribes. That of course is as it should be. It raises the issue, though, of whether the tribes are simply more capable of managing and protecting those assets than is the Interior Department. If so, obviously the sensible policy is to assist tribes in managing the resources rather than creating a duplicative and intrusive federal system to do so.

It is troubling as well that the trust as currently constituted is premised on a presumption of Indian incompetence. This presumption goes far in explaining why it has become so very ineffective in modern times. Whatever may have been true in 1900, Indians simply do not need the protection of the trust to defend their interests in their property in 2005. Moreover, it should always be remembered that this view of Indians as the incompetent wards of the United States gave rise in Indian law doctrine to the notion that the Congress possesses plenary power to do as it chooses with Indian property, including selling that property without the consent of the tribal owners. That fact alone is reason enough to seek a new definition to the federal–Indian trust relationship.

Certain elements of the trust are beneficial and should be retained. Trust lands and income derived directly from trust land are largely immune from state and federal taxation, for example. There is no reason that tribes should suffer the disabilities of trust status in order to enjoy the advantage of tax immunity. Additionally, current Supreme Court doctrine attaches great significance to the trust status of property when determining the extent of tribal jurisdiction. Tribal authority over these lands should remain intact even without the intrusive federal supervision that trust status has bred. Other advantages also arise from the federal obligation to protect the beneficial interests of tribes and individuals in trust lands. There is no reason that tribes should not continue to enjoy such advantages while at the same time enjoying greater freedom to manage that property as the tribe chooses.

Needless to say, any change in the attributes of Indian trust property requires the consent of the affected tribes. Redefinition of how trust lands will be managed is a perfect opportunity for tribe-by-tribe negotiations that result in specific procedures, and consequences for failures to abide by those procedures, for the management of trust lands. The tribes are likely to have very different priorities, and the current one-size-fits-all approach to trust reform is clearly inadequate to meet the needs of all tribes.

Conclusion

Indian policy for 218 years has swung wildly between policies that presume the imminent disappearance of the tribes, and policies that foster an ongoing role for tribes in American federalism. It may be that this policy schizophrenia has come to an end, and that tribes have won a permanent place in the American governmental system and a perpetual and unique relationship with the federal government. If this is true, it hardly marks the end of tribal efforts to reform policy. Many challenging and complex issues remain to be resolved, and the best efforts of tribal, state, and federal policymakers will be required to address them. These issues, however, are in a sense only the details of the armistice. If the great war for survival has been won, and I believe that it *has* been won, this is indeed a Golden Era of federal Indian policy.

Notes

1. Lewis Meriam, *The Problem of Indian Administration: Report of a Survey Made at the Request of Hubert Work, Secretary of the Interior, and Submitted to Him, February 21, 1928* (Baltimore: Johns Hopkins University Press, 1928). Hereafter cited as *Meriam Report*.

2. J. D. C. Atkins, *Annual Report of the Commissioner of Indian Affairs to the Secretary of the Interior for the Year 1887* (Washington, D.C.: U.S. Government Printing Office, 1887), xxi–xxiii.

3. Estelle Reel, *Annual Report of the Commissioner of Indian Affairs to the Secretary of the Interior for the Year 1900* (Washington, D.C.: U.S. Government Printing Office, 1900).

4. *Meriam Report*, 12–13.

5. Dwight D. Eisenhower, "Statement by the President upon Signing Bill Relating to State Jurisdiction over Cases Arising on Indian Reservations, August 15, 1953," *Public Papers of the President of the United States: Dwight D. Eisenhower, 1953* (Washington, D.C.: Office of the Federal Register), 564.

6. "Termination of Federal Supervision: The Removal of Restrictions over Indian Property and Person," *U.S. Statutes at Large*, 67: B132.

7. Felix S. Cohen, "The Erosion of Indian Rights, 1950–53: A Case Study in Bureaucracy," *Yale Law Journal* 62 (1953): 348, 390.

8. Lyndon Baines Johnson, "Special Message to the Congress on 'The Forgotten American' March 6, 1968," *Public Papers of the Presidents of the United States: Lyndon Johnson*, part 1 (Washington, D.C.: Office of the Federal Register, 1968): 335.

9. Richard Nixon, "Special Message on Indian Affairs July 8, 1970," *Public Papers of the Presidents of the United States: Richard Nixon* (Washington, D.C.: Office of the Federal Register, 1970): 564–567, 576.

10. *Native Vote 2004: A National Survey and Analysis of Efforts to Increase the Native Vote in 2004 and the Results Achieved*, First American Education Project, May 2005, 32–33.

11. *Duro v. Reina*, 495 U.S. 676 (1990); *United States v. Lara*, 541 U.S. 193 (2004).

12. See P. L. 103-263, §5(b) (May 31, 1994), codified at 25 U.S.C. §476(f).

13. *Cobell v. Norton*, No. 1: 96CV01285 (D.D.C.) (Judge Lamberth).

An Overview and Patterns in Federal Indian Law

21

WALTER ECHO HAWK

I AM GOING TO PRESENT TODAY AN OVERVIEW of federal Indian law, its changes over time, and where we stand today in those patterns. I will also provide my thoughts, as an Indian law practitioner, about what the future trends of Indian law may be. Many topics have been discussed in this symposium, relating to the encounter between the two cultures that was initiated by the Lewis and Clark Expedition as their canoes paddled up the Missouri River into this region of the world. My topic is going to focus on the law that pertains to the survival of the Native people and the Native tribes who greeted Lewis and Clark.

My tribe, the Pawnee tribe, was not among the tribes that actually greeted Lewis and Clark. Their canoes came up the Missouri River, which was the eastern boundary of the Pawnee Nation. We call it Kitswaruksti, which means "the Holy River." In the summer of 1804, the Pawnee Nation was on its summer buffalo hunt in our tribal buffalo hunting grounds, as were the Oto tribe and the Omaha tribe. However, Lewis and Clark were able to round up some of the Oto chiefs, who engaged in a discussion with them, and the Americans came bearing gifts at that time and were seeking commerce and trade with the Indian Nations of the Great Plains and the region of the Louisiana Purchase. One of my ancestors on my Oto side, as I am related to the Oto on my grandmother's side, was one of the chiefs that greeted Lewis and Clark at that time. His name was Shunga Tonga, which means "Big Horse." Today, that name is a Shunatona family. Many of you will know members of the Shunatona family. My grandfather, Chief Babe Shunatona, has a peace medal that was given to him at that time by Lewis and Clark—a Thomas Jefferson medal. He complained at the time, in the diaries of Lewis and Clark, that the other chiefs got a bigger medal than he did, so they gave him a bigger-sized medal.

I want to focus on federal Indian law from the time of Lewis and Clark up to the present, and more specifically, to provide just an overview of the historical patterns in federal Indian law and my thoughts as to the future trends in that field of law. At the outset, the role of law has always had a very powerful effect on the survival of the Indian tribes, Native American culture, tribal land, and tribal political rights in the United States. Law has always been fundamental to the survival of those Native interests.

When the Lewis and Clark Expedition entered into the Great Plains on their voyage of discovery, they encountered a very complex tribal world. They found that every inch of the Louisiana Purchase was occupied by very powerful Indian tribes, who had resided throughout the region from time immemorial, occupying their aboriginal lands in this very vast domain. And yet, by the year 1871, when Congress acted to end the treaty-making era, the United States had effectively conquered and colonized the entire Louisiana Purchase. The tribes' lands had pretty much been taken at that point through a series of treaties. The tribes had been removed in just a short period, about sixty-five years, to small reservations—remnants of their former aboriginal lands—and they had been militarily defeated, conquered, and colonized by the United States. My question today is: were those actions legal? Were those actions lawful under American law? That is what I want to pose to you this afternoon.

I will address four subjects. First, I would like to talk a little bit about what is "law" itself and what is the place of law in society. Secondly, I will define federal Indian law and discuss the role it has played historically, either to harm Native Americans or to protect Native Americans. Federal Indian law has been used both ways—as a shield or as a sword—a shield to protect the rights of Native people or a sword to pierce through the heart of their sovereignty and their cultural rights as Native people. Third, I will discuss the historical patterns as to when the law has been used as a sword, when the law has shifted back to be a shield. We do have a history of pendulum swings between those two uses of the law with respect to Natives in the United States. And finally, I want to provide some of my own thoughts about the future trends of federal Indian law.

The Concept of Law

What is law? A dictionary definition of law is that law is simply "a system or body of rules, principles, and regulations and standards that are prescribed by a government." The laws that are prescribed by a government are derived from legislation, from customs, and from policies, and they are broadly accepted throughout the society and recognized and enforced by the courts. These rules affect the condition of the society through their observance of these rules and regulations. Ideally, the law is a set of rules of civil conduct that is supposed to reflect the values of the society that created the law. It is intended to serve that society, to protect that society's institutions and interests, and it is conservative in that respect.

Professor Carey Vicenti has spoken in the past about the role of law, how it is supposed to not only protect our very best values and codify that into a system of rules and principles, but at the same time protect the very institutions that created the law itself, the institutions that make up society. It is supposed to promote the prevailing notions of justice at any given time in history that are held by the particular society—that which is right, that which is moral, should be promoted by the various laws that society makes for itself. In that fashion, law identifies lawful conduct—what is lawful—by providing a logical rationale and a justification for state action and conduct about national policies.

Being lawful implies, or imports, some sort of a moral content, an ethical content. It must be right because it is legal. It must be right because it is lawful. Our society has declared that certain policies or actions are lawful. So it imports an ethical element as well. Being legal merely connotes that you have complied with the rules, but lawful, at the larger connotation, imports some ethical and moral elements into action.

Finally, law does change. It is supposed to change over time to keep step with society's changing needs and society's changing values. In short then, the law, which we will be discussing this afternoon, from a practical standpoint, is simply a manmade institution, and its purpose is to serve and protect the society or the government that created it.

There are a couple of popular misconceptions about law, in my view. I know I had them as a younger man before I went to law school, and even in my younger days as an attorney. Many people, including myself, tend to equate law, or the rules of law, the principles of law, with universal truth of some kind—we think that the law is wise, like biblical law or some natural truism that stands true throughout the test of time. We see that in concepts such as "wisdom of Congress" in making these laws or the "discretion of judges" to decide cases and apply principles of law in the cases. But I submit that there are very few laws or rules of law that are, in fact, universal truths. What may seem right or just or correct or accurate to one generation may look foolish to the future generation that changes the law. The law is always being amended, repealed, aggregated, and changed over time, so whatever the lawmakers of the past century may have thought was right and just has been repealed over time.

So there are very few universal truths that we will find in the law. The Constitution of the United States embodies many things that are close to universal truths, but even it itself has been amended and added to over time.

The second misconception is that many people tend to equate law with justice. If it is law, it must be equated to our concept, our notion, of justice. But that, again, is not necessarily true in all instances, either here in the United States or in other countries. For example, to cite an extreme example, apartheid was perfectly legal and perfectly lawful under the law of apartheid South Africa. The double standard and the discriminatory treatment of the native people by the apartheid government of South Africa was all done in accordance with the law of that nation. It was lawful conduct, but it was not necessarily justice. The same is true with Nazi Germany, to cite another extreme example. That regime was again supported by German law at that time, and under that German law, horrible, horrendous atrocities were committed—genocide, the most horrible things imaginable, were perfectly legal and lawful under German law. They were promulgated by the government, widely accepted and enforced by the courts, and rationalized. Not in all instances, then, can we say that law equals justice.

American law, to bring it closer to home, over history has also supported, justified, and rationalized many injustices in the history of our nation. Slavery, to cite one, was imbedded in the U.S. Constitution—the notion that another human being is property, and rationalized by the U.S. Supreme Court in very eloquent opinions. That was the law of the land, but it was not a just law. It was not justice. The same thing with the separate but equal doctrine of *Plessy v. Ferguson*,[1] where the Supreme Court, our best judicial minds of that day, very eloquently rationalized the separate but equal doctrine that discriminated against black Americans for many generations until repealed by *Brown v. Board of Education*.[2] I would submit today that many of the laws pertaining to Native Americans fall into that same category—that Native Americans and the lands within the Louisiana Purchase were conquered, colonized, in accordance with American law at the time in question. In short, laws can be used by governments either as a tool for evil or for good.

The Role of Law in Indian Affairs

I would like to consider the origins of federal Indian law since the time of Lewis and Clark. During my review of the law, I want you to think about this question: has the United States' conduct and actions toward its Native people from Lewis and Clark always been lawful under American law?

As indigenous people, the Native tribes of this region suffered the same fate that indigenous people suffered on colonization that most native people across the world suffered: that is, the appropriation of their land, the destruction of their indigenous habitat, and the assimilation or destruction of their traditional ways of life. Legal scholars and legal thinkers in the United States have some very legitimate questions to ask about the law that sanctioned colonization of America. For example, American law, as I'll discuss in more detail later, sanctioned the taking of Indian land. How did the United States acquire legal title from the tribes? Was it legal? If it wasn't legal, what is our recourse? The United States actually bought the Louisiana Purchase from France, so France is the one who sold the Indian land to the United States. That is like me selling your land to someone.

What about the United States' relocation policies and their removal policies, where President Andrew Jackson marched the Cherokee Nation out of the State of Georgia on the Trail of Tears and moved them to Oklahoma. Was that legal? Was that lawful action on the part of the United States? What about the use of military force? Between the time that Lewis and Clark and the American "Big Knifes," our Pawnee name for Americans, entered this region in 1804, it was less than sixty-five years later that the tribes had been subjected to a military conquest. The use of military force—was that legal? Was that lawful? What about the assimilation policy of the U.S. government to stamp out the Native cultures, to remove the children into federal boarding schools, to the ban on Native religions that the BIA promulgated in its "Code of Indian Offenses"? Were these actions lawful? Were they legal? I submit to you that they were at that time. They were all perfectly lawful activities. The list could go on—the history of grave robbing, the double standard on grave robbing, destruction of our Native American sacred sites, our holy places, that have gone on and continue to go on—perfectly legal.

If all of these actions were legal, then the law was used as a sword to harm the Indian people under U.S. law. But on a more positive note, what about the establishment of our Indian reservations? Was that legal? What about the right of Indian tribes to have self-government? How did that come about under American law? What about the treaty hunting, fishing, and gathering rights that the courts have protected in certain periods in our history? Are those just special privileges? What about the casinos and the new Indian wealth pouring into the reservations that makes a lot of people very jealous? Are the casinos legal under American law?

The answers to these questions are very complex. They involve an inquiry into history, and we can look to federal Indian law to try to analyze and understand these answers. Historically, we will see some pendulum swings and shifts in federal Indian law between its use as a sword and its use as a shield to protect Native rights. But regardless of pendulum swings, the law has always played a fundamental role in American Indian affairs and remains so to this day, and will into the future. It is a very powerful force that affects the very survival of Indian tribes and Native people as indigenous people, and their bundle of political, cultural, human, property, and political rights in the United States in a very real and literal sense.

Defining Federal Indian Law

The body of federal Indian law is just that, the body of law concerning Indian affairs. It was created by:

- treaties: we are the only minority group in the United States that has treaties with the government;
- statutes: there are thousands of federal statutes that pertain only to Indians; they are all codified in volume 25 of the U.S. Code;
- executive orders: the president promulgates executive orders from time to time that affect Indian affairs;
- agency regulations: literally thousands of federal regulations affecting all aspects of Indian life and governments in the United States;
- court decisions: each year the U.S. Supreme Court decides vital cases affecting core interests of Indian tribes.

These sources of law define and implement the relationships among the United States, Indian tribes, and the various states. This is a body of law that originated from, and continues to be derived from, federal law, not state law. It is founded not on race, according to the Supreme Court in *Morton v. Mancari*,[3] but on the political relationships between Indian tribes and the U.S. government.

The field of Indian law is very broad from a substantive standpoint. It entails constitutional law, international law, tax law, family law, administrative law, jurisdiction law, civil procedure law, trust law (as we see in the *Cobell* case), and other aspects. From a substantive viewpoint, it is a very broad, dynamic, and vibrant area of the law. Each year it grows; it's refined through very important laws and court decisions. It's practiced in state courts and federal courts. It's practiced in the halls of Congress, in the state legislatures and federal agencies. And many of the practitioners are Native American attorneys themselves.

When I graduated from law school, there were just a handful in 1973—perhaps less than ten. Today, there are probably several hundred, several thousand non-Indian lawyers that practice this field. The practice of Indian law and the victories in Indian law have been an integral part of the American Indian sovereignty movement since the 1950s up unto the present. We have seen the rise of Indian Nations into the large sophisticated governments that dot the American landscape now throughout the Louisiana Purchase. Charles Wilkinson, in his recent book *Blood Struggle*, gives credit, and rightly so, to our distinguished tribal leaders for the rise of the Indian Nations: their determination and their courage and their bravery and their honesty and their leadership for achieving the successes.[4] But as David Getches, dean of the Colorado Law School and former director of the Native American Rights Fund, has noted, the federal Indian law made much of that possible: the significant court decisions in the modern era that I want to talk about.

But I want to add that some of the sources of federal Indian law are in international law, an important source of that body of law. The treaties are an important source of that law. Federal law and the U.S. Constitution and the treaty clauses are another important source. Supreme Court decisions are another important aspect of the law, as are federal statutes that I have talked about, including executive orders. Tribal law, the laws passed by the tribal governments themselves that are important in tribal courts, are another important source of federal Indian law. State law has very little to say about federal Indian law. And now there is even a movement for international standards—the UN draft Declaration on the Rights of Indigenous Peoples is an attempt by Native peoples to move into the international arena to establish international minimum standards for the rights of indigenous peoples.

Origins of Federal Indian Law

The development of federal Indian law began in earnest shortly after Lewis and Clark came into this region through the Marshall trilogy of cases that were decided by the Supreme Court. The Supreme Court began the task of defining the sovereignty and landholdings of American Indian tribes and their place in U.S. society. This was led by the Chief Justice, John Marshall, who wrote the decisions of three cases between 1823 and 1832. Those decisions enunciated principles that endure today, both being good or bad depending on how you look at them. But the upshot of these decisions established the cornerstone and foundation of federal Indian law as we know it today.

In effect, those decisions gave to the United States all of the powers of a conqueror with respect to Native people. With the stroke of his pen, supported by legal rationales, Justice Marshall set forth the cornerstone. In doing so, he agonized, as being an honest man I guess, about how to justify and to rationalize from a legal standpoint the United States' control over Indian Nations who at that time, practically speaking, especially in the Louisiana Purchase, were largely independent and powerful nations who owned land and occupied land located outside of the boundaries of any state. This is how he did it.

The first case was *Johnson v. McIntosh*,[5] which was decided in 1823, nineteen years after Lewis and Clark entered this region. The issue in this case was whether an Indian Nation could sell its land to anyone other than the United States. The tribe in that case wanted to sell its land to an individual. But the U.S. Supreme Court held that the tribes could not sell their land to anyone other than the United States. But it's the logic of that holding that had profound implications, because the Chief Justice reasoned that the tribe could not sell what it did not own. He reasoned that the tribe did not own the land because of the European Doctrine of Discovery.

The European Doctrine of Discovery was broadly accepted at that time among the nations of Europe who were engaged in colonizing the rest of the world. It was an understanding among the European nations that the first European nation to "discover" a foreign land was the only entity to whom the natives could sell their land. But John Marshall took that doctrine one step further in *Johnson v. McIntosh* to mean that, in the United States, discovery actually conferred legal title in fee simple absolute upon the discovering nation. There was some support for this remarkable notion that mere discovery, bouncing along on the coast in the ships of Columbus, or paddling a canoe up the Missouri River, literally conferred title on the United States. That explorers could have the power to claim land discovered by them on behalf of the countries that commissioned their exploration or voyages was commonly accepted at that time by the colonial powers in Europe. One can trace the origins of the theory to the Catholic Church. In May of 1493, Pope Alexander VI issued a papal bull declaring that "whereas Columbus had come upon lands and people undiscovered by others well disposed to embrace the Christian faith, all lands discovered or to be discovered in the name of the Spanish Crown in the region legally belong to Ferdinand and Isabella."[6] Marshall took that doctrine to heart and enlarged it in his Doctrine of Discovery.

Under that legal doctrine, the coming of Lewis and Clark through this region acted to transfer legal title of Indian lands to the United States. According to Marshall, the tribes were only left with the right of occupancy that could be extinguished at the pleasure of the United States. He justified it, not only by relying on this Doctrine of Discovery, but also stating "the tribes of Indians inhabiting this country were fierce savages whose occupation was war and whose subsistence was chiefly drawn from the forest. To leave them in possession of their country was to leave the country a wilderness."[7] At the same time, he expressed some doubts about the morality of this theory and the legal fictions it rested upon, but he nonetheless embraced them and applied them. So *Johnson v. McIntosh* had sweeping implications for the taking of Indian land, making it all perfectly legal according to the U.S. Supreme Court. The doctrine was used to justify colonialism. The doctrine has also

218 WALTER ECHO HAWK

spawned a well-developed scholarly debate among legal thinkers about the morality of that part of the origins of federal Indian law—the roots of modern federal Indian law.

The second case was *Cherokee Nation v. State of Georgia*,[8] in which the State of Georgia sought to drive the Cherokee Nation out of Georgia because it wanted the land. So the State of Georgia declared that the Cherokee government was disbanded and illegal under Georgia state law. The Cherokee Nation brought suit in federal court, challenging that state edict. But when it got to the U.S. Supreme Court, the Supreme Court refused to hear the case, saying they didn't have any jurisdiction to hear this case. The reason was that the plaintiff, the Cherokee Nation, is not a foreign nation. At that time, the federal court had jurisdiction to hear cases only between two states (state versus state), a state versus the citizen of another state, citizen versus a citizen of two different states, or a state versus a foreign nation. In those instances, the federal courts could hear the case. The Court examined those criteria and said that an Indian tribe fits none of them. In particular, an Indian tribe is not a foreign nation. John Marshall then proceeded to define what exactly are these Indian tribes. He admitted that they have governments. They occupied territory. They were not located within the boundaries of any state. But they did not meet the European standards of nationhood. He stated that they are not foreign nations but "dependent, domestic nations." They have no right of external sovereignty. They are dependent upon the United States. They only have the right of occupancy by title. And he further bolstered this new definition with the trust doctrine. The tribes are in a state of *pupilage* and their relation to the United States resembles that of a ward to its guardian. What is this state of pupilage? It was unilaterally assumed by the United States. Was it involuntary servitude? I am now a ward? The *Cherokee Nation v. State of Georgia* case was used to harm the Cherokee Nation by refusing to hear their case when Georgia tried to disband and outlaw their government. In doing so, Marshall gave birth to this notion of domestic dependent nationhood that endures to this day. Tribes are viewed as domestic dependent nations. They have the right of only internal sovereignty to govern their own affairs—self-government. They can't conduct foreign relations. This state of pupilage and the relationship of a ward that created the birth of the Indian trust doctrine endures to this day and is being discussed in the *Cobell* case, and the United States is not carrying it out very well. Indians have not fared too well under the trust doctrine because a ward doesn't have many legal rights. If you are not a citizen and you are ward, that means the state can do things to you. You don't have a First Amendment right, or equal protection, or due process rights, liberty rights. You are virtually without legal protection when you are in a state of pupilage under the trust doctrine.

The final case was *Worchester v. State of Georgia*,[9] decided in 1832, where Georgia arrested a white man for being in Cherokee territory without a state permit. The law was kind of like DWI—driving with Indians without a state permit. Here, the Supreme Court held that the State of Georgia really didn't have the authority to enforce its laws in Indian territory. That case created two foundation principles in federal Indian law that, again, endure to today. First, reservation boundaries are a barrier to state jurisdiction. And, second, the tribes have their internal sovereignty. They are free to make their own laws and be governed by them, free from state intrusion, unless Congress deems otherwise. These are bedrock principles.

The Treaty Period

There have been pattern swings during the treaty period in the history of federal Indian law, from 1540 to 1871. Treaties were entered into. The United States treated Indian Nations as sovereigns, duly ratifying over 370 treaties. The treaties ceded enormous blocks of land to the U.S. government, and the tribes relinquished their interests in those ceded lands, except in rare cases where they reserved their treaty hunting and fishing rights. The impact of these treaties was to drastically shrink the tribal land base. But the treaties also reserved reservations and protected the remaining property rights of the tribes.

The second thing of significance that occurred in this period was, again, the Marshall trilogy, which set out the foundation for federal Indian law—defining tribes as domestic dependent nations with inherent rights of internal sovereignty. Their reservations are territories that are barriers to the active intrusion by the state. There is a federal trust relationship, and only Congress, not the courts, can alter these bedrock principles. With that, we see the rise of plenary power of Congress over Indians and Indian affairs.

Congress Is King

From 1871 to 1959, Congress was king. It exercised unbridled and absolute power over Indian affairs, not limited by the constitutional protections. Statutes were enacted without any consultation with the Indian people. You talk about a harsh, mean-spirited legislative atmosphere—that is what occurred during this period, and it makes the goings on in D.C. today pale, as far as being extremely harsh, mean-spirited laws with no Native representation. And this trend led to the low point, the rock-bottom place that Native Americans hit by the 1950s. During this period, the pattern shifted to Congress and away from the courts.

The U.S. Supreme Court decided, in *Lone Wolf v. Hitchcock*,[10] that Congress can abrogate these treaties and that it could do so under its plenary power. But the Court said we must presume that Congress will exercise discretion to abrogate these treaties in a just manner, because it is the trustee. Congress is "governed by such considerations of justice as would control a Christian people in their treatment of an ignorant and dependent race." That was the assumption. You could abrogate these treaties, but we know you are going to be a good guy and only do it in a just way for their own good.

The abrogation and plenary powers were exercised by Congress with a vengeance:

- The Allotment Act of 1887, where Congress carved up the remaining reservation land base until a majority of that land was gone;
- The Major Crimes Act of 1885, overturning *ex parte Crow Dog* and bringing in state criminal jurisdiction over offenses between Indians on their own reservation;
- A bright spot—the Indian Citizenship Act of 1924, but that was too little too late, as tribes were under strict federal control, absolute federal control;
- The Termination Act of 1953, where Congress terminated the political relationship for over 100 tribes, severing them from the political relationship, disbanding them to acquire their land, to assimilate them out into mainstream society;
- Public Law 280, passed around the same time, which granted state jurisdiction over civil and criminal jurisdiction in Indian Country.

The impact of this legislative period, when Congress was king, was that by the 1950s, according to Charles Wilkinson in *Blood Struggle*, Native America had hit rock bottom. Population had shrunk to a mere quarter of a million from 5 million in 1900. The land base had shrunk to just 48 million acres—today it's 56 million. There was abject poverty throughout Indian Country, iron rule of the reservations by the BIA, assimilation, and discrimination. Education had been completely taken away from the tribes with Indian boarding schools, and there was almost complete encroachment by the federal and state governments. This was a very bad end to the era when Congress was king. We learned hard lessons about the exercise of absolute power, and it should give pause to all of us as Americans—this abuse of plenary power that went on in a democracy. How far could it really go, and how far would it go if unchecked and unbridled?

The Modern Era

Commencing in 1959 until about 1985, the law, for the first time, became a shield to protect Native rights. Using these foundation principles, we saw a golden age of federal Indian law when the Supreme Court built upon, authenticated, and strengthened these foundation principles in a modern-day context. *Williams v. Lee*, in 1959,[11] said that the State of Arizona had no jurisdiction to hear a lawsuit by a white merchant to collect a debt from tribal Indians on the reservation, vindicating tribal sovereignty in a modern context and affirming its adherence to the foundation principle that the reservation boundary is a border. *McClanahan v. State of Arizona Tax Commission*, in 1973,[12] said that the State of Arizona could not collect tax on income earned on the Navajo Reservation. This was followed by several other Supreme Court decisions, finally recognizing the tribes' power to tax. In *California v. Cabazon Band of Mission Indians*, in 1987,[13] the Supreme Court allowed gaming on reservations even if it was contrary to state and local laws. And a whole host of decisions based upon those foundation principles acted to limit state authority, to uphold tribal authority to govern their own reservation, and to uphold and enforce our treaty rights. The impact of Indian law during the modern era was, again, to facilitate the rights of the Indian Nations. The enormous progress, Charles Wilkinson says, was an important American social movement which ranks up there with the civil rights movement, the women's movement, and any other kind of important historical movement in the history of our nation.[14]

We saw that movement in this period. Congress supported it through proactive legislation, expanding the tribal powers beyond the reservation in the Indian Child Welfare Act, NAGPRA legislation, and other laws that Congress amended to treat tribes as states. The executive branch promulgated the Indian self-determination policy in 1970. All of this launched the resurgence of tribal government. The land base increased. The population was in the millions at that time. Business grew. Governments grew and became more sophisticated. There were tribal colleges, natural resource protection, and an explosion of Native culture. But, unfortunately, this trend ended prior to the 1990s.

Backlash: Postmodern Era

We entered into a new, backlash, postmodern era in the 1990s. Under Bush and Reagan appointees, the courts began a general retreat from the foundation principles to a more subjective balancing, where the justices tried to balance interests according to their perceptions of the way things ought to be in modern society, and guided primarily by the desire to protect non-Indian interests. David Getches documented seventeen major decisions decided by the Court between 1982 and 1996 that took this tack of not deciding on foundation principles, but on the subjective vicissitudes of what was the Court's majority perception of the way things are.[15] That has led to an approach that bends tribal sovereignty to fit the Court's perspective of what things ought to be and defines tribal values by the policies and values and goals of non-Indian society. Thereby, the Court is not being a bulwark against state intrusion on Indian Country and a general demotion of rights. I could cite the cases and the new rules retreating from the canons of statutory construction, but all I can say is, it is a very scary time we are in right now. Congress does not appear to be a major factor at this point in time. It appears to be neutralized. It has overturned some adverse Supreme Court decisions, like the *Duro* case on criminal jurisdiction regarding nonmembers,[16] the *Smith* case was overturned on peyote use,[17] but Congress has not been a very big factor in the last year or two, and our administration is not particularly friendly.

Future Trends

As for future trends, will the law be a sword or a shield in the future? That is the paramount question facing us. I think that the Supreme Court will continue to be bad in the foreseeable future. Justice O'Connor, who has not been that good to begin with, has resigned and will probably be replaced by someone worse. Congress, again, is impossible to predict. It just depends on the vicissitudes and the outcome of elections. International remedies are one area that Native people are investigating.

But I feel that tribal governments will continue to grow despite an adverse legal climate and despite an adverse political climate, because Indian tribes have become entrenched in the American social fabric and legal landscape. We are not going anywhere. We are indigenous to this land, and history has shown a remarkable determination to survive. And I also feel that Native culture will continue to thrive, maybe not through the law, but through growing public appreciation for our beautiful cultures and, maybe, public education.

Notes

1. *Plessy v. Ferguson*, 163 U.S. 537 (1896).
2. *Brown v. Board of Education*, 347 U.S. 483 (1954).
3. *Morton v. Mancari*, 417 U.S. 535 (1974).
4. Charles Wilkinson, *Blood Struggle: The Rise of Modern Indian Nations* (New York: Norton, 2005).
5. *Johnson v. McIntosh*, 21 U.S. 543 (1823).
6. "Inter Caetera," May 3, 1493, in *European Treaties Bearing on the History of the United States and Its Dependencies to 1648*, ed. Frances Gardiner Davenport (Washington, D.C.: Carnegie Institution of Washington, 1917), 75–78.
7. *Johnson v. McIntosh*.

8. *Cherokee Nation v. State of Georgia*, 30 U.S. 1 (1831).

9. *Worchester v. State of Georgia*, 31 U.S. 515 (1832).

10. *Lone Wolf v. Hitchcock*, 187 U.S. 553 (1903).

11. *Williams v. Lee*, 358 U.S. 217 (1959).

12. *McClanahan v. State of Arizona Tax Commission*, 411 U.S. 164 (1973). See also *Kahn v. State of Arizona Tax Commission*, 411 U.S. 941 (1973).

13. *California v. Cabazon Band of Mission Indians*, 480 U.S. 202 (1987).

14. Wilkinson, *Blood Struggle*, xiv.

15. David T. Getches, "Beyond Indian Law: The Rehnquist Court's Pursuit of States Rights, Color-Blind Justice, and Mainstream Values," *Minnesota Law Review* 86 (December 2001): 267.

16. *Duro v. Reina*, 495 U.S. 676 (1990).

17. *Employment Division, Oregon Department of Human Resources v. Smith*, 494 U.S. 872 (1990).

THE ENVIRONMENT AND LAND   VI

As Long as the Water Flows: A Century of Blackfeet Water Lost from the St. Mary Canal and the Milk River Drainage

22

RICHMOND CLOW

ON MAY 8, 1805, in what is now north-central Montana, the Corps of Discovery crossed the mouth of the *river which scolds at all others* flowing from the northwest into the Missouri River. During the past winter stay with the Mandan, the Hidatsa had described the river to the Corps by its color. When Meriwether Lewis reached its mouth, he observed that it was "the colour of a cup of tea with the admixture of a tablespoon of milk."[1] He had hoped the Milk was the highway to the northern Saskatchewan River, but its origin is on the western Blackfeet Reservation.[2] The Corps never witnessed three future events: first, the tribe's future use of the Milk and St. Mary waters; second, the policies that diverted water away from the reservation; and third, tribal efforts to regain control of their water.

The St. Mary and Milk Rivers both traverse the western edge of the Blackfeet Reservation, but they are part of two different drainages. The Milk originates from reservation springs creating the North Fork and the South Fork of the Milk River that flow northeast, joining in southern Alberta, where they become the Milk River. It reenters the United States over 100 miles east of the Blackfeet Reservation and is a tributary of the Missouri, which is part of the Mississippi River complex. Hudson Bay Divide separates the Milk from the melting mountain snows and glaciers to the west, so these waters do not reach the Milk—often keeping its flow low.[3] The St. Mary lies west of the Hudson Bay Divide and originates from the glacier streams and snow melt in Glacier National Park. It flows east through a twenty-mile lake–river complex, then turns north to Canada and is part of the Hudson Bay drainage system, but water can fluctuate from a low winter to a high summer.[4]

The Milk and St. Mary rivers remained in Blackfeet territory based on treaty boundaries. Consequently, nineteenth-century tribesmen used both rivers to water horses, to hunt in the riparian zones, and for domestic purposes. After the starving winter of 1883–1884, the Blackfeet escalated their use of St. Mary and Milk waters, building inexpensive water diversions to irrigate hay lands producing winter supplies for their stock.[5] Between 1891 and 1895, tribesmen constructed over twenty-two miles of ditches to divert water for reservation agriculture and domestic needs (see table 22.1).[6] They were able to construct these ditches because the reservation was "finely watered."[7] Indian Service Irrigation Inspector Walter H. Graves concurred, observing: "There is an abundance of water on the [Blackfeet] reservation, and it appears to be fairly accessible for diversion to areas of irrigable land."[8]

In 1893, they produced 1,700 tons of hay with their small, efficient, low-cost water diversions. By 1898, they irrigated 5,900 acres, mostly for hay.[9] In 1896, Indian Inspector C. C. Duncan observed: "if they can be induced to continue their present efforts in raising and caring for cattle they will be on a self-supporting basis."[10] That year, Blackfeet ranchers owned 20,000 cows and registered over 500 individual tribal brands at the agency. Fewer than 100 were drawing rations.[11]

Table 22.1.   Water Ditches Constructed by Blackfeet for Tribal Use, 1891–1895

Ditches Built or in Existence in 1891–1892	
Agency Ditch, Agency	2 miles
Agency Ditch, Curly Bear	1 mile
Stiffarm's Ditch (8 miles east of Agency)	1 mile
Green Grass Bull's Ditch (8 miles west of Agency)	0.59 mile
Running Craine's Ditch (8? miles west of Agency)	1 mile
Two Medicine Ditch (Two Rivers)	3 miles
Lateral Bear Chief	0.50 mile
Cut Bank Johns Ditch	2.11 miles
Ditches Built in 1893–1895	
Bull Shoes, etc. (4 miles west of Old Agency)	3.06 miles
Willow Creek, Kipps Ditch	0.77 mile
Willow Creek, Galbreaths Ditch	0.48 mile
New Agency Ditch	1.12 miles
Government Boarding School Ditch	1.39 miles
Cut Bank to Willow Creek	
Section 1	
Section 2	
Section 3	
Main Lateral	4.85 miles
	(22.87 total miles)
Unnamed Ditch on Cut Bank Creek (1 mile below Agency)	Undisclosed length

Source: N. E. Jenkins to the Commissioner of Indian Affairs, April 16, 1898, Blackfeet Irrigation, Special Case 190, RG 75, National Archives.

In 1898, the Blackfeet were irrigating 700 acres with diverted North Fork and South Fork Milk River waters. Between them, 1,800 cubic feet per minute flowed through these two small streams, and even more water flowed through the St. Mary River, where 2,500 acres were described as having the potential for irrigation. The western Milk and St. Mary rivers were the largest reservation water sources and were near irrigable lands.[12] Reservation streams provided the Blackfeet with water to develop a cattle industry.

Cattle grazing and low-cost irrigation had made the Blackfeet nearly self-sufficient on their unalloted reservation, but late nineteenth-century congressional policies to allot reservations, to build extensive on-reservation Indian irrigation projects, to sell surplus tribal lands, and to open ceded territories to homesteading destroyed tribal independence. Complementing these policies was the development of reclamation projects to deliver water to arid lands. Collectively, these decisions worked against the Blackfeet, destroying their self-sufficient cattle industry and ending their control of the Milk and St. Mary rivers, but not their right to the water.

The 1887 Northwest Commission began the disposition process when commissioners John V. Wright, Jared W. Daniels, and Charles F. Larabee discussed land cessions and separate reservations for tribes living on the northern border of Montana Territory. Tribal leaders consented to divide their common lands into the Blackfeet, Fort Belknap, and Fort Peck Reservations and open the ceded lands to homesteading. Congress approved the agreement in May 1888.[13]

The ceded lands had little water, forcing the homesteaders to claim water, and the "first water right" in the Milk River valley was filed in 1889 near the Fort Belknap Reservation.[14] Since Congress was willing to find water for the homesteaders, believing that with work and money these arid lands would bloom, Edwin S. Nettleson, chief engineer of the Department of Agriculture, proposed a St. Mary interbasin water transfer through an all-American canal to divert water to north-central Montana farms.[15] With St. Mary water, he wrote, "there is plenty of fine irrigation land awaiting only the touch of water to make it produce magnificent crops.[16] Since this proposal would adversely impinge on upstream Blackfeet water users, Indian Service irrigation engineer Ross Cartee asked that any St. Mary diversion benefit the reservation. He wrote in 1895: "There is a reservoir proposition on Milk River that will be of great benefit if made use of, especially so as in dry season, Milk River is practically dry also [on the reservation]."[17]

Water diversion discussions continued that fall when William C. Pollock and George Bird Grinnell introduced the St. Mary–Milk River project in September 1895 to Blackfeet leaders, informing them they had to discuss reservation irrigation canal construction. William Conrad, president of the

Conrad Investment Company, a "prominent northern Montana land and water developer," attended the negotiations[18] and commented, "I think it would
be a good thing if this [St. Mary River to Milk River] canal was built. You
might want this water in different places on the reservation where this ditch
runs. This is a canal running [from] St. Mary's Lake across to Milk River that
I refer to especially."[19]

These discussions led to an agreement between the Blackfeet Nation and
the United States in 1896. Article VIII states: "It is further agreed that whenever, in the opinion of the President, the public interests require the construction of . . . canals and irrigating ditches, through any portion of the
reservation, right of way shall be and is hereby granted for such purposes."[20]

At the height of the tribal water use, their control of the water was slip-
ping away, but Pollock assured Commissioner of Indian Affairs Daniel M.
Browning "that the water rights of the Indians will not be in any way im-
paired by the cession agreement, and that they have retained enough wood
and water for their uses for all time." Satisfied, Browning informed Congress
that Blackfeet water rights still remained, claiming: "I am satisfied that in making this agreement the water and timber rights of the Indians have received
due consideration of the commissioners and have been preserved intact."[21]

The Americans were not alone; Canadians also had designs on St. Mary
water.[22] The latter were concerned "that in the absence of any international law governing diversions of water flowing across national boundaries, there was no way to prevent the planned [all-American] diversion . . .
in Montana."[23] The Alberta Irrigation Company countered by constructing a canal in 1898 to divert St. Mary Canal water near Cardston, claiming both a prior right to the St. Mary water and that they had won the war
for St. Mary water.[24]

To deny the Canadians' water, Congress authorized a northern Montana
land reclamation investigation in 1900. The following year, U.S. Geological
Survey engineer Cyrus C. Babb located a 300-mile American canal beginning
at the western edge of the Blackfeet Reservation, from a proposed St. Mary
storage facility, to carry water to where the Milk River reenters Montana.
This would keep "the water in the United States for the entire course [and]
that would deprive Canadians of water."[25]

Despite heated words, American engineers knew that an international water war was unlikely because diplomacy was a high priority if the United
States was to protect nontribal water users on the lower Milk River.[26] Even
President Theodore Roosevelt realized that compromise was crucial, despite
his threat to build an all-American canal.[27] On the other hand, Canadians had
witnessed American aggressiveness toward Mexico over the Rio Grande and
wanted to avoid a conflict over the Milk and St. Mary waters.[28] When the

Canadians began constructing their southern Alberta "Spite Ditch" to transfer Milk River water back to the St. Mary, diplomacy became urgent.[29]

In 1905, U.S. Reclamation Service officials met Alberta Irrigation Company officers and together determined that the waters of the two rivers should be divided along the following formula: one-third of the Milk River and two-thirds of the St. Mary River waters going to Canada. But Americans stalled until Canadians agreed that St. Mary water would flow through the Milk River without Canadian interference.[30]

Diplomacy succeeded in 1909.[31] Secretary of State Elihu Root promoted a good-neighbor policy and "hemispheric solidarity" toward Canada to remove the stigma that America had transformed the Monroe Doctrine into a policy of justifying American intervention. Chandler P. Anderson, special State Department counsel, oversaw the International Boundary Waters Treaty Act that British Ambassador to the United States James Boyce and Secretary Root signed on January 11, 1909.[32]

This treaty is interesting from the vantage point of origin protection, which can be identified as an inherent right of a sovereign. A classic statement regarding a nation's control over water is found in the 1909 treaty.[33] In Article II, both Canada and the United States "reserves to itself . . . exclusive jurisdiction and control over the use and diversion, whether temporary or permanent, of all waters on its own side of the line."[34] These words were written one year after the U.S. Supreme Court had defined tribal implied reserve water rights in *United States v. Winters*.[35] The 1909 boundary waters treaty had ignored tribal rights on both sides of the international border.

Article IV required that the Milk River and the St. Mary River be treated "as one common stream for the purposes of irrigation and power." The waters were divided "equally between the two countries, but in making such equal apportionment more than half may be taken from one river and less than half from the other by either country so as to afford beneficial use to each." In addition, the treaty provided "that in the division of such waters during the irrigation season, between the 1st of April and 31st of October, inclusive, annually, the United States is entitled to a prior appropriation of 500 cubic feet per second of the waters of the Milk River, or so much of such amount as constitutes three-fourths of its natural flow, and Canada is entitled to a prior appropriation of 500 cubic feet per second of the flow of the St. Mary River, or so much of such amount as constitutes three-fourths of its natural flow." In turn, the United States obtained the right to use the Milk River as a canal to transport St. Mary River water to Havre farms.[36]

Since water problems were inevitable, Article III created an International Joint Commission with representation from both nations empowered to make future treaty changes. The Joint Commission changed Article IV in 1921, increasing the flow to 666 cubic feet per second, and ordered the stream volume measured constantly, which continues today.[37] The St. Mary River–Swift Current Creek waters were then distributed to dams and canals on the lower Milk River Project.[38] The Sherburne Dam site offered protection for the St. Mary Canal from Swift Current Creek's spring floods, providing economic storage potential, and Swift Current Creek's heavy runoff that may "be required to satisfy the water rights of Canada under the treaty of January 11, 1909."[39] The 1909 treaty, the 1921 modification, and the water diversion's structures denied the Blackfeet use of their water and assisted in developing off-reservation economies east of the reservation.

Cyrus Babb declared the 1909 treaty removed every obstacle to the project. The treaty "contemplated the enhancement of the water supply of Milk River by diversion of water of the St. Mary River drainage basin." To Babb, the 1909 treaty made the Milk River from its Blackfeet headwater origins to the lower Milk River valley a canal for St. Mary River water destined for the lower Milk River Project. During the diversion canal and storage facility planning, engineers "recognized that no person, commission or judicial tribunal would determine with certainty . . . what portion of the water in the stream [Milk River] constituted the natural flow of the Milk and what constituted the increased supply from the St. Mary River and St. Mary storage reservoir intended to be constructed."[40]

Construction plans began before the conclusion of the 1909 treaty. On March 25, 1905, Secretary of the Interior Ethan Allan Hitchcock took $1 million from the Reclamation Fund to initiate construction.[41] In early January 1906, Montana Senator Joseph M. Dixon informed the Havre newspaper that construction would start "confounding all international claims and contentions."[42] Building began in July 1906, and on July 1, 1917, the project was completed and 49,866 acre-feet of water was transferred from the St. Mary to the Milk River. In 1919, Sherburne Reservoir contributed 28,828 acre-feet for downstream water users. This interbasin water transfer provided Chinook and Harlem, Montana, with domestic water until the winter freeze prevented further canal diversions from the St. Mary River west of Hudson Bay Divide.[43] The completed project eliminated Blackfeet control and use of these waters.

Congress compensated the Blackfeet for the St. Mary division of the Milk River project in 1913. The Department of the Interior paid $10,937.86 as "just compensation" for damages and the right of ways affecting 2,863.93 acres of tribal lands to construct the lower St. Mary Reservoir and diversion canal. For individuals, Congress divided $2,439.60 among twenty-seven tribesmen for damages to and right of ways across allotments.[44]

With that paltry payment ninety-two years ago, the United States took control of reservation waters for downstream users, and neither the tribe nor the Office of Indian Affairs was able to compete politically with the collective power of the Reclamation Service and their political allies in the Department of the Interior who had the support of influential state and congressional leaders.

Despite the odds, the tribe's attempts to keep their water began before the 1909 treaty. William Conrad fired the first volley, diverting water from Birch Creek on the southwest reservation border. In January 1905, U.S. Justice Department Attorney Carl Rasch filed suit, *United States v. Conrad Investment Company*, claiming that Conrad deprived the tribe of water and they were entitled to "*all* the waters of the creek, beyond what was currently used by the Indians and the United States on the reservation to meet future needs consistent with the purposes for which the reservation was established."[45]

Drought struck north-central Montana as the *Conrad* case began, forcing Rasch to postpone his work on the *Conrad* case to focus on Fort Belknap Reservation lower Milk River rights where nontribal irrigators deprived tribal farmers of water. He filed *Winters v. United States* in July 1905. This was not a basinwide adjudication, and since the Milk River was "never . . . officially quantified," trouble has abounded from that time forward.[46] Three years later, the U.S. Supreme Court ruled that the Fort Belknap Reservation had an implied reserved water right that began when the reservation was created in 1888. The Court ordered upstream water users to release 5,000 miners' inches to fulfill tribal water rights, based on the need to fulfill the nation's reservation agricultural policy.[47]

Since *Winters* involved Milk River water, some asked if the ruling applied to the upstream Blackfeet users. In 1906, Milk River Project supervising engineer H. Savage wrote after the district court ruled in favor of Fort Belknap's reserved water rights: "I do not see why the Blackfeet Indians might not make claim to waters of the St. Mary River, with equal propriety." He added: "it is apparent that claims will be made to every asset and irrigation water supply is one of . . . controlling importance."[48] After *Winters*, the *Conrad* case ended, and the court followed the *Winters* ruling affirming Blackfeet rights to reservation waters, but they were denied access to their Milk and St. Mary waters due to the political power of outside interests.

From the project's completion until today, the Blackfeet have been left without water from these two rivers that are being diverted to benefit downstream water users—a classic case of tribal resources being used to develop outside communities while the reservation gets poorer. One expert observed that "virtually all the St. Mary waters arrives when the non-Indians can use it."[49] To ensure that tribal members do not use the water, Canada, America, and international monitors have installed instruments to detect unauthorized stream diversions.

One Blackfeet rancher has retold the decades of tribal frustration and mis-understanding over their inability to use the St. Mary–Milk Rivers flowing near their homes. During his younger days, he watched people monitor wa-ter levels and hid from the water checkers. He played in the empty flumes, but always watched, because water checkers scared him. Not only did the monitors frighten him, but "all his life it confused him to live next to the canal and flumes where it crosses the river and not understand why they couldn't use it." Living near the St. Mary River and diversion canal, today he is forced to pump groundwater for stock. A few tribal members pump water from the canal under cover of night to avoid water-checker detections.[50]

In 1952, with the McCarran Amendment, Congress waived "federal sov-ereign immunity in certain types of water-rights cases, permitting the U.S. government to be joined in general stream-adjudication proceedings in state tribunals."[51] Twenty-five years later, this opened the door for water-basin ad-judication when "the United States Supreme Court declared that certain states have jurisdiction to quantify" tribal water rights, basing their decision on the need to proceed with general watershed adjudication as the McCarran Amendment intended.[52] Montana then created the Reserved Water Rights Compact Commission in 1979 to negotiate with tribal Nations and made the Milk River a priority, since three reservations, two wildlife refuges, the Milk River Project, and domestic users are along the watershed.

After decades of exclusion, the Blackfeet Nation moved to reclaim con-trol over their water. In 1975, the Blackfeet Tribal Council passed resolution 34-75, declaring that the "Blackfeet Tribe are the owners and have the prior and paramount rights to all waters arising on, flowing by, through, over or un-der the Blackfeet Reservation." To carry out that claim, the tribe created a water rights office and wanted all tribal members to receive maximum bene-fits from tribal waters.[53]

In reviewing past water activities, the Tribal Council condemned the Sec-retary of the Interior for entering "the Blackfeet Indian Reservation and has constructed Sherburne Dam and maintains a reservoir on the Blackfeet Indian Reservation and has confiscated, taken and diverted away from the Blackfeet Indian Reservation the waters of the St. Mary's River and likewise the wa-ters of the Milk River for the benefit of the Milk River Federal Reclamation Project and by that conduct not only violates the Tribe's vested rights, but likewise unconscionably wastes huge quantities of water from the St. Mary and Milk Rivers."[54] Ira New Breast, a tribal biologist, added that in 1909, "there was across-the-board discrimination and we were left out of the treaty . . . and . . . now we'd like it to be revisited."[55]

The tribe's determination to regain control of their western waters, along with the increasing demand for water, convinced Montana Governor Judy

Martz to ask the International Joint Commission to review their 1921 order. There was a note of urgency because the State of Montana and the Bureau of Reclamation were "evaluating the options for meeting existing and future water needs of a number of native American tribes that reside within the basin as well as the Milk River water users that suffer significant water shortages."[56]

The Blackfeet did not support Martz. The "tribe has both aboriginal and treaty reserved rights to water in the two rivers" whose waters have cultural and economic importance to the Blackfeet." Tribal representatives protested that tribal rights were not considered in the building of the diversions, a troubling situation in the light of the *Winters* ruling. Tribal rights were never even mentioned in the 1921 International Joint Commission order. The Reclamation Service built the diversion facilities for off-reservation users, and the structures did not benefit the Blackfeet Nation, but "serve as potential barriers to full recognition of the Tribe's rights . . . [and] the Blackfeet Tribe is now having to deal with the consequences of these failures." The tribe wants to ensure full representation and support in any review, because the past "is not a history of which the United States can be proud." The tribe supports review but did not support reopening the 1921 order.[57] One potential reason may be that reopening the review might reduce the volume of water going to the United States and the tribe.

The International Joint Commission, which "prevents and resolves disputes between the United States . . . and Canada" held public meetings in July 2004.[58] A working group was formed and made the Blackfeet Nation a permanent member. They are the most crucial participant. First, any renovations or repairs to the system involve tribal reserved water rights. Second, the Fort Belknap Water Rights Compact included all the Milk River's natural flow, which depends on the St. Mary–Milk River structures to deliver the water, "subject to the [water] claims of the Blackfeet Nation." Third, most of the diversion structures are on the Blackfeet Reservation, and "they must be seen as an equal partner in rehabilitation of the St. Mary Facilities." Four, the Blackfeet Nation and the State of Montana "are in negotiations for a water rights compact that will include claims for water from the St. Mary and Milk Rivers."[59]

As the water negotiation process continues, the Blackfeet Nation will be the most important party who possess a reserved tribal water right dating from 1855. When they decide on the size and use of that right, their water may not pass anymore through the reservation for outsider use. The Blackfeet may keep or sell their water, creating an uncertain future for current users.[60] Malta rancher Bruce Hould wants the Blackfeet to determine their reserve water rights, because "they're a key player in that thing" in the future of the Milk

River Project.[61] The Blackfeet Nation, like other western tribes, has the ability to shift the balance of water power, taking water from current users, leaving Malta rancher Bruce Hould without water.[62]

When the Corps of Discovery stopped at the Milk River 200 years ago, they never conceived of the development of implied tribal reserve water rights, or tribes empowered to control their waters at the expense of the nontribal communities that would follow the Corps of Discovery on their nation-building mission.

Notes

1. Gary Moulton, ed., *The Journals of the Lewis and Clark Expedition*, vol. 4, April 7–July 27, 1805 (Lincoln: University of Nebraska Press, 1983), 124.

2. Moulton, *Journals of Lewis and Clark*. Moulton errs in writing that the Milk River's origin is in Glacier National Park, 129n.

3. B. E. Jones and R. J. Burley, *Water Supply of St. Mary and Milk River, 1898–1917*, Department of the Interior, U.S. Geological Service, Water Supply Paper 491 (Washington, D.C.: U.S. Government Printing Office, 1920), 140; R. E. Thompson Jr., *Natural Flow and Water Consumption in the Milk River Basin, Montana and Alberta, Canada*, U.S. Geological Survey, Water Resources Investigations, Report 86-4006, 1986, 3; Donald F. Putnam, ed., *Canadian Regions: A Geography of Canada* (Toronto: J. M. Dent, 1952), 346.

4. Jones and Burley, *Water Supply of St. Mary and Milk River*, 18–19; Putnam, *Canadian Regions*, 8, 346.

5. *Annual Report of the Commissioner of Indian Affairs*, 1886, 389.

6. N. E. Jenkins to the Commissioner of Indian Affairs, April 16, 1898, Blackfeet Irrigation, Special Case 190, RG 75, National Archives.

7. Provisice McCormack to the Secretary of the Interior, September 28, 1893, Blackfeet, Reports of the Inspections of the Field Jurisdictions of the Office of Indian Affairs, 1873–1900, Roll 3, Microcopy 1070, National Archives and Records Service.

8. Walter H. Graves to the Secretary of the Interior, September 23, 1899, Blackfeet, Reports of the Inspections of the Field Jurisdictions of the Office of Indian Affairs, 1873–1900, Roll 3, Microcopy 1070, National Archives and Records Service.

9. *Annual Report of the Commissioner of Indian Affairs*, 1893, 712.

10. C. C. Duncan to the Secretary of the Interior, October 3, 1896, Blackfeet, Reports of the Inspections of the Field Jurisdictions of the Office of Indian Affairs, 1873–1900, Roll 3, Microcopy 1070, National Archives.

11. *Annual Report of the Commissioner of Indian Affairs*, 1896, 175.

12. Jenkins to the Commissioner of Indian Affairs, April 16, 1898.

13. U.S. Stat. 261–266.

14. *Reclamation Project Data*, U.S. Department of the Interior, Bureau of Reclamation (Washington, D.C.: U.S. Government Printing Office, 1961), 343; Carl Mar-

tin Gunderson, "The History of the Milk River Valley" (MA Thesis, Montana State University, 1951), 127.

15. Edwin S. Nettleson, "Artesian and Underflow Investigation," *Irrigation*, Senate Ex. Doc. No. 41, Part 2, Serial 2899, 52nd Congress, 1st Session, 105; *Milk River Project*, Montana, Project History, 1902–1911, vol. 1, 5–6, U.S. Reclamation Service, Department of the Interior, Roll 76, Microcopy 96, RG 115, National Archives. Hereafter cited as the Milk River Project History.

16. Nettleson, "Artesian and Underflow Investigation."

17. *Annual Report of the Commissioner of Indian Affairs*, 1895, 181.

18. John Shurts, *Indian Reserved Water Rights: The Winters Doctrine in Its Social and Legal Context, 1880s–1930s* (Norman: University of Oklahoma Press, 2000), 124–125.

19. Proceedings of the Meetings of Commissioners for Reduction of Indian Reservations, Blackfeet Reservation, Microfiche No. 174, Indian Jurisdiction Files.

20. Charles Kappler, *Indian Affairs: Laws and Treaties*, vol. 1 (Washington, D.C.: U.S. Government Printing Office, 1903–1904), 605–607.

21. "Blackfeet Reservation," U.S. Senate, 54th Congress, 1st Session, *Senate Documents*, No. 118, Serial 3350, 5.

22. For a study of Canadian irrigation history, see Lawrence C. Lee, "The Canadian–American Irrigation Frontier, 1884–1914," *Agricultural History* 40, no. 4 (1966): 271–283. Lee stresses the importance of cooperation between the United States and Canada in settling their water disputes.

23. N. F. Dreisziger, "The Canadian–American Irrigation Frontier Revisited: The International Origins of Irrigation in Southern Alberta, 1885–1909," *Historical Papers, 1975* (Canadian Historical Association, 1975), 214–218.

24. Dreisziger, "The Canadian–American Irrigation Frontier Revisited," 218–219; Edward Wahl, *This Land: Geography of Canada* (Toronto: University of Oxford Press, 1961), 346.

25. Milk River Project History, vol. 1, 5–6.

26. *Bureau of Reclamation Project Feasibilities and Authorizations: A Compilation of Findings of Feasibilities and Authorizations for Bureau of Reclamation Projects of the Department of the Interior*, U.S. Department of the Interior, Bureau of Reclamation (Washington, D.C.: U.S. Government Printing Office, 1949), 311–315. Hereafter cited as Project Feasibilities and Authorizations.

27. Gunderson, "The History of the Milk River Valley," 131.

28. Dreisziger, "The Canadian–American Irrigation Frontier Revisited," 219–220.

29. Thompson, *Natural Flow and Water Consumption*, 2.

30. Thompson, *Natural Flow and Water Consumption*, 221–222.

31. Bureau of Reclamation, 1949, 311.

32. Thompson, *Natural Flow and Water Consumption*, 2; Richard W. Leopold, *Elihu Root and the Conservation Tradition* (Boston: Little, Brown, 1954), 62–63, 67, 100; Philip Caryle Jessup, *Elihu Root*, vol. 2 (New York: Dodd, Mead, 1938), 97–98, 98f.

33. Thompson, *Natural Flow and Water Consumption*, 12–13.

34. "Treaty between the United States and Great Britain Relating to Boundary Waters between the United States and Canada, Proclaimed May 13, 1910," *Papers Relating*

to the Foreign Relations of the United States (Washington, D.C.: U.S. Government Printing Office, 1915), 532–540. Hereafter cited as Boundary Waters Treaty.

35. *Winters v. United States*, 207 U.S. 564 (1908).

36. Boundary Waters Treaty, 532–540.

37. David J. Lystrom, Representing the United States, and R. A. Halliday, Representing Canada, "Report to the Joint Commission on the Division of the Waters of the St. Mary and Milk Rivers," 1996; Thompson, *Natural Flow and Water Consumption*, 2.

38. *Reclamation Project Data*, 344–345.

39. St. Mary Storage Unit, Milk River Feature History, 1914, vol. 10, 59–67, U.S. Reclamation Service, Department of the Interior, RG 115, Roll 86, Microcopy 96, National Archives.

40. Milk River History Project, vol. 2, 34.

41. Project Feasibilities and Authorizations, 314–315.

42. As quoted in Gunderson, "The History of the Milk River Valley," 133.

43. Milk River Project History, vol. 16, 334–335, 275.

44. E. B. Meritt to the Blackfeet, December 19, 1913, File: Damages Assessed for Right-of-Way, Lower St. Mary Lake Reservoir, Box 1167, Blackfeet Agency, RG 75, National Archives and Records Center, Seattle, Washington; E. B. Meritt to the Director of the U.S. Reclamation Service, December 27, 1913, File: Damages Assessed for Rights-of-Way, Lower St. Mary Lake Reservoir, Box 167, Blackfeet Agency, RG 75, National Archives and Records Center, Seattle, Washington. Norris Hundley, in work on *Winters v. U.S.*, only mentions the 1909 treaty and does not locate the St. Mary or Milk Rivers as originating on the Blackfeet Reservation. See Norris Hundley, "The 'Winters' Decisions and Indian Water Rights: A Mystery Reexamined," *Western Historical Quarterly* 13, no. 1 (1982): 44.

45. Shurts, *Indian Reserved Water Rights*, 63.

46. For a critical study of the *Winters* decision, see "Indian Reserved Water Rights: The *Winters* of Our Discontent," *Yale Law Journal* 88, no. 8 (1979): 1690.

47. *Winters v. United States*.

48. H. Savage to the Chief Engineer, U.S. Reclamation Service, March 22, 1906, Milk River Water Rights, 1906–1909, Milk River Project Files, 1902–1911, Bureau of Reclamation, RG 115, National Archives.

49. Hundley, "The 'Winters' Decisions and Indian Water Rights," 41.

50. Betty Mathews to author, January 15, 2005. Letter in possession of author.

51. Lloyd Burton, *American Indian Water Rights and the Limits of the Law* (Lawrence: University Press of Kansas, 1991), 27.

52. Burton, *American Indian Water Rights and the Limits of the Law*, 36.

53. The Blackfeet Tribe, Browning, Montana, Blackfeet Tribal Resolution No. 34-75, September 10, 1975, Reserved Water Rights Compact Commission, Helena, Montana.

54. The Blackfeet Tribe, Browning, Montana, Blackfeet Tribal Resolution No. 56-83, November 2, 1982, Reserved Water Rights Compact Commission, Helena, Montana.

55. As quoted in Ali Macalady, "Tribe Calls Dam a Trout Trap," *High Country News*, February 28, 2000, 1, Internet Archives Copy.

56. Judy Martz to Dennis L. Schornack, April 10, 2003. Papers of the St. Mary–Milk River Canal, International Joint Commission.

57. Statement of the Blackfeet Tribe to the International Joint Commission, 2004, Papers of the St. Mary–Milk River Canal, International Joint Commission.

58. International Joint Commission, "Basic Fact Sheet," *Public Consultation Sessions on St. Mary and Milk Rivers Water Apportionment*, 1, Papers of the St. Mary–Milk River Canal, International Joint Commission; "IJC Completes Appointments to St. Mary and Milk Rivers Administrative Measures Task Force," 1, Papers of the St. Mary–Milk River Canal, International Joint Commission.

59. "St. Mary Rehabilitation Working Group Process Agreement as Adopted by Consensus on June 23, 2004," 10–11, Papers of the St. Mary–Milk River Canal, International Joint Commission.

60. *Missoulian*, April 7, 2004.

61. *Great Falls Tribune*, November 19, 2003.

62. Daniel B. Wood, "Tribes May Shift Delicate Water Balance in West," *Christian Science Monitor*, October 26, 1999, electronic edition.

How the Land Was Taken: The Legacy of the Lewis and Clark Expedition for Native Nations

23

REBECCA TSOSIE

HE TOPIC OF THIS SYMPOSIUM is both fascinating and provocative. What are the enduring effects of the Lewis and Clark Expedition for Native Nations? As we contemplate the impact of the Lewis and Clark Expedition, we consider the past, present, and future of Native Nations, providing not only a much-needed snapshot of where we are, but also a vision of where we are headed. It is our own expedition into consciously creating the world that we aspire to. Historian James Ronda has asserted that "exploration journeys" are "all about the imagination's encounter with the physical world," which produces "new knowledge" and understandings, situated in particular places and narratives.[1] To me, federal Indian law is a body of doctrinal law that non-Native jurists have constructed to adjudicate Native and non-Native rights to tangible and intangible resources, including rights to land, sovereignty, cultural resources, and natural resources. With ownership comes control over resources and knowledge. The Lewis and Clark Expedition manifested a basic structure for the new knowledge and understanding that would be necessary to craft the body of law that would determine the ownership of lands and resources. The cultural dynamic that resulted from this expedition has been, and continues to be, played out in a host of venues. By bringing this dynamic to consciousness, we can engage in a critical appraisal of what its impact has been on the lives and destinies of Native peoples, and what Native people must do to reclaim the agency of thought and action necessary to achieve true self-determination in the contemporary global world.

Because this paper is focused on Native land rights, I will start by offering the very basic view that, at the time of contact, Native peoples "owned" every

240

square inch of land now comprised within the United States, in the sense that they exercised all of the rights generally associated with ownership (e.g., use, enjoyment, possession, right to alienate, right to exclude). Of course, at that time, there was no country called the United States. The sovereign nations of Europe claimed the lands owned by the sovereign Native Nations in the Americas. Thus, the whole idea of how Indians "lost" their lands traces back to a fundamental doctrine that imagined the nature of sovereignty and the relationship of sovereignty to land title: the Doctrine of Discovery.

The Lewis and Clark Expedition and the Doctrine of Discovery

The American public is fascinated with the Lewis and Clark Expedition. James Ronda asserts that the act of "reconsidering Lewis and Clark" is important to Americans, because in this process "we consider ourselves, not as an act of self-indulgence but as an act of self-discovery."[2] The Lewis and Clark Expedition is emblematic of the birth of a new nation carved out of "foreign soil." In the minds of the American people, Native people are incorporated into the creation story of America, and Native narratives of place and history become subsumed within American law and history. Thus, an important part of our project in this symposium is to differentiate the "American narrative" from the narratives of Native peoples, and to document the past, present, and future of Native America according to tribal narratives and worldviews.

In a material sense, Lewis and Clark mapped and documented the character and extent of a new nation. In a symbolic sense, they appropriated the places, images, and character of the people they encountered to construct an "American epic," including a new frontier—the "American West"—that would be vital to the creation of the nation. The result was to incorporate Native peoples into the political and legal structure of America, not as foreign sovereigns and not as citizens, but with a peculiar hybrid status termed "domestic, dependent nations." The brash glory of the Lewis and Clark Expedition also carries a darker underside: "discovery" and "conquest" are the twin faces of federal Indian law.

The Doctrine of Discovery as Emblematic of Western Norms

An issue to consider at the outset is whether the jurisprudence of "discovery" that has had such a profound impact upon Native peoples represents a "past" set of beliefs and norms about Native/non-Native encounters, or whether it continues to be of significance. As Robert Williams has demonstrated, the Doctrine of Discovery originated in medieval Europe as a means for European nations to justify their conquests of "non-Christian" peoples during the Crusades. The Doctrine of Discovery was imported into federal Indian law by Chief Justice John Marshall's 1823 opinion in *Johnson v McIntosh*.[3] The litigants in that case were two non-Indians, each of whom sought to maintain the paramount claim of title to the same land. The plaintiffs had received title to the land through grants directly from the Indian tribes who were in original possession of the lands, while the defendants had received title through later grants made by the federal government. In this case, Chief Justice Marshall held that the character of the Native people was such that they could not be recognized as holding the full rights and title to their ancestral lands at the time of contact, as would be the case had they been "civilized" nations. Marshall portrayed Native people as "fierce savages, whose occupation was war, and whose subsistence was drawn chiefly from the forest. To leave them in possession of their country, was to leave the country a wilderness; to govern them as a distinct people, was impossible, because they were as brave and as high-spirited as they were fierce, and were ready to repel by arms every attempt on their independence."[4]

The inevitable consequence of this situation, according to Marshall, was a bifurcated system of legal rights, which stemmed from the international Doctrine of Discovery. Because the Native peoples of the New World were "uncivilized," the doctrine of "conquest" that governed the relationship between civilized subjects of conquered nations and their conquerors, and generally permitted existing property rights to survive the political transition of governance, could not apply. Rather, Marshall crafted a modified version of the Doctrine of Discovery, which typically governed the first ownership of "vacant" lands. Under this rule, the first European sovereign to "discover" and "take possession" of lands occupied by Native peoples received the sovereign title to such lands. The Native peoples retained a more limited "right of occupancy," which essentially allowed them to maintain their actual use and possession until the sovereign "extinguished" the Native peoples' right to occupy "by purchase or conquest." According to this account, Native people were fully capable of transferring their right of occupancy to a third party, but it was not the type of "property right" that would be enforced under American law in the American courts.

Professor Robert Williams calls the Doctrine of Discovery a "discourse of conquest," and asserts that it confirmed the superior rights of Europeans to lands occupied by the "savage" Indians, encouraged white settlement of Native lands on the theory that, in the hands of Native people, these were "wastelands," and vested authority in the United States to regulate the Indians' dispossession according to the "national interest."[5] According to Professor Williams, the *McIntosh* decision institutionalized European racism and colonialism into American law and negated Native peoples' human rights by claiming that they were not equal to "civilized" Europeans.

The *McIntosh* opinion also influenced Chief Justice Marshall's subsequent opinions in the Cherokee cases, which formulated the notion of Native political identity as "domestic, dependent nations," whose rights to self-governance were qualified and limited by the superior sovereignty of the U.S. government. The legal issue in the Cherokee cases was whether the State of Georgia could enforce its laws within the boundaries of the Cherokee Nation. In *Cherokee Nation v. Georgia*,[6] the Cherokee Nation brought suit against the State of Georgia in an effort to enjoin enforcement of state laws that sought to foreclose the exercise of Cherokee legislative and judicial authority. Chief Justice Marshall authored the plurality opinion, finding that the Supreme Court lacked constitutional authority to hear the case because the Cherokee Nation was not a "foreign nation" for purposes of the Article III grant of jurisdiction over controversies between a foreign nation and a domestic state. Marshall found that the Indian tribes were "domestic dependent nations" because they "occupy a territory to which [the United States asserts] a title independent of their will, which must take effect in point of possession, when their right of possession ceases."[7] During this interval, the Indian tribes were "in a state of pupilage. Their relation to the United States resembles that of a ward to his guardian. They look to our government for protection; rely upon its kindness and its power; appeal to it for relief of their wants; and address the President as their Great Father. They and their country are considered by foreign nations, as well as by ourselves, as being . . . completely under the sovereignty and dominion of the United States."[8]

In a later opinion, *Worchester v. State of Georgia*, the Supreme Court further defined the character of the Cherokee Nation as a "domestic, dependent nation" and elaborated on the protective role of federal power, by holding that Georgia's laws could not extend into the Cherokee Nation's territory because "The Cherokee nation . . . is a distinct community, occupying its own territory, with boundaries accurately described, in which the laws of Georgia can have no force, and which citizens of Georgia have no right to enter, but with the assent of the Cherokees themselves, or in conformity with the treaties, and with the acts of Congress. The whole intercourse between the United States and this nation, is, by our Constitution and laws, vested in the government of the United States."[9]

The "Marshall Trilogy" effectively defined the subordinate sovereignty and land rights of Native peoples in relation to the superior sovereignty and title of the U.S. government. Although the Cherokee cases clearly confirm the political status of Indian tribes as "nations," they are not considered "foreign nations" because they exist within the territorial boundaries of the United States, because the commerce clause distinguished "foreign nations" from "Indian tribes," and because, through treaties such as the Cherokee Treaty of Hopewell, some Indian Nations had placed themselves under the "sole protection" of the United States. Marshall's conception of the relationship between the Indian Nations and the federal government has at least three enduring components. First, tribal sovereignty is clearly tied to geographical boundaries. Tribal sovereignty enjoys its fullest expression within tribal territory, often designated as "Indian Country." Second, the concept of Indian tribes as "domestic, dependent nations" establishes the paramount authority of the federal government with respect to Indian Nations, and the lack of state power within Indian Country. This notion receives constitutional support through the commerce clause, which gives Congress the sole and exclusive right to regulate trade with "foreign nations, among the several states, and with the Indian tribes." Finally, the trust relationship between the federal government and the Indian Nations is at the core of the relationship and is founded on the federal government's "duty to protect" the Indian Nations. As future cases would explain, the federal government's commerce clause authority could be employed on behalf of Native Nations by enacting statutes to protect their welfare.[10]

Each of these concepts plays an important role in understanding Native land claims under U.S. law. However, I want to emphasize that in all of these cases, there are competing cultural constructions about the significance of the land. It is a mistake to focus on the doctrinal claims as a feature of federal Indian law without also taking into account the significance of the claims in a cultural sense.

Native Lands and Narratives of Place and Identity

"We are the land," writes Laguna author Paula Gunn Allen of the relationship of native peoples to the land that has sustained and nurtured them for countless generations.[11] "More than remembered, the Earth is the mind of the people as we are the mind of the earth. . . . It is not a means of survival. . . . It is rather part of our being, dynamic, significant, real." Allen highlights the fact that the earth is commonly seen as a means of physical survival when in fact it is simultaneously the source of "cultural survival" for Native peoples. For the "indigenous peoples" of this land, particular geographic areas are often constitutive of cultural identity. Many Indian Nations speak of the specific "origin place" of their people as being attached to a river, mountain, plateau, or valley. This origin place becomes a central and defining feature of the tribe's religion and cultural worldview. Charlotte Black Elk, for example, relates that the Lakota creation story tells of the emergence of the Lakota people from the caves within the Black Hills, which are called "Wamaka Og'naka Icante"—the "heart of everything that is."[12] The land also becomes a way to designate the cultural universe of a particular Indian tribe. For example, the Tewa of New Mexico see their world as bounded by four sacred mountains, the same mountains that were seen by the first four pairs of sibling deities as they were sent out to explore the world in the Tewa's origin story.[13] The Tewa cosmology is structured around these mountains and the associated bodies of water, spirit entities, shrines, directions, and colors that characterize these mountains and establish the place of the Tewa people within this universe. The Navajo, or Diné, people have an analogous structure, locating themselves within the confines of four sacred mountains, and articulating a relationship between the people, the land, and the spirit entities through a distinctive set of narratives, and social and religious connections. Although the Navajo and the Tewa are culturally quite distinct and different from each other, both groups perceive that they have a responsibility to care for these sacred elements of their universe, and both maintain a strong belief that there is an appropriate balance between human beings and the natural world which must be preserved in order to ensure continual survival.

There is a second sense in which "place" is significant to Native peoples. In his book *Wisdom Sits in Places*, anthropologist Keith Basso documents the ethical precepts that derive from specific places and mark the cultural evolution of a people throughout history.[14] According to one Apache elder, "The land is always stalking people. The land makes people live right. The land looks after us. The land looks after people."[15] According to Basso, the Apache names for geographical locations provide specific descriptions of their physical characteristics (for example, "White Rocks Lie Above in a Compact Cluster") and, in that sense, they operate like a map, defining the boundaries of the Apache's ancestral lands. However, place names are also used very specifically to transmit knowledge about particular events that occurred at these places, which not only links the Apaches to their ancestors in a historical sense, but also provides a code of appropriate moral behavior by which each generation should live. The place name, then, evokes not only a picture of the place, but also a story to "make you live right."[16] The ethical lessons of the land are seen as pivotal in constructing a set of principles to guide right action, and they apply to successive generations equally. The late Ronnie Lupe, an esteemed tribal leader for many years, expressed sadness that there was a marked loss of this knowledge among the young people, and said that the lack of knowledge about what happened at these places may lead some young people to get into trouble.[17]

The cultural connections between Native peoples and the land are quite misunderstood among non-Indians. Non-Indians typically see this as a "romanticized" notion that is of limited utility in a modern era. The "mystical" aspect of this relationship is often used to discount the reality of Native rights to the land, most commonly, by the notion that Indian people lacked any conception of "ownership." While it is true that no Native people employed the concept of the "fee simple" or maintained written land titles prior to the arrival of the Europeans, there is a rich tradition of "rights" and "responsibilities" that accompanies Native narratives about the land. In the broader sense of "ownership," Native peoples most definitely maintained political and cultural claims to their ancestral lands.

The Legacy of Discovery

The legacy of "discovery" is a profound clash of narratives. At a symbolic level, the transformation of "Native" lands to "American" lands occurred through the mapping and naming of Native lands. Throughout their expedition, for example, Lewis and Clark mapped the mountains, valleys, rivers, and other natural features of the land they traversed. In some cases, they recorded the French names or Native names that had already been given to these natural features. However, in most cases, Lewis and Clark named the places according to their own experience (e.g., whether the water was "muddy" when they visited it), or through incidents that occurred when they visited the places (e.g., the day they ran our of flour), or in commemoration of people that were important to them (e.g., the "Judith River" after Clark's fiancé; "Clark's Fork," after himself). This was a "renaming process" designed to transform indigenous understandings of the land into an "American" understanding, and to supplant Native narratives with a new "American" narrative.

At a policy level, the United States used the law of nations and the rule of "discovery" to assert that it acquired title from France and Great Britain, although the Indian people were largely in undisturbed possession and occupancy of these lands. The Lewis and Clark Expedition was intended to gather the information necessary to appropriate Native title and further restrict the free movement of Native peoples across their traditional lands. Thomas Jefferson, the primary architect of the Lewis and Clark Expedition, gave specific instructions to Meriwether Lewis to "find a navigable waterway from St. Louis to the Pacific Ocean, to make contact with the Indians he encountered, and to document all that he observed en route."[18] In this sense, the Native peoples were seen as "both objects of scientific study and as sources of geographic information."[19] The Lewis and Clark Expedition was the precursor to nineteenth-century Indian policy. President Jefferson understood that the

United States could become a powerful nation only if it could annex lands west of the Mississippi. In 1803, when he assumed office, there were several significant obstacles to westward expansion, including the limited options for transportation and the lack of knowledge about the nature and characteristics of the western lands. The area was largely unmapped at the time, and popular mythology speculated that these lands harbored exotic creatures, such as wooly mastodons, as well as erupting volcanoes. In a confidential communication to Congress recommending exploration of the western lands, Jefferson mentioned the necessity of securing as much information about the Indians as possible in order to develop appropriate strategies to deal with their growing resistance to transferring any further lands to Europeans.[20] Specifically, Jefferson called for two measures: first, to encourage the Indians to abandon hunting and take up agriculture, which would necessitate "less land and labor" and "maintain them better than their former hunting lifestyle"; and second, to "multiply trading houses among them, and place within their reach those things which will contribute more to their domestic comfort than the possession of extensive but uncultivated wilds." Jefferson elaborated on the latter point in a letter to William Henry Harrison, which calls for encouraging the "good and influential individuals" among the Indians to "run into debt, because we observe that when these debts get beyond what the individual can pay, they become willing to lop them off by a cession of lands."[21]

By advocating for the "civilization" of Indian people and encouraging their dependency upon European trade goods, Jefferson set the stage for nineteenth-century federal Indian policy, which centered upon the dispossession of native peoples from their lands. Many land claims cases of the twentieth century trace back to these policies. In the next section, I will distinguish doctrines that allow Indian Nations to receive compensation for takings of their land and also highlight the operative pieces of federal legislation which have contributed to the loss of Native lands. By studying Native land claims cases, we can understand the legal mechanisms that have been employed to take Native lands.

Colonialism and United States Law and Policy: How the Indians "Lost" Their Lands

U.S. federal Indian law has consistently distinguished between the "aboriginal title" interests of Native peoples, which are essentially rights to use and enjoyment of land so long as the U.S. government has not extinguished this title, and "recognized title," which occurs through federal action which confirms the tribal property interests (generally a "reservation") under federal law by treaty, statute, or in some cases by an executive order that is later ratified through congressional action. Only takings of "recognized title" are compensable under the Fifth Amendment of the U.S. Constitution, which provides for "just compensation" whenever property is taken by the federal government for a "public purpose."[22] However, tribes sometimes encounter difficulty proving that the government action that took their lands was in fact a "taking" and not an exercise of the federal government's legitimate authority as "trustee" over tribal lands, which includes the power to sell such lands out of trust, as it did during the allotment era of the late nineteenth and early twentieth centuries. The Dawes Allotment Act of 1887 was designed to break up the collective landholdings of the Indian Nations by allotting Indian reservations in fee simple parcels to individual tribal members and selling the "surplus land" to non-Indian settlers. In the 1903 case of *Lonewolf v. Hitchcock*, the Supreme Court described congressional power to allot a treaty reservation as virtually absolute and beyond the ability of the courts to adjudicate.[23] In 1980, this ruling was modified by the Supreme Court in *United States v. Sioux Nation*, which held that federal actions with respect to tribal property would receive scrutiny under the due process clause.[24] In that case, the federal government had made no effort to offer the Lakota people fair compensation when it enacted legislation in 1877, removing the Black Hills from tribal ownership. The Black Hills are sacred land to the Lakota and many other Plains Indian Nations, and they were located within the reservation that was created by the 1868 Fort Laramie treaty with the Lakota. The Court held that, through the 1877 Act, the federal government had committed a "taking" under the Fifth Amendment, compensable with damages for the value of the land taken in 1877 (estimated at $17.5 million) plus the accrued interest from 1877 until the present (estimated at over $400 million).

A very different legal regime applies to takings of "Native title." In *Tee-Hit-Ton Indians v. United States*, the Supreme Court held that federal takings of Native aboriginal title are not compensable under the Fifth Amendment because this interest merely entitled "permission from the whites to occupy" such lands.[25] The interest "is not a property right," said the Court, "but amounts to a right to occupy which the sovereignty grants and protects against intrusion by third parties, but which right of occupancy may be terminated and such lands fully disposed of by the sovereign itself without any legally enforceable obligation to compensate the Indians."[26]

Although Native title is not compensable as a constitutional matter, certain federal statutes have enabled tribes to be compensated for takings of their Native title interests, including the federal Nonintercourse Act, first passed in 1790, which required federal consent to transfer lands out of tribal ownership and voided conveyances that did not have such consent, and the Indian

Claims Act of 1946, which was intended to settle all Native land claims in order to pave the way for the ultimate assimilation of Native peoples into American society. Before engaging this legislation, however, this paper offers a brief survey of the federal policies and laws that have divested Indian Nations of much of their lands.

Colonial Era (1492–1776)

During the colonial era, the European nations employed the Doctrine of Discovery to claim sovereign title to lands in the "New World" and to divest the Native Nations of any claim, except the right of occupancy. In fact, however, the Doctrine of Discovery operated largely at the level of theory. Great Britain and France were among the European nations that executed treaties with the Indian Nations to gain cessions of land and political alliances. These treaties recognized the Indian Nations as sovereign governments with exclusive rights to their lands, thus necessitating a mutual and voluntary surrender of interest before European colonists could take possession. Prior to the War of Independence, the British colonies were required to abide by the Proclamation of 1763, which forbade cessions of land west of the Appalachian Mountains without consent of the British Crown. This document represented the sovereign's need for centralized management of relations with the Indian Nations in order to avoid conflict and warfare. In 1764, the Crown attempted to extend this centralized authority to the management of trade between agents of the British Crown and the Indian Nations.[27] This plan, however, was never formally approved and was only partially implemented before it was abandoned altogether in 1768.

The Confederation Period (1776–1789)

A major shift in relations with the Indian Nations occurred as a result of the push by the British colonies for independence. At this point, the colonies challenged all aspects of British policy, including the Proclamation of 1763, and entered intensive negotiations with the Indian Nations to secure political and military alliances.

With respect to the Proclamation of 1763, land speculators drew on a policy statement that applied to the colonies in India, which asserted that the colonies could directly negotiate with East Indian representatives for land acquisitions. Envisioning the ultimate independence of the colonies, these land speculators "purchased" vast tracts of land from the Indian Nations.

The treaties of this era exemplify the political relations that existed between the colonial governments and the Indian Nations. For example, the 1778 Treaty of Fort Pitt with the Delaware Nation speaks of the United

States' engagement in a "just and necessary war" with Great Britain and entreats the Delaware Nation to "give free passage through their country" and to offer up any "warriors" of the Delaware Nation that were willing to join the troops of the United States in a military alliance. The document calls for a mutual and bilateral political relationship between two sovereigns, including consent to punish citizens of the other sovereign in tribunals that offer mutual justice. The document further invites the Delaware Nation to join the present confederation of the United States and form a state with political representation in Congress, at such time as this would be found "conducive to the mutual interest of both parties."[28]

In 1781, the United States approved the Articles of Confederation, in which Article IX vested the Continental Congress with the "sole and exclusive right and power of . . . regulating the trade and managing all affairs with Indians not members of any of the states; provided, that the legislative right of any state within its own limits be not infringed or violated."[29] This provision was intended to secure the benefits of centralized management of Indian affairs (e.g., to keep the peace with the Indian Nations), while still recognizing the political autonomy of the former colonies, who were actively involved in securing further land cessions. In *Oneida Indian Nation v. New York*,[30] the Second Circuit Court of Appeals upheld the legality of two treaties between the Oneida Nation and the State of New York, which took place prior to the ratification of the U.S. Constitution, on the theory that Article IX of the Articles of Confederation preserved the right of the state to purchase lands directly from the Indian Nations.

The Nonintercourse Act

That situation changed when the U.S. Constitution was ratified in 1787. As Chief Justice Marshall noted in his famous trilogy of Indian law cases, the commerce clause of the Constitution recognized the exclusive authority of Congress to regulate trade with the Indian Nations, including any cession of tribal lands. The first Congress acted immediately to assert this exclusive control by enacting the Trade and Intercourse Act of 1790, also known as the Nonintercourse Act, which prohibited the sale of Indian lands to any person or to any state without first securing permission from the federal government. The 1790 Act was, by its terms, temporary, leading to the enactment of several similar laws in subsequent years, and culminating in the enactment of the 1834 Trade and Intercourse Act, which is intended to be permanent and binding on all states and third-party purchasers, and is currently codified at 25 U.S.C. 177. In recent years, several Indian Nations have successfully litigated their continuing right to lands that were removed from tribal possession in violation of the Nonintercourse Act. In *Joint Tribal Council of the Passamaquoddy Tribe v. Morton*,[31] the Passamaquoddy tribe (which was then not federally recognized) prevailed in its claim seeking a declaratory judgment that the tribe was entitled to federal protection under the Indian Nonintercourse Act at the time that its lands were taken by the State of Maine in violation of the Nonintercourse Act. This holding ultimately led to the Maine Land Claims Settlement Act, which settled claims on behalf of the Passmaquoddy, Penobscot, and Maliseet Indians to large portions of Maine.[32] Through this legislation, the affected tribes received federal recognition and other benefits, including a monetary settlement designed to enable the tribes to acquire trust lands. The Act also formally extinguished the tribes' aboriginal title claims.

The Removal Period (1835–1861)

The federal government's removal policy inspired some of the most devastating losses of tribal landholdings, resulting in the complete exclusion of many groups from any portion of their aboriginal landbase. The Removal Act was an outgrowth of the dissatisfaction expressed by the states about the existence of autonomous tribal enclaves within state boundaries. After the War of 1812, the federal government became more responsive to state concerns because it no longer perceived the Indian Nations to hold an important balance of power in the United States' claim to nationhood. The removal process began slowly, with the federal government encouraging Indian Nations to voluntarily consent to move westward in treaties that promised Indian Nations permanent political autonomy once they were outside state boundaries. However, toward the end of the 1820s, the federal government became much more coercive. President Andrew Jackson, who was elected in 1828, was a fervent supporter of Indian removal. In the wake of the Cherokee cases, which held that the State of Georgia had no right to impose its laws on the Cherokee Nation, removal was seen as the only solution to an intractable problem. The Removal Act of 1830, designed to use Congress's exclusive authority over Indian affairs to gain further land cessions, spoke of securing the "consent" of Indian Nations to remove to western lands. However, in the Southeast, the removal of Indian Nations such as the Cherokee, Choctaw, Chickasaw, Creeks, and Shawnee to the "Indian Territory" was primarily a military and forcible operation. Tribes in the Northeast were also coerced to sign removal treaties, although the political environment was different in these areas, and for many tribes, such as the Menominee and Ho-Chunk (Winnebago), this only resulted in a partial removal of the Indian Nations.[33] The net effect of the removal policy was not only to divest the tribes of their aboriginal homelands, but to break down tribal autonomy, in some cases breaking

Indian Nations into fractionated political units and, in other cases, forcing distinct Indian Nations to occupy lands in common with tribes that had not been historical allies and did not share a common cultural basis.

Reservation Policy (1861–1887)

The federal government also asserted its exclusive authority to regulate trade with the Indian Nations by entering into numerous treaties with Indian Nations to secure further cessions of their lands. The goal of the treaty policy was to reserve smaller tracts of land under the protection of federal agents as "reservation lands." The treaty policy vastly circumscribed the traditional aboriginal use areas of Indian Nations to smaller tracts of land that were under the legal ownership of the United States but held for the beneficial use of Indian people. In addition to the goal of acquiring as much land as possible for white settlement, reservations were seen as necessary to keep Indian people separate from white settlers, to minimize conflict between the two groups, and also to start the "civilization" process. The treaty reservations, of course, were portrayed to the Native Nations as their "permanent homelands." In actuality, however, the federal government would periodically reopen negotiations with the tribes to gain further land cessions. Thus, for example, the Lakota, Cherokee, and other Indian Nations entered a series of treaties with the United States, each of which was designed to procure further land for white settlement, but each of which was accompanied by several benefits (e.g., monetary payments, rations, promises of education) designed to entice the tribes to consent. In 1871, the U.S. Congress officially ended the treaty-making process with Indian Nations, inspiring the use of more coercive mechanisms to divest the tribes of their lands (e.g., purported "agreements" which were then "confirmed" by congressional action).

During the treaty era, the United States signed over 370 treaties with Indian Nations, which resulted in the loss of nearly 2 billion acres of Indian lands when the treaty-making period ended in 1871 (the last treaty was made and ratified in 1868).[34] The Indian Nations retained approximately 140 million acres of land on about 200 reservations.[35] Thus, while Indian treaties do acknowledge tribal sovereignty, and in that sense are important political instruments, they also served as the legal means to extinguish title to vast sums of aboriginal lands.

The Allotment Period and Forced Assimilation (1871–1934)

The nineteenth century and early part of the twentieth century marked an intensive effort of federal policy designed to break down tribal political autonomy and acculturate individual Indians to the norms of Western society.

The reservation policy facilitated this effort by placing the administrative responsibility for Indians on a reservation in the hands of a non-Indian agent. The Indian agents were often Christian missionaries who saw the need to Christianize Indians and "civilize them" by transforming tribal lifeways into an agrarian model. The assimilation policy was multifaceted. The use of Indian agents and the formation of "tribal police" that operated under the Code of Federal Regulations to punish infractions—such as marriage to multiple wives, or the ceremonial gifting of family property through "potlatch" or "giveaway" ceremonies—supplanted traditional tribal governance structures and enforced the norms of Anglo-American culture by penalizing contrary Native norms. The boarding-school policy broke down Indian family units and educational systems, and forced Indian children to speak English, become Christians, and learn skills that would serve them in non-Indian society (such as household labor or farm labor).

An important component of this policy was to break the norm of "tribalism" altogether and institute a social norm that would exalt the individual/nuclear family structures of non-Indian society. This policy was implemented in the context of landholdings by the allotment policy, which sought to allot tribally held lands into separate lots or parcels that were assigned to tribal members for a permanent home. These "trust allotments" were to be of an appropriate size for an individual or family farm unit, and the benefit of such ownership often included access to farm implements and training in agrarian pursuits. The allotment policy was an informal part of several treaties with Indian Nations from the 1850s to the end of treaty-making in 1871. However, the allotment policy became pervasive with the enactment of the 1887 General Allotment Act, which gave the federal government the authority to negotiate with Indians on any reservation to allot the reservation and sell all "surplus" lands that remained after the tribal members each received their share.

The Allotment Act resulted in a devastating loss of tribal lands. According to Vine Deloria Jr. and Clifford Lytle, Indian landholdings were reduced from a total of 138 million acres in 1887 to 48 million acres in 1934, when the Indian Reorganization Act officially ended the allotment policy.[36] The net loss of tribal lands in acreage, of course, does not correlate to the net loss in the value of tribal lands. The federal officials in charge of allotting the reservations often allotted the lands of poorest quality (measured in terms of suitability for irrigation or timber harvesting) to tribal members, reserving the prime lands to be sold to non-Indian settlers in order to entice them to move to reservation lands. The allotment policy also had several other negative consequences for Indian Nations and tribal members. The trust restriction on sale or alienation of allotments to tribal members was designed to be temporary (twenty-five years), and could be lifted at an earlier time upon proof of the "competency" of the allottee. Once the trust restriction was lifted, the lands could be sold and taxed by the state, which resulted in the loss of further Indian lands by sale to non-Indians or by tax foreclosure actions. The allotment policy also resulted in a peculiar checkerboard effect of ownership on the reservation, interspersing Indian allotments with non-Indian fee lands. This arrangement has inspired tremendous jurisdictional challenges on the reservation. In addition, through successive generations, tribal allotments that were once sufficient for a particular land use have been fractionated into shares of marginal value. The multiplicity of owners has led to problems with efficient land use. In fact, the land use policies of the Bureau of Indian Affairs (BIA) for many years advocated leasing of tribal allotments to non-Indian farmers, ranchers, and timber companies. The lease revenues were often below market and resulted in a further loss of value in the lands retained in Indian ownership.

Federal Land Policies in the Twentieth Century

The federal government's Indian land policies in the twentieth century have been very uneven. The Indian Reorganization Act (IRA) of 1934 ended the allotment policy; however, other than extending the trust restriction on allotments in perpetuity, the Act did little to alleviate the negative effects of allotment, which continue to plague Indian Nations in the present day. Overall, the IRA had a benevolent approach to tribal land rights. On the other hand, the termination policy of the 1950s was as devastating to the affected tribes as the nineteenth-century policies, such as the removal policy. In 1955, House Concurrent Resolution 108 expressed the "policy of Congress" to secure "equal citizenship" for Indian people by "freeing them from federal supervision and control" as rapidly as possible. The "termination" of federal supervision and control technically referred to the severance of the federal trust relationship with an Indian Nation, including the sale and disposition of tribal assets, including land and natural resources. The ultimate goal of termination was that the "tribe" would no longer have any viable purpose, and that individual Indians would move to urban areas and live exactly like their non-Indian neighbors. The BIA's relocation policy, designed to encourage Indians to move from the reservation to urban areas and participate in educational programs and job training, was an important adjunct to this policy. The federal government purportedly "selected" the tribes for termination on the basis of their ability to make that transition. This meant that the tribes that were more "successful," as measured in socioeconomic terms, were deemed fit for termination. Not surprisingly, however, many of the tribes selected for termination possessed incredibly valuable timber and mineral resources. The Klamath tribe in Oregon and Menominee tribe of Wisconsin, for example, both possessed reservations with rich timber resources. Each tribe selected for termination was then required to agree to an administrative "plan" to effect termination, which generally included the abolishment of the reservation, sale of Indian lands and natural resources, and a payment distribution to tribal members. Without fail, the tribes selected for termination suffered terribly, being divested of valuable reservation lands as well as the political identity that sustained their survival as distinct nations within the United States.

During the termination era, approximately 109 tribes and bands were terminated.[37] Although there has yet to be an accurate accounting of the impact of termination, it is estimated that over 1.3 million acres of Indian lands and approximately 12,500 individuals were affected by termination.[38] Overall, the termination policy resulted in a net loss of about 3.2 percent of all remaining tribally held land.[39] It should be noted that some of the Indian Nations that were terminated later were reinstated to federal status and, in some cases, regained portions of the lands that they lost. However, this was a bitter struggle for most tribes, and the residual effects of this federal policy are overwhelmingly negative.

Summary

In 1970, President Richard M. Nixon called for an end to termination and for a commitment to tribal self-determination. This statement ushered in what has been called the "era of self-determination," most notably represented by the Indian Self-Determination and Educational Assistance Act of 1975,[40] which empowered the Secretary of the Interior and the Secretary of Health and Human Services to contract with, and make grants to, Indian tribes and other Indian organizations for the delivery of federal services. The self-determination policy and statutes enacted pursuant to the policy uphold the federal trust responsibility and the bureaucracy that has resulted from the trust, but seek to empower Indian Nations to make decisions about the administration of federal policy on their lands and for their membership. In that sense, the policy maintains a commitment to tribal self-governance, although it is not the same vision of political autonomy and agency that is represented under the doctrine of self-determination under international law.

Since the end of termination, there has not been any overt federal policy designed to remove lands from Native ownership. (What do they retain today?) In the next section of the paper, I will address how Indian Nations have dealt with the historic loss of tribal lands.

Responding to the Historic Loss of Tribal Lands: The Land Claims Process

Overall, Indian Nations have employed three primary strategies in the effort to deal with the historic loss of tribal lands.

First, many tribes have litigated their land claims as actions for damages, largely pursuant to the Indian Claims Commission Act and special jurisdictional statutes that were passed to enable such claims for particular tribes.

Second, many tribes have used funds derived from land settlements and from gaming revenues or other economic development initiatives to purchase lands. In some cases, the lands purchased are outside the reservation. In other cases, the lands purchased are within the reservation, and these purchases are designed to reconsolidate tribal landholdings within the reservation. Many of the reacquisition cases involve the issue of petitioning to take the lands into trust.

Third, in some cases, tribes have successfully petitioned to have Congress restore lands that are of particular importance to the tribe or that were taken for "temporary" federal purposes, such as for military installations. I will refer to these cases as encompassing claims for "repatriation" of tribal lands.

This section of the paper responds to the first category, and the next section of the paper will discuss the second two categories.

An Overview of the Indian Land Claims Process

As the above discussion illustrates, the federal government divested Indian nations of their lands through many different legal instruments and through a variety of policies, which are at best described as "misguided" but are more appropriately understood as "immoral," and perhaps downright "evil." The United States, of course, is a sovereign nation and, like all sovereign nations, is immune from suit for its misfeasance without its consent. In 1855, the Court of Claims was established for the American people to litigate their claims against the United States under a carefully circumscribed list of possible actions. Interestingly, Indian claims were expressly excluded from the jurisdiction of the Court of Claims on the ground that Indians were not American citizens. Until 1946, Indian claims against the United States could be litigated only if Congress passed special legislation authorizing the suit. This was a cumbersome process that resulted in over 140 distinct jurisdictional acts that authorized particular tribes to sue for particular claims. If the tribal claimant, through its government-appointed attorney, prevailed, the amount of any award was routinely "offset" by the value of any "gratuities" that had been given to the tribe, such as the value of health and education services, farm implements, and commodities. Not surprisingly, the federal government rarely was required to pay out more than 50 percent of the award.

In 1946, Congress enacted the Indian Claims Commission Act (ICCA) as a vehicle to extinguish all pending Indian claims with a "final settlement" and pave the way for the termination of the federal government's trust relationship with the tribes, thus ending the financially onerous obligation to support the tribes. Congress saw the necessity of assembling a tribunal that would have specialized knowledge about Indian claims and could do its work efficiently. Thus, the Act established a three-member commission (later enlarged to five members) to adjudicate Indian claims. The claims had to have arisen prior to 1946 and were required to be filed by August 13, 1951. No other statute of limitations applied, nor was the defense of laches applicable. Initially, Congress envisioned that the commission could complete its work within five years. However, the commission's tenure was extended several times before it was finally dissolved in 1978. Claims that arose after 1946 were required to be filed directly in the Court of Claims.

Under Section 2 of the ICCA, the commission was authorized to adjudicate five different causes of action:

1. Claims in law or equity arising under the Constitution, laws, or treaties of the United States and executive orders;
2. All other claims in law or equity, including those sounding in tort, that raise claims against the federal government (an extension of the Federal Tort Claims Act);
3. Claims which would result if treaties, contracts, or agreements between the tribe and the United States were revised on contract principles (fraud, duress, unconscionable consideration, mistake);
4. Claims arising from takings by the United States of lands owned or occupied by the claimant without payment of compensation (this section opened the door for aboriginal title claims);
5. Claims based upon fair and honorable dealings that are not recognized by any existing rule of law or equity (a catch-all category designed to account for "moral wrongs").

Most of the cases brought under the Indian Claims Commission Act encompassed claims to redress uncompensated cessions of Indian land, forcible removals from aboriginal lands, to force the United States to adhere to express treaty obligations, or to impose liability upon the United States for its failure to properly manage tribal funds and other trust assets. Although the ICCA did not expressly provide that recovery was limited to monetary damages, this was expressed in the legislative intent of the statute, and the tribes' non-Indian lawyers were motivated to litigate these cases for monetary damages because they were eligible to receive 10 percent of the claims award. Importantly, the payment of any claim by the federal government constitutes a full discharge of liability on the part of the United States and precludes any further litigation. Thus, Indian Nations like the Lakota, who revised their initial claims to seek return of the land, rather than monetary damages, have been barred from any further litigation after payment of the judgment, regardless of their refusal to accept the award.[41] Similarly, autonomous bands who dissented from the decision of a larger tribal unit to bring claims under the ICCA have been held to be bound by the ensuing judgment.[42]

Over $800 million had been awarded to Indian tribes under the ICCA, leading some commentators to view this statute as a positive force for tribal claimants. I would like to discuss two categories of cases—those for extinguishment of aboriginal title and those for takings of recognized title—to demonstrate the difference in the doctrines of property law that apply and the impact of these doctrines on Indian Nations. I have selected current examples of cases litigated under these principles to illustrate the contemporary impact of the doctrines of the ICCA and related statutes.

The Aboriginal Title Cases

As the Court recognized in this case, aboriginal title claims encompass the right of Native peoples to use and occupy lands that they had held for "time immemorial." Aboriginal rights include subsistence rights exercised in a manner consistent with their ancient custom and practice. Aboriginal title includes a legally enforceable right of possession; however, it is subordinate to the fee simple, and upon extinguishment, the fee holder has full possession and use of the land. Until extinguishment, however, tribes maintain the right to bring legal action against trespassers, including an action for accounting, even if they no longer physically occupy the land. As the Supreme Court held in the *Oneida* case, the federal Nonintercourse Acts provide the basis for the principle that Indian Nations have a federal common-law right to sue to enforce their aboriginal title rights.[43] The operative question in all of these cases is whether the federal government has acted to extinguish the tribe's aboriginal title. As the Supreme Court noted in *United States v. Santa Fe Pacific Railway*,[44] extinguishment can occur "by treaty, by the sword, by purchase, by the exercise of complete dominion adverse to the right of occupancy, or otherwise."

The most recent aboriginal title case in the United States is *Alabama-Coushatta Tribes of Texas v. United States*.[45] The *Alabama-Coushatta* case is the culmination of an extraordinarily complex set of litigation brought by the Alabama-Coushatta tribe of Texas to vindicate its aboriginal title claims. The tribe's original claim arose prior to 1946, but the tribe failed to bring the claim within the statutory deadline of August 13, 1951. The tribe maintained that it had not received written notice about the ICCA or its terms prior to the deadline, and was able to confirm this through pieces of correspondence. In 1975, the tribe unsuccessfully tried to intervene in another action, brought by the Caddo Nation of Oklahoma. Finally, in 1983, Congress passed House Resolution 69, authorizing the tribe to bring its claim in the U.S. Claims Court. The tribe duly filed its action on February 22, 1984, asserting aboriginal title to approximately 6.3 million acres.

In its 2000 decision, the Federal Claims Court review panel vacated an earlier 1996 ruling and found that the tribe had established aboriginal title to approximately 5.5 million acres of land in east Texas by 1830, and that subsequent land grants and settlements did not extinguish the tribe's aboriginal title. The panel concluded, however, that the United States could only be held liable for damages with respect to 2.8 million acres of these lands, which were illegally occupied by settlers after 1845, when Texas achieved statehood, and which the U.S. government failed to protect on behalf of the tribes pursuant to its trust responsibility. The panel found that the United States had no liability for any dispossession of aboriginal title that took place prior to 1845, when the lands were annexed into the United States. The panel further found that the tribe's claim persisted until 1954, when the tribe's federal trust status was terminated. The Alabama-Coushatta tribe's federal trust status was formally restored in 1985 by the Ysleta del Sur Pueblo and Alabama-Coushatta Tribes of Texas Restoration Act. The next phase of the litigation will calculate the damages from a negotiated "date of taking" until 1954.

The Alabama-Coushatta case is widely considered a victory for Native land rights in the modern era. It is interesting to compare that case with other cases where the Native claimants have not prevailed, often due to political or economic concerns. One such case is *State v. Elliott*,[46] in which a group of Abenaki fishermen claimed that they should be exempt from the State of Vermont's fishing license requirements based upon their "aboriginal title" to the land and its associated resources. The Abenaki tribe was a large historical Indian Nation that encompassed several subgroups, in this case, the Missiquoi. Although the tribe lacked federal recognition, this was not the key to the Vermont State Supreme Court's finding that the fishermen lacked aboriginal rights. The court accepted the assertion that the Abenaki constitute an "Indian tribe" for the purposes of maintaining "aboriginal title" rights, but found that the Abenaki's aboriginal rights were extinguished through a series of historical events, prior to Vermont's admission to the Union in 1791. After asserting the same general legal framework identified in the Alabama-Coushatta case, the court emphasized that "extinguishment is irrevocable; once it takes place, Indian title cannot be revived." The court then went on to discuss a series of land grants, commencing with a set of 1763 grants made by the governor of New Hampshire to several third parties and ending with a series of acts designed to confirm land titles (and separate these from conflicting claims by New York and New Hampshire) prior to Vermont's admission to statehood in 1791.

In the *Elliott* case, the court could not identify any action taken by the British Crown or the United States that affirmatively extinguished Native title. Rather than insisting upon such an event, the court maintained that "extinguishment may be established by the increasing weight of history." Based upon the cumulative effect of many historical events, the Court concluded that there had been actual settlement and appropriation to the exclusion of competing claims, and that Congress had ratified this upon Vermont's admission to statehood.

In so ruling, the Vermont State Supreme Court foreclosed the Abenaki tribe from pursuing further remedies under the Nonintercourse Acts. Consistent with *Alabama-Coushatta*, the U.S. government would have no liability for damages for failing to protect Indian tribes from the actions of third parties prior to the time the state was admitted to the Union. The *Elliott* case illustrates the lack of political power in a tribe that lacks federal recognition, and the obvious effort of the state court to protect land titles in the state of Vermont from the type of "cloud" that emerged in other eastern land claims cases when the tribe was recognized as having an aboriginal claim in a currently heavily populated area of the state. This latter point leads into the discussion of the economic consequences of recognizing "Native title."

The *Dann-Western Shoshone* litigation exemplifies the economic consequences of aboriginal title cases. In 1951, certain members of the Shoshone tribe sought compensation under the ICCA for the loss of aboriginal title to lands located in California, Colorado, Idaho, Nevada, Utah, and Wyoming. Eleven years later, the Indian Claims Commission entered into an interlocutory order holding that the aboriginal title of the Western Shoshone had been extinguished in the latter part of the nineteenth century.[47] The commission later awarded the Western Shoshone in excess of $26 million in compensation, which was later affirmed by the Court of Claims.[48] On December 6, 1979, the Clerk of the Court of Claims certified the commission's award to the General Accounting Office, which, under the relevant statute, automatically appropriated the amount of the award and deposited it for the tribe in an interest-bearing trust account in the U.S. Treasury.

The Western Shoshone Nation historically comprised several autonomous bands, many of whom had dissented from the decision to pursue monetary damages for the appropriation of their ancestral lands. Due to the inability of the bands to agree to a plan of distribution for the $26 million judgment, the funds were not distributed. Two Shoshone sisters, Mary and Carrie Dann, who were members of one of the autonomous bands, continued to graze their cattle in the disputed area, contending that they still maintained aboriginal title to the land. When the United States brought an action in trespass against the sisters, they defended the suit by contending that their aboriginal title to the land precluded the government from requiring grazing permits.

In *United States v. Dann,* the U.S. Supreme Court held that "payment" occurred within the meaning of the Indian Claims Commission Act when the funds were placed by the United States into a Treasury account for the Shoshone tribe, thus releasing the federal government from further claims to continuing aboriginal title.[49] The Court based its decision on the two articulated purposes of the ICCA: the first to dispose of the "Indian claims problem with finality" in response to a study that had concluded that there ought to be a "prompt and final settlement of all claims between the Government and its Indian citizens; and the second, to transfer from Congress to the Indian Claims Commission the responsibility for determining the merits of Native American claims.

The practical implications of the decision are significant. The opinion implicitly holds that a monetary judgment by the ICCA extinguished aboriginal title, and also holds that a minority group within a tribe who maintains such an action can determine the rights of all other members of the tribe, assuming that the petitioning group otherwise meets the standing requirements to maintain an action under the ICCA. The Court reserved the question of whether the Danns could possess individual, as well as tribal, aboriginal rights, noting that these are not foreclosed by the "final discharge" language of the ICCA with respect to tribal claims that are certified for payment. Although the Dann sisters chose not to litigate the claim of individual aboriginal title on the merits, the Ninth Circuit Court of Appeals did issue a ruling in support of the position that the Dann family's grazing or use rights in the affected area were established prior to the time that the Taylor Grazing Act established an exclusive mechanism to secure such rights, and that, procedurally, the Danns were entitled to litigate this claim.[50]

The Dann sisters instead chose to actively resist the U.S. Bureau of Land Management's effort to enjoin the Danns' "trespass on federal lands" and efforts to seize their livestock. In 1993, the Dann sisters, represented by the Indian Law Resource Center, filed a complaint with the Inter-American Commission on Human Rights, alleging violations of the American Declaration of the Rights and Duties of Man, as well as other international human rights norms and principles. In September of 2002, the commission ruled in favor of the Danns, concluding that the Danns "did not play a full or effective role in retaining, authorizing, or instructing the Western Shoshone claimants in the ICC process," and that the finding of extinguishment was "not based upon a judicial evaluation of pertinent evidence, but rather was based upon apparently arbitrary stipulations as between the U.S. government and the Temoak Band regarding the extent and timing of the loss of indigenous title to the entirety off the Western Shoshone ancestral lands." This ruling, however, is purely advisory and carried no binding effect on the United States, which continues to maintain that the ICCA was a fair and efficient statute to address Native land claims. Even after the ruling, the BLM has continued to actively prosecute the Danns for their trespass on what it perceives to be "federal land."

The Recognized Title Cases

Another very important category of land claims cases involves Native claims for the appropriation of treaty-guaranteed lands and other reservation lands under "federal" trust status. Here, the Fifth Amendment to the Constitution protects the tribes' land claims, unlike the aboriginal title cases. However, the land claims in this category are sometimes difficult to articulate because of the plenary power and trust doctrines within federal Indian law, which give the U.S. Congress the authority of a "trustee" to make alternative dispositions of tribal lands, which can include sale or transfer of the lands, when deemed to be in the "best interest" of the Indians. That principle stems from the 1903 case of Lone Wolf v. Hitchcock, in which the Supreme Court upheld the legality of the allotment statute which broke up the Kiowa, Comanche, and Apache Reservation confirmed by the Treaty of Medicine Lodge in violation of that treaty's express requirements that any further land cessions must be approved by three-quarters of the adult males of the tribes.[51] The Court found that "plenary authority over the tribal relations of the Indians has been exercised by Congress from the beginning," and constituted a "political question" outside the scope of review of the federal courts. Thus, Congress was free to pass a statute which unilaterally abrogated an Indian treaty in full or in part, including the provision with respect to land rights, because the Indian people, as dependents, had no right to consent. Rather, Congress, as the trustee, might be compelled to make a "partition and disposal of tribal lands" on relatively short notice, and could not be expected to do so only with tribal consent. Moreover, Congress possessed "full administrative power" over tribal property, and so long as it was acting in "good faith," such dispositions are merely a "change in the form of investment of Indian tribal property." Thus, because most of the allotment statutes required the tribes to be compensated for the loss of tribal lands designated as "surplus lands" available for purchase by non-Indians, the allotment statutes are generally seen as a benign exercise of the trustee's authority. The ICCA left such claims open to the extent that tribes could prove misfeasance, such as duress and coercion, or to the extent that the value offered was so minimal that a "moral wrong" could be found. Damages were paid for these claims without the interest award that accompanies constitutional takings.

In comparison, where tribes were able to prove that the trustee did not act in good faith and merely used its power to appropriate lands from the Indians for the public benefit without any attempt to offer compensation, constitutional redress is available. The classic case on this doctrine is the *Sioux Nation* case.

The Fort Laramie Treaty of 1868 between the United States and the various autonomous bands and political units (Lakota, Dakota, Nakota) of the Sioux Nation established the Great Sioux Reservation, an expansive area that included much land comprised within the contemporary states of Montana, Wyoming, North Dakota, South Dakota, and Nebraska, and included the Black Hills. The Fort Laramie Treaty, which was solicited by the United States, guaranteed the Sioux people the absolute and undisturbed occupation of these lands, including the sacred Black Hills, in perpetuity in exchange for the Sioux Nation's agreement to cease military warfare against the United States and allow safe passage of American citizens across the Bozeman Trail. The United States pledged that it would protect the Sioux Nation's possessory rights against trespassers and that no further land cessions would be effective unless signed by three-quarters of the adult Indian males occupying these lands.

Less than a decade later, the United States reneged on its treaty promises and enacted an 1877 statute that vastly diminished the Great Sioux Reservation, appropriating the Black Hills and other valuable lands. Although the United States purported to have secured the consent of the Sioux people, it was clear that the agreement was a product of coercion and starvation and was secured after an official military order to force the Sioux people to locate to the Agency and to cease hunting and fishing on their traditional lands. The document lacked the agreement of the requisite number of Sioux males and did not give any compensation other than a commitment to continue rations. The substandard rations, much of which never even made it to the Indian people but were illegally sold by corrupt government contractors and agents, were designed to "compensate" the Indians for the loss of land of incomprehensible cultural value and an estimated economic value in excess of $100 million, not counting the wealth in extracted gold, uranium, and timber. In 1889, the remaining Great Sioux Reservation was broken up and allotted in order to separate the various bands and break any military alliances that would threaten the United States' interest.

In 1920, Congress passed a special jurisdictional statute authorizing the Sioux to bring suit in the Court of Claims for the taking of the Black Hills by the 1877 Act without just compensation in violation of the Fifth Amendment. The case, handled by a local attorney, ended up being dismissed in 1942 as a "moral claim" not compensable under the Fifth Amendment. After the Indian Claims Commission Act was passed in 1946, the Sioux Nation revived its claim. The Claims Commission found that the 1877 Act was a taking under the Fifth Amendment, and that the Black Hills had been acquired through "unfair and dishonorable dealings." The commission awarded the Sioux claimants a sum of $17.5 million, plus accrued interest. The Court of Claims reversed this decision in part, finding that the 1942 decision barred relitigation of the constitutional claim under the doctrine of *res judicata*, but sustained the damages judgment without accrued interest (estimated at $90 million at the time) under the statutory cause of action in the ICCA.

In 1978, Congress passed a statute allowing the Court of Claims to review the takings claim without regard to the defenses of *res judicata* and collateral estoppel. The Court of Claims then found that there had been a taking and that the Sioux Nation could recover the principle sum of $17.5 million plus accrued interest at 5 percent annual interest since 1877, resulting in a total award of over $105 million. That case ultimately went to the U.S. Supreme Court, which affirmed the Court of Claims judgment, and clearly repudiated the "political question" doctrine of *Lone Wolf*. In this case, the Court held, Congress had not made a "good faith effort" to give the Indians full value of the land, which would sustain the notion of congressional power to transmute tribal property "from land to money." Because Congress had not done this, it had violated its trust duty to the Indian people. The Court affirmed congressional power to condemn Indian land under its eminent domain power for another "public purpose." However, the Court held that when Congress is acting in the exercise of its eminent domain power, it must pay Indians "just compensation" under the Fifth Amendment.

Note that the *Sioux Nation* case is widely perceived as a victory for Indian people. However, the doctrinal subtext of the case clearly states that tribal interests are not entitled to any greater protection than property interests of private non-Indian citizens. Thus, Indian Nations, such as the Seneca, have been divested of huge portions of their treaty-guaranteed reservations to facilitate "public projects" like the Kinzua Dam. Justice Black, who dissented in that case, would have protected Indian peoples' treaty rights under a stricter standard, on the theory that "Great Nations, like great men, should keep their word." However, the eminent domain power has been sustained again and again, so long as "just compensation" has been paid. The "just compensation" award is purely a function of the economic value of the land. The cultural value of the land is not even a factor in the inquiry.

Thus, the second consequence of this doctrine for Native people is that, as in the *Dann* case, a final payment of the judgment into a Treasury account constitutes full satisfaction of the claim and precludes any further litigation on the subject. The Sioux Nation has never accepted payment of the monetary judgment and continues to assert that it maintains legal rights to the land under the Treaty of Fort Laramie. The Sioux Nation's subsequent attempts to litigate the claim in a way that would vindicate its right to use, possession, or cultural access to the actual lands (and an ability to preclude culturally harmful uses such as uranium mining) have all failed on the theory of *res judicata* and collateral estoppel. Nor have any of the Sioux Nation's efforts to protect its interests under the free exercise clause of the First Amendment been sustained.[52] Although Congress possesses the power to make a political solution (e.g., through a settlement act that would provide for return of some lands in the Black Hills to the tribe in combination with monetary compensation), none of the proposed solutions have garnered enough political support to result in legislation.

Responding to the Historic Loss of Native Lands: Land into Trust and Repatriation of Tribal Lands

In an article I co-authored with Wallace Coffey, the current chairman of the Comanche Nation, we spoke of "cultural sovereignty" as "the effort of Indian nations and Indian people to exercise their own norms and values in structuring their collective futures."[53] The notion of "cultural sovereignty" is intended to capture the essence of an Indian Nation's "inherent sovereignty," and is located within the cultural and political structures of a specific Nation. It does not come "from" the federal government, nor can it be accurately defined by the federal courts. The expression of "cultural sovereignty" is uniquely that of a distinctive Indian Nation. In the article, we suggested that cultural sovereignty evoked an ethic of "repatriation" of land, wisdom, and cultural identity. These components are vital to the continued exercise of tribal sovereignty in the modern era.

Cultural sovereignty, as it relates to land and resources, is being exercised in a number of ways. Many Indian Nations are acquiring lands outside the reservation and attempting to place them in trust status. Some Indian Nations are exploring ways to protect cultural resources located off the reservation, within the boundaries of their traditional lands.[54] And Indian Nations are litigating to preserve their treaty rights to hunt, fish, and gather resources outside the reservation.[55] The crucial intersection of political and cultural sovereignty is represented by each of these efforts. This section of the paper discusses some contemporary efforts by Native peoples to repatriate lands that were taken from them, examines the current controversies over land consolidation and taking land into trust, and evaluates tribal efforts to protect significant places (e.g., sacred sites) that are located off reservation.

Repatriation of Tribal Lands

Today, Indian Nations are actively attempting to rebuild their land bases and mitigate the devastating legacy of allotment. The most compelling instances of cultural sovereignty involve cases in which Native people actually fought for and achieved repatriation of tribal lands. Most of these cases involve lands that were taken by the federal government for a specific and limited purpose—for example, for use in connection with a military installation—that is no longer appropriate. Because the lands are still in federal ownership, they can be transferred back to the affected Indian Nation without involving myriad political issues that would arise if the lands were in private or state ownership. An example of this occurred in 2000 when the Department of the Army transferred 4,900 acres of land at Lake McFerren on the former Fort Wingate Army Depot in New Mexico to the Bureau of Indian Affairs for the Navajo and Zuni tribes.[56] These lands constituted the first part of a projected transfer that would involve 21,881 acres. Malcolm Bowekaty, who was governor of the Zuni Pueblo at the time, described the transfer as "the first big step to reclaiming our ancestral grounds" and "a tribute to our forefathers who always told us to have patience and tolerance." Similarly, the Navajo Nation's president, Kelsey Begaye, expressed the happiness of the Navajo people that they were able to "come back to the land or the land has come back to us." The partnership between the Navajo Nation and the Zuni Pueblo was a notable instance of tribal cooperation in the exercise of cultural sovereignty.

There are also instances where Indian Nations have successfully repatriated sacred lands that were incorporated into federal public land preserves. The classic example is the Taos Pueblo's repatriation of Blue Lake, which is a very sacred site to the Taos Pueblo and is a fundamental part of their continuing cultural and religious practices.[57] In 1906, President Theodore Roosevelt appropriated Blue Lake from the Taos Pueblo when he established the Taos Forest Reserve, which was ultimately incorporated into the Carson National Forest. For many years, Pueblo elders and leaders traveled to Washington, D.C., annually to testify before Congress and petition for the return of Blue Lake. Finally, in 1970, President Nixon signed House Resolution 417, which restored 48,000 acres of land, including Blue Lake, to the Taos Pueblo. Acoma poet Simon Ortiz has described the dedication of the Taos people as "truly epic" and tied to the power of an oral tradition and daily lived practice that affirmed the continued existence of Blue Lake as Taos land, even while it was in federal "ownership."

These claims have been handled on a case-by-case basis, necessitating congressional legislation to effect the land transfer. Although there have been proposals to pass broader legislation authorizing the transfer of sacred sites on public lands to Indian Nations, none of these effort has been successful.[58] There are often many contentious political issues to resolve, depending upon the existing use of the affected lands, including objections by recreational users of public lands[59] and even objections by other tribes, where a particular tribal claim is seen as damaging to an interest of another tribe.[60] Thus, it is unclear what type of federal legislation would best meet the needs of Indian Nations for repatriation of ancestral and sacred lands.

Land Consolidation and Land into Trust Issues

In 1934, the Indian Reorganization Act formally ended the allotment policy that devastated many reservations across the United States due to loss of land and an inability to effectively manage those interests that remained in Native ownership but were badly fractionated. To ameliorate the problems caused by allotment, Congress authorized the Secretary of the Interior to purchase lands in trust for the benefit of individual Indians or tribes as part of the IRA, and more recently, Congress has passed additional legislation directed toward the need for land consolidation.

LAND INTO TRUST.   Congress envisioned the need for land to be taken into trust as part of the Indian Reorganization Act. Section 5 of the IRA (codified at 25 U.S.C., Section 465) authorized the Secretary of the Interior to acquire any interest on lands, water rights, or surface rights for Indians "within or without a reservation" through "purchase, relinquishment, gift, exchange or assignment." When such lands are acquired, they are taken in the name of the United States and held in trust for the Indian tribe or individual Indian for which the land is acquired, and thereafter, the lands are deemed to be exempt from state and local taxation. Section 465 applies to all tribes, whether or not they are formally under the IRA.[61] In 1980, the Department of the Interior issued regulations at 25 C.F.R., Part 51, to guide the secretary's Section 465 authority. These regulations were amended in 1995 to address concerns raised by state and local governments about the impacts of decisions to take land into trust on those governments, and the broad discretion that had been exercised by the secretary over such decisions.

The regulations provide that land may be acquired in trust status only "when such acquisition is authorized by an act of Congress," although Section

465 is generally used to supply that authorization. The purposes and standards
for such acquisition include a determination that "the acquisition of land is
necessary to facilitate tribal self-determination, economic development, or
Indian housing."[62] Applications commence with a written request to the secretary to take the land into trust title.

If the lands are located within or adjacent to an existing Indian reservation, there must be a formal notification of the state and local governments
that have regulatory jurisdiction over the land to be acquired and a thirty-day
comment period for them to respond.[63] Applicants then have a period of time
to respond to any concerns raised. Once the application is complete, the secretary is required to consider several factors, such as compliance with the National Environmental Policy Act (NEPA), the impact on the state and local
governments that would result from removing the lands from the tax rolls, and
any jurisdictional problems or conflicts over land use that are likely to arise.
In order to satisfy NEPA, the applicant must either secure a Finding of No
Significant Impact (FONSI) on the environment or conduct an exhaustive
Environmental Impact Study (EIS).

If the lands are located outside the reservation and are not contiguous to
existing reservation boundaries, all of the above requirements must be met,
and in addition, the application must specify the location of the land relative
to both state boundaries and the boundaries of the tribe's existing reservation.[64] The same requirements for notice to state and local governments and
an opportunity to respond apply, and the regulations further specify a height-
ened standard of scrutiny to be applied by the secretary. As the distance between the tribe's reservation and the land acquired increases, the secretary
"shall give greater scrutiny to the tribe's justification of anticipated benefit
from the acquisition." The tribe must also submit a business plan for any such
lands acquired for business purposes.

The land into trust process requires a full title examination, and distinguishes
the treatment given to lands that will be used for gaming, as opposed to
nongaming uses. If the land to be acquired in trust is nongaming related, the
secretary has delegated the exercise of his discretion to approve the acquisition
to the regional offices of the BIA. On the other hand, if the land is to be used
for gaming purposes (including supplemental uses such as a parking lot), the approval must be issued from the Washington, D.C., offices of the BIA. In addition, Section 20 of the Indian Gaming Regulatory Act (IGRA) of 1988
(codified as 25 U.S.C. 2719) expressly prohibits the use of newly acquired lands
for gaming purposes, with narrowly defined exceptions. Some of these exceptions are specified to particular tribes or regions. However, generally, the provision recommends taking such lands into trust for gaming purposes only if this
would be in the best interest of the Indian tribe and its members, would not

harm the surrounding community, and the governor of the state in which the land is located consents to the secretary's determination.[65]

The issue of land into trust continues to be politically divisive, and attempts to revise the current regulations to facilitate the process for Indian tribes have failed due to the opposition expressed by state and local governments over the loss of the tax base, control over economic development and land use, and potential jurisdictional conflicts.

LAND CONSOLIDATION   The problems attendant to fractionation of allotments were apparent as early as the 1930s. In 1960, both the House and Senate undertook comprehensive studies of the problem, which indicated that one-half of the approximately 12 million acres of allotted trust lands were held in fractionated ownership, with over 3 million acres held by more than six heirs to a parcel. With each generation, the problems intensified, leading Congress to enact a comprehensive piece of legislation in 1983, the Indian Land Consolidation Act (ILCA).[66] The Act authorized the buying, selling, and trading of fractional interests and provided for the escheat to the tribes of land ownership interests of less than 2 percent. The escheat provision was invalidated by the U.S. Supreme Court in *Hodel v. Irving* as a taking of a vested property interest under the Fifth Amendment of the Constitution without payment of "just compensation."[67] The Supreme Court reasoned that the escheat provision was unconstitutional because there could be tangible economic value in a fractional interest and the statute "effectively abolishes both descent and devise of these property interests." Although Congress had tried to resolve the constitutional problems in 1984 amendments to the statute by limiting its effect to shares of minimal economic valuation and offering property owners the right to devise their interests to any other owner of the affected parcel, the Court held that the amendments were also unconstitutional under the Fifth Amendment in its 1997 ruling in *Babbitt v. Youpee*.[68]

The Indian Land Commission Act was again amended in 2000 to address the fractionated heirship problem and the constitutional challenges.[69] The 2000 amendments attempted to address the constitutional problem through restrictions which make certain heirs and devisees ineligible to inherit in trust status (e.g., non-Indian spouses) and require that certain interests be held by the heirs and devisees as joint tenants with rights of survivorship. The legislation also provided for the consolidation of fractional interests. Tribes and individual owners can now consolidate their interests by purchase or exchange with fewer restrictions. The legislation also sought to enhance economic development opportunities by encouraging the use of negotiated agreements, recommending standardization of procedures and relaxing owner consent requirements. Finally, the legislation extended the secretary's authority to acquire fractional interests at fair market value through the Indian land acquisition pilot program, with the establishment of an Acquisition Fund and authorized annual appropriations to fund the program. While many of the provisions were immediately effective, the inheritance restrictions were not, and efforts continue to resolve the probate issues before final implementation of these provisions.[70]

Sacred Sites Dilemma

Many sites of religious and cultural significance to contemporary Indian Nations are located off reservation, on federal public lands, state lands, and even on lands in private ownership. Due to the tendency of American jurisprudence to privilege the interests of property "owners," Indian Nations have encountered substantial difficulty in their efforts to ensure access to such sites and to protect these places from harm. The American Indian Religious Freedom Act of 1978 specifies that it is "the policy of the United States to protect and preserve for American Indians their inherent right of freedom to believe, express and exercise" their traditional religions. The statute was specifically designed to recognize that Native religions are often premised on practices that are quite distinctive from those of other religions, and may require access to and use of particular lands and geographic places. However, the statute does not contain any legally enforceable cause of action.

Because of this, Native Nations sought protection for sacred sites under the First Amendment free exercise clause of the U.S. Constitution. Although some lower federal courts were initially willing to recognize such claims where the sacred site was "central" to the practice of a continuing Native religion, the Supreme Court rejected the theory in the context of a Native sacred sites claim on federal land in *Lyng v. Northwest Indian Cemetery Protective Association*.[71] That case involved a claim by several tribes in northern California that the proposed construction of a road through a federally owned wilderness area would jeopardize their ability to continue necessary religious practices that were vital to the continuation of their religions. The Supreme Court held that the free exercise clause did not even apply to a government road construction project because the government was the land owner and the project was the product of an entirely neutral administrative decision. Even though anthropologists commissioned by the government confirmed that the construction of the road would virtually destroy the ability of the tribes to practice their religion, Justice O'Connor's opinion maintained that the First Amendment must "apply to all citizens alike, and it can give none of them a veto over public programs that do not prohibit the free exercise of religion." The Court's opinion further finds that the "Constitution does not . . . offer to reconcile the various competing demands on the government" that arise from a pluralistic society. On the contrary, to do so in favor of the Indian plaintiffs in this case would be to require "de facto beneficial ownership of some rather spacious tracts of public property." An additional problem has been raised in the context of the establishment clause. For example, in the *Bear Lodge* case,[72] the NPS issued a voluntary ban on hiking at the Devil's Tower National Monument in order to accommodate Native religious use during the month of June. A group of recreational rock climbers challenged the policy as a violation of the establishment clause. Although the Court of Appeals did not consider the issue on the merits, because it found that the mountain climbers lacked standing, the Court described the policy as essentially designed to serve cultural, educational, and historical purposes, and therefore was not designed to uphold one religion against all others.

Today, sacred sites issues on public lands are subject to the requirements of two federal executive orders, designed to protect tribal interests.

The first order, the 1996 Executive Order on Indian Sacred Sites,[73] was intended to protect the interests of Indian Nations in preserving sacred sites from harmful development activities. The executive order requires federal agencies with responsibility for the management of federal lands to (1) accommodate access to and ceremonial use of Indian sacred sites by Indian religious practitioners; (2) avoid adversely affecting the physical integrity of such sites; and (3) maintain the confidentiality of such sites. The executive order offers agencies considerable discretion in achieving these goals and requires them to adhere to these goals only if "practicable" and only to the extent "permitted by law." Furthermore, the action must not impair "essential agency functions." The executive order further specifies that it does not create any right, benefit, or trust responsibility that would be enforceable "at law or in equity."

The second order, the 2000 Executive Order on Consultation and Coordination[74] with Indian Tribal Governments, acknowledges the government's trust responsibility to federally recognized Indian Nations and establishes specific requirements that agencies must follow as they develop and execute policy actions that affect Indian Nations. This executive order is important in the context of federal public lands policy because it requires consultation with Indian Nations with respect to actions that affect tribal interests. As a result of this executive order, most federal agencies have now designated an official with primary responsibility for implementing this order. The "Indian liaison" in each agency was charged with developing regulations to implement the policy and for outreach efforts to tribal communities. As might be expected, the effectiveness of each agency varies, and there is still widespread disagreement over what an adequate "consultation" with tribal officials requires.

Cultural resources on public lands may also receive some protection through the provisions of the 1966 National Historic Preservation Act (NHPA),[75] which requires federal agencies to assess the impacts of development activities on significant historic resources, including any structure, area, or district listed or eligible for listing on the National Register of Historic Places. The NHPA is primarily a procedural statute, and section 106 of the statute imposes detailed consultation requirements upon the agencies undertaking the activities. If an agency fails to comply with its responsibilities, the agency and its permittees may be enjoined from proceeding with the undertaking.[76] Sites that have religious or cultural significance to Indian Nations may be eligible for listing on the National Register even if they are essentially "natural"—as opposed to "manmade"—properties.[77] The NHPA covers "Traditional Cultural Properties," which are sites that are associated with the cultural practices and beliefs of a living community and are important in maintaining the community's continuing cultural identity. Thus, the NHPA may provide a means to protect places that are considered sacred to an Indian Nation or several Indian Nations.

Under the 1992 amendments to the NHPA, if a proposed federal undertaking might affect a site that is eligible for listing on the National Register as a Traditional Cultural Property, the agency must consult with the tribe as part of the Section 106 process. This requirement applies regardless of the ownership status of the land. In addition, Section 470(d) of the statute sets a model for cooperative management of "historic properties of Indian tribes" by specifying that the secretary "shall foster communication and cooperation between Indian tribes and the State Historic Preservation Officers in the administration of the national historic preservation program to ensure that all types of historic properties and all public interests are given due consideration," and encourages tribes to work cooperatively with the federal agencies and the preservation officers in the "identification, evaluation, protection, and interpretation of historic properties."

Emerging Challenges

As we move forward into this new century, many of the things that Native people have come to view as the "norm" for federal Indian policy may be challenged. Let me mention a few areas of concern.

First, many Native people and non-Natives have intensified their challenge to the continuing utility of the trust doctrine. The Supreme Court in the Navajo Nation and White Mountain Apache trust cases has narrowed the cause of action for a compensable breach of trust to situations where the federal government has assumed a nearly exclusive management of tribal property, has committed itself in writing to trust management of these resources, and has committed some act of waste or misappropriation that follows common-law principles for breach of a trust by a fiduciary. The *Cobell* litigation[78] has inspired many federal policymakers to call for an end to the trust, and thus to the potential liability of the federal government. Many proposals have been advanced, to privatize these interests and to advocate that tribes and individual Indians protect their own interest through nongovernmental mechanisms. Indeed, the entire premise of "self-determination" and "self-governance" is that tribes become the managers, assuming the benefits and the risks of this decision-making authority.

So, what does this mean for tribal lands? Recently, Lance Morgan, the CEO of Ho-Chunk Enterprises, Inc., gave a talk at ASU's law school in which he advocated for the end of trust status for Indian lands. He cited figures illustrating the significant economic value of tribal lands and resources, but he claimed that Indian people are unable to capture the value of these resources because of the onerous restrictions that apply to Indian lands and are inconsistent with efficient economic use of such lands. There is certainly a great deal of truth to this as a factual statement, and the problems with efficient use of tribal lands and allotted lands are legendary. However, is this the time to dispense with the trust, or is there another way to look at that doctrine that will protect Indian Nations from the risks and harms of the market system without hampering their ability to gain the full economic value of their resources?

That difficult question ties into another issue, which is jurisdiction. Mr. Morgan's premise was that anyone should be able to own land in fee within the reservation, but that tribes should still have jurisdiction as governments over that land. However, the Supreme Court's jurisprudence has increasingly narrowed the scope of tribal jurisdiction over non-Indian-owned land on the reservation. Under the doctrines of *Montana* and *Strate*,[79] tribes lack jurisdiction to regulate non-Indians on non-Indian fee land within the reservation, and they lack jurisdiction to adjudicate tort cases between non-Indians arising on state-owned right of ways that run through the reservation. Under the doctrine of *Atkinson*,[80] the same rationale was applied to the Navajo Nation's attempt to tax a non-Indian hotel and its guests, even though the primary reason for non-Indian tourism at the hotel was to enjoy the cultural experience of visiting the Navajo Nation! We are even starting to see incursions of state authority on tribal land and over tribal members. The lower federal courts have begun to extend *Strate's* doctrine to cases where a tribal member is involved in a highway accident, and in the *Hicks* case, the Supreme Court authorized a search by state game officials of a tribal member's home on the reservation for evidence of an off-reservation crime. The operative distinction in all of these cases is not purely the status of the land, but rather the status of the persons involved. If all parties are tribal members, the Court has shown little interest in divesting the tribe of jurisdiction. However, anytime the tribe is seeking to exercise jurisdiction over a nonmember, the Court's jurisprudence becomes much more restrictive, presumably on the theory that nonmembers' individual rights are not adequately protected by laws such as the Indian Civil Rights Act, which largely submit civil rights cases to exclusive tribal jurisdiction.

Many people continue to believe that Congress can enact legislation that would "cure" the jurisdictional problems caused by the Supreme Court's jurisprudence. This may be true, but it is difficult to place that level of trust in a political body that is, after all, comprised of representatives of the states. Moreover, the Supreme Court in decisions such as *Lara*[81] has set the stage for a conversation about the ability of Congress to legislate in a way that violates American constitutional norms. There is a balance of power between the federal courts and Congress, but the boundaries have not been fully illuminated in the area of federal Indian law.

The last thing I will share with you on this is the Supreme Court's recent decision in *City of Sherrill, New York v. Oneida Indian Nation*.[82] This case involved land within the city of Sherrill to which the Oneida maintained unextinguished aboriginal title and which was also comprised within the Oneida's 300,000-acre reservation that had been taken by New York in violation of the 1795 Nonintercourse Act. The Oneidas thus had a clear possessory claim under federal law, and this claim was enhanced because of the status of the land at the time of transfer as a federally confirmed reservation under the 1794 Treaty of Canandaiga.

The Oneida's treaty lands were "purchased" by the State of New York, and many of the Oneidas were moved from their reservation lands to Wisconsin. Some Oneidas stayed in New York, but the individual Oneidas who remained sold the lands in question to the State of New York in the 1840s. After positive case law from the Supreme Court affirming the continuing validity of Oneida possessory rights to areas that were improperly ceded under the Nonintercourse Acts, the Oneida Indian Nation purchased several parcels of land within its original reservation. In this case, the Oneidas maintained that these properties were exempt from state taxation, including the assessed property taxes. The City of Sherrill initiated eviction proceedings in state court, and the Oneida Nation sued Sherrill in federal court. In this case, the Oneidas sought equitable relief, prohibiting currently and in the future the imposition of property taxes, as well as a declaratory judgment against the county that the properties in Madison are tax exempt.

The Second Circuit affirmed the district court ruling in favor of the Oneidas, reasoning that the parcels qualify as Indian Country because they were part of a treaty reservation that had never been disestablished or diminished. The Supreme Court, however, reversed this decision and held that the tribe could not exercise sovereignty over these parcels unless they were placed in trust status pursuant to the federal statutory and regulatory framework, and that the state was free to tax until then. Why? The Court articulated three reasons. First, the United States had been indifferent to the illegality of the state "purchase" and governance of the lands at issue. Second, the properties are currently of substantial economic value, which was not the case 200 years ago, and it has been only "lately" that the Oneidas sought to "regain ancient sovereignty over land converted from wilderness to become part of cities like Sherrill." And finally, the area is now over 90 percent non-Indian in population and in land use, leading to the "justifiable expectations" of the people living in the area that New York is the jurisdictional authority and not the Oneida Indian Nation.

In other words, *Sherrill* has now negated the long line of cases saying that only the federal government has the authority to diminish or disestablish a reservation. This one no longer exists because of the "long passage of time," and the "justifiable expectations" of the non-Indians that now populate the area, and frankly, because non-Indians are responsible for the current "value" of the lands. They were a "wilderness" in the hands of the Oneidas, and now they are urban economic centers, and the shift in jurisdiction would be so "disruptive" that it might disturb this scheme. The Court specifies that the sole remedy for the Oneidas is to go through Section 465 and the regulations to petition for trust status for the land, which then would imply immunity from state taxation.

So, the bottom line is: do Indian Nations really want to give up "trust" status for Indian lands?

The Future of Native Property Rights

My assigned topic was "land rights" and I have kept to that topic. I want to suggest, however, that the Doctrine of Discovery and the policies of the nineteenth century with respect to land are now being applied in other areas of "property" law. Today, cases like *Bonnichsen*[83] seek to extend the rationale of the Doctrine of Discovery to Native claims to ancestral human remains, on the theory that, because they cannot be scientifically or culturally tied to a contemporary Native group, they are the "common property" of Americans and thus can be scientifically studied without any need to comply with the requirements of NAGPRA. This is also a growing assumption about genetic material. The DNA of Native people is valuable to researchers because Native peoples constitute "population isolates" who often maintain distinctive group markers that might be used to ascertain the origin of human populations or might be used to craft a gene patent for use in health research. While current laws do specify that research subjects must be given "informed consent," the prevailing doctrine holds that once cells, blood, and tissue are removed from a human subject, these are no longer the "property" of the individual and can be used at will by researchers for any research that is otherwise permissible under existing law. How will Indian Nations respond to the newest applications of the Doctrine of Discovery? I will leave that thought for all of you to consider, and I thank you for your time and attention today.

Notes

1. James P. Ronda, "Counting Cats in Zanzibar, or Lewis and Clark Reconsidered," *Western Historical Quarterly* 33, no. 1 (2002): 5, 17.

2. Ronda, "Counting Cats," 9.

3. *Johnson v. McIntosh*, 21 U.S. (8 Wheat) 543 (1823).

4. *Johnson v. McIntosh*.

5. Robert A. Williams Jr., *The American Indian in Western Legal Thought: Discourses of Conquest* (New York: Oxford University Press, 1990).

6. *Cherokee Nation v. State of Georgia*, 31 U.S. 1 (1831).

7. *Cherokee Nation v. State of Georgia*.

8. *Cherokee Nation v. State of Georgia*.

9. *Worchester v. State of Georgia*, 31 U.S. 515 (1832).

10. See, e.g., *United States v. Kagama*, 118 U.S. 375 (1886) (Major Crimes Act); *Lonewolf v. Hitchcock*, 187 U.S. 553 (1903) (allotment legislation).

11. Paula Gunn Allen, "Iyani: It Goes This Way," in *The Remembered Earth: An Anthology of Contemporary American Literature*, ed. Geary Hobson (Albuquerque: University of New Mexico Press, 1990), 191.

12. Rebecca Tsosie, "Sacred Obligations," *UCLA Law Review* 47 (2000): 640, 122n.

13. Alfonso Ortiz, *The Tewa World: Space, Time, Being, and Becoming in a Pueblo Society* (Chicago: University of Chicago Press, 1969), 19.

14. Keith H. Basso, *Wisdom Sits in Places: Landscape and Language among the Western Apache* (Albuquerque: University of New Mexico Press, 1996).

15. Basso, *Wisdom Sits in Places*, 38, quoting Annie Peaches.

16. Basso, *Wisdom Sits in Places*, quoting Benson Lewis, who describes the name of a particular mountain as being "like a picture. Stories go to work on you like arrows. Stories make you live right. Stories make you replace yourself."

17. Basso, *Wisdom Sits in Places*.

18. Stephen Dow Beckham, *Literature of the Lewis and Clark Expedition: A Bibliography and Essays* (Portland: Lewis and Clark College, 2003), 7.

19. Ronda, "Counting Cats," 12–13.

20. Thomas Jefferson, "Confidential Message Recommending a Western Exploring Expedition, 18 January 1803," in *A Compilation of the Messages and Papers of the*

Presidents 1789–1897, vol. 1, ed. James D. Richardson (Washington, D.C.: U.S. Government Printing Office, 1899), 352, quoted in Juan F. Perea, *Race and Races: Cases and Resources for a Diverse America* (St. Paul, Minn.: West Group, 2000), 184.

21. "Thomas Jefferson to William Henry Harrison 27 February 1803," *Writings of Thomas Jefferson*, vol. 10, ed. Andrew A. Lipscomb (Washington, D.C.: Thomas Jefferson Memorial Association of the United States, 1904), 369–371, quoted in Perea, *Race and Races*, 184.

22. *Tee-Hit-Ton v. United States*, 348 U.S. 272 (1955).

23. *Lone Wolf v. Hitchcock*.

24. *United States v. Sioux Nation* 448 U.S. 371 (1980).

25. *Tee-Hit-Ton v. United States*.

26. *Tee-Hit-Ton v. United States*.

27. Robert N. Clinton, Carole E. Goldberg, and Rebecca Tsosie, *American Indian Law: Native Nations and the Federal System: Cases and Materials* (Newark: LexisNexis, 2003): 22.

28. Clinton, Goldberg, and Tsosie, *American Indian Law*, 4–5.

29. Clinton, Goldberg, and Tsosie, *American Indian Law*, 23.

30. *Oneida Indian Nation v. New York*, 860 F.2d 1145 (2nd Cir. 1988).

31. *Joint Tribal Council of the Passamaquoddy Tribe v. Morton*, 528 F.2d 370 (1st Cir. 1975).

32. 25 U.S.C. 1721–1735.

33. Clinton, Goldberg, and Tsosie, *American Indian Law*, 27.

34. Imre Sutton and Ralph L. Beals, *Irredeemable America: The Indians' Estate and Land Claims* (Albuquerque: University of New Mexico Press, 1985), 36.

35. Sutton and Beals, *Irredeemable America*.

36. Vine Deloria Jr. and Clifford M. Lytle, *American Indians, American Justice* (Austin: University of Texas Press, 1983), 10.

37. Charles F. Wilkinson and Eric R. Biggs, "The Evolution of the Termination Policy," *American Indian Law Review* 5 (1977): 139, 151–154.

38. Wilkinson and Biggs, "The Evolution of the Termination Policy."

39. Wilkinson and Biggs, "The Evolution of the Termination Policy."

40. 25 U.S.C.A. 450a–450n.

41. *United States v. Sioux Nation*.

42. E.g., Dann litigation.

43. *County of Oneida v. Oneida Indian Nation of New York*, 470 U.S. 226 (1985).

44. *United States v. Santa Fe Pacific Railway*, 314 U.S. 330 (1941).

45. *Alabama-Coushatta Tribes of Texas v. United States*, 2000 WL 101352 (Fed. Cl. June 19, 2000).

46. *State v. Elliott*, 616 A.2d 210 (Vt. 1992).

47. *Shoshone Tribe v. United States*, 11 Ind. Cl. Comm'n 387, 416 (1962).

48. *Western Shoshone Identifiable Group v. United States*, 40 Ind. Cl. Comm'n 318 (1977), affirmed *Temoak Band of Western Shoshone Indians v. United States*, 593 F.2d 1994 (Ct. Cl. 1979).

49. *United States v. Dann*, 470 U.S. 39 (1985).

50. *United States v. Dann*, 873 F.2d. 1189 (9th Cir. 1989).

51. *Lone Wolf v. Hitchcock*.

52. See case re: Bear Butte, *Fools Crow v. Gullet*, 706 F.2d 856 (8th Cir., 1983).

53. Wallace Coffey and Rebecca Tsosie, "Rethinking the Tribal Sovereignty Doctrine: Cultural Sovereignty and the Collective Future of Indian Nations," *Stanford Law and Policy Review* 12, no. 2 (2001): 191, 196.

54. See, e.g., *Muckleshoot Indian Tribe v. U.S. Forest Service*, 177 F.3d 800 (9th Cir. 1999), upholding tribe's claim that the USFS had not fulfilled its obligation under the National Historic Preservation Act to minimize the adverse effect of transferring a portion of the tribe's ancestral transportation route under a land swap with a private landowner who sought the land for logging.

55. See, e.g., *Minnesota v. Mille Lacs Band of Chippewa Indians*, 526 U.S. 172 (1999), holding that tribe retained its off-reservation hunting, fishing, and gathering rights originally secured in an 1837 treaty.

56. See Rebecca Tsosie, "The Conflict between the 'Public Trust' and the 'Indian Trust' Doctrines: Federal Public Land Policy and Native Nations," *Tulsa Law Review* 39 (2003): 306–307 and notes 212–215.

57. Tsosie, "The Conflict between the 'Public Trust' and the 'Indian Trust' Doctrines," 307.

58. See, e.g., H.R. 2419, 108th Congress, Section 6(a), sponsored by California Representative Rahall, which would have authorized federal agencies to transfer sacred lands into trust for the benefit of an Indian tribe or tribes so long as the tribes would agree to "manage the land in perpetuity to protect that sacredness."

59. See Bear Lodge case: a group of recreational hikers opposed the NPS plan to accommodate tribal religious concerns by imposing a voluntary ban on hiking during the month of June. *Bear Lodge v. Babbitt*, 175 F.3d 814 (10th Cir, 1999).

60. See Virginia de Leon, "Tribe Longs for Home," *Spokane Review* 8 (September 2003): A1, discussing the efforts of the Wenatchi tribe to regain their lands within an 1855 treaty reservation, which were subsequently taken and incorporated into the Wenatchee National Forest and the tribe relocated to the Colville Reservation, where it is now one of the twelve bands that constitute the Confederated Tribes of the Colville Reservation; to date, the Yakimas have opposed the plan due to concerns over their fishing rights, which were part of the 1855 treaty.

61. See Indian Consolidation Act of 1983, 25 U.S.C. 2202, specifying that Section 465 is applicable to "all tribes" and supersedes any other provision of federal law that would restrict the acquisition of lands by a tribe.

62. 25 CFR 151.3.

63. 25 CFR 151.10.

64. 25 CFR 151.11.

65. See *Keweenaw Bay Indian Community v. United States*, 136 F.3d 469 (6th Cir. 1998), discussing application of the gubernatorial concurrence of section 2719 to a parcel of land in Michigan acquired immediately prior to the enactment of IGRA and placed into trust after the statute's enactment.

66. See *Hodel v. Irving*, 481 U.S. 704 (1987).

67. *Hodel v. Irving*.

68. *Babbitt v. Youpee*, 519 U.S. 234 (1997).

69. See Testimony of Ross Swimmer, Special Trustee for American Indians, U.S. Department of Interior, before the Committee on House Resources, June 23, 2004.

70. Testimony of Ross Swimmer, discussing American Indian Probate Reform Act of 2004.

71. *Lyng v. Northwest Indian Cemetery Protective Association*, 485 U.S. 439 (1988).

72. *Bear Lodge v. Babbitt*.

73. Exec. Order 13007, 61 Fed. Reg. 26771 (May 24, 1996).

74. Exec. Order 13175, 65 Fed. Reg. 67249 (November 6, 2000).

75. P. L. 89-665, 80 Stat. 915 (1966), codified at 16 USC 470 et seq.

76. See, e.g., *Pueblo of Sandia v. United States*, 50 F.3d 856, 859 (10th Cir. 1989).

77. 16 U.S.C. 470 (f).

78. *Cobell v. Norton*, No. 1:96CV01285 (D.D.C.) (Judge Lamberth).

79. *Montana v. Crow Tribe of Indians*, 523 U.S. 696 (1998) and *Strate v. A-1 Contractors*, 520 U.S. 438 (1997).

80. *Atkinson Trading v. Shirley*, 532 U.S. 645 (2001).

81. *United States v. Lara*, 541 U.S. 193 (2004).

82. *City of Sherrill, New York v. Oneida Indian Nation*, C. Ct. (March 29, 2005).

83. *Bonnichsen et al. v. United States et al.*, 357 F.3d 962 (9th Cir. 2004).

24

Concluding Keynote Address:
From Battlefields to Boardrooms:
A Rich Complexity of Enduring Pride
and New Achievements

JAMES D. NASON

I
T IS AN HONOR TO OFFER A FINAL COMMENT on the many informative, insightful, and inspiring presentations that have characterized this conference. These have demonstrated that at least one thing has not changed over the years—we still have strong and committed leaders in our communities, and I know that we will continue to be guided by their wisdom, insights, and accomplishments in the future.

It is not possible for any one person to accurately sum up the state of Indian Country today. There has been and is far too much diversity of our experience and our cultures to do much justice to such an attempt, so I would like instead to offer a few reflections on at least some of what has been presented.

In considering our rich complexity of culture, belief, expression, and experience, it seems to me that family histories can evoke much of the change that has taken place. In some respects this may also be a more familiar way for us to grasp the enormity of what has happened to and within our communities over the past 100 or 150 years.

A cousin and I recently reflected on just how much our family has changed through time. Our great-grandmother was born in the preservation years, before the Medicine Lodge treaty of 1867, and grew to be a remarkably strong woman. During her lifetime, tribal membership more than doubled from the 2,400 people on the rolls in 1880, although we had numbered about 20,000 just a hundred years before. Unlike many, she survived smallpox as a child and lived a very long life, not leaving us until the 1950s at the age of ninety-four.

When our grandmother and grandfather were born, the Comanche Nation had just been placed on reservation land under the eyes of the U.S. Army detachment at Fort Sill in Oklahoma. They had allotment land and ran a combined ranch and farm. Our great-uncles fought in World War I, and came home as professional gamblers among other things. One of our great-uncles became a government Indian agent, and was even an agent for our own tribe (which gave our grandmother endless opportunity to tell her brother about everything she thought was wrong). One of our great-aunts achieved some success in Hollywood as an actress in early films.

Our uncles tried their hands at lots of things but had only limited success, and both substance abuse and family instability plagued many of them, as well as others in our family. None of them stayed in Oklahoma, and none of them married within the tribe. Our grandfather and grandmother were fluent speakers of Comanche, and our grandfather was apparently well known as a singer at the gatherings that took place in the Wichita Mountains before World War II. But our grandparents decided it was best not to speak Comanche to their children and, sometime around 1920, just stopped.

My father and his siblings never thought about being Indian one way or the other. My father was a cowboy and worked on ranches in Texas and even Mexico. Most of these ranches were Anglo and English owned, of course. Like so many others, he became part of the urban movement during and after World War II and moved to Los Angeles, where he confronted a largely foreign way of life (indeed, to some, a different planet). By this time our family had experienced significant changes in family life, livelihoods, education, their knowledge of the world, religion, and all that went with attempts to adapt and become, in various ways, Americans. In the process our family leased and finally lost their allotment lands, moved to many different places, and lost touch with many aspects of what represented traditional life—although not the family stories that tell us not only who we had been as a family, but also who we were as tribal members. Indeed, as a child I was always struck by the immediacy of those stories of our past—how alive they were, and how recent it all seemed to have happened, as if those notable events and battles had been just last week, or last month.

I do not mean to suggest that this is in any sense a unique history, or an unusual set of experiences. I do suggest that it begins to bring home to us, along with countless other comparable family histories in tribal communities, the stupendous changes that occurred, and the challenges that our families faced and met and even overcame in just the last 150 years. In other words, we don't have to look very far to see how much has happened in many of our communities.

Earlier Reviews of Native American Status
Other people have tried, at various times in the past, to review these kinds of changes and to sum up, in a collective way, the status of Native North America, or at least Native Americans in the United States.

Schoolcraft's History
Perhaps one of the earliest of these efforts was made by Henry Rowe Schoolcraft. In 1822, at the age of twenty-nine, Schoolcraft had already done surveys of what was then the frontier and had been named the Indian agent at Sault Sainte Marie. He married a woman of Ojibwa descent and through her relatives began collecting Indian cultural lore. He became a well-known member of scholarly societies, was highly regarded as an ethnologist, and published extensively about Indians, with some of his work being the inspiration for Longfellow's poem *Hiawatha*. He was also commissioned to write the first major survey of the Indian tribes of the United States, a project ordered by Congress. This survey, *The History of the Indian Tribes of the United States: Their Present Condition and Prospects*, was published in six volumes between 1851 and 1857.[1]

In his preface to the last volume, he said: "The Indians have been prejudged, misjudged, and subjected to harsh judgments in various ways."[2] In 166 chapters comprising 756 pages in just this last volume, he proposed to correct those faults by examining the history, languages, nature, and culture of American Indians, with thoughts on prehistory and other matters as well as a census and an attempt to summarize economic conditions and prospects. Schoolcraft's approach and findings were both sympathetic and simplistic.

He firmly believed that Indians required white assistance in order to become industrious and civilized, which also meant becoming Christian and becoming educated. He thought this would happen through boarding schools, the adoption of agriculture, and avoiding ardent spirits. He believed that Indian survival depended on the "colonization plan" (i.e., relocation) that was then a government policy. Although he was considered very sympathetic to Indians, he had scant regard for Indians who rejected this approach, and even less hope for their future: "Regarding the numerous tribes of Indians who rove over the interior of the continent, between the Missouri River and the Pacific Ocean, and who are yet fascinated with the pursuit of the chase—who yet reject the principles of civilization, and still delight to rob and murder—it requires no spirit of prophecy to predict their progress, or their end."[3]

In light of the annihilation or remnant status of many eastern tribes, Schoolcraft believed that it was necessary and desirable to relocate tribes to western lands where Indian Nations could develop. He thought, along with others, that the five civilized tribes (the Creeks, Seminoles, Choctaws, Chickasaws, and Cherokees) would form the core of a future independent Indian government west of the Missouri. He expected this government to have its own assembly, led by educated Indians, and to have congressional representation. He did not think it possible for Indians educated beyond the state of Indian society to be assimilated into American society: "They will be avoided as members of a peculiar caste, seek in vain for employment and encouragement and yet be useless if they return to their own people."[4] Prophetic words indeed, given the history of many Indians out of boarding schools.

Schoolcraft thought the creation of a multitribal national group was possible for several reasons. First, he believed that no civilized white people would ever settle the vast area from the Rocky Mountains east to a line running from Winnipeg in the north to Corpus Christi in the south—a line that crosses the Missouri River about Vermillion, an area thought to be a great American desert. Second, he believed that the hallmarks of civilization—including piety, thrift, virtue, and temperance—would help overcome what he regarded as the Indians' "innately suspicious character and the over-estimate they [attach] to independence," which had led them to refuse to confederate.[5] In other words, the only hope for Indians was to become like other Christian Americans, and yet, not seek assimilation into American society but instead form their own confederation linked to the U.S. government through Congress.

His comments on the population decline of Indians, with an 1850s estimate of 379,264 in all of the United States, similarly reflected his belief that only agricultural communities could survive. While being perhaps the best data available at the time, his population data for 189 tribes and other kinds of Indian groups was rough at best, with such entries as "Washington Indians east of the Cascades."[6] In a similar manner, his representation of the economic status of Indians in America had only two parts: the amount of money given by the government to Indians as per capita payments or other treaty obligations; and the general agricultural productivity status of tribes. In other words, his survey was a history designed to eulogize the wisdom of the federal government's policies based on the belief that the only Indian problem was the failure of some tribes to recognize the benefits of Christianization, civilization, and relocation.

The Meriam Report

Seventy-one years later, the next major national survey of the status of Native Americans in the United States was completed. This was the Meriam Commission report, named after Lewis Meriam. Published in 1928, it is often spoken of as the most significant survey of conditions in Indian Country in the twentieth century. Commissioned by the government, an independent team of scholars traveled 25,000 miles and visited some ninety-five communities before producing their devastating 872-page report, *The Problem of Indian Administration*.[7] Among other things, the report concluded that the allotment system had been a dramatic failure; that Indian property rights were consistently at risk, and Indians had been subjected to serious exploitation; that educational and health services were far below even minimum acceptable standards; and that Indian community life was plagued by severe poverty, poor nutrition, high disease rates, a lack of access to preventive medicine, and a lack of economic enterprise even where it was feasible, and was hampered by an ineffective government bureau.

The writers of the Meriam Report believed that Indians should be and would be assimilated into the general population, should exercise the privileges of citizenship (which so many were denied then, through various state and local mechanisms), and would ultimately contribute services and taxes to the commonwealth. They believed that significant changes would have to be made to support Indian communities and Indian property rights, as well as major new educational and health programs. Education was seen as the key, in large part, in dealing with what they saw as a "retarded" state of the Indian "race." They urged the prompt settlement of claims against the government, and wanted the role of the government to be as a vigorous guardian of Indian advancement through a significantly altered Indian Service that would "hasten the day when there will no longer be a distinctive Indian problem and when the necessary governmental services are rendered alike to whites and Indians by the same organization without discrimination."[8] They also did not believe that Indians would be able to continue many aspects of their traditional life as they were either absorbed into the prevailing civilization or "fitted to live in the presence of that civilization with at least a minimum standard of health and decency,"[9] although they also imagined that Indians should have a "proper race pride and self respect."[10]

The Meriam Report provided a new foundation for reformers to seek improvements, and led to the Indian Reorganization Act under Bureau of Indian Affairs Commissioner John Collier, who had earlier been an outspoken critic of the government. But much of what had been recommended, and especially land reforms, was abandoned by the government because of lobbying pressures from western ranchers and eastern railroad interests, who clearly had much to lose were changes made. Indeed, they also forced Collier out of office. By 1945, the presence on Indian lands of more than one-third of all U.S. mineral resources in the form of coal, oil, gas, and uranium spurred western Republicans to get rid of reservation lands altogether, an effort that in part led to the terminations of the 1950s.[11]

The American Indian Chicago Conference

Thirty-two years after the Meriam Report, in 1960, Sol Tax, an anthropologist at the University of Chicago, approached the National Congress of the American Indian for their support for a national Indian discussion about common concerns. An Indian steering committee recommended state and regional meetings that culminated in a conference in Chicago in 1961 with 460 Indian representatives from ninety tribes. Their report and recommendations were based on several fundamental principles, among the most important being the preservation of Indian heritage in meeting the threat posed "by the presumption of being absorbed by the American society."[12] The prologue began by stating:

> We believe in the inherent right of all people to retain spiritual and cultural values, and that the free exercise of these values is necessary to the normal development of any people. . . . We believe that the history and development of America show that the Indian has been subjected to duress, undue influence, unwarranted pressures, and policies which have produced uncertainty, frustration, and despair. . . . We believe in the future of a greater America. . . . In such a future, with Indians and all other Americans cooperating, a cultural climate will be created in which the Indian people will grow and develop as members of a free society.[13]

Their proposals to achieve this future covered a wide-ranging set of legislative, economic, health, educational, legal, treaty, and other issues. Aside from ending the policy of termination, other recommendations included not only increasing educational assistance in all areas, but directly involving Indians in planned change, especially in economic development. Development projects, they noted, had been hampered by incomplete projects, arbitrary decision-making, disasters in relocation policy, and lack of access to employment and funds for land purchases. They also saw the clear need for support for new housing standards and low-cost housing development, as well as long-term credit at low interest for housing needs.

They sought an end to discriminatory health services for Indians, new preventive health programs, and expanded health services. Like the Meriam Report, they echoed the desire that the Indian Bureau be primarily an educational support service that would help eliminate high student dropout rates, arbitrary transfer policies, and discriminatory education access, as well as establishing adult and vocational education programs for all Indians, including those not in reservation communities.

Within the legal arena, they recommended the restoration of lands still in public domain, the prompt completion of the Indian Claims Commission work, the reassertion of Indian ownership of reservation lands and Indian water rights, new surveys of reservation boundaries, and the imposition of a requirement that Indians approve any transfer of civil or criminal jurisdiction to states. These recommendations were related to the insistence that treaties be kept intact and maintained, and that self-government be maintained for tribal communities. Their report ended with this statement:

> What we ask of America is not charity, not paternalism, even when benevolent. We ask only that the nature of our situation be recognized and made the basis of policy and action. In short, the Indians ask for assistance, technical and financial, for the time needed, however long that may be, to regain in the America of the space age some measure of the adjustment they enjoyed as the original possessors of their native land.[14]

A Consistent Pattern

There have been other surveys, other reviews, of varying degrees of accuracy and coverage, and many of the coffee-table books about Indians in America that have appeared in the last two decades also contain forecasts into the Indian future. All of the surveys I've mentioned here were the products of a particular time and perspective of that time. Schoolcraft's history, for example, consulted only government agents and others—not Indians—and emerged with a viewpoint that was unabashedly laudatory of the government's actions and policies. It was a stridently colonialist document that saw the need for Indians to become like—but always live apart from—Christian Americans.

In sharp contrast to this, the Meriam Report was based on extensive consultation with Indians. It attempted a critical appraisal of not only conditions in Indian Country but also of government agency policies and practices that had helped to create those conditions. And, of course, the Chicago report was written by Indians about Indian perspectives on problems and concerns affecting Indian communities. Over the course of this conference, we have heard noted Indian and non-Indian scholars and professionals reflecting on the past, present, and potential future of Indian communities and the issues they confront.

American Indian Nations: Yesterday, Today, and Tomorrow—A Review

In all of the reviews done in the past, we see essentially the same problems being voiced, and often the same frustrations being expressed, and many of the same recommendations being made. The most important variation, of course, is the shift from the separatist views of Schoolcraft, to the assimilation in the Meriam Report, to the assertion of a cultural pluralist model put forth

by the Chicago Conference representatives, who saw no contradiction in being Indian, and protecting and promoting Indian heritage, while also being in
other respects modern members of American society. This issue of Indian
identity, especially in the face of continuing stereotypes of all sorts, and the
related concerns with the maintenance of language, tradition, and heritage,
continues to be important today, as we've heard in the stimulating presentations made by Suzan Shown Harjo, Narcisse Blood, and Carey Vicenti.

And there are clearly new expressions of such concerns, including the
manner in which the media deals with Indians, as noted by Mark Trahant,
Tim Johnson, and Jennifer Perez. We have only to examine issues ranging
from Makah whaling to natural resource issues to criminal reporting to see the
wide range of stereotypes, political bias, and other aspects being interjected
into media coverage. At the same time, Native American journalists and the
growth of Native American media are also having an impact in presenting a
more balanced view.

Of course, being Indian is inexorably linked for many people with the existence of Indian tribal communities, and this raises questions of enrollment,
tribal sovereignty, and even the basic demography issues of who is identified
as Indian. Stephen Greymorning spoke to the issue of blood quantum guidelines established by the government and related concerns with tribal membership, while James Shield and Roy Gardner reviewed problems in gaining,
or regaining, federal recognition for their tribes, the Little Shell Chippewa
and Chinook, respectively. Helen Scheirbeck highlighted the status of many
eastern tribes with respect to the ongoing matters of tribal recognition, a perspective made more compelling by her personal reflections on Lumbee history and Lumbee achievements. Tribal recognition by federal or state
governments continues to be an issue which has sometimes even split Indian
interests and concerns, engendering intercommunity and even intracommu-
nity conflict. Of the more than 600 tribes in the United States, more than
500 are federally recognized, and another 26 or so are recognized by a state
government, but the remainder are unrecognized.[15]

Matthew Snipp has provided us with important insights into the historical
and contemporary changes in Indian populations, and few subjects could have
more dramatic implications for us. When we consider that by 1900 many scholars here and abroad believed that Native American peoples would shortly be extinct—as social and political groups if not as distinct populations—the changes
that have since occurred are as astonishing as they are wonderful. There are, of
course, still major problems in many places that negatively impact Native American demography, and these have been touched upon by others here as well, including the dramatic post-1950s growth of an urban Indian population and
continuing unemployment and poverty in some of our communities.

The change in the drastic population decline of past centuries has also led to new discussions about Indian identity as the older, racist, "blood quantum" arguments about tribal membership are reexamined, along with questions of who is or might be legally Indian, or culturally Indian, or socially Indian—issues reflected in basics such as access to education funds and other services. There is no single answer to how Indians remain Indian while also being successful in the broader American society, anymore than there is a single meaning to what is or might be "traditional." It all depends.

As Phillip Deloria said recently: "Here, then, is one of the paradoxes of Indian Country in the Twentieth Century: if Indians change, their culture is considered contaminated and they lose their 'Indianness.' If they do not change, they remain Indians, but are refused a real existence in the modern world."[16]

Issues of heritage are pivotal concerns for Indian communities and find expression in a wide array of topics. In this conference we've heard from Emil Her Many Horses and David Penney about both traditional and contemporary art. David Penney asks us to reconsider the nature of art, and be mindful of the nature of all that might be considered Indian art. Emil Her Many Horses wonderfully reviewed the maintenance of individual family traditions of art through his examination of Northern Plains beadwork. The arts have proven crucial in many places over the past 100 years, in not only maintaining and sometimes redefining Indian heritage, but they have also been a major economic force in many Indian communities. Today's art market for Indian arts and crafts is a multibillion-dollar-a-year enterprise, and has generated its own concerns and laws aimed at protecting what is authentically Indian from forged, imported, and otherwise deceptively produced and marketed knockoffs.

Others speakers, Carmelita Wright and Jim Northrup, have spoken to us about the special issues that confront Indian writers, particularly as they deal with community traditions as well as publishing contracts. Drawing upon a rich history of story-telling and oral literature, contemporary Indian authors and poets have given us award-winning literature in many genres, from historical fiction, regional novels, and satires to poetry, as they explore our connectedness to the past, our confrontations with the present, and our hopes for the future.

For a great many Indian people, the Native Americans Grave Protection and Repatriation Act (NAGPRA) has represented a major national victory in the struggle for sovereign protection of key elements of our heritage, including the protection of our ancestors' bodies. Jim Pepper Henry discussed this from the perspective of new Indian-sensitive policies and practices of collection management at the National Museum of the American Indian, a part of what is globally the "indigenization" of museums. David Hurst Thomas explored this vital law and its consequences looking at the Kennewick Man legal case and urges compromise and collaboration over such issues. Not simply a law about our sacred objects and our ancestors, this is also important criminal law and even more important sovereignty law. The recent court decision about one ancestor, known in the media as "Kennewick Man," has drawn a new line in the sand about tribal rights and federal law. As one of the lead attorneys for a tribe involved in this case has said recently: "The case is a microcosm of the struggles that tribes face today. Tribes must battle to explain their rights to the non-Indian community, to fight off exploitation from the scientific community, and to assert their sovereignty against state and federal governments that are usually opposed to their interests."[17] We have not, I am sure, heard the last of this issue yet.

One of NAGPRA's consequences has certainly been to spur the development of new tribal museums, cultural centers, and other heritage institutions, as Lisa Watt has discussed in her review of the current status of this important area of tribal heritage control and heritage education. In 1981 there were about 40 such institutions in the United States, and now there are more than 170, with new facilities being built every year. These are important because they give us control over our own heritage. Not only do they play significant roles in education and research in their own communities, Native American museums and cultural centers also offer those in other communities the opportunity to explore and understand far better Indian heritage and history from an Indian perspective, something often lacking in public school curricula and materials.

Every earlier review has focused on educational issues, and this conference paid significant attention to this topic. Education clearly remains a major concern and focus with historical inadequacies of educational access, quality of education, involvement of families, and even educational content along with inequities in student discipline confronting us. At the same time, it is clear that we have many more Indian professionals in our communities than ever before, and their presence is making a difference, just as our determination to gain greater control over the educational destinies of our children is also significant.

Many of the presentations in this conference, including that of Earl Barlow, address the varied and important educational landscape and the impact of federal policies. How important it has been is reflected by the fact that in 1900 more than half of all Bureau of Indian Affairs (BIA) staff were in education, and the major share of the BIA budget went to schools. This pattern remained true for many years, and education remains a major focus in the current BIA billion-dollar-plus budget. Despite this, we see some of our tribal schools falling into a state well beyond decrepitude through lack of federal funding, while continuing issues in the education of Indian children in public schools are right at the forefront of community concerns in far too many places.

Of equal importance is the educational challenge in the maintenance of our languages, especially with the 1990 U.S. Census reporting only 282,000 speakers over the age of five nationwide, with 224,000 of those in the western United States.[18] This vital nationwide concern for Indian communities has been reviewed by Margaret Field, Darrell Kipp, and Joyce Goodstriker, who examine in particular the success of immersion programs, one of many contemporary approaches in keeping our languages alive.

The emergence of tribal colleges, and the role they are playing in providing technical, professional, and general educational services, is clearly a huge step forward, as the presentations by Gerald Gipp and James Shanley have indicated. They have also shared with us the challenges that remain. Since the founding of Navajo Community College in 1968, more than 33 Indian colleges have been established in some 11 states, with the majority being in North and South Dakota and Montana. While all of these offer students associate degrees with relevant tribal course content, some offered by elders, other colleges now also offer baccalaureate degrees. The role of tribal colleges may be critical, but of equal interest has been the decades-old presence of American Indian Studies programs in American universities, a mixed history that has been discussed by Duane Champagne and is of special interest to many of us who were involved in creating such programs decades ago. Many programs still face formidable obstacles in their attempt to impact the educational programs of universities, and while some now offer graduate degrees for those who wish to pursue this subject area, others are experiencing budgetary cutbacks and questions of mission, purpose, and marginalization.

Health issues have always, since contact, been literally a life and death matter for our communities, both because of what was deliberately done to us as well as by what has not been done for us. Nutrition, especially in light of the diabetes epidemic in Indian Country, has been highlighted in the presentations of Marietta King, Pauline Matt, and Rosalyn LaPier. Billy Mills has reminded us of the need to work at taking care of ourselves, and finally, although not strictly a health concern, Polly La Tray has spoken to us of the special problems that confront Indian military veterans who face post-traumatic stress, health, employment, and other challenges even in the face of federal attempts to cut back benefits.

We are all also well aware that some of the problems we encounter are still due to blatant discrimination, ongoing attacks against the sovereignty of our communities, and other legislative and legal actions that affect our lives. Janine Pease spoke on civil rights within the context of redistricting, and a history of Indian voting rights, including recent law cases and the growing importance of the Indian vote in many locales. Lenor Scheffler discussed the complex arena of multijurisdictional problems within reservation communities, a matter of considerable concern, given the number of non-Indians living on tribal lands. Elouise Cobell has reviewed for us the still astonishing multibillion-dollar saga of the Indian Trust Funds, and the lawsuit that seeks to settle this matter once and for all—perhaps even within our lifetimes. The significance of changes in federal Indian policy on our communities has also been reviewed by Kevin Gover, who traces the limitations of the 1930s reformers, the disasters of relocation and termination policies, and the subsequent forty-year period of favorable presidential leadership and policy, even as Supreme Court decisions were attacking sovereignty. His thoughts about future government options are compelling.

Walter Echo Hawk reminds us that law is not necessarily justice, or even lawfulness, in his eloquent review of federal Indian law and the impacts of shifts in that law on our tribes, while Oren Lyons has spoken of the much larger international arena within which indigenous rights concerns are being discussed within a worldwide context. While I personally hold little hope for any Indigenous Convention within the United Nations in the near future, these continuing discussions have raised the level of awareness about Native American rights and concerns within the context of the much broader indigenous rights movement. Federal legislation, of course, has a much more immediate and direct impact on our lives, and is often generated in ways that make their origin and character difficult to understand. This in turn presents a real and daily challenge to tribal leaders, who must deal with the consequences of such legislation. Alan Parker expanded this discussion with his review of tribal–state agreements and also raised the issue of tribal and other indigenous community treaty making.

Our political strength within American society is growing, and in some areas the Indian vote is key. Jonathan Windy Boy has presented us with his perspective on working within state politics, while Senator Ben Nighthorse Campbell has urged us to work politically within the national political arena where so much that is vital to our interests can be influenced, particularly in defending treaty rights and sovereignty through legislative actions. In some areas, such as Montana, there are more Native Americans in political positions and much greater interest in securing the Indian vote. We have problems within our own tribal governments, as we all know, but strong and informed effective leadership remains critical to our collective national and individual tribal success, and we were fortunate enough to have Tex Hall speak to this issue, and to the complexity of concerns that confront tribal and national leaders.

Central to earlier reviews and certainly still in our minds today have been the questions of resources, and particularly land. In this conference we have been fortunate enough to hear a number of wonderful presentations about both land and water resources. Narcisse Blood and Richmond Clow have addressed resource issues, while Denise Stiffarm, George Horse Capture Jr., and Harold Main have focused on water rights, considered by many to be one of the next major cases of tribal–government confrontation, by examining a case at Fort Belknap. Rebecca Tsosie has reviewed the legal history of land seizures, from the medieval European Doctrine of Discovery and its application here, contrasting so sharply with Indian perspectives about the land, and the ensuing legal mechanisms which took our lands. Cris Stainbrook has also examined current landholdings, and new changes to Indian ownership of lands, especially pertinent as many tribes regain lands formerly lost through allotment, fraud, and other actions.

Overall, this conference has provided us with new insights into many of the most critical issues that have been and continue to be of significance to Indians in the United States, as well as a few glimpses into the near future and the challenges that await us there.

We Are Still Here

As we progress into the twenty-first century, 513 years after 1492 and 200 years after the Lewis and Clark Expedition reached Great Falls, it seems clear that many of the devastating impacts that have affected Native Americans are being or have been overcome, while others still remain, along with entirely new challenges. During this conference we have been presented with regional examples of both these challenges and our successes. We know that Indian Country is both wide and diverse, and that many other examples of both challenges and successes are out there for us to explore and from which we can learn important lessons.

Traditional belief systems have not disappeared, and neither have traditional family and social groups which also lie at the core of our communities. Continuing issues of substance abuse and related problems still confront us, but are also the focus of our resources and energies. Elders remain a vital part of our communities, but have lower life expectancies and poorer health than other Americans, especially because of the ravages of tuberculosis, alcoholism, diabetes, and pneumonia. Health issues remain critical in some areas, and especially so for elders, but our numbers are increasing.

The drop in the Indian populations of the coterminous United States from an estimated 7 million in 1492 to only 250,000 in 1900 (a decrease of almost 97 percent) has changed, with the 2000 U.S. Census now reporting that more than 4 million Americans were identified as Indian.[19]

Equally significant, and challenging, is the fact that so many Indians live off-reservation and in urban centers, a fact that may also be linked to the increase in the numbers of Americans who identify themselves as being Indian or of Indian descent. As Snipp noted, more than 12 million Americans now claim some Indian ancestry, thus making Indian ancestry one of the top ten identified by Americans.

Although it was not specifically addressed at this conference, economic development activities are major areas of focus for many tribes. Gaming income is being used, for example, to leverage other economic enterprises and bring both increases and stability to tribal employment, thus changing for many the desperate poverty that was so commonplace at the beginning of the twentieth century. Are there still economic problems? Yes, there are. Are all Indians above the poverty level? No. Are we making gains? Yes, it's clear that we are. While our lands went from 155 million acres in 1881 to only 59 million acres by 1910, with further losses thereafter, we now see many tribal governments regaining land, and expanding their landholdings in significant ways.[20] Whether we can maintain control over our natural resources and continue to regain resources remains to be seen.

Everywhere there is increased pride in being Indian, and this is matched by the marked increase in educational programs and materials that are being generated within our tribes and devoted to our heritage, and our languages. Language preservation and the expansion of those who speak our languages in our communities continue to be widespread concerns as well as the focus of much effort by communities and organizations.

Our arts in all areas are expanding in what some have called the new Indian artistic renaissance. We've heard about this in the reviews of traditional and contemporary graphic and sculptural arts and in literature at the conference, but it's also true in music, theater, film, and even couture. The number of important young artists who are maintaining artistic traditions as well as expanding the scope of Indian arts in entirely new media and forms of expression is breathtaking and increasingly attracting attention on the international art scene.

Everywhere we look, we see a stronger determination to protect our autonomy, our sovereignty, our rights of self-determination, and our traditions and heritage. We also see the emergence, especially in the last 100 years, of new activism to achieve these ends, as well as new intertribal organizations that have united our common concerns and placed them in national political and legal arenas. Through these we have made real gains, including new laws like NAGPRA, which at last give most of our deceased the same rights against desecration as other Americans, and which allow us to regain control over much of our traditional sacred materials that were lost to us in the nineteenth and twentieth centuries. And this reflects what is most common for all Indians throughout the last century and before—our central concern with maintaining or regaining control over our own lives, our own destinies, within the context of being a part of America, a country that has fought us, and for which we have fought, a country that has harmed us and tried to change us, just as we have in some ways been helped by it and have also changed it. There is new nationwide unity and new organizations to represent this unity in dealing with attempts to change our tribes, our lives, and our futures in ways contrary to our interests. We have indeed gone from battlefields to corporate and other boardrooms, where power struggles are different, but no less important.

No one can predict the future. No one can say with certainty what will next present itself as a major challenge to our communities, or how well we will succeed in meeting those challenges. Perhaps what we can say has already been said by one of the organizers of this conference, George Horse Capture: "We are here now, have been here for thousands of years, and we will always be here. We have fooled them all."[21]

Notes

1. Henry Rowe Schoolcraft, *History of the Indian Tribes of the United States: Their Present Condition and Prospects* (Philadelphia: Lippincott, 1857; facsimile, Historical American Indian Press, no date).

2. Schoolcraft, *History of the Indian Tribes*, xi.

3. Schoolcraft, *History of the Indian Tribes*, 521.

4. Schoolcraft, *History of the Indian Tribes*, 553–554.

5. Schoolcraft, *History of the Indian Tribes*, 523.

6. Schoolcraft, *History of the Indian Tribes*, 686–689.

7. Lewis Meriam et al., *The Problem of Indian Administration*, Institute for Government Research, Studies in Administration (Baltimore: Johns Hopkins University Press, 1928).

8. American Indian Charter Convention, "Selection from the Meriam Survey Summary," 3–34, AICC, University of Chicago (Ann Arbor: Edwards Brothers, 1961): 4.

9. AICC, "Selection from the Meriam Survey Summary," 3.

10. AICC, "Selection from the Meriam Survey Summary," 5.

11. Judith Nies, *Native American History* (New York: Ballantine Books, 1996): 306, 330.

12. American Indian Charter Convention, *The Voice of the American Indian: Declaration of Indian Purpose*, AICC, University of Chicago, 1961, 4.

13. AICC, *The Voice of the American Indian*, 5.

14. AICC, *The Voice of the American Indian*, 20.

15. Sharon O'Brien, *American Indian Tribal Governments* (Norman: University of Oklahoma Press, 1989), 90.

16. Phillip Deloria, "The Twentieth Century and Beyond," in *The Native Americans*, ed. Betty Ballantine and Ian Ballantine (Atlanta: Turner, 1993), 402.

17. Dan Sadowsky, *Ancient Remains Trigger a Modern Court Battle*, 2005, www.lclar.edu/dept/chron/kennewickmans04.html.

18. U.S. Census Bureau, *American Indian Languages Spoken at Home by American Indian Persons 5 Years and Over in Households: 1990* (Table 3), 1995, www.census.gov/population/socdemo/race/indian/ailang3.txt.

19. Russell Thornton, "Population," in *Native American in the Twentieth Century*, ed. Mary B. Davis, 461–464 (New York: Garland, 1994); and U.S. Census Bureau, *The American Indian and Alaska Native Population: 2000*, 2002, C2KBR/01-15.

20. Nies, *Native American History*, 304.

21. Nies, *Native American History*, 307.

Bibliography

American Indian Charter Convention. "Selection from the Meriam Survey Summary," 3–34. AICC, University of Chicago. Ann Arbor: Edwards Brothers, 1961.

———. *The Voice of the American Indian: Declaration of Indian Purpose*. AICC, University of Chicago, 1961.

Deloria, Phillip. "The Twentieth Century and Beyond." In *The Native Americans*, ed. Betty Ballantine and Ian Ballantine. Atlanta: Turner, 1993.

Meriam, Lewis, et al. *The Problem of Indian Administration*. Institute for Government Research, Studies in Administration. Baltimore: Johns Hopkins University Press, 1928.

Nies, Judith. *Native American History*. New York: Ballantine Books, 1996.

O'Brien, Sharon. *American Indian Tribal Governments*. Norman: University of Oklahoma Press, 1989.

Sadowsky, Dan. *Ancient Remains Trigger a Modern Court Battle*. 2005. www.lclar.edu/dept/chron/kennewickmans04.html.

Schoolcraft, Henry Rowe. *History of the Indian Tribes of the United States: Their Present Condition and Prospects*. Philadelphia: Lippincott, 1857. Facsimile, Historical American Indian Press, no date.

Thornton, Russell. "Population." In *Native American in the Twentieth Century*, ed. Mary B. Davis, 461–464. New York: Garland, 1994.

U.S. Census Bureau. *American Indian Languages Spoken at Home by American Indian Persons 5 Years and Over in Households: 1990* (Table 3). 1995. www.census.gov/population/socdemo/race/indian/ailang3.txt.

———. *The American Indian and Alaska Native Population: 2000*. 2002. C2KBR/01-15.

Index

Taylor, Jonathan Ed, 15
team mascots, 13–18, 19–20; perceived
    by non-Native general public, 14–16
technology, pre-Columbian, 39–40
Tee-Hit-Ton Indians v. United States, 248
Temoak Band, 262
Temporary Assistance for Needy
    Families (TANF), 12
termination, 191–92, 195, 220, 254–55,
    284; as assimilation, 193–94;
    renunciation of, 195; restoration, 196
Termination Act (1953), 3, 31, 220
terra nullius, 40
Tewa, 245
Texas, 28n21
Thomas, David Hurst, 289
Thornton, Russell, 43
Thune, John, 161
Tiipaay, 100
Time Magazine, 160
Tlingit, 77–78
tobacco, 42
Tofoyo, Margaret, 56
tourist art, 54. *See also* art
trade, 250
Trade and Intercourse Act. *See*
    Nonintercourse Act
Trademark Act, 10
trademarks, racist, 10–11, 17
Traditional Cultural Properties. *See*
    sacred sites
Trahant, Mark, 287
Trail of Tears, 113
treaties, 2, 14, 19, 21, 113, 215, 252;
    and American Indian identity, 24;
    constitutional protection, 98n16; and
    education, 88, 93; and tribal
    museums, 73–74. *See also individual
    treaties*
Treaty Beer, 15
Treaty of Canandaiga (1794), 274
Treaty of Fort Laramie. *See* Fort
    Laramie treaty
Treaty of Fort Pitt (1778), 249–50

Treaty of Medicine Lodge, 262
treaty period, 219
tribal authority, 219, 221; legal cases,
    203–4; persistence of, 222;
    restoration, 203–4
tribal colleges, 112–13, 115–18, 119,
    121–22, 133; challenges, 118–19,
    120–21
tribal language: and culture, 107–8,
    113–14, 118–19, 120, 126–27; in
    private school, 108–11; revitalization,
    105–8, 110–11. *See also* Piegan
    Institute
tribal law, 216; newspapers, 152
tribal museums, 70, 71–74; challenges,
    74–75; history, 70–71; model
    museums, 75–80; planned, 80–81
Tribal Self-Governance Act, 196–97
tribal sovereignty. *See* tribal authority
tribalism, opposition, 253
Tribally Controlled College or
    University Assistance Act (1998),
    116, 142
Tribally Controlled Community
    College Assistance Act (1978), 116,
    142, 197
tribes: and biological and cultural purity,
    25; government, 2–3, 5; historic vs.
    created, 205–6; intermarriage, 124,
    126–27; recognition by U.S.
    government, 29–34; sovereignty, 2–3,
    5, 24, 66–67; use of blood quantum
    standards, 25–26. *See also individual
    tribes*; Self-Determination Policy;
    treaties
Truman, Harry S., 192
Tsimshian, 77–78
Tsosie, Rebecca, 292
tuberculosis, 2
Tulsa Coalition Against Racism, 12
Turtle Mountain Band, 31–32. *See also*
    Little Shell Chippewa; Pembina
    Chippewa
typhus, 42

About the Contributors

Dr. Earl J. Barlow (Blackfeet) served as a teacher, principal, coach, and superintendent for the Flathead Reservation and in the Browning and Stevensville, Montana, school districts. He served under the Montana Superintendent of Public Instruction. In 1979, Barlow joined the Bureau of Indian Affairs as Director of the Office of Indian Education. He later served as Area Director for the Minneapolis Area for the BIA, retiring in 1994.

Dr. Gregory R. Campbell is a cultural anthropologist who is interested in health issues, particularly among Native Americans. He has conducted ethnographic field research among Native Americans of the Great Plains. His research interests are social epidemiology, demography, social organization, ethnic studies, and critical anthropology. He earned a Ph.D. from the University of Oklahoma in 1987, and he serves as chair of the Anthropology Department as well as being the curator of ethnology for the Department of Anthropology anthropological collections.

Dr. Duane Champagne (Turtle Mountain Band of Chippewa) is professor of sociology and American Indian studies, a member of the Faculty Advisory Committee for the UCLA Native Nations Law and Policy Center, and acting director of the Tribal Learning Community and Educational Exchange (TLCEE). Champagne was director of the UCLA American Indian Studies Center in 1991–2002 and editor of the *American Indian Culture and Research Journal* in 1986–2003. He has authored or edited over ninety publications. Champagne's research focuses primarily on issues of social and cultural change in both historical and contemporary Native American communities.

Dr. Richmond Clow received a Ph.D. in 1977 from the University of New Mexico. He received the Robinson Award for lifetime achievements in history from the South Dakota Historical Society in 2004. Prior to joining the University of Montana in 1984, Clow worked at the Institute for Native American Studies at the University of South Dakota. His career includes service as program director for a South Dakota Committee on the Humanities in 1982–1983, and he was a proposal writer and research director for the Bureau of Indian Affairs (Rights Protection Branch) in 1980–1983. He has written six books and numerous articles on American Indians and South Dakota history.

Walter Echo Hawk (Pawnee) is a senior staff attorney of the Native American Rights Fund. He received a political science degree from Oklahoma State University and a J.D. from the University of New Mexico. He has worked on cases involving Native American religious freedom, prisoner rights, water rights, treaty rights, and reburial and repatriation rights. He is admitted to practice law before the U.S. Supreme Court, the Colorado Supreme Court, and the U.S. Courts of Appeals for the 8th, 9th, and 10th Circuits. His publications include the award-winning book *Battlefields and Burial Grounds*. He has received various awards, including the American Bar Association's Spirit of Excellence Award for legal work in the face of adversity, and the Civil Liberties Award from the American Civil Liberties Union of Oregon "for significant contributions to the cause of individual freedom."

Dr. Margaret Field is chair of the Native American Studies program at San Diego State University. She earned a Ph.D. in linguistics at the University of California at Santa Barbara in 1998 and has worked extensively in indigenous language revitalization with the Navajo Nation and tribal groups in California.

Ray Gardner (Chinook) is vice chair of the Chinook Indian tribe and is a descendant of Huckswelt, the last chief of the Willapa tribe and a signature signer of the Treaty of 1851. He is currently chair of the Natural Resources/Fisheries Committee, is vice chair of the Health Board, and serves on a variety of other committees within the community. Gardner has worked in state government since 1991 at the Utilities and Transportation Commission and is the liaison for the Native American Tribes and Law Enforcement agencies for the State of Washington.

Dr. Gerald E. Gipp (Standing Rock Sioux) has served as executive director of the American Indian Higher Education Consortium since 2001. He graduated from Ellendale State Teachers College and earned his M.Ed. and Ph.D. in educational administration from Pennsylvania State University. Gipp has served as a school administrator, teacher, and coach in North Dakota, Montana, and South Dakota, and he was program director at the National Science Foundation and executive director for the Intra-Departmental Council on Native American Affairs with the U.S. Department of Health and Human Resources. He also was the first American Indian appointed as deputy assistant secretary for the Office of Indian Education in the U.S. Department of Education. He was president of Haskell Indian Nations University and on the faculty of Pennsylvania State University.

Kevin Gover (Pawnee Tribe of Oklahoma) joined the Arizona State University College of Law faculty in July 2003. After he received his B.A. from Princeton's Woodrow Wilson School in Public and International Affairs in 1978, Gover worked as a specialist for the American Indian Policy Review Commission, a research group chartered by Congress to study a wide range of issues important to Native Americans. He received his J.D. from the University of New Mexico in 1981 and served for two years as a law clerk to U.S. District Judge Juan Burciaga. Gover served as assistant secretary of the interior for Indian Affairs in 1996–2001 and was a partner in the Washington, D.C., office of Steptoe & Johnson LLP, focusing on federal law relating to Indians and on Indian tribal law.

Dr. S. Neyooxet Greymorning holds joint appointments as associate professor in Anthropology and Native American Studies. He is a political anthropologist conducting research among indigenous peoples of Australia, Canada, New Zealand, Timor, and the United States. Greymorning's research interests include indigenous sovereignty issues, contemporary Native American issues, and Native American language retention. He earned a Ph.D. from the University of Oklahoma in 1992 and served as director of the Arapaho Language and Culture Project for the Wyoming Indian Schools. He is executive director of Hinono'eitiit Ho'oowu' (Arapaho Language Lodge) in Wyoming.

Suzan Shown Harjo (Cheyenne and Hodulgee Muscogee) is a poet, writer, lecturer, curator, and policy advocate. She is president and executive director of the Morning Star Institute, a national Native rights organization founded in 1984 for Native peoples' traditional and cultural advocacy, arts promotion, and research. Harjo is one of seven prominent Native people who filed *Harjo et al. v. Pro Football, Inc.*, regarding the name of the Washington football team, before the U.S. Patent and Trademark Board in 1992. The case is currently on appeal. She has been a columnist for *Indian Country Today* (2000–2006) and was a founding trustee of the National Museum of the American Indian and

318 ABOUT THE CONTRIBUTORS

a guest curator of the Peabody Essex Museum. She has been the curator for numerous exhibits at many museums across the country.

James Pepper Henry (Kaw Nation of Oklahoma and Muscogee Creek Nation) is assistant director for community services at the National Museum of the American Indian. He manages a wide variety of Native community-oriented programs and services: training (internships, workshops, and museum technical assistance), electronic initiatives (radio and Internet), repatriation, and the museum's culturally sensitive collections care program that includes policy development and management (care, handling, and treatment) of certain religious, ceremonial, and other sensitive materials in the museum's stewardship. He has been active in Native American repatriation efforts for the Kaw Nation as director of the tribe's Kanza Museum and tribal Historic Preservation Officer, and as the former repatriation program manager for NMAI, and he has worked to promote Native American art, culture, and heritage as curator at the Institute of Alaska Native Arts in Fairbanks and the Interstate Fire House Cultural Center in Portland, Oregon, and as interim curator of American Indian Art at the Portland Art Museum.

George Horse Capture (A'aninin Gros Ventre) retired as senior counselor to the director and special assistant for cultural resources at the National Museum of the American Indian, Cultural Resources Center, in Suitland, Maryland. He earned a B.A. in anthropology from the University of California, Berkeley, in 1974 and an M.A. in history from Montana State University, Bozeman, in 1979. He was awarded an Honorary Doctorate of Letters from Montana State University in 1996. Horse Capture taught college classes and served as a curator for the Plains Indian Museum of the Buffalo Bill Historical Center in Wyoming for eleven years. His professional pursuits also include publishing, lecturing, and consulting for museums and other cultural institutions around the country.

Chandler Jackson is director of the John F. Reed Library at Fort Lewis College in Durango, Colorado. Prior to moving to Fort Lewis, he was director of the library at the University of Great Falls, and he was one of the organizers for the Confluence of Cultures Symposium at the University of Montana in May 2003 and for Lewis and Clark Bicentennial events in the Great Falls area. His research interests include the American West and the plight of the American Indians during the nineteenth century.

Tim Johnson (Mohawk) is executive editor of *Indian Country Today*. Johnson has worked as deputy assistant director of community services at the National Museum of the American Indian, where he also founded their magazine, *American Indian*. He is also co-founder of *Native Americas Journal* at Cornell University.

Darrell Robes Kipp (Blackfeet) is executive director of the Piegan Institute in Browning, Montana, which he founded in 1987. The institute is dedicated to the preservation of Blackfeet language and culture and sponsors the Nizipuhwahsin School, which is a Blackfeet language immersion school for youth age five through twelve.

Dr. James D. Nason (Comanche) is curator of Pacific and American Ethnology, Burke Museum of Natural History and Culture, University of Washington. He received his Ph.D. from the University of Washington in 1970. His research interests include culture contact and culture change, social organization, material culture, museology, Micronesia, Polynesia, and North American Indians. In 2002, Nason was awarded a National Park Service National NAGPRA grant for research on the use of portable X-ray fluorescence spectrometers in detecting deadly residues on cultural objects. Since 1989 he has played several roles in the development of the National Museum of the American Indian: as a member of the Smithsonian's search committee for the NMAI director, as a member of the architectural program design team for both the Cultural Resource Center and NMAI's mall building, as a member of the circle of advisors in developing the main exhibition plan, and most recently as a member of NMAI's Seminar and Symposium Programs Advisory Committee.

Senator Ben Nighthorse Campbell (Northern Cheyenne) served in the U.S. Senate from Colorado in 1992–2004, the first American Indian to serve in the Senate in more than sixty years. He received a B.A. in physical education and fine arts from San Jose State in 1957. Campbell is a self-employed jewelry designer and rancher. He was elected to the Colorado State Legislature in 1982 and served in the U.S. House of Representatives in 1987–1992. As a senator, he initiated legislation to establish the National Museum of the American Indian within the Smithsonian Institution.

Dr. Janine B. Pease (Crow) is vice president for American Indian Affairs at Rocky Mountain College, and she has owned her own consulting firm, specializing in tribal colleges and universities program development and strategic planning. She served as a senior program development specialist to the Achein Lifelong Learning Center at the Institute of American Indian Arts in Santa Fe, the American Indian College Fund in a commissioned study on Native

American language immersion, and Sinte Gleska University for international indigenous higher education initiatives. Pease was president of Little Big Horn College from 1982 to 2000, during which time the college became accredited, built a comprehensive curriculum and campus facility, and founded a two-year curriculum around the Crow Indian language, culture, and knowledge. From 1975 to 1979, she headed the Adult and Higher Education Programs of the Crow Central Education Commission. She has also worked in higher education positions in Washington and Arizona and has a Ph.D. in higher education from Montana State University. When MSU celebrated its centennial, Pease was named to the Centennial Graduates: one hundred distinguished graduates from the first one hundred years of the university's history.

Dr. David Penney is vice president of exhibitions and collections strategies at the Detroit Institute of Arts. He received a B.A. from New York University in 1978 and Ph.D. in art history from Columbia University in 1989. He has been at the DIA since 1996 in a variety of positions. His many publications include *Native North American Art* (2004), *Arts of Native North America* (1998), and *Masterpieces of Native American Art* (1996).

Dr. James Shanley (Assiniboine) is currently serving his twenty-first year as president of Fort Peck Community College in Poplar, Montana. Shanley graduated from Poplar High School and is a Vietnam veteran. He has a doctorate in educational administration from the University of North Dakota, and he has worked in Indian education for over thirty years, primarily with tribal colleges.

James Parker Shield (Chippewa Cree) is vice chair of the Little Shell Chippewa Band in Great Falls, Montana. He has served on the staffs of Congressman Dennis Rehberg and Governor Ted Schwinden. He has also served as state coordinator of Indian affairs. He is currently chair of the Native American Local Government Commission.

Dr. C. Matthew Snipp (Oklahoma Cherokee and Choctaw) is professor of sociology at Stanford University and a faculty affiliate of the Center for Comparative Studies of Race and Ethnicity. His current research and writing deals with the methodology of racial measurement, changes in the social and economic well-being of American ethnic minorities, and poverty and unemployment on American Indian reservations. He has served on several advisory working groups evaluating the 2000 U.S. Census and two National Academy of Science panels charged with designing the 2010 Census. He currently serves as a member of the Census Bureau's Racial and Ethnic Advisory Committee and is a member of the Board of Scientific Counselors for the Centers for Disease Control and the National Center for Health Statistics.

Dr. David Hurst Thomas is curator of anthropology at the American Museum of Natural History, New York, a founding trustee of the National Museum of the American Indian, and adjunct professor at Columbia University and the City University of New York. In 1989, he was elected to the National Academy of Science. He earned his Ph.D. in anthropology from the University of California at Davis and is the author of numerous books, monographs, and scientific articles. His research focuses on aspects of Americanist archeology, including human adaptations to the harsh Great Basin area of the western United States, environmental archeology on St. Catherines Island, Georgia, and paleoenvironmental evidence suggesting that two major droughts struck the western United States within the last millennium. Thomas and his team have also been excavating the ruins of a Spanish Mission south of Santa Fe. This project includes high-school-age interns who are descendants of the local Hispanic and Pueblo Indian communities. Thomas's recent book *Skull Wars* looks at the relationships and tensions between Native American and anthropological communities, seeking ways to build bridges between the groups' diverse perspectives.

Mark Trahant (Shoshone-Bannock) is editor of the editorial page of the *Seattle Post-Intelligencer*, and he has held several positions for the *Seattle Times*, the *Moscow-Pullman Daily News*, the *Salt Lake Tribune*, and the *Arizona Republic*. Trahant has been chair and chief executive officer at the Robert C. Maynard Institute of Journalism Education, which provides training to help news media reflect diversity in content, staffing, and operations. For the past two years, he has been a juror for the Pulitzer Prize and was a finalist himself, for national reporting in 1989, for a series on federal Indian policy.

Rebecca Tsosie (Yaqui) is professor of law at Arizona State University and executive director of ASU's Indian Legal Program. She was appointed Lincoln Professor of Native American Law and Ethics in 2001. She joined the faculty of the College of Law in 1993, after practicing with the law firm Brown & Bain. Tsosie graduated from UCLA School of Law in 1990 and clerked for then Vice Chief Justice Stanley G. Feldman. She is co-author of a federal Indian law casebook, *American Indian Law: Native Nations and the Federal System*. She serves as a Supreme Court Justice for Fort McDowell Yavapai Nation, and she received the American Bar Association's 2002 Spirit of Excellence Award.

Lisa J. Watt (Seneca Nation of Indians, Iroquois Confederacy) is a museum consultant working with tribes and nontribal groups nationwide. She has nearly twenty years of programming and fundraising experience in the museum field at the local and national levels. Her professional museum experience includes service with the Office of the Assistant Secretary for Museums, Smithsonian Institution; the Museum at Warm Springs, Warm Springs, Oregon; and the Portland Art Museum, Portland, Oregon. She was also director of the museum project for the Confederated Tribes of Grand Ronde in Grand Ronde, Oregon. Most recently, she gathered the information for the first-ever national survey on the state of tribal museums and cultural centers, visiting nearly sixty reservations and seventy tribal facilities.